From Biblical Interpretation to Human Transformation

*Reopening the past
to actualize new possibilities
for the future*

From Biblical Interpretation to Human Transformation

*Reopening the past
to actualize new possibilities
for the future*

Essays honoring Herman C. Waetjen

Editors

Douglas R. McGaughey
Cornelia Cyss Crocker

Chora-Strangers

Published by:

Chora Strangers
c/o Douglas McGaughey
Department of Religious Studies
Willamette University
900 State Street
Salem, Oregon 97302
USA

email: info@chora-strangers.org
website: http://www.chora-strangers.org

Cover: 'Black Jesus' by Nicholas Mukomberanwa (1940-2002)

From Biblical Interpretation to Human Transformation: Reopening the past to actualize new possibilities for the future

ISBN-13: 978-097-761300-7
ISBN-10: 0-9776130-0-3

Library of Congress Control Number: 2006920755
Printed in the United States of America

Table of Contents

Part I: Hermeneutics and the Act of Reading

Part II: Critical Interpretations

Part III: Constructive Application

Preface

The structure of this Festschrift is based on Herman's own three-fold interest in hermeneutics and interpretation theories, in Biblical exegesis and interpretation of Biblical texts, and in integrating what human beings study and teach with how they live and act. Hence, the contributors to this Festschrift have focused their articles on three areas of investigation: hermeneutics and the exploration of different theories and models of interpretation; critical exegesis and interpretation of particular Biblical texts; and practical application of insights derived from Biblical scholarship. The first section on hermeneutics contains essays by John H. Eliott (University of San Francisco), Douglas R. McGaughey (Willamette University, Salem, OR), and Eung Chun Park (San Francisco Theological Seminar, San Anselmo, CA). In these articles, the authors reflect on how readers approach and interpret Biblical texts and how one's hermeneutical stance will influence what is perceived and understood in a given book or passage. The second section contains critical interpretations of Biblical passages by Robert B. Coote (San Francisco Theological Seminary, San Anselmo, CA), Cornelia Cyss Crocker (Graduate Theological Union, Berkeley, CA), Joseph Kang (Theological Seminary of the Evangelical Lutheran Church of Russia and Other States, St. Petersburg), Luise Schottroff (Pacific School of Religion, Berkeley, CA), Robert H. Smith (Pacific Lutheran Theological Seminary, Berkeley, CA), Theodore Louis Trost (University of Alabama, Tuscaloosa, AL), and Antoinette Clark Wire (San Francisco Theological Seminary, San Anselmo, CA). With one exception all articles tackle passages from the New Testament and deal with issues that arise out of the early Christian movement and remain important for Christians to this day. Finally, the contributions by Denise M. Ackermann (University of Western Cape, South Africa), James R. Cochrane (University of Cape Town, South Africa), Douglas E. Oakman (Pacific Lutheran University, Tacoma, WA), and Gerald West (School of Theology, University of Natal, Pietermaritzburg, South Africa) all reflect the location of their authors at the nexus of theology and politics. The practical insights that these authors have derived from their Biblical-theological work show the profound implications and applications that the study of the Bible can have for the social-political realm. Taken together, these three sections of essays reflect the movement in Herman's own work and teaching from hermeneutics to critical interpretation to thoughtful application of what he gleaned from the Biblical text.

We would like to thank Herman for his work in the church and the academy! How fortunate we are to have been able to learn and work with you. You have taught and mentored many of us, you have challenged us to look deeply into the Biblical text and to think critically about its message. You have taught us to question our assumptions about the Bible and theology, about reading and interpretation. You have engaged us in vigorous dialogue and exhilarating debate. In celebration, we present to you some of our own scholarly efforts. May the next quarter-century of your life be filled with satisfying research, new insights, much writing, and many more joyous times together.

Douglas McGaughey
Cornelia Cyss Crocker

Author Biographies

Denise M. Ackermann

Denise Ackermann was Professor of Christianity and Society at the University of the Western Cape, South Africa, until her retirement in 2000. Since then she has been an Extraordinary Professor at the University of Stellenbosch in the Department of Practical Theology, teaching courses on "The History of Christian Spirituality", "Gender, Culture and Religion", and "A Theological Perspective on HIV and Aids". Her latest book is *After the Locusts: Letters from a Landscape of Faith"*(Eerdmans, 2003).

James R. Cochrane

James R. Cochrane is Professor in the Department of Religious Studies at the University of Cape Town, South Africa. He received BSc and Ph.D. from UCT, and his MDiv from Chicago Theological Seminary. A past editor of the J*ournal of Theology for Southern Afric*a and of the ecumenical quarterly *New South African Outlook*, he is the author of *Circles of Dignity: Community Wisdom and Theological Reflection* (Fortress, 1999) and *Servants of Power: The Role of English-Speaking Churches [in South Africa], 1903-1930*, as well as some eight edited books and sixty journal articles or book chapters. He directs the Research Institute on Christianity and Society in Africa (RICSA) and leads the UCT-hub of the African Religious Health Assets Programme.

Robert B. Coote

Robert B. Coote is professor of Old Testament at San Francisco Theological Seminary and the Graduate Theological Union. Late in his career, his interests have gravitated to, among other things, two longstanding puzzles, one of the academy, the other of the church: how Isaiah got composed, and how a historical perspective on the Bible can live in the church.

Cornelia Cyss Crocker

Cornelia Cyss Crocker has served Presbyterian congregations for six years and currently teaches New Testament at Pacific Lutheran Theological Seminary in Berkeley, California. Her publications include *Reading First Corinthians in the Twenty-first Century* (New York, London: T&T Clark International, 2004) and several articles on 1 Corinthians, the Gospels according to John and Mark, Mikhail Bakhtin, and biblical interpretation.

John H. Elliott

Rev. Dr. John H. Elliott, Professor Emeritus of Theology and Religious Studies, University of San Francisco, San Francisco, CA (1967-2001) and clergyman of the Evangelical Lutheran Church of America, is author of numerous books and articles on the New Testament and its social world, including *A Home for the Homeless* (Minneapolis: Fortress, 1981/1990), *What is Social-Scientific Criticism?* (Minneapolis: Fortress, 1993), *I Peter* (Anchor Bible 37B, New York: Doubleday, 2000) and, most recently, "Worthy is Christ:" A Modern Hymn and Its Apocalyptic Pedigree" (*Currents in Theology and Mission* 30/6 [2003]: 406-422. E-mail: elliottj@usfca.edu.

Joseph Kang

Joseph Kang was born in Korea. He received a Th. B. and Th. M. from Hankuk Theological Seminary in Seoul, Korea, and an STD from San Francisco Theological Seminary, San Anselmo, CA. He served First Virginia Korean Presbyterian Church in Annandale, VA and Washington Youngnak Presbyterian Church, MD from January1981, and has been a Mission Co-worker of Presbyterian Church (USA) since 1990, where he was a Professor of New Testament at Zomba Theological College, Malawi, Africa, and Professor of Biblical Studies at ELCROS-Theological Seminary, St. Petersburg, Russia. hanjoekang1@aol.com.

Douglas R. McGaughey

Douglas R. McGaughey is Professor and Chair of the Departments of Religious Studies and Classical Studies at Willamette University in Salem, Oregon. He received his Ph.D. in Christian Theology from The Divinity School at The University of Chicago and is an Elder in the United Methodist Church. He is the author of *Strangers and Pilgrims: On the Role of Aporiai in Theology* (De Gruyter, 1997) and *Christianity for the Third Millennium: Faith in an Age of Fundamentalism and Skepticism* (Univ. Press of America, 1998).

Douglas E. Oakman

Douglas E. Oakman is Associate Professor of Religion at Pacific Lutheran University. He received his Ph.D. in New Testament from the Graduate Theological Union in Berkeley, CA, and is an ordained minister in the Evangelical Lutheran Church in America. He is the author of *Jesus and the Economic Questions of His Day* (Edwin Mellen, 1986) and with K. C. Hanson the award-winning *Palestine in the Time of Jesus: Social Structures and Social Conflicts* (Fortress Press, 1998). Connoisseur of classical jazz, avid railfan, and Ham Radio enthusiast, the author resides in Washington State with wife Deborah and son Jonathan; another son Justin lives with wife Joanna in St. Paul, Minnesota. Email: oakmande@plu.edu

Eung Chun Park

Eung Chun Park is Professor of New Testament at San Francisco Theological Seminary and Graduate Theological Union, Berkeley. He is the author of *The Mission Discourse in Matthew's Interpretation* (Tübingen: Mohr-Siebeck, 1995), *The Gospel for the World: Studies in the Acts of the Apostles* (Seoul: Institute for Biblical Studies, 1997), and *Either Jew or Gentile: Paul's Unfolding Theology of Inclusivity* (Westminster John Knox, 2003).

Luise Schottroff

Born in Berlin, Germany, in 1934, Luise Schottroff studied Protestant Theology at the Universities of Bonn, Mainz and Göttingen. She was awarded the Dr. theol. in 1961and the second doctorate (Habilitation) in 1969. In 1961, she married Willy Schottroff. She taught New Testament Studies at the Universities of Mainz and Kassel; at the latter she inaugurated an interdisciplinary doctoral program in Feminist Exegesis and Feminist Theology. Since 2001, she is Visiting Professor of New Testament at Pacific School of Religion and the Graduate Theological Union at Berkeley, CA.

Robert H. Smith

Robert H. Smith has served as Christ Seminary-Seminex Professor of New Testament at Pacific Lutheran Theological Seminary in Berkeley, California since 1983. He has known Herman Waetjen since the late 50's when he was a graduate student at Concordia Theological Seminary in St. Louis and Herman was a young instructor in philosophy. Smith's books include commentaries on Matthew (1989), Acts (1970), Hebrews (1984), and Revelation (2000). He has also published *Easter Gospels: The Resurrection of Jesus according to the Four Evangelists* (1983).

Theodore Louis Trost

Theodore Louis Trost is Associate Professor in Religious Studies and New College at The University of Alabama, Tuscaloosa. He has also served as Visiting Professor in the College of the Humanities at Carleton University in Ottawa, Canada. He is the author of *Douglas Horton and the Ecumenical Impulse in American Religious History* (2002) and several articles and book chapters including, most recently, "The Passion and the Compassion of the Christ" in *The Role of Christology in the United Church of Christ* (2005), edited by Scott Paeth. He is the founding member of the musical entourage *Thaddaeus Quince and the New Originals*, whose third album is "The Wrest" (2004).

Gerald O. West

Gerald West is Head of the School of Theology at the University of Natal in Pietermartizburg, South Africa. He received his Master's and Ph.D. from Sheffield University in Sheffield, England. He is author of *Biblical Hermeneutics of Liberation: Modes of Reading the Bible in the South African Context* (New York: Maryknoll 1995, and Cluster Publications, 1995), *The Academy of the Poor: Toward a Dialogical Reading of the Bible* (Sheffield: Sheffield Academic Press, 1999), and was co-editor of *The Bible in Africa: Transactions, Trends, and Trajectories*, (Leiden: E.J. Brill, 2000).

Antoinette Clark Wire

Antoinette Clark Wire is Professor Emerita of New Testament Studies at San Francisco Theological Seminary and the Graduate Theological Union. She has written on Pauline theology, gospel miracle story traditions and women's leadership in Early Christianity. Her publications include *The Corinthian Women Prophets: A Reconstruction through Paul's Rhetoric* (Philadelphia: Fortress, 1990) and *Holy Lives, Holy Deaths: A Close Hearing of Early Jewish Storytellers* (Atlanta: Society of Biblical Literature, 2002). She is also studying biblical interpretation and oral-composed songs in contemporary Chinese Christianity.

Hermeneutics
and the Act of Reading

Articles in this section focus on how readers approach and interpret Biblical texts and how one's hermeneutical stance will influence what is perceived and understood in a given book or passage.

Hunting for Homosexuals at Corinth

Exegetical Tracking Rules and Hermeneutical Caveats[1]

John H. Elliott

The hunt for homosexuals at Corinth and elsewhere in the biblical communities presents a particularly prickly problem of contextual reading and interpretation. Its involves, among other things, a clash of ancient and modern sexual concepts, constructs, and frames of reference. Attempts at using allegedly relevant biblical texts as moral guidelines today are subject to serious exegetical and hermeneutical constraints.

Vorgeschichte und Einleitung

The honoree and I have a history that goes "way back" in time, Lutheran time. We first met in 1956 at Concordia Seminary, St. Louis, where Herman was teaching courses on modern continental philosophy, as I recall. On furlough from completing a doctorate at Tübingen, Germany, he not only was one of our frischgebackene Dozenten, he also took an interest in my personal life, encouraging me too to take the German doctorate plunge. I did so, but at Münster in Westfalen where Dortmunder Kronen reigned supreme (1960-63). I returned stateside in November 1963 to teach at the same seminary from 1963-1967, while Herman had since departed and was stirring up Lutheran dust elsewhere. We caught up with each other again in California where I took up residence with the Jesuits at the University of San Francisco in 1967 and he moved in on the Presbyterians at San Francisco Theological Seminary in San Anselmo, CA. Alte Freunde now united as Kollegen at the Graduate Theological Union in Berkeley and as war-protesting academics meeting regularly not only in demonstrations but also as members of the BASTARDS. As the Bay Area Seminary for Theology and Related Disciplines, we organized to compare the Viet Nam War to another war of liberation in biblical time, the Maccabean revolt. The goal of the seminar was to figure out a way of merging traditional exegesis with the research and perspectives of the social sciences so as better to understand the complexities of the politics of first-century Palestine and twentieth-century Washington, D.C. Out of this effort at multi-disciplinary analysis came several books by our honoree, myself, and others of the group, including Norman Gottwald's pioneering classic, *The Tribes of Yahweh.*

A hallmark of Herman's approach to biblical interpretation has always been his concern with the broader hermeneutical dimensions of the Scriptures and of his craft as exegete. In addition, Waetjen the exegete-hermeneut has always also been Waetjen the churchman, a theologian witnessing to the church and for the church in society. Among the issues currently challenging the church and its social witness there is none producing as much heat and as little light as the hot potato of the place and role of homosexuals in the church and its offices of leadership. As Herman has been involved

---

1   A slightly different version of this essay appears in *Biblical Theology Bulletin* 34/1 (2004), pp. 17-40 under the title: "No Kingdom for Softies? Or, What Was Paul Really Saying."

in years of study of this issue among the Presbyterians,[2] so I have had a part in the seemingly interminable official studies commissioned by the Evangelical Lutheran Church of America. The essay that follows has gone through several transmogrifications over the years to fit specific themes of specific conferences.[3]

The biblical text on which this essay shall concentrate is a passage of 1 Corinthians (6:9-10) that is widely regarded as relevant to the topic of "what the Bible says on homosexuality." In my analysis of this text and its bearing on the topic at hand, I shall be demonstrating what are regarded by exegetes around the world as the appropriate steps to take in order to arrive at the meaning of any biblical text in its literary, historical, geographical, economic, social, and cultural contexts. This issue of exegetical method, it has become clear to me, is as much a part of the problem regarding the topic, as is the issue of homosexuality itself. In the heat of confrontations over the place and role of homosexuals/gays, and lesbians (and bisexuals and transgender persons) in religious communities today, astounding ignorance and red-hot emotion all too often displace sound knowledge of how to read the Bible and how to make rational use of our extensive knowledge of the psychological, biological, social, historical, theological, ethical, and spiritual dimensions of human sexuality.

As to the use and abuse of the Bible in discussions of this issue, it is clear that much of the upset and disagreement among ordinary folk is traceable to a confusion, or worse, an ignorance, as to how to read, interpret, and apply the Bible to this and other pressing problems of our time.[4] Clarity is needed on four points: (1) how to analyze a biblical passage exegetically; (2) the hermeneutical principles guiding any exegetical undertaking; (3) the content of the investigated texts themselves—what they state and do not state; where unclarities of meaning, nuance, and implication of the original Hebrew, Greek, and Aramaic formulations are present; how and why translations vary and represent culturally-specific interpretations; how the meaning of each biblical text is controlled and limited by its complex of contexts (literary, historical, geographical, economic, social, cultural); and (4) the hermeneutical guidelines concerning the use of any biblical text to shape and inform theological and ethical decisions today. I shall address these points as space allows, and at the conclusion I shall recall some of the broader hermeneutical principles in play.

---

2   His published article on "Same-Sex Sexual Relations in Antiquity" (1996) is one result of this research.

3   An initial draft was commissioned by and presented to a Task Force of the ELCA on Human Sexuality on 4/5/1991. The final report of this Task Force was published in November 1991 under the title, "Human Sexuality and the Christian Faith. A study for the church's reflection and deliberation." This report was studied (or at least discussed) in most (or at least some) of the ELCA congregations, but produced no ELCA-wide consensus and no resolution of the issue. Since then, two subsequent ELCA-wide studies of this issue have followed, each supposedly designed to correct or improve (read: domesticate) the previous studies. Of such institutional studies, as of books, there is never an end. The commissioning of task forces and studies has become--in end effect, if not in design--a tactic for tabling or "deep-sixing" topics too hot to handle and for going along with the current cop-out policies of "don't ask, don't tell."

4   This is to say nothing about the second main area of ignorance: unenlightenment concerning what is currently known regarding sex, sexuality, sexual identity, sexual behavior in all their dimensions and expressions today.

The Greek Text of 1 Corinthians 6:9-10—Preliminary Considerations

The Greek text reads as follows:

6:9 ἢ οὐκ οἴδατε ὅτι ἄδικοι θεοῦ βασιλείαν οὐ κληρονομήσουσιν; μὴ πλανᾶσθε: οὔτε πόρνοι οὔτε εἰδωλολάτραι οὔτε μοιχοὶ οὔτε μαλακοὶ οὔτε ἀρσενοκοῖται   6:10 οὔτε κλέπται οὔτε πλεονέκται, οὐ μέθυσοι, οὐ λοίδοροι, οὐχ ἅρπαγες βασιλείαν θεοῦ κληρονομήσουσιν.

The terms thought to bear specifically on the issue of homosexuality are μαλακοὶ and ἀρσενοκοῖται.

The first problem for most bible readers will be their inability to read this Greek text. So they shall have to resort to a translation and this introduces problems of its own. Every translation is an interpretation. This is the case because all languages encode information from their respective social and cultural systems and no two social or cultural systems are identical—alike in some respects but never completely identical. Thus translations always run the risk of using culture-specific or modern terms and concepts (so that the reader can understand) but terms that are alien to the cultures of the texts being translated. Our 1 Corinthians text is a classic case of this translation and interpretive problem. When "homosexuals" or "homosexual perverts" is used to translate μαλακοὶ οὔτε ἀρσενοκοῖται (as does the RSV and the TEV, respectively, for example), a modern, post-Enlightenment, late 19th century term, "homosexual," is used to translate one or two Greek terms that literally mean "soft males" and "males who lie with males." This represents a serious problem, however, since "homosexual" and "homosexuality" are conceptual constructs of recent time and have no ancient counterparts in any ancient language.[5]

Other biblical versions prefer different translations such as *Weichlinge, Knabenschänder, catamites, sodomites, invertidos, afeminados, effeminate.* Each of these expressions, of course, also is culturally laden. The startling differences among translations indicate serious problems concerning the sense of the original terms and make one wonder which, if any of them, comes closest to the meaning and implications of the original Greek terms. More on the translation problem anon. For the moment these observations should suffice for demonstrating that even the claim that this text has bearing on the topic of "homosexuality" is open to serious question. This illustrates an important, yet regularly overlooked, hermeneutical point: relevancy of certain biblical texts to certain theological or moral issues is often in the eye of the beholder. We frequently see what we have been taught to see or what we wish to see—and not always what is actually there. Thus an accurate reading of the Bible never starts with a translation but with the original text—a step impossible for the majority of Bible readers. From the very getgo, they are thus quite dependent on the opinion of "experts,"—translators, commentators and decoders, who themselves in the case of 1

---

5   The term "homosexual" was first coined by the Austrian-Hungarian Károly Mária Kertbeny (Benkert) in 1869 (two pamphlets in German). It was then introduced into English in the 1890s by Charles Gilbert Chaddock in his translation of R. Krafft-Ebbing's *Psychopathia sexualis* (2d ed. of the German original of 1887). Thereafter it was included in the *Oxford English Dictionary* (1892). The word was invented to designate persons who manifested a particular sexual profile reflecting a particular modern construct of gender and sexual differentiation quite divergent from the prevailing gender construct(s) of the ancient world.

Cor 6:9 have reached no agreement on the translation or meaning of terms thought to be relevant to the topic of homosexuality.

Usage of these Greek terms in their linguistic context is essential to consider here. But before doing this, it will be helpful for us to first examine the literary and rhetorical context of which 1 Cor 6:9-11 is a part. Limitations of space require brevity on this point. Here are some points that have a substantive bearing on the meaning and thrust of 6:9-11.

The Situation at Corinth and Paul's Response in General

The letter of 1 Corinthians was written by Paul about the year 55 CE or so to a small community of Jesus followers that Paul had helped establish in the seaport city of Corinth a few years earlier. In this letter Paul answers a series of questions (7:1-16:12) contained in a letter the Corinthians had sent him, and mounts a powerful critique of, and evangelical response to, a bevy of competing factions, economic divisions, and socio-cultural discriminations that were tearing apart the community. Recent adherents to the faith coming from a diversity of social, economic, ethnic and cultural backgrounds had different "takes" on the implications of Paul's gospel and its social and ethical implications. Self-designated "spirituals" were claiming superiority over the "physicals;" the wealthy and powerful were disdaining the poor and powerless; the wise demeaned the foolish; the "strong" claimed superiority over the "weak;" the party of one leader opposed parties claiming allegiance to other leaders. Confusion reigned regarding the nature of salvation—was it salvation *of* the body or liberation *from* the body? Devaluations of materiality, physicality, and sexuality were asserted in the name of some "more advanced" knowledge (*gnosis*). Notions of freedom from communal obligations and social responsibility were thought by some (the elites in particular) to be the logical consequence of Paul's gospel of freedom. This confusion and strife was accompanied by a plethora of moral problems (around issues of sexual conduct, litigation against fellow believers, the eating of food dedicated to idols, behavior at worship) that had surfaced in this fledgling community. These problems threatening to destroy the struggling beachhead of the messianic sect at Corinth evoked from the apostle Paul one of the most sustained and powerful assertions of the unity of believers in Christ to be found in all the New Testament.

The problems addressed in chapter six form part of a discussion of immoral behavior (*porneia*) extending from 5:1 to 6:20. The theme of *porneia,* in fact, runs through this section from start to close. Of the 13 occurrences of this family of terms in 1 Corinthians, all but two (7:2; 10:8) are located in chs. 5-6.[6] The meaning of these terms can vary from a vague form of "sexual immorality" (whose specific nature is unstated) to "idolatrous engagement in polytheistic cult" to "unlawful sexual intercourse"of persons not married to "selling use of one's body for compensation," with context always determining specific meaning. Israelites and followers of Jesus conventionally associated *porneia* with outsider Gentiles and their forms of polytheistic worship, so that *porneia* could always be a term for "idolatry." This association is evident in 1 Corinthians in the juxtaposition of terms in 5:9 (*pornois,*

---

6   *Porneia*: 5:1; 6:13; 6:18 ("flee *porneia*;" cf. 10:14, "flee idolatry"); 7:2; *porneuô*: 6:18; 10:8 (2x; allusion to Num 21:5-6; cf. 10:14); *pornê* (6:15, 16); *pornos* (5:9, 10, 11; 6:9).

eidôlolatrais) and 6:11 (*pornoi, eidôlolatroi*), and in the linking of worshiping idols (10:7, 14) with "indulging in immorality" (10:8). The related nouns *pornos* and *pornê*, used in a literal sense, could designate a male or a female "prostitute," respectively; and *porneia*, "prostitution." [7] Or they could denote "fornicator" and "fornication," or, more generally and less sexually specific, "immoral person" and "immorality." They too, however, appear in biblical contexts treating idolatry and apostasy, and, used figuratively, could denote foreign governments hostile to God and God's people[8] or persons practicing idolatry and "whoring after foreign gods."[9] The kindred verb *porneuô* could mean either, literally, "to practice prostitution" (e.g. 1 Cor 6:18) or, figuratively, "to practice idolatry."[10] Thus, *porneia* and related terms in the Bible could denote either actual or metaphorical prostitution, "peddling one's body" literally or figuratively. In the latter case, the terms refer to idolatrous and immoral behavior typical of *Gentiles*, including, but not restricted to, sexual behavior proscribed in Torah or viewed as incompatible with God's will.

In chapters 5 and 6 of 1 Corinthians, Paul introduces and addresses specific instances of immoral behavior (*porneia* etc.) occurring in the Corinthian community of believers: a case of incest (5:1, 9), activity as prostitutes (6:13?, 6:16, 18), commerce with prostitutes (6:16, 18), and a related case of inappropriate interaction with unjust/unrighteous unbelievers (6:1-8) which, as its context suggests, Paul also regards as an instance of *porneia*. The verses attached to 6:1-8, namely vv. 9-11, continue on the theme of *porneia* as they include *pornoi* and *eidôlolatrai* (v. 9) in a list of persons excluded from the kingdom of God. Chapter seven introduces a new topic, marriage (7:1-40). The *porneia* of which Paul speaks (7:2) appears not to be selling oneself as a prostitute and engaging in idolatry, but rather sexual intercourse outside of marriage.

Chapter five opens with mention of a case of incest (5:1), a type of *porneia* even condemned by Gentiles, Paul notes. Thus the *pornoi* referred to a bit later (5:9, 10) could be understood as perpetrators of incest. On the other hand, since they appear here in 5:9 and 5:10, as in 6:9-10, in traditional lists of various types of immoral persons, the term *pornoi* might have the more general sense of "sexually immoral persons" or "fornicators." In any case, Paul's chief concern in 5:1-12 was to denounce this act of incest within the Corinthian community because it undermined the moral and social integrity of the believing community as a whole. The believers are urged to "remove him from among you" (5:2) and to "purge the evil one from your midst" (5:13).[11]

Thus, in regard to 1 Cor 5:1-11 and the case of incest within the community, this instance of *porneia* was seen by Paul as something that could contaminate the entire community (as leaven "contaminates" a lump of dough). From this perspective,

---

7   LSJ list "catamite" as the first meaning for *pornos* and "sodomite" as the second. For the LXX and NT they propose the rendition "fornicator." This is one of LSJ's less felicitious entries.

8   E.g. Isa. 1:21; Jer 3:3; Ezek. 16:30-31, 35; Rev.17:5

9   E.g. Hos 6:10; Jer 3:2,9; 2 Kgdm 9:22; Rev 19:2.

10 E.g. Hos 9:1; Jer 3:6; Ezek 23:19; Rev 17:2; 18:3, 9. The sexual aspects of pagan cults made possible this equation of idolatry and fornication.

11 The OT prohibition of incest appears in Deut 22:30 (HT: 23:1; cf. 27:20; Lev 18:8; 20:11). But the excommunicating injunction, "purge the evil one from your midst," was employed repeatedly in Deuteronomic legislation in relation not only to incest but to a variety of community-threatening acts (13:6, 17:7, 19:19, 22:24; 24:7).

therefore, the perpetrator had to be expelled (5:2, 13) and delivered to Satan with the goal of freeing the community of this contaminating "malice and evil" (5:8) and of seeking his ultimate repentance and salvation (5:5). Ethically, Paul's strategy for dealing with this situation assumes (a) a group of believing insiders demarcated from immoral outsiders (5:12); (b) an infecting and polluting power of *porneia* capable of corrupting the entire community (as leaven does a lump of dough); (c) the cultural (Israelite) association of leaven with malice and evil (5:8) and the Christian identification of Jesus Christ as paschal lamb (associated with unleavened bread, 5:7); and (d) the effectiveness of social excommunication as a controlling discipline for maintaining ideological and social cohesion. These assumptions regarding the necessary demarcation of believing, holy insiders from nonbelieving, unholy outsiders and concerning the infectious and contaminating power of immorality and unholiness inform all of 5:1-6:20 and its ethical strategy and in fact the letter as a whole.

The exhortation of chapter 6 is related thematically to that of chapter 5 and was likewise guided by these assumptions. What relates the issues of litigation (6:1-8), conduct barring admission to the kingdom of God (6:9-11) and intercourse with prostitutes (6:12-20) to the preceding case of incest is a similar social problem and a similar Pauline response inspired by a similar set of assumptions: (1) the unacceptable association of holy insiders (6:1, 11, 19) with "unjust/unrighteous" outsiders (6:1), including prostitutes (6:16), and even the submission of the holy ones to inferior outsiders' legal judgment (6:1-8); (2) discord within the community (6:1-8) and the pollution affecting the entire Body of Christ through members' association with prostitutes (6:15-20; cf. 6:11); and (3) a libertine (6:12, 13) and arrogant (cf. 5:2, 6) attitude of certain Corinthians that "all things are lawful" (6:12; cf. also 10:23 in regard to eating idol meat and brotherly scandal), a slogan apparently implying that for the believers there are no moral norms or principles or sanctions now governing moral conduct and no reasons for distinguishing members of the Christ community from others.

In response, Paul insisted that (1) since believers have been "washed, sanctified and justified" (6:11b), they are a new and holy people (6:1, 11), different from the way they were prior to their baptism and inclusion into the believing community (6:11a). (2) As members of a holy community, they are superior to unjust/unrighteous outsiders (*adikoi*, 6:1, 2-4) and therefore should avoid subjecting themselves to the outsiders in their courts of law (6:1, 4, 6). (3) They should rather settle disputes among themselves (6:2, 5), and preferably eliminate these legal disputes among believers altogether (6:7-8). (4) There are indeed moral principles and standards operative for believers. Believers are called to a morality superior to that of unjust/unrighteous (*adikoi*, 6:1, 9) outsiders, who will not inherit the kingdom of God (6:9). Ten examples of such unjust/unrighteous persons are mentioned (6:9-10) and some of the Corinthians were among them prior to their baptismal washing, their being made holy, and their being made just/righteous (6:11). (5) All things are indeed lawful, but not all things are advantageous for the good of the whole community (6:12; 10:23, 33; 12:7); that is, for the building up of the Body of Christ. This is a fundamental ethical principle that is reiterated throughout the letter (cf. 8:1-13; 10:23-11:1; chs. 12-14) and that is meant to guide conduct aimed at overcoming the basic problem of dissension and division within the community.

The issue of communal dissension and disunity is raised at the very outset of the letter (1:10), and throughout the letter Paul takes up and responds to various types of its manifestation: competing factions, envy and strife (1:10-17; 3:1-23); conflicting, boastful claims to knowledge and wisdom (2:1-16; 3:18-23; 4:6-21) concerning sexual matters (chs 5-7); eating meat devoted to idols (8:1-13; 10:1-11:1); eucharistic celebration and worship (11:1-14:40); and the Christian understanding of death and resurrection (1:18-25; 15:1-58). In general, Paul aims at enabling the factious Corinthians to see themselves as the one communal entity, one integral Body of Christ (6:15, 19; 10:16-17; 11:27; 12:1-13:13) and to behave accordingly. Thus the aim of the believers as constituents of this new collective reality, the "Body of Christ," should be to live not as independent individuals ("just me and Jesus"), but as persons incorporated into the crucified and resurrected body of Jesus Christ (6:15, 17; 12:12-13), to strengthen and build up this collective body (8:1; 10:23), to maintain undivided devotion to the Lord (7:35), and with this collective body to glorify God (6:20). Membership in (a) the *ecclesial Body of Christ*, in other words, has specific ethical implications regarding the consumption of (b) the *eucharistic body of Christ* and the use of (c) *one's physical body* now united with the Body of Christ.

This examination of the wider and more immediate literary and rhetorical contexts of 6:9-10 has surfaced several items that bear on the meaning of these verses, their specific terms, and the thrust of Paul's thinking and exhortation.

1. The letter as a whole (a) addresses problems of congregational disparities, dissension, discrimination, and division, (b) argues that the attitudes and conduct responsible for these problems are incompatible with membership in the collective Body of the crucified and resurrected Christ, and (c) calls for behavior aimed to demonstrating and maintaining communal cohesion and ideological commitment to God, Jesus Christ, and one another. In regard to 6:9-10, this means that whatever the sense of these verses might be, it must be consistent with this integrating and unifying aim of the letter as a whole.

2. In regard to 5:1-6:20, the more immediate context of 6:9-10, the chief concern of this section is with types of *porneia* that are damaging the ethical integrity and communal cohesion of the group, and that are incompatible with membership in the Body of Christ. With respect to 6:9-10, this means that the behavior that Paul condemns in vv. 9-10 is proscribed because, from Paul's perspective, it is linked with *porneia* and is typical of outsider Gentile behavior, and because it pollutes and contaminates the holy community of believers and violates the integrity of the Body of Christ.

3. In his treatment of the issue of believers litigating with fellow believers in the courts of law of nonbelieving outsiders (6:1-11), Paul objects that the holy believers (RSV: "saints," 6:1) are inappropriately submitting themselves to the judgment of the unjust/unrighteous (*adikoi*) unbelieving (6:1, 6) outsiders. In reality, however, it is God's holy ones (i.e. we ourselves who have been made holy in baptism, 6:11) who will judge the world (6:2) and angels (6:3), and thus "how much more concerning

matters of this life!" (6:3). Believers, in fact, should not be litigating at all with one another, and should rather suffer injustice (*adikeisthe*). But instead, they unjustly treat (*adikeite*) and defraud one another (6:7-8). The issue of this passage thus is that believers should not behave unjustly with one another and should not submit their disputes to the judgment of unbelieving outsiders who are unsanctified, unjust, and morally inferior.

4. Continuing on the issue of justice-injustice as well as one the theme of *porneia*, Paul then in vv. 9-11 reminds his audience that "unjust/unrighteous persons" (like those of whom he has been speaking, 6:1) will not inherit the kingdom of God (v. 9a). To illustrate further examples of unjust/unrighteous persons not inheriting the kingdom of God, he lists ten types of such unjust persons (vv. 9b-10) and comments that some of the Corinthians were in fact such persons prior to their baptism and conversion. However, through baptism they have been "washed, sanctified, and justified"— implying their inclusion in the holy Body of Christ (6:14, 17, 19-20). The ethical implication is that baptism and incorporation in the holy body of Christ entails a severance from unjust/unrighteous persons and non-engagement in the conduct typical of such persons.

The hermeneutical importance of this last observation is that the list, of which the terms crucial to our subject are a part, is cited to exemplify types of unjust/unrighteous persons who will not inherit the kingdom of heaven (6:9, 10). Whatever the terms *malakoi* and *arsenokoitai* might mean, their function in this letter is the same as that of the other terms of the list: to exemplify unjust/unrighteous persons--persons different from the holy believers and outside the kingdom of God.[12]

Homosexuals at Corinth?

Within this general and more immediate context of the letter occurs a list of persons (1 Cor 6:9b-10) that contains two terms at the heart of our investigation, terms that have often been cited as evidence that the Bible condemns homosexuals and homosexual behavior. The words so understood are *malakoi* and *arsenokoitai*. They are quite rare and their meanings, very problematic. Several observations are in order here.

First, the terms are part of a larger list of persons declared to be excluded from the kingdom of God (6:9b-10). This list, in turn, is similar to, and expands upon, two previous lists of immoral persons presented in ch. 5. A comparison of the lists indicates that they are similar in some respects and different in others.

The shortest of the three is that of 5:10. It mentions four types of "immoral" persons inhabiting human society outside the believing community: *pornois*, ("immoral persons"? "prostitutes"?, clients of a prostitute? perpetrators of incest?), greedy persons (*pleonektais*), robbers (*harpaxin*), and idolaters (*eidôlolatrais*). This list, says Paul, illustrates types of immoral *outsiders* of whom he was *not* speaking in his earlier letter (5:9a, 11a) when he encouraged the Corinthians "not to associate with immoral persons (*pornois*)" (5:9). Avoidance of such persons out there in society, he

---

12 Peter Zaas (1988) correctly stresses the close relation of the lists to the situation of the letter and discusses their rhetorical function.

said, would have been impossible from a practical point of view (5:10b). Furthermore, judging outsiders is not the task of believers but rather the job of God (5:12-13a).

In that earlier letter (described in 5:11) he in fact discouraged association and dining with certain types of *fellow believers*; namely a "brother" who was either a *pornos*, a greedy person (*pleonektês*), an idolater (*eidôlolatrês*), a reviler (*loidoros*), a drunkard/boozer (*methyos*), or a robber (*harpax*). It is believers *within* the community whose conduct was and is Paul's concern (5:12a) and he now commands the Corinthians to "drive out," excommunicate, the evil person (*ponêron*; cf. "evil," 5:8) from their midst (5:13b), that is, the male committing the *porneia* of incest mentioned in 5:1-8 and already targeted for exclusion (5:2, 5, 7-8). Thus the "immoral persons" mentioned in 5:10 were nonbelieving *outsiders*, not believing insiders. The list of 5:11, on the other hand, concerns immoral types of *fellow believers*. Nevertheless, the lists mention the same types of immoral persons, except that the longer list of 5:11 adds "reviler and drunkard."

The list in 6:9-10 is longest of the three. It includes all the types listed in 5:10, all those of 5:11, and adds four further terms, "adulterers" (*moichoi*), *malakoi*, *arsenokoitai*, and "thieves" (*kleptai*), inserting them as a block of four between "idolaters" and "greedy persons."

The following comparative table displays the similarities and differences of the three lists. Terms of 5:11 added to those of 5:10, and terms of 6:9-10 added to those of 5:10 and 5:11 are italicized.

1 Cor 5:10	1 Cor 5:11	1 Cor 6:9-10
immoral	immoral	immoral
greedy	greedy	idolaters
robbers	idolater	*adulterers*
idolaters	*reviler*	*malakoi*
	drunkard	*arsenokoitai*
	robber	*thieves*
		greedy
		drunkards
		revilers
		robbers

Size of lists and sequence of terms vary. Moreover, 1 Cor 5:11 lists *singular* terms, in contrast to the *plural* terms of 5:10 and 6:9-10. 1 Cor 5:11 enumerates types of immoral believer *insiders*, whereas 1 Cor 5:10 and 6:9-10 list types of immoral *outsiders*. All three lists commence with the term *pornoi/pornos*, which links all these lists to the general theme of *porneia*/immorality and to Paul's earlier injunction not to associate with *pornois* (5:9). As already noted, the semantic range of *pornos* is broad and its meaning here far from certain. It could denote immoral persons, or male prostitutes, or clients of a prostitute, or perpetrators of incest, any one of which meanings would have ties to the context.[13] The increasing size of the lists could suggest Paul's moving toward a climactic and inclusive conclusion in ch. 6 where the

---

13 "Immoral persons" would be consistent with 5:1, 9 and the immoral litigaters of 6:1-8. "Male prostitutes" or "clients of a prostitute" would be consistent with 6:15-18. "Perpetrators of incest" would fit the content of 5:1.

most comprehensive list is given as illustration of behavior excluding persons from the kingdom of God. The longest list, 6:9-10, is either the source from which the terms of 5:10 and 11 are excerpts (so Scroggs 1983) or a Pauline expansion of the previous lists through the intentional addition of the terms *adulterers, malakoi, arsenokoitai,* and *thieves* (so Zaas 1988). The first three of these terms would be germane to a sexual implication of *porneia* in 5:1-6:20, but not the fourth. On the whole, the lists involve vices stereotypically associated by the Israelites with Gentile outsiders and proscribed within the House of Israel and the Jesus movement. Here their function appears primarily illustrative and, except for *pornos/pornoi,* involve activities not at the heart of Paul's concern.

The contents of the lists refer to types of persons or actions conventionally proscribed in Greco-Roman culture (e.g. greedy, robbers, revilers) or Israelite culture (all terms). Similar "vice lists" appear in Gal 5:19-21 and Eph 5:5 with the statement that such persons will not inherit the "kingdom of God," an expression rarely employed by Paul. Of the four instances in his authentic letters (Gal 5:21; 1 Cor 6: 9, 10; 15:50), half appear here and in three cases the phrase accompanies vice lists (here in 6:9 and 10 and in Gal 5:21). Such lists or catalogues of vices were a typical component of Israelite moral exhortation[14] and were adopted and used by members of the Christ movement as well.[15]

The lists of 1 Cor 5:10, 5:11 and 6:9-10 appear to have belonged to this stock of ethical and hortatory tradition, of which Paul and many other Christian authors made use. The fact that language concerning "not inheriting the kingdom of God" also accompanied some of these lists and that the phrase was rarely employed by Paul (except where he cites lists), make its virtually certain that these vice lists in 1 Corinthian were not composed by Paul, but were adopted and adapted by him from existing tradition. This likelihood is strengthened by the fact that in this letter Paul frequently uses the expression "do you not know" (1 Cor 6:9a) to introduce and recall sources or points of knowledge with which he expected his audience to be familiar.[16] It is also evident, moreover, that the formulation of the source, "will not inherit the kingdom of God,"—so unusual for Paul--inspired Paul's own statement, "do you not know that unjust/unrighteous persons *will not inherit the kingdom of God.*" Paul worded his own statement (6:9a) to fit the language of the source he was about to cite (6:9b-10).

The function of the list of 6:9b-10 was to provide examples of the "unjust/unrighteous persons" mentioned in 6:1 and 6:9a (so also Zaas 1988:626-27). They are like, or even comprise, nonbelieving outsiders to whom the Corinthian believers should not be taking their internal disputes (6:1-8). Only one of the terms of the list, however, is directly linked to the chief theme of 5:1-6:20, *porneia,* and that is

---

14 See Wis. 14:25-27; Sir 7:1-21; *1 Enoch* 8:1-4; *2 Enoch* 10:4-6; 34:1-2*; 2 Bar.* 73:4; 1QS 4.9-11; 10:21-23; *T. Reub.* 3:3-6; *T. Dan* 1:6; *T. Sim.* 3:1; *T. Dan* 2:4; *T. Jud.* 16:1; Philo, *Sac.* 32 147 vices!]; Jos. *Ag. Ap.* 2.19-28; *T. Mos.* 7:3-10.

15 See Matt 15:19/Mark 7:21-22; Rom 1:29-31; 13:13; 1 Cor 5:10-11; 6:9-10; 2 Cor 12:20-21; Gal 5:19-21; Eph 4:25-31; 5:3-13; Col 3:5-9; 1 Tim 1:9-10; 6:4-5; 2 Tim 3:2-5; Tit 3:3, 9; Rev 21:8; 22:15; cf.also *Did.* 2-5; 5:1-2; Herm. *Mand.* 8.3; *Sim* 6.5.5; 9.15.3; Polyc. *Phil.* 4:3; 5:2, 3; 6:1). On these catalogues or stock lists of vices and virtues and their employment by Greek and Roman moralists as well as Israelite and early Christian authors see Vögtle 1936; Wibbing 1959; and Kamlah 1964.

16 See 1 Cor 3:16; 5:6; 6:2, 3, 9, 15, 16, 19; 9:13, 24; cf. also Rom 6:16; 11:2.

the first term mentioned, namely *pornoi*. Thus it is clear that this list and those of chapter five are not at the heart of Paul's argument, bur rather enumerate stock vices used to illustrate types of behavior inconsistent with membership in the Body of Christ and with having been "washed, sanctified, and justified." (6:11).

There are several exegetical implications of these observations concerning 6:9-11 for our analysis of the terms *malakoi* and *arsenokoitai*. (1) Vv. 9-11 are a continuation and conclusion of a Pauline condemnation of litigation against fellow believers in the courts of law of "outsiders'" (6:1-8). (2) The list in vv. 9-10, like those of 5:10 and 5:11, was not composed by Paul but taken over by him from available hortatory tradition. (3) The list in vv. 9-10, like those of 5:10 and 5:11, has only an illustrative function and is peripheral to the heart of Paul's exhortation. The lists could all be excluded with no damage to Paul's argument. They are supplemental, not essential. (4) In the list, *pornos* is the only term related to the chief theme of 5:1-6:20, namely *porneia* and its avoidance. None of the other terms is connected with Paul's argument or essential to points he is making in 5:1-6:20, including *malakoi* and *arsenokoitai*.[17] (5) The terms *malakoi* and *arsenokoitai* occur only here in 1 Corinthians and are not a specific focus of Paul's attention. (6) At this point in our study, it is not certain what their meaning is, why they are present in this list, and what role they have in the point Paul is making. One thing however is clear: whatever weight and moral significance these two terms have, must be shared by all the terms in the list. Or, to put it another way, being *malakoi* or *arsenokoitai* is no better or worse than being any other kind of person included in the list. Types of immoral or unjust people are listed here, but not graded. No vice, including *malakoi* and *arsenokoitai*, receives particular comment or censure.

The terms *malakoi* or *arsenokoitai* occur nowhere else in 1 Corinthians and are unique to 1 Corinthians among the genuine Pauline letters. The latter term, *arsenokoitai*, appears in the Deutero-Pauline letter of 1 Timothy (1:9-10), never again in the NT and only rarely thereafter. The former term, *malakoi*, appears only twice more in the NT (Matt 11:8/Luke 7:25) and thereafter, combined again with *arsenokoitai*, in a quotation of 1 Cor 6:9 contained in Polycarp's letter to the Philippians (5:3). Given the rarity of this lexical combination in the Greek world generally, the lack of Pauline and biblical contexts for determining what Paul might have meant by the terms in 1 Corinthians is especially problematic. Thus it is hardly surprising that there is at present no scholarly consensus concerning their meaning and significance in 1 Corinthians or concerning their relevance to the issue of homosexuality.

There is as much disagreement among the Bible translations as there is among the commentators. A comparison of Bible translations illustrates the diversity or confusion concerning the assumed meaning of these terms and how that meaning is best rendered in modern languages.

Vulgate	neque molles neque masculorum concubitores
Luther	noch die Weichlinge noch die Knabenschänder
Zürcher	noch Lustknaben noch Knabenschänder

17 Beyond this context, "idolaters" (6:9; cf. 5:10, 11) is related to the issue of idolatry taken up in 8:1-11:1.

KJV	nor effeminate nor abusers of themselves with mankind
Goodspeed 1923	or sensual or given to unnatural vice
Moffatt 1926	catamites, sodomites
Bible de Jerusalem 1961	ni dépravés, ni gens de moeurs infames
Jerusalem Bible 1966	catamites, sodomites
New JB 1985	self-indulgent, sodomites
Knox New Testament	the effeminate, the sinners against nature
La Biblia 1990	ni los afeminados, ni los homosexuales
La Sacra Bibbia 1984	nè gli effeminati, nè i sodomiti
NAB 1990	nor boy prostitutes nor practicing homosexuals
NEB 1970	guilty of …homosexual perversion
Nueva Biblia Espanola:	invertidos, sodomitas
RSV 1946	nor homosexuals
RSV 1971	nor sexual perverts
New RSV 1989	male prostitutes, sodomites
Revised English Bible	sexual pervert
TEV 1976	or homosexual perverts
Weymouth New Testament	nor men guilty of unnatural crime

Another hermeneutical note: the number of different translating terms and the semantic differences among these terms is both remarkable and depressing. With ordinary Bible readers encountering such different versions of the biblical text in one language alone, to say nothing of differences across cultures, how could it ever be hoped that religious bodies appealing to this Corinthian text could ever reach agreement on what it originally meant and what meaning it might continue to have today? John Boswell (1980:338-339), summarizing only some English versions of this text, put it mildly when he stated that this translational variation "inspires skepticism, and close examination suggests that no modern translations of these terms are very accurate." I would add that the above comparison also makes vividly clear the tendency of modern translations to ascribe meanings to these terms that reflect *modern* conceptions of persons labeled "homosexual," their behavior and moral evaluation, that may have little or nothing to do with the meaning of the Greek terms in their original cultural context. In other words, this passage, to which hunters for homosexuals in the Bible have attributed so much significance, offers a classic case of *eisegesis* displacing *exegesis*, inadvertently reading *into* the text what supposedly is to be elicited *from* a text. The translations tell us as much, if not more, about the culture and values of the translators than they do about the culture and values of Paul and his sources.

Perhaps we as readers or translators or interpreters can never entirely avoid this danger of ethnocentrism any more than we can change the ocular lenses with which we view all so-called "reality." As modern readers of ancient and culturally alien texts, none of us possesses "immaculate perception." But surely we can make an effort at some modest degree of objectivity. One step in this direction is to ask, like a field anthropologist would ask of a native tribe she or he was studying, what do the natives mean by these words? With what values and perceptions, attitudes and even worldviews are these terms connected? What did these terms possibly mean in their original historical, social and cultural context? Let us first consider *malakoi*, then *arsenokoitai*.

Malakoi

The Greek adjective *malakos* literally means "soft." The term *malakoi*, a masculine plural form used here as a substantive, means, literally, "soft males." In its only other NT occurrence, the Q logion of Matt 11:8/Luke 7:25, it appears twice as a substantive neuter plural, *malaka* (literally, "soft things"), which in context denotes "soft clothing." Addressing the Galilean crowds about John the Baptizer, Jesus asked, "Why then did you go out? To see a man clothed in *soft clothing*? Behold, those who wear *soft clothing* live in kings' houses." The ironic point of this rhetorical question is only clear from the narrative and the cultural context. John, the hearers/readers had already learned in Matt 3:1-10, was a wildman prophet like those of old, preaching in the desolate wilderness of Judaea, clothed with a course and definitely unrefined leather girdle and chowing down on locusts and wild honey while denouncing the holy Pharisees and the priestly elite of being "snake bastards." [18] John was anything but an aristocratic wealthy fop given to the luxuries and refinements of life! In this only other occurrence of *malakos* in the NT, the word indicates an item of apparel illustrating the economic-social-cultural distinction between robust moral people like Jesus and his predecessor John, on the one hand, and rich elite "softies," on the other. In first century Palestine, real men don't eat quiche and don't wear soft clothes! Honest, reliable, salt-of-the-earth people (from the 97% lower class) have no connection with kings' houses, expensive threads, and the soft life (enjoyed by only 3% or less of the population, its "upper crust").

Could the term *malakos* have such class implications here in 1 Corinthians? If the hermeneutical principle often appealed to in the hunt for homosexuals in the Bible were brought into play—"let scripture interpret scripture"—a case could be made that "soft males" here in 1 Cor 6:9-10 implies decadent "rich men" who are always ripping off poor folk (like the Enron swindlers or Charles Keating or Neil Bush or Michael Milkin or Kenny Boy Lay...or —I cease for lack of space and spirit). Paul's cultural context allows this as a possibility since in a world where all goods were seen as in scarce and limited supply, rich people were always viewed suspiciously as rapacious thieves expanding their wealth and profiting at the expense of others (Malina 1979, 1986, 2001:81-133). Such a meaning, moreover, would be consistent with several of the other terms of the list e.g. "thieves, greedy persons, robbers." On the other hand, "soft males" could also possibly refer to males with soft physical features, soft skin, hair, or cheeks, or soft and gentle in their nature. Or might it imply males who were "soft-headed" or "weak-willed" persons, "lacking in self-control" (LSJ, *s.v.*). Or could it mean "ill males," given the fact that its noun, *malakia*, denoted "sickness, debility, weakness" (BDAG 613). Without extensive knowledge of the cultural context, how could one decide which of these alternatives is more plausible for a first-century audience at Corinth? And yet how often some rush to claim that the term means "homosexuals" without further exegetical ado? One thing is absolutely certain: the

---

18 The parallel Lukan account (7:18-35) combines in one unit what Matthew narrates in two separate accounts (3:1-10; 11:7-19).

word was no technical, conventional term for males who engaged in sex with other males. It had no sexual connotation in Matthew and Luke and if it did so in 1 Cor 6:9, this must be demonstrated on other than linguistic grounds.

Here is where ancient views of males and females, their differing natures and modes of behavior—that is, ancient constructs of gender-- become relevant.[19] Ancient Mediterraneans viewed human beings as either male or female, each with nature-given, distinctive, gender-based personal features, social ranking and behavioral scripts. The ideal male was seen as rational, physically strong, daring, bold, courageous, competitive, socially and sexually aggressive, rough and tough, hard and hairy, protector of his home and family and embodiment of the family's honor (its public reputation and status) symbolized in his blood, male organ and testicles. The ideal female was his physical, mental, and moral opposite. She was emotional more than rational, physically weak, reticent, modest, sensitive, socially and sexually vulnerable, smooth and gentle, soft and depilated, nurturer of her home and family and embodiment of her family's shame (the vulnerability of its honor) symbolized in her blood, breasts and vulva. Since the world of the Bible was a patriarchal world whose dominant ideas, values, and worldviews were those of the dominant free males, the male was regarded—they regarded themselves-- as superior "by nature" and the female, inferior, just as the traits ascribed to the male were judged superior to those ascribed to the female. He was dominant and ruled; she was subordinate and was ruled. He was on top, she was on the bottom (in bed and everywhere else). He was active; she was passive. He gave; she received. His organ was a plow; hers was a field. He was the "sower;" she was the "soil."[20]

Given this notion of the inferiority of females, male to male friendships were preferred to male to female relationships. Achilles Tatius, in his story *Leucippe and Clitophon,* has one of his characters articulate a prevalent view concerning the preference for boys over women:

> "To me you sound less like a beginner in sex than an old pro, surrounding us with all these female complications. Now listen to what I have to say in defense of boys. Everything women do is false, both words and actions. Even if a woman appears to be beautiful, it is the laborious contrivance of make-up. Her beauty is all perfume, or hair dye, or potions. And if you strip her of all these devices, she'll look like the jackdaw in the fable, stripped of all his feathers. A boy's beauty isn't fostered by the scent of myrrh or by other false odors; a boy's sweat smells sweeter than all women's perfumes..."

Accordingly, in this macho-oriented culture, for a male to appear in any way whatsoever as "womanish" was a horror and an immediate occasion for public censure and ridicule. For him to display any feature associated with females was to deny his identity and responsibility as a male, a distortion of how nature and the gods intended him to be. The same script applied to females in reverse: any display on their part of "masculine" traits was a violation of their feminine identity as established by nature

19 Our honoree discusses elements of ancient gender constructs in his 1996 essay.
20 For ancient sources and secondary literature on this ancient construct of male and female genders see Delaney 1987; Halperin 1990:15-40, 41-53;Halperin et. al. 1990; Malina 1990; Dean-Jones 1991; Malina and Neyrey 1991; Winkler 1991; Williams 1999; Elliott 2000 500-599; Malina 2001:27-57.

and the gods, and constituted conduct earning public censure and reproach. According to this cultural script, then, for males to be called "soft" (a quality of females) could have constituted a potent public put-down, similar to certain males today being called "pussies" or "cunts" or "bitches." For males to prefer being soft and adopting other "feminine" characteristics was disgraceful, repugnant, and a bid for public condemnation. In other words, for males to be "effeminate" was a gross violation of moral norms and expectations concerning honorable male conduct. To be sure, this does not mean that such boundary-crossing behavior never happened. Rather when it did, it was open to damaging public ridicule and a debilitating loss of honor, reputation, and status. For the ancients it was a short step from "effeminate" male youth ("fairies," "fruits," "sissies" they would be called today) parading around like women to the assumption that these "faggots" or "queens" assumed the passive, receptive role of women in sexual intercourse with older men and became their "bitches," as our contemporary jargon puts it.

It is crucial here to recognize the fact that sex, as understood by the ancient Greeks (that is, the dominant males), centered on the *male* sexual equipment, the erect penis or phallus, and phallic penetration of a receptive partner (Halperin 1990:130). Sex, in other words, was phallically conceived, defined, and artistically depicted. To be "masculine" was to possess and wield a phallus, to be aggressive, to dominate, to be "on top" physically and socially. To be "feminine" was to lack a penis, to be passive, submissive, penetrated, and physically and socially "below" the male. This explains not only the relative lack of male interest in what females did with one another (unless surrogate phalluses [aka dildoes] were involved).[21] It also explains a major vantage point from which male character and behavior was viewed and evaluated.

In the numerous ancient references to male-male sexual relations, where censure was expressed, it focused chiefly on the disgrace of young males abandoning or at least compromising their masculinity and assuming the position and role of inferior, passive, and receptive females (Dover 1989:100-109).

Israelites shared this perspective. For example, Philo, an Israelite contemporary of Paul, commenting on the ancient residents of Sodom, dwelled on the horror of emasculation:

> "Men mounted males without respect for the sexual nature (*physin*) which the active partner shares with the passive. Then as little by little they accustomed those who were by nature men [who had been born male] to submit to play the part of women...not only did they emasculate (*malakoteti*) their bodies by luxury and voluptuousness, but they worked a further degeneration in their souls and, as far as in them lay, were corrupting the whole of mankind" (*On Abraham* 135-136).

Philo's concern was less with male-male coitus per se and more with how such intercourse distorted gender roles and promoted the disgraceful *effeminization* of the passive male partner. Similar disgust with males "changing the order of their nature" into females and females doing likewise is registered by the Israelite moralist, Pseudo-

---

21 Halperin notes (1990:136) that Plato is "the only writer of the classical period to speak about sexual desire between women" (*Symposium* 191E 2-5).

Phocylides (1 cent BCE-1 cent CE)[22] and by Paul in Rom 1:26-27.[23] The effeminate males, by the way, were youths, not children. They were pubescent boys (*paides*) who had reached puberty but had not yet grown beards. At the same time, they were not adult males on the same physical, economic, or social level as their partners but were inferior in terms of both age and social station (Halperin 1990:20-21). In this respect, male-male sexual relations mirrored and replicated the unequal pattern of male-female relations (Dover 1989: 16, 84-85). Attested male-male sexual relations in antiquity were, with few exceptions, between *unequal* partners, with the older, socially superior male pursuing, dominating, and on occasion "corrupting" the younger inferior boy (Halperin 1990:20-21)

Philo's treatise, *On the Contemplative Life*, (59-62) illustrates several of these features of male to male sexual relations as viewed by Israelites in Paul's time: the assumed inferiority of females to males; the "disease of effeminacy;" male to male sexual relations as older males to boys (and the respective terms for "beloved" and "lover"); the symbolizing of intercourse between males as sowing seed among rocks and stones; and his rationale for the condemnation. Describing the first of Plato's two types of banquets, Philo writes:

> "In Plato's banquet, the talk is almost entirely concerned with love (*erôtos*), not merely with love-sickness of men for women, or women for men, passions recognized by the laws of nature, but of men for other males (*andrôn arresin*) differing from them only in age. For, if we find some clever subtlety dealing apparently with the heavenly Love and Aphrodite, it is brought in to give a touch of humour. The chief part is taken up by the common vulgar love (*erôs*) which robs men of the courage which is the virtue most valuable for the life both of peace and war, sets up the disease of effeminacy (*thêleian de noson*) in their souls and turns into a male-female hybrids (*androgynous*) those males who should have been disciplined in all the practices which make for valour. And having wrought havoc with the years of boyhood and reduced the boy to the grade and condition of a girl (*erômenês*) besieged by a lover it inflicts damage on lovers (*tous erastas*) also in three most essential respects, their bodies, their souls, and their property. For the mind of the lover (*tou paiderastou*) is necessarily set towards his darling (*ta paidika*) and its sight is keen for him only, blind to all other interests, private and public; his body wastes away through desire (*epithymias*), particularly if his suit is unsuccessful, while his property is diminished by two causes, neglect and expenditure on his beloved *(ton erômenon)*. As a side growth we have another greater evil of national importance. Cities are desolated, the best kind of men become scarce, sterility (*steirôsin*) and childlessness (*agonian*) ensure through the devices of these who imitate men who have no knowledge of husbandry by sowing not in the deep soil of the lowland [i.e. coitus with the female] but in briny fields and stony and stubborn places, which not only give no possibility for anything to grow but even destroy the seed deposited within them [i.e. anal coitus with young males who cannot conceive].[24]

---

22 Pseudo-Phocylides, lines 190-92: "Do not transgress with unlawful sex the limits set by nature. For even animals are not pleased by intercourse of male with male" (*lekhos andrôn*; cf. Lev 18:22, 20:13 *miškab zakûr*, in the rabbinic sources). And let women not imitate the sexual role of men" and Line 215. "Guard the youthful prime of life of a comely boy, because many rage for intercourse with a man."

23 "Their [those suppressing the truth, 1:18] females exchanged natural relations for unnatural, and the males likewise gave up natural relations with women and were consumed with passion for one another."

24 The metaphor of sowing in rocks and stones was used already by Plato (*Laws* 838E). It presumed the

In another treatise, *On the Virtues*, Philo explains the prohibition of Deut 23:5 ("a woman shall not wear anything pertaining to a man, nor shall a man put on a woman's garment") as assuring in regard to the male that "no trace, no merest shadow of the female, should attach to him to spoil his masculinity" (*Virt.* 18), and that "in such matters the real man should maintain his masculinity, particularly in his clothes, which, as he always wears them by day and night, ought to have nothing to suggest unmanliness(*anandria*)" (*Virt.* 20).

These sentiments were in keeping with the Israelite insistence that social order, like the natural order, is maintained by respecting the distinctions among things that the Creator established from the beginning. As Israel conceived the creation of life, trees, plants and living beings of the water, earth, and air were each created "according to their own kind" and belonged properly to the domain of either earth, water or air (Gen 1). This feature of creation required that God's people respect the distinctions set by God, abhor all anomalies that failed to fit a specific class, and never mix those entities that God specifically separated (Lev 11; Deut 14:3-20). Behind this system of classification and regulation of life lay a fundamental concern for order in society and in the cosmos, which in Israel, was spelled out in a system distinguishing "clean" from "unclean," "pure" from "impure," "holy" from "profane," as anthropologist Mary Douglas has so brilliantly shown in her classical cross-cultural studies on purity and pollution (Douglas 1966, 1970, 1975). Anomalous creatures were abominated as unclean and were forbidden for food: "I am the Lord your God, who have separated you from the peoples. You therefore shall make a distinction between the clean beast and the unclean; you shall not make yourselves abominable by beast or bird or anything with which the ground teems, which I have set apart for you to hold unclean. You shall be holy to me; for I the Lord am holy, and have separated you from the peoples, that you should be mine" (Lev 20:24-26). In this same spirit, Torah declared that "a woman shall not wear anything that pertains to a man, nor shall a man put on a woman's garment, for whoever does these things is an abomination to the Lord your God" (Deut 22:5).

This abhorrence of mixing the not-to-be-mixed extended to animals, seed, and cloth as well. "You shall not let your cattle breed with a different kind; you shall not sow your field with two kinds of seed; nor shall there come upon you a garment of cloth made of two kinds of material" (Lev 19:19; Deut 22:9). "You shall not plow with an ox and an ass together. You shall not wear a mingled stuff, wool and linen together" (Deut 22:10-11). The distinctiveness of male and that of female was understood as established by God in accord with the established distinctiveness of all created things. Social order required observance of these distinctions. For males or females to violate these boundaries and exchange their "God-given" and "nature-determined" roles was to violate Torah and seriously undermine the order to which Torah pointed—the argument that Paul mounted in his letter to the Romans (1:18-32).

Throughout the ancient world, for males to adopt the ways of females and "effeminize" themselves, to morph from lads into ladies, as it were, was looked upon with loathing and excoriated with an entire arsenal of labels: *thêlydrias, thylyprepês,*

---

wide-spread symbolizing of male-female intercourse as "sewing seed" (the male) in fertile soil (the female), ploughing (the male) a field (the female), in all cases of which, of course, the male is the active penetrater and the female, the passive penetrated.

ektethêlymmenos, gynnis (can also mean *castratus*), *gynaikanôr, gynaikias; androgynos, batalos, bakêlos, kinaidos, kinaidologos.* Latin labels included *effeminare, effeminatus, effeminatio;   mollis; delicates; scortum (exoletum;, prostibulum;;* cf. also *kinaidoi* and *pathici* (male prostitutes). Entire peoples were put down by the Greeks as effeminates/faggots:" Lydians, Persians, Medes, Phrygians, Amazons, Babylonians, Armenians, Syrians, Libyans, Carthaginians, Ionians, Athenians, Corinthians, Cyprians, Rhodians, Sybarties, Tarentines, even Romans (*Or. Sib.* 5.167)--often because of their "feminine" attire or because they were perceived to be under the domination of women (e.g. Amazons or Phrygians worshipping Cybele or Syrians worshipping Dea Syria; cf. also "female" attire of Dionysos and Priapos). For males to make themselves up as females (*thêlynesthai)* was to act "against nature" (Diog. Laert.6.65; Seneca., *Ep.* 122.7) and an "illness" (Seneca, *Contr.* 2.1), as Philo also put it. Fine, soft material, silk, musslin etc was "female" attire, as was donning colored or purple clothing, long robes, much underclothing; fine footwear, elaborate head coverings (especially the mitre), and jewelry; showing attention to hair care; being beardless; depilation of body hair; delighting in cosmetics and perfume, and looking like a female in bodily appearance and gait (wagging of hips, inclining of head); unsteady eyes and gaze; high voice, lisping; and luxury and a soft way of life.[25] These are elements of prevailing constructs of female and male gender, utterly misinformed scientifically, yet universally held notions related to the loathing of effeminacy that festered in the ancient macho-obsessed world and shaped its language, social relations, and behavioral scripts.

From a cultural perspective, it is quite possible that with *malakoi* Paul was referring to this type of "soft males." He then would have been speaking of "effeminate males," just as Jerome, Luther, KJV, Knox, and the Spanish and Italian versions consider to have been the case. Such effeminate males, beside depilated dandies, could have included entertainers acting as women, transvestites (in modern parlance), eunuchs (castrated and hence emasculated = "effeminated") or even males with long hair. According to Paul, males wearing long hair were acting contrary to their nature and were behaving as effeminates looking like women. Paul makes this point when trying to explain and justify the differences in attire between men and women (1 Cor 11:2-16). Surely it is not proper, he insists, for a woman to pray to God with her head uncovered (v. 13).

> Does not nature itself teach you that a man wearing his hair long brings disgrace upon himself? But a woman wearing her hair long brings honor upon herself, since her hair was given to her [by God and nature] as a covering (vv. 14-15).[26]

The Church Fathers, as Boswell (1980:339-41) has observed, did not use *malakos* but rather other terms for "effeminate," but they were certainly preoccupied with effeminacy (for which the related noun *malakia* sometimes was used).[27]

---

25 On effeminacy in the ancient world see Herter 1959.
26 For an Israelite and a Greek expressing the same thought see Pseudo-Phocylides 212. ("Long hair is not fit for boys, but for voluptuous women") and Epictetus, Disc. 3.1.25-31.
27 See Clement of Alexandria, *Paedagogus/Instructor*, Book 2. chs. 3, 4, 5, 6, 7, 8; for *paederastia*, see *Paed.* 2.10.83.5; 2.10.86.2). Effeminates were lumped together with prostitutes, violators of graves, murderers, thieves (Greg. Naz. c. 1.2.2.496f; John Chrys., in *Ioh. h.* 33 [32].3; in 2 Tim h. 6.4; in Hebr.

Another aspect of Greek culture relevant to our topic was the emotional and *loving relationships* that could develop between a younger "soft" male, a "beloved" (*erômenos*, related to *eros*, "love") and an older male suitor, the "lover'" (*erastês*) or "lover of the boy" (*paiderastês*). In the male-oriented and male-dominated culture of the time, such male-male love relationships often were preferred to male-female relations, especially by those wishing to avoid procreation in their sexual activity. In such love relationships involving young free males, their submission to senior lovers and their temporary adoption of the passive "feminine" role was acceptable under the condition that they felt no erotic desire for their elder partner but submitted only out of love. "The boy," Socrates emphasized in Xenophon's *Symposium* (8.21), "does not share in the man's pleasure in intercourse, as a woman does; cold sober, he looks upon the other drunk with sexual desire."[28] "It was clearly unacceptable, after all, Halperin aptly observes (1990:130), for the future rulers of Athens to exhibit any eagerness or desire to submit themselves to anyone, especially to their (eventual) peers."

For Israelites, intentional avoidance of the primary command to be fruitful and multiply (Gen 1:28) was a grave violation of Torah and came under severe censure. Philo's criticism of the lover-beloved relationship (*Contemp.* 59-62 cited above) included this point as well as other features of this partnership.

In a further extension of this cultural construct, *malakos* could also designate males, particularly young boys, who made their bodies soft and smooth by shaving and powdering them (as did women) and who sold themselves as *male prostitutes* (BDAG 613). The appearance of *malakoi* in the 1 Cor 6 list along with *pornoi*, and *moichoi* ("immoral/prostitutes" and "adulterers") would, in fact, favor this sense, as would the mention of prostitution in 6:15-20. In our modern culture, Robin Scroggs (1983:106) points out, such youth would be "call-boys," young males who have sex with older males for pay, "who walked the thin line between passive homosexual activity for pleasure and that for pay." The term "prostitute" implies sex for pay, then as now. So if *malakoi* in 1 Cor 6:9 and its source was referring to young male ; prostitutes (this sense appears to be assumed by the Zürcher version, NRSV, and NAB), it may have been the sex-for-pay angle that was deplored. In classical Athens, the hiring of young male prostitutes by senior males was a known practice, but the passive male prostitute himself, when he reached his majority, was barred from admission and participation in the public assembly (*ekklêsia*) because his earlier abandoning of his maleness in playing the receptive role impugned his character and honor as a male (Halperin 1990: 88-112; see also Krenkel 1978). While such a situation is conceivable, there is an even more likely scenario where pay was not a factor but rather unacceptable male passive and submissive behavior.

Here again the male-dominated Greek and Roman cultural context is important to keep in mind. Male to male relationships were prized over male-female relationship,

---

h. 2.4; inscr. alt. 1) and were disallowed from the Christian assemblies (Clem. Alex. *Paed.* 3.19.3, ref. to Deut 22:5; cf. Philo, *Spec. Leg.* 1.325; *Virt.* 18-21; Jos., *Ant.* 4.301; Clem. Alex. *Strom.* 2.81.3; Tert. *Spect.* 23) and with ref. to 1 Cor 6:9 (Tert. *Pud.* 16; Joh. Chrys. *Illum. Cat.* 1.25). See also Petersen 1989.

28 See also related expectations expressed in Aristophanes's *Clouds* (979-80) and Halperin 1990:130-33 for discussion of this conventional view as contrasted to Plato's new and more egalitarian (and idealist) vision of reciprocal love between lover and beloved.

since males were ranked superior to females (by other males, of course). Females, on the other hand, were viewed as misbegotten or defective males. They were necessary for reproduction and extending the family line and for doing all the shunt work at home. But actual friendships of equals or relationships of patrons and clients were normally forged only between males. Secondly, in Greco-Roman circles, education of males among elites (i.e. those who set the standards) conventionally involved the separation of young males (ca. 8 years) from their mothers and home, and their entrustment into the care of an older male friend or relative of the family who would assume responsibility for the boys' formal education. This older male was known in Greek as a *paiderastês*, a "pederast," i.e. a "lover/friend "(*-erast*) of a "boy" (*ped-*, from *pais*) whose education (*paedeia*) was being advanced.[29]

Such an arrangement could and often did lend itself to abuse, including sexual predation on the part of the pederasts and their subjection of the young male to sexual misuse and humiliation. A testament to this development was the transformation of the Greek myth of Zeus' love for the beautiful youth Ganymede (reflecting and justifying "natural" and divinely sanctioned male-male relationships) into the "dirty old man" account of lecherous Zeus lusting after the dandy Ganymede. This produced the term *catamitus* in Latin (a Latin formulation derived from the word "Ganymede" in Greek) for the male passive partner in a male-to-male sexual relationship.[30] *Catamitus*, in turn, was transliterated into English as "catamite." Though such male relationships were commonplace among the elites, the sexual abuse possible in this relationship, as well as the general disapproval of males behaving as females, was a frequent target of moral scorn. The modern biblical versions translating *malakoi* with "catamites" (Moffatt, JB) may have had this development in mind. The Greco-Roman myth, like the institution of pederasty itself, could have been known in Corinth among believers from a Gentile background. Among those of Israelite origin this would have been less likely since neither the myth nor the educational convention was an element of Israelite culture.[31]

If *malakoi* in 1 Cor 6:9 designated either young males who were under the *tutelage* of older males or who were *lovers* of these older males and submitted to them sexually, or if they were young males who submitted sexually to older males *for pay*, then the adjacent term *arsenokoitai* could have denoted the elder male partners. In the former case, it could have been the corrupt and corrupting institution of pederasty that was found odious; in the latter case, it could have been the sex-for-pay factor. Already in antiquity, paying for something as natural as sexual intercourse, degraded and shamed the act. What these two possibilities have in common is the fact that both cases would involve males taking on a perceived female role, submitting themselves to other males as though they were females, receiving in their anus the penis of the penetrating male and thus making "cunts" of themselves.[32]

---

29 On pederasty see Marrou 1964: 50-62, 479-82; Cartledge 1981; Patzer 1982; Koch-Harnack 1983; Percy 1996; Nissinen 1998:57-62, in addition to coverage in the works listed above in Note 19.

30 On the Zeus-Ganymede myth see Lewis 1983, Dover 1989:196-197.

31 Philo does not employ the noun *paederastia* but does use the verb *paederasteô* (*Spec.* 2.50; 3.37; *Hypoth* 7:1) and the noun *paederastês* (*Decal.* 168; *Spec.* 3.39; 4.89; *Contempl.* 52, 61) only in reference to sexual relationships involving older males with younger males.

32 When in post-biblical times (and only then), the sin of the Sodomites was no longer understood to be

The blurring or eradication of sexual boundaries, which were thought to have been established by nature, the gods, or the God of Israel, also drew Paul's censure and condemnation in his letter to the Romans (1:18-32) where "exchanging natural relations for unnatural" meant males behaving as females and females behaving as males. In this dishonorable distortion of nature and violation of God's will, it was not the sexual intercourse per se that was the bone of contention, but rather males pusillanimously acting as passive females or treating other males as females, and females presumptuously acting as aggressive males with other females and the latter cooperating in this transgression of sacred boundaries.

Arsenokoitai

The term *arsenokoitês,* the singular of *arsenokoitai,* is most unusual. It is not attested in Greek literature prior to 1 Corinthians, and it appears only rarely thereafter. In the Bible it appears only in 1 Cor 6:9 and 1 Tim 1:10, in both instances in vice lists pre-existing the writings in which they were included. The list of 1 Timothy (1:9-10) is presented to exemplify types of unjust persons for whom the law was laid down (1:8):

> The law is not laid down for the just person (*dikaios*, v. 9) but for the lawless and disobedient, for the ungodly and sinners, for the unholy and profane, for murderers of fathers and murderers of mothers, for manslayers, for immoral persons/prostitutes, for *arsenokoitai,* kidnappers, liars, perjurers and whatever else opposes sound teaching (1:9-10)

The list of 1 Timothy serves the same general purpose as the list in 1 Corinthians 6; namely to exemplify *unjust* persons engaged in conduct viewed as incompatible with the gospel (1 Tim 1:11) or membership in the community of the faithful (1 Cor 5-6). The precise meaning of *arsenokoitai* is just as uncertain in 1 Timothy as it is in 1 Corinthians. Bishop Polycarp of Smyrna, writing in the first half of the second century to the church at Philippi, mentions both terms in his encouragement of young men or recent converts (5:3) to "be blameless in all things" and remove themselves from "worldly cravings." Selecting language from the list of 1 Cor 6:9-10 he warns that "neither *pornoi* nor *malakoi* nor *arsenokoitai* will inherit the kingdom of God" so that "it is necessary to refrain from such things." Here too is a list but it is reduced to just three terms presumably relevant particularly to those enticed by the "cravings" (*epithymiai,* 5:3) of this world. This text is no clearer than its source on the specific meaning of these terms or their possible social or moral implications. As in 1 Corinthians, they are representative. Here, however, they are examples of "craving of

---

inhospitality and rape of strangers (as it was throughout the biblical literature) but was thought to be the males of Sodom copulating with other males, Sodom and "sodomy" became terms for *male same-sex sexual intercourse* as well as *anal intercourse*, no matter by whom it was practiced. Neither Genesis 19 nor the Bible in general , of course, says anything of this, but one could imagine the contorted development of thought: the association of Sodom with male-male sexual intercourse would have presumed that the males of Sodom copulated with the visitors (regarding them as human males and not sexless angels) and this would have involved anal intercourse. Ergo "sodomy" "must" cover both *male-male sexual intercourse* and *anal intercourse*. That anal intercourse was practiced not only by males with males but males with females does not seem to have occurred to those who would find here in Genesis 19 a prohibition of male-with-male sexual relations. On the invention of the conceptual construct "sodomy" see Jordan 1997.

the things in the world" from which believers should be "cut off."[33] Jerome, translating centuries later for a Latin-speaking audience, rendered *arsenokoitai* in both 1 Cor 6 and 1 Tim 1 with the same Latin phrase, *masculorum concubitores*, lit. "male bed-fellows of males"—an expression as unspecific in Latin as is the original Greek. However, the meaning of *arsenokoitai* is to be established, it is clear that, like *malakos*, it is no technical or conventional term for males who have intercourse with other males.

In brief, the meaning of *arsenokoitai* (*arsenokoitês* in the singular) is as uncertain as the meaning of *malakoi,* and its occurrences are even fewer.[34] The components of *arsenokoitês* are *arsen* ("male") + *koitê* ("bed," "marriage-bed;" or figuratively, "sexual intercourse" ["go to bed with"]; or sexual emission [occurring in bed]). The *gender* of the word alone is ambiguous, occurring in a declension denoting either males or females. Thus it could denote "*females* lying/sleeping (around) with males" as well as "*males* lying" (Boswell 1980:345, n.27). It is also uncertain whether *arsen* is to be understood as *object* or *subject*: i.e. a male or a person who lies *with men* (= object) or a *male who lies* with both women and men (as preferred by Boswell). Related terms beginning with *arseno* or *arreno* employ the form as subject: *arsenogenês* ("male"), *arsenothymos* ("male-minded"), *arsenomorphos* (having the form of a male"), *arrenophanês* (having a male appearance), thereby giving weight to the latter alternative. On the other hand, Jerome's translation, *masculorum concubitores* ("males bedding with males), takes *arseno* as object.

Virtually no light is shed on the issue by extra-biblical texts. Contemporary Greek and Roman authors, when discussing male-male sexual relations, never use the term. The same is true of the Church Fathers, who, while commenting frequently on male-male sexual relations and drawing on a large vocabulary for this subject, never use the term *arsenokoitai*. This could suggest that the term *arsenokoitai* had no connection whatsoever with male same-sex behavior.

John Boswell sees the term referring to "male prostitutes capable of the active role with either men or women" (1980:344) and *malakoi* as possibly meaning "masturbators" (1980:338-53). Inclusion of male prostitutes in this list of proscribed activities would be consistent with the condemnation of prostitution, both commercial and cultic, in Israel and the early Church. This sense of the term would also fit the context of 1 Cor 5:1-6:20 where prostitution is also discussed (6:15-20). On the other hand, *arsenokoitai* meaning "male prostitutes," would involve a redundancy if *pornoi*

---

33 The verb occurs in a proscription of behavior presented in *Sib. Or.* 2.73 ("Do not *arsenokoitein*, do not betray information, do not murder") but again its context sheds little light on its specific meaning; for the infinitive see also *Acts of John* 36. The *Apology of Aristides,* a 2d century CE Christian text, contains a list of Gentile vices that ends with *arsenokoitia* (9:13); cf. also 9:8-9 (they are "mad after males"[*arrenomaneis*] and the question about whether a god can be an adulterer or "corrupter of males" [*androbatês*]).

34 Another hermeneutical comment: Determining the possible meaning(s) of the term *arsenokoitai* is made difficult by its rarity in the Greek world and by its presence in the NT in lists whose terms are not all expressly related to their literary and rhetorical contexts. In neither 1 Corinthians nor 1 Timothy do the authors focus directly on *malakoi* and *arsenokoitai* by commenting further on them and explaining their relevance to the points being made. While the factor of *literary* context is not completely irrelevant to a determination of meaning, its is not as helpful with respect to these terms as it is in most other cases.

at the outset of the list also meant "male prostitutes" rather than the more general "immoral males" or "males engaging in incest."[35]

Robin Scroggs (1983:83, 107-08), speculates that the term *arsenokoitês* may have been a Greek translation of the Hebrew *miškab zakûr* ("lying with a male"), a Rabbinic expression found in the Talmudic interpretation[36] of Lev 18:22 and 20:13: "With a male you shall not lie the lyings of a woman" (Lev 18:22, Scroggs' literal translation) and "If a male lies with a male the lyings of a woman, both of them have committed an abomination" (Lev. 20:13). The Hebrew formulations of Lev 18:22 and 20:13 are obscure and unclear and the virtually equivalent LXX formulations are no clearer.[37] As a pair, *malakoi* and *arsenokoitai*, Scroggs suggests, could have designated the passive and active partners respectively in male with male sexual intercourse.[38] This paring of the two terms, however, is unique, occurring nowhere else in the entire Bible, and thus is in no way a standard expression. Moreover, the Rabbinic sources are much later than Paul and probative evidence of any actual connection of *arsenokoitês* with an earlier Hebrew term or with the two texts of Leviticus has not been presented. Of the three NT texts claimed to refer to male-with-male sexual relations (Rom 1:18-32, 1 Cor 6:9 and 1 Tim 1:10), none refers explicitly to, or quotes, Lev 18:22 or 20:13.

Frederick Danker, lexicographer non pâreil, in the BDAG entry on *arsenokoitês*, also considers the component parts of the term and mentions as analogous a word occurring in extra-biblical Greek, *mêtrokoitês*, meaning "one who has intercourse with his mother (*mêtêr*)" (BDAG 135). He thus renders *arsenokoitês* "a male who engages in sexual activity w[ith] a pers[on] of his own sex, *pederast*...of one who assumes the dominant role in same-sex activity" (BDAG 135). This coincides with Scrogg's view that in 1 Cor 6:9 "*malakos* points to the effeminate call-boy" and *arsenokoitês*, to "the active partner who keeps the *malakos* as a 'mistress' or who hires him on occasion to satisfy his sexual desires" (1983:108). Accordingly, "a very specific dimension of pederasty is being denounced with these two terms," a disapproval voiced frequently in the Greco-Roman world on the topic. "Romans forbade pederasty w[ith] free boys in the Lex Scantinia, pre-Cicero" (BDAG 135) and in general distanced themselves from male same-sex relations and labeled it "the Greek vice." Second Temple Israel

---

35 Boswell is followed by Countryman (1988:127-28, 202); Wright (1984), on the other hand, rejects Boswell's proposal; see Peterson (1986) for informative observations. The hunch that *malakoi* means "masturbators" ignores, in my opinion, the large body of evidence attesting the antipathy toward effeminacy as the operative cultural value here, and introduces an activity that is only infrequently mentioned in ancient sources. It is also difficult to imagine how Paul could have viewed masturbation as an example of injustice (see 6:9a).

36 See *b. Šabbat* 17b; *b. Sukkah* 29a; *b. Sanhedrin* 82a; *y. Berakhot* 9.50.13c.

37 Lev 18:22 LXX: *Kai meta arsensos ou koimêthêsêi koitên gynaikeian*, lit., "And with a male you shall not lie the woman lying/bed." Lev 20:13 LXX: *Kai hos an koimêthêi meta arsenos koitên gynaikos*, lit. "And whoever lies with a male the lying/bed of a woman..." In neither the Hebrew nor the Greek is it clear what exactly is forbidden: males lying with other males as they would with women so as to engage in some form of sexual intercourse ("lyings of a woman" suggesting *sexual intercourse*), or, more specifically, males assuming the female passive role when lying sexually with other males ("lyings of a woman" suggesting the *passive, receptive role*).

38 In this case, the *malakoi* would have certainly been young boys who were adolescents who had not yet grown beards, since "male prostitution," at least as we know from classical Athens, "was largely the province of those below the age of majority" (Halperin 1990:90).

condemned male same- sex sexual relations and likewise considered it practiced only by "the other guys," deploring it as a typical Gentile vice.[39]

The corruption of young boys by predatory older males came under heavy censure throughout the ancient world. Occasion was given to the vice by the opportunity older males had given the cultural preference for male-male relations in general and the operation of pederasty as an educational arrangement. The deviant aspect of pederasty was not the relationship as such, but the "effeminizing" of the younger males and their *abuse* by their senior tutors/lovers. In this relationship, older, established powerful males could and did abuse their younger, weaker, and socially inferior male partners. Thus we find the warning issued by an Israelite writer, "Guard the youthful prime of life of a comely boy, because many rage for intercourse with a man/male" (Pseudo-Phocylides, line 215 [1 cent BCE-1 cent CE]). Discussing the vices of an evil man, Philo observes that in regard to his tongue, belly, and genitals (*ta gennêtika*),

> "He misuses them for abominable lusts and forms of intercourse forbidden by all laws. He not only attacks in his fury the marriage-beds of others, but even plays the pederast (*paiderastôn*) and forces the male type of nature to debase and convert itself into the feminine form, just to indulge a polluted and accursed passion." (*Special Laws* 2.14.50)

His comment on the residents of Sodom in Abraham's time (*On Abraham* 135-136, cited earlier) expressed similar notions. The description reflects pagan practices of Philo's own time, which he imagined to have typified the residents of Sodom in Genesis 19, where none of these particulars is mentioned.

Emasculation and effeminization of males given to the "female disease" and the complicity of the active partners in this vice are also denounced even more extensively by Philo in his commentary on various violations of the 6th Commandment of the Decalogue and the obligation to procreate:

> "Much graver than the above [certain tactics used for avoiding conception in sexual intercourse and "ploughing the hard and stony ground," 32-36] is another evil, which has ramped its way into the cities, namely pederasty/love of boys (*to paiderastein*).[40] In the former days the very mention of it was a great disgrace, but now it is a matter of boasting not only to the active but to the passive partners who habituate themselves to endure the disease of effemination (*noson thêleian*, lit., the "female disease"), let both body and soul run to waste, and leave no ember of their male sex-nature to smoulder. Mark how conspicuously they braid and adorn the hair of their heads, and how they scrub and paint their faces with cosmetics and pigments and the like, and smother themselves with fragrant unguents. For of all such embellishments, used by all who deck themselves out to wear a comely appearance, fragrance is the most seductive. In fact, the transformation of the male nature to the female is practiced by them as an art and does not raise a blush. 38. These persons are rightly judged worthy of death by those who obey the law, which ordains that the man-woman hybrid (*ton androgynon*) who debases the sterling coin of nature should perish unavenged, suffered not to live

---

39 See *Jub.* 7:20-21; 13:17; 16:5-6; 20:5-6; *T. Naphtali* 3:4-5; 4:1; *T. Asher* 7:1; *T. Benjamin* 9:1; *T. Levi* 14:6; *2 Enoch* 10:4; 24:2; 3 Macc 2:5; *Sib. Or.* 3:185, 594-600; 5:166-67; 5:386-96; *Let. Aris.* 152; Pseudo-Phocylides, 3, 190, 191, 215; Philo, *Abr.* 135-36; *Spec.* 3.37-39; *Contempl.* 59-62; *Q.Gen* 4.37; Jos., *Ag. Ap.* 2.37.273-75.

40 Philo appears to be resuming his interpretation of Leviticus 18 begun in 3.3.12, so that these words would constitute his comment on Lev 18:22 (and 20:13).

for a day or even an hour, as a disgrace to himself, his house , his native land and the whole human race. 39. And the lover (*ho de paiderastês*) of such may be assured that he is subject to the same penalty. He pursues an unnatural pleasure and does his best to render cities desolate and uninhabited by destroying/wasting the means of procreation [i.e. his semen]. Furthermore he sees no harm in becoming a tutor and instructor in the grievous vices of unmanliness and effeminacy (*anandrias kai malakias*) by prolonging the bloom of the young and emasculating (*ekthêlynôn*) the flower of their prime, which should rightly be trained to strength and robustness. Finally like a bad husbandman he lets the deep-soiled and fruitful fields lie sterile, by taking steps to keep them from bearing, which he spends his labour night and day on soil from which no growth at all can be expected. 40. The reason is, I think, to be found in the prizes awarded in many nations to licentiousness and effeminacy (*malakias*). Certainly you may see these man-woman hybrids (*androgynous*) continually strutting about through the thick of the market, heading the processions at the feasts, appointed to serve as unholy ministers of holy things, leading the mysteries and initiations and celebrating the rites of Demeter. 41. Those of them who by way of heightening still further their youthful beauty have desired to be completely changed into women and gone on to mutilate their genital organs (*ta gennêtika*), are clad in purple like signal benefactors of their native lands, and march in front escorted by a bodyguard, attracting the attention of those who meet them. (*Special Laws* 3.7.37-41. LCL modified).

Philo's "androgynes" (man-woman hybrids) were decidedly not homosexuals (as that term is understood today) but were imagined as males with *both* male and female sexual characteristics. The disgrace in which they were involved for Philo lay not in same-sex coitus, but in the partners' dishonoring of maleness, the wasting of the senior partner's power to procreate, and the passive partner's assuming the "female disease" and adopting the ways of women. The prohibition of adultery, on which this discussion is a commentary, forbids the violation of a married male's honor by the stealing/controlling of his wife. Philo's concern with maintaining the honor of malehood by eschewing effeminacy is consistent with the Decalogue's protection of male honor by prohibiting the theft of his chief property.

It may well be that Paul shared this view of his compatriot, Philo, and that a perceived violation of the gender boundaries understood as set by God and nature earned for both *malakoi* and *arsenokoitai* their place in the list cited by Paul. In this view, both passive and active partners in a male-with-male sexual interaction colluded in a degradation of male virtue and male honor and thereby brought shame on all manly males. The submissive partner was a passive patsy and receptive like a female. The active partner cooperated in the dishonoring of the passive male and in many instances even subjected the youth to further modes of physical abuse, economic subservience, insult, and social shaming.[41]

If *arsenokoitai* denoted not senior males who *loved* boys but older males who *preyed sexually on and abused* young males, then it would be a synonym of the more common word *paidophthoros*, "corrupter of boys/children" (see *Testament of Levi* 17:11; *Barn.* 10:6). The related verb *paidophthorein*, "to corrupt boys/children,"

---

41 In this kind of liaison, the senior male was usually married to a woman and accustomed to regular coitus with women. In no case did he restrict himself to only male-male coitus. Thus even if *arsenokoitai* is taken as a reference to such senior males, they hardly fit the definition of "homosexual" as understood today (males oriented to and engaging exclusively with other males in sexual relations).

appears in Christian lists of prohibited activities in *Didache* 2:2 and *Barnabas* 19:4; cf. also 10:6. Another list of vices characterizing "the way of death" (*Didache* 5:1-2) includes "corrupters of God's creatures" (*phthoreis plasmatos theou*), a formulation also included in a similar list of vices characterizing "the way of the Black One [Satan] in the *Letter of Barnabas* 20:1-2. The combination of *arsenokoitai* with *malakoi* makes this conceivable in the case of 1 Cor 6:9 (contrast 1 Tim 1:10 where only *arsenoikoitai* occurs). Again, however, we are dealing only with possibilities on top of unclarities.

Renderings of *malakoi* and *arsenokoitai* by a *single* expression such as "homosexuals" (RSV 1946), or "sexual pervert" (Revised English Bible 1989), or "homosexual perverts" (TEV 1966) or "men guilty of unnatural crime" (Weymouth NT 1943) are, in any case, "lexically unacceptable" (BDAG 135), apart, I would add, from their incorrectness in other respects. Along with the concepts of "heterosexuality" and "bisexuality," the concept of "homosexuality, "is a modern construct, as is the notion of "perversion" as currently defined. All these concepts are modern in their conceit and formulation. They are absent from the world of the Bible and alien to its thought, which knows nothing of "sexual identity" or "sexual orientation" and which rather attends to specific persons voluntarily involved in specific acts. In regard to the lexical aspect of the terms *malakoi* and *arsenokoitai*, neither in and of itself states anything about "unnatural" or "perversion," or "crime."

A Summmary of the Foregoing Analysis and Exegetical Conclusions

Consideration of whether or not 1 Corinthians 6 condemns, or says anything about, homosexuality requires attention to several interrelated factors.

1. *The lexical factor.* The terms *malakoi* and *arsenokoitai* are rare in the Bible; *arsenokoitai* appears nowhere in the Greek language prior to 1 Corinthians and rarely thereafter. Their meanings are ambiguous and uncertain. They were not technical or standard terms for persons who engaged in male-to-male sexual intercourse or even for "males who love other males." *Malakos* means "soft." It is possible that in this context it had a sexual implication, but this is not certain. It cannot be assumed, as its only other NT occurrences make clear. The word *arsenokoitai* is more likely to have had sexual implication, by virtue of its components ("males" + "bed") and its similarity to the expression of Lev 18:23 and 20:16 as Scroggs has argued. This too, however, is not certain and cannot simply be assumed. With a sexual implication, *malakoi* could have designated "effeminate" males adopting the ways of women. It is also possible that *malakoi* and *arsenokoitai* formed a pair of words that designated passive and active male partners in a same-sex sexual relationship. But this is only possible and cannot be assumed. Even if the terms are supposed to have had sexual overtones, the precise nature of the relationship and the sexual behavior is unstated by Paul. All translations or interpretations offer no more than conjectures. They are best left as vague as are the original Greek words: "soft males" and "males who lie with males."

2. *The factor of literary context.* The terms are part of a traditional Israelite pre-Pauline list of persons not inheriting the kingdom of God. Some of the persons and their actions are sexual in nature ("adulterers," possibly *pornoi,* if meaning "prostitutes" or "males engaging in incest" rather than "idolators" or merely "immoral persons"), but not the majority of the remaining terms ("idolaters," "greedy," "drunkards," "revilers," "robbers"). Moreover, aside from the term *pornoi,* which is mentioned first and hence given pride of place, no term is singled out as especially pernicious; all have equal weight. The list in its totality does not have a sexual focus. No stress is given to the terms *malakoi* and *arsenokoitai* in particular. The theory that they were added by Paul to fit the general theme of *porneia* in 5:1-6:20 (as argued by Zaas 1988) is made doubtful by the fact that Paul says nothing about them anywhere else in his letter and never employed them or this list in any other of his extant genuine letters.

There is also the *factor of cultural context* and that will be discussed below in connection with the evaluation of translations.

3. The *factor of rhetorical function.* Paul employed this list in 1 Cor 6:1-11 not to make a point about sexual activity, but to respond to a *legal* problem that had social, not sexual, ramifications. Believers were suing one another in outsider pagan courts of law and submitting their cases to persons Paul considered unjust judges (6:1-8). Unjust/unrighteous persons like these, Paul said, will not inherit the kingdom of God (6:9a). The persons enumerated in vv.9b-10 illustrate kinds of such unjust/unrighteous persons and behavior. The focus of 6:1-11 is on *justice/injustice* and the *internal* settling or elimination of brotherly disputes so as to preserve and enhance the unity of the community. The *function* of the list, in other words was to illustrate kinds of unjust/unrighteous persons who will not inherit the kingdom of God. Injustice is the focal issue, not sexual activity, sexual sins, or sexual "perversions." In terms of the letter's message in general, we can join Zaas (1988:629) who insists that "we must agree with Scroggs that Paul is not using these catalogues to argue against specific vices like *arsenokoitia,* but in a broader sense, as part of an argument about 'harming the body', about the sanctity of the brotherhood, and about the separation of church and world."

It is in the light of these three exegetical factors that the determination of the meaning and function of *malakoi* and *arsenokoitai* in this context is to be made.

4. The great disparity among Bible translations and commentaries indicates that there has been and remains no consensus concerning the *meaning* of these terms, whether they involve sexual matters, let alone "homosexual" or same-sex activity, what activity or social relations the terms might imply, and what might qualify these activities or relations as immoral. While many questions must remain open for lack of probative evidence, a few things are clear and certain.

4.1. Neither *malakoi* nor *arsenokoitai* can be translated with "homosexuals," a term of modern coinage and shaped by modern conceptions of gender, gender identity, and sexual orientation (against the RSV 1946, TEV 1976, NEB 1971, NAB). The concept of "sexual orientation" and its distinction from "sexual practice" also are foreign to the ancient world and alien to its prevailing mentality. The modern translation "invertidos" (Nueva Biblica Espanola) is wrong for the same reason; the concept of sexual inversion is a modern one unknown in the ancient world. Versions mentioning "perversion" (NEB) or "pervert(s)" (RSV 1971, TEV, Rev. EB) are likewise wrong on this score. All these translations are reflections of modern psychological concepts anachronistically attributed to Paul and his source.

4.2. Also incorrect are all translations that collapse the two terms *malakoi* and *arsenokoitai* into *one* modern expression such "men guilty of unnatural crime" (Weymouth), "homosexuals" (RSV 1946), "homosexual perversion" (NEB 1961), or "sexual perverts" (RSV 1971), or "homosexual perverts" (TEV).

4.3. The choice of "sodomites" for *arsenokoitai* (Moffatt, JB, NRSV 1989, Nueva Biblica Espanola, Sacra Bibbia) also is inappropriate and likewise should be eliminated. The term *arsenokoitai* itself had no inherent connection with Sodom and its sin. It is the translators alone who make the association, apparently on the inferred but unproved web of assumptions that (1) *arsenokoitai* refers to male to male sexual intercourse; (2) that the sin of the residents of Sodom as narrated in Genesis 19 was not that of inhospitality (as the story and later biblical references to Sodom indicate) or violent raping of visitors (as Gen 19 indicates), but voluntary sexual intercourse among males, so that (3) the persons identified in the list and by Paul as *arsenokoitai* are best identified as "sodomites." Whether "sodomites" involves only the *choice of sexual partners* (males preferring males) or the *mode* of sexual intercourse (anal intercourse) is a question on which proponents of this inaccurate rendition make no comment. As a consequence some modern state courts of law in the United States still criminalize anal intercourse (even between married heterosexual partners because legislators are guided and motivated by the erroneous translation of 1 Cor 6:9 and an equally misinformed understanding of Genesis 19 and its cultural context.

4.4. Translations of *malakoi* such as "sensual" (Goodspeed), or "depraved" (BJ), or "self-indulgent" (NJB 1985) have the virtue of a vagueness that parallels the vagueness of "soft." They could have a sexual implication, but not necessarily so. Consequently, these translations make the verses irrelevant to the question of whether 1 Cor 6:9-10 has a bearing on male-to-male sexual relations or on the modern issue of homosexuality, except to imply a negative answer to both questions.

4.5. The KJV rendition of *arsenokoitai* as "abusers of themselves with mankind" does not indicate the type or domain of the self-abuse. Though "self-abuse" became a designation for masturbation in the Victorian period, it is not likely implied here, given the accompanying words, "with mankind." A social activity, in other words, is implied —unless the translators regarded male to male sexual intercourse as a form of mutual masturbation. Its pairing with "effeminate" probably points to a sexual implication of *arsenokoitai*. The only thing certain is that the translating expression emphasizes *abuse* as the immoral aspect of this term.

5. The specific connotations of *malakoi* and *arsenokoitai* were determined by the knowledge, perspectives, concepts, values, norms, practices and institutions of the Greco-Roman world, Hellenistic Israel, and the fledgling Jesus movement. This

cultural framework included a patriarchal, male-oriented and male-dominated society, the valorization of male-male relationships over male-female relationships (except for child production), the economic and social importance of family increase as such, the scorn of effeminacy; the educational and cultural institution of pederasty and its potential abuses; the power and pollution of sex; and cultic prostitution viewed as idolatry. *Preferable translations* are those that reflect and are consistent with these social and cultural factors.

5.1. Versions that suggest that the original terms were pointing to persons behaving "unnaturally," or "contrary to nature," are culturally plausible (Goodspeed, Knox, Weymouth), since *nature* (and nature's Creator or God) was believed to have established the characteristics (physical, mental, moral) and behavioral scripts of all males and females. Persons acting contrary to nature were seen by Israelites like Paul as acting contrary to the will of God and hence as "sinful" and "immoral." In his letter to the Romans (1:18-32) Paul argues thusly, censuring males and females who have acted contrary to their natures and "exchanged natural relations for unnatural" (1:26, 27).[42] The problem with inferring an appeal to nature here in 1 Corinthians 6 is that the terms themselves and the text in which they are embedded say nothing explicit about "nature" or the "unnatural." The idea is rather in the minds of the translators who seem to view and translate *malakoi* and *arsenokoitai* in the light of Rom 1:18-32. Also damaging to this view is the fact that other terms of the list involve actions that are not "unnatural" but all too natural and typical of the human condition (immorality, idolatry, adultery, theft, greed, drunkenness, reviling). *Malakoi* and *arsenokoitai* may imply actions that would have been viewed by some in Paul's world as "unnatural;" but Paul does not make that case here and it is best to avoid language suggesting that he does.

5.2. Closer still to Paul's cultural world and to what he does say in 1 Corinthians are the versions that render *malakoi* as "effeminate(s)" (Vulgate, KJV, Luther, La Biblia, La Sacra Bibbia) or "Lustknaben" (Zürcher), or "catamites" (Moffatt, JB1966), or "boy/male prostitutes" (NAB, NRSV), and *arsenokoitai* as "males sleeping with males" (Vulgate), or "corrupters of boys" (Luther, Zürcher), and possibly " (male) abusers of themselves with mankind" (KJV). . While not technical Greek terms for males engaged sexually with other males and while not commonly employed, these words could be pointing to various male-to-male sexual relations that in Paul's time were practiced by the Greeks, tolerated with exasperation by the Romans, and denounced by the House of Israel as typical of Gentile degeneracy and moral depravity. The problem with the behavior and/or the relations is that in some way they were seen to violate the gender boundaries set by nature (and God), with males assuming the passive role and inferior position of females, and their male partners being complicit in this distortion of maleness and masculine honor. In regard to the institution of pederasty, while the relationship of older males to younger boys once had a useful educational function, it eventually became an occasion for abuse, commercialization, and corruption. Older men forced themselves on young boys,

---

42 Note the similar appeal to nature that Paul makes in deploring long hair on males but encouraging it for females (1 Cor 11:14).

abusing them physically, using them as play things (Lustknaben) and, in some cases enticing them to literally peddle their asses for sex and sesterces. Dandified and perfumed boys, on the other hand, switched from active to passive, shaved and powdered their bods, assumed the posture and role of receptive, soft females, bid out their butts to the highest bidders, and for the sake of money and the protection of powerful patrons played the role of the passive lover (like Ganymede to Zeus) as long as necessity demanded, occasion permitted, and time allowed.

5.3. If the terms *malakoi* and *arsenokoitai* had a sexual implication for Paul and his source, it is possible that one of the above scenarios lay behind this sexual connotation. *Malakoi* could have denoted "effeminate males." Or, if *malakoi* and *arsenokoitai* formed a pair of words indicating some kind of sexual relationship and behavior, *malakoi* could have designated "boys playing the passive role of females in male to male sexual relations of beloved and lover," or "boys playing the passive role of females in male to male sex-for-pay transactions. *Arsenokoitai*, in turn, could have denoted the dominant, and often abusive, male partners who were complicit in these acts of male humiliation or sex for pay and of older males corrupting tender boys."

5.4. While none of these options can be proved as envisioned by Paul, each is at least lexically possible and contextually plausible. With such meanings, this pair of terms would be semantically compatible with the other terms of the list, each of which denotes some form of excess (greed, drunkenness) or type of conduct condemned by Israel's God or the *mos maiorum,* the customs of the ancestors (immorality, idolatry, adultery, theft, reviling). With these meanings they would also fit the context of 6:1-11 and join the other terms listed in vv. 9-10 as indicating types of unjust/unrighteous persons excluded from the kingdom of God. This possibility is also compatible with what is known about sexual relationships, sexual values, and sexual norms in Paul's period. It must be acknowledged, however, that these are only *possibilities* that are more likely than other alternatives. The available evidence does not allow a definitive conclusion or a *dernier mot.*

6. In the ancient world of the Bible, in contrast to the present, no distinction was drawn between personal sexual "orientation," on the one hand, and behavior on the other. Persons were classified according to their origin (blood line and locality), looks, and behavior—external factors, not internal states--since only external features were visible and verifiable. God could look inside and alone knew the heart. The terms in the lists cited in 1 Corinthians and elsewhere in the NT and secular world refer *not* to persons of a particular *condition*, i.e. the "condition" of adultery, theft, greed, etc., but to persons engaging in specific violent, abusive, immoderate, socially destructive or religiously proscribed *acts*. Paul and his ancient contemporaries regarded the persons and implied actions enumerated in the lists of 1 Corinthians 5 and 6 as agents capable of choosing between moral or immoral modes of behavior, and their preferences, whether good or evil, as free and deliberate choices. Desire and choice were the operative forces, not "orientation."

7. A passage of the 1-2 century Epistle of Barnabas could relate to 1 Cor 6:9 and in any case offers a sobering eye-opener concerning the state of knowledge about sexual

matters in Paul's age. In this passage (*Barn.* 10:6-8) reasons are given for the food prohibitions in Leviticus and the classification of certain animals as "unclean:"

> But furthermore, he [Moses] says [Lev 11:5;cf. Deut 14:7], "You shall not eat the hare." Why? Do not, he means, be a corrupter of boys (*paidophthoros*) or like such people, because the hare grows a new anus every year, and their number is proportionate to its years [cf. Aelianus, *De Natura Animalium* 1.25; Clement of Alexandria, *Paedagogus* 2.10.83-84 etc.]. But "neither shall you eat the hyena" [not in Lev or OT, but added by the author of Barnabas]. Do not, he means, be an adulterer or corrupter (*phthoreus*) or like such people. Why? Because this animal changes its sex every year, and is at one time male, at another, female. But he also rightly abhorred the weasel [Lev. 11:29; cf. Aelianus, *De anim.* 2.55]. Do not, he means, be like those males who, we learn, because of their uncleanness, do what is forbidden with their mouth; and do not associate with unclean women who do what is forbidden with their mouth; for this animal conceives through the mouth.[43]

If *arsenokoitai* in 1 Cor 6:9 is seen to denote older males *sexually corrupting* young boys, then this passage of Barnabas illustrates the theological and ethical reasoning underlying the early Christian censure of this practice. From a hermeneutical perspective, the text illustrates the need for great caution in the use of any biblical argument based on "what is natural" or "what nature teaches." As our knowledge of nature has changed drastically since ancient time, so must our ethical reasoning once based on "what nature teaches." This text of Barnabas also illustrates how weak and arbitrary ethical rules are that are based on an allegorical mode of interpretation.

8. *Paul's concern* in citing the list in which these terms are contained was to illustrate modes of unjust behavior typical of Gentile unbelievers and to proscribe such behavior as inimical to the moral and social integrity of the believing community and incompatible with its holiness. These are behaviors that do not exhibit but rather inhibit love—a focus on and concern for others of one's primary group, like the love one has towards one's family (8:1; 13:1-13). In 1 Corinthians, it is this love serving to maintain and build up the unity of the community, the body of Christ, that is Paul's vital concern. The list in 6:9-10 enumerates the types of persons who are unjust/unrighteous. Within the argument that Paul is making here, the persons of this list illustrate types of such unjust/unrighteous persons who, like believers who put themselves before the needs of the group, drag their fellow believers into pagan courts of law, and ignore the communal well-being of the Corinthian faithful. The listed persons do not practice justice, they -do not act in love toward their fellows, and they do not contribute to the building up of the communal Body of Christ.

---

43 In the famous and regularly used *Loeb Classical Library series*, the English translation of the Greek text of *Barnabas* is abruptly interrupted at this point and Latin is substituted for English—apparently to avoid offending the sensibilities of its vulnerable readers. It is, however, this "real dirty stuff" that reveals not only the ignorance of the ancients but also the puritanicalism of modern scholars. This bizarre explanation offered in Barnabas is repeated almost verbatim by Clement of Alexandria (d. ca. 215 CE) in his *Paedagogus* 2.10.

Some Broader Hermeneutical Observations—Exegetical and Hermeneutical Principles and Implications

1.   The body of the letter of 1 Corinthians opens with Paul's stress on "Christ crucified" and the paradoxical power of the gospel (1:18-31). It closes with a resounding affirmation of the resurrection of Christ and of all believers (15:1-58). Between opening and close, more attention is given to sexual issues than in any other NT writing. This indicates that, for Paul, crucifixion and resurrection set the hermeneutical framework within which sexual issues are to be viewed and treated. Those who today claim to stand within the Pauline tradition can be expected to follow Paul's lead. If this present paper were a study of Paul's view on sexuality in general, this is precisely the direction I would have taken. I would have shown how Paul's insistence on the unity and inclusiveness of the believing community as the Body of Christ, his concern with the consolidation of that body through love and putting the brother or sister before self, his interweaving of Christ's personal body (crucified and resurrected), Christ's social body, the church, and Christ's eucharistic body, and his emphasis on the creating and recreating action of God bringing a new eschatological, physical and social reality into existence all established a context for comprehending his teaching on sexual relations and responsibilities.

2.   The present essay, however, is more narrow in scope and has focused on a subordinate issue and a passage, 1 Cor 6:9-10, that has been claimed to speak of and condemn "homosexuals" and "homosexuality." The conclusion of the study is that this claim is unsubstantiated, erroneous and methodologically misguided.

2.1.   Accurate translation and interpretation requires that words, phrases, and sentences be understood and interpreted always with reference to their literary, historical, social and cultural context(s). Any translation or interpretation ignoring this principle of contextuality will inevitably misrepresent and distort the meaning of the original text. This is the *hermeneutical principle of contextual interpretation*. Many translations or interpretations of *malakoi* and *arsenokoitai* violate this principle of contextual interpretation, as indicated above.

2.2.   Since *malakoi* and *arsenokoitai* are not technical or recurrent terms for same-sex sexual relations, it is not certain that they relate in any way to the issue of same-sex sexual relations then or now. The adjective *malakos* meaning "soft" could denote various features of things or persons depending on context, only some of which had sexual implications. In its only other NT occurrence, it meant "soft" (modifying clothing) with no sexual overtones whatsoever. The noun *arsenokoitês* is so rarely attested that a precise meaning (as indicated by usage) is impossible to determine, though the components of the word and its combination with *malakoi* could suggest possibilities with sexual implications.

3.   Certain renditions of *malakoi* and *arsenokoitai* are linguistically possible and culturally plausible, but not exegetically demonstrable beyond the shadow of doubt.

3.1.   In the light of Paul's male-dominated, male-oriented, machismo-driven culture, it is *possible but not certain* that *malakoi* and *arsenokoitai* denoted effeminate and domineering male partners respectively in abusive or commercialized sexual relationships. This meaning, however, is a *supposition* based on what is known about the culture of Paul's world and on semantic possibilities (but not certainties) of the terms themselves.

The *hermeneutical significance* of this uncertainty is the severe limits it sets on the use that can be made of these terms today for theological or ethical purpose. The relevant hermeneutical principle governing the use of ancient texts in modern settings states that *where meanings of terms are unclear and implications of terms uncertain in the original text, great caution is required in the use of these terms in theological or ethical reasoning.* No ethical rules can be based on unclear concepts. Theological doctrines and ethical rules cannot be based on exegetical suppositions and conflicting modern translations. Any attempt to do so leads only to unclarity concerning the rules themselves, confusion concerning the rationale behind their formulation, and inconsistency in their enforcement. Accordingly, the lexical ambiguity and semantic uncertainty of the terms *malakoi* and *arsenokoitai* in 1 Cor 6:9 advise extreme caution regarding the theological and ethical use of this passage today.

3.2. What *is* certain is that neither term can accurately be translated "homosexuals," and neither word relates to the phenomenon of homosexuality as currently defined and understood. Claims that this passage and these terms speak to the issue of "homosexuality" *as defined and understood today* are erroneous, because neither Paul nor any other biblical author or any author at all from antiquity had any term for, or concept of, what is defined today as a "homosexual."[44] "The idea of the homosexual person as one who is exclusively or predominantly attracted to members of the same sex," William Countryman (1988:118) has correctly stressed, "appears to have been unknown to them [i.e. ancient Greeks and Romans]. Assuming that "human beings are attracted sexually both to their own and the opposite sex," these ancients, including Paul and his contemporaries, "lacked even a behavior–based category for people who showed a fixed preference for partners of the same sex." The Finnish exegete Marti Nissinen (1998:118) similarly aptly insists that "[t]he modern concept of 'homosexuality' should by no means be read into Paul's text, nor can we assume that Paul's words in 1 Corinthians 6:9 'condemn all homosexual relations' in all times and places and ways; so also Petersen 1986. The meanings of the words are too vague to justify this claim, and Paul's words should not be used for generalizations that go beyond his experience and world." To claim that *malakoi* and *arsenokoitai* were "homosexuals" would be as anachronistic as claiming that *methysoi* (1 Cor 6:10) were "alcoholics" or "addicts" or that *loidoroi* (1 Cor 6:10) were "trash talkers" or that *pleonketai* (1 Cor 6:10) were rapacious "capitalists." It would be as ethnocentric as claiming that Jesus was viewed as an "extrovert" or Paul as a "libertarian" or "leftwing progressive." It would be like imagining that ancient Mediterraneans thought and behaved like middle class Americans. Translating *malakoi* and *arsenokoitai* with "homosexuals" is as anachronistic and ethnocentric as claiming that Paul and the biblical authors were aware of X and Y chromosomes, sexual orientation, and HIV.

---

44 Stressing the difference between ancient and modern "mentalities" concerning sexual relations and same-sex sexual relations, the German Lutheran exegete Wolfgang Stegemann makes the same point; see Stegemann 1993a, 1993b, 1998a, 1998b.

4. Whatever meanings are accepted for these terms today, an attempt to use them today for theological and ethical purpose faces further hermeneutical constraints posed by their *literary context and rhetorical function.* The fact that *malakoi* and *arsenokoitai* are part of a list used by Paul to illustrate unjust/unrighteous persons in a context dealing with injustice (1 Cor 6:1-11) has several hermeneutical implications.

4.1. If an attempt is made to find theological and ethical significance in this text for today's situation, then all terms of 6:9-10 must be weighted equally today, as they were by Paul. There can be no singling out of *malakoi* and *arsenokoitai* as of greater importance or gravity and no ignoring the other types of persons censured by Paul. If it is held today that *malakoi* and *arsenokoitai* are excluded today from the kingdom of God and from the Church "because the Bible demands it" (with reference to these verses), then this censure must include *all* the vices of 6:9-10. One must then also exclude from the kingdom of God today all who are immoral (or prostitutes or engaged in incestual relationships), all idolaters, adulterers, thieves, greedy persons, drunkards, revilers, and robbers. And vice versa: the manner in which these other vices are evaluated in a contemporary ethic will, for the sake of consistency, apply to *malakoi* and *arsenokoitai* as well. If greed or drunkardness or reviling are no longer viewed as activities preventing inheritance of the kingdom of God, then the same will have to be true of the actions of *malakoi* and *arsenokoitai*, whatever they may be.

4.2. This *hermeneutical principle of consistency* applies, by the way, to the theological and ethical treatment of other supposedly relevant texts such as Lev. 18 (degrees of incest, intercourse during menstruation, adultery, males "lying with males the lyings of females," bestiality, idolatry) and Lev 20 (child sacrifice, engagement in magic, cursing parents, incest, males lying with males the lyings of females, bestiality, intercourse during menstruation, distinction of clean and unclean animals and food), Romans 1 (idolatry, gender role reversal, unholy and dishonorable conduct and the twenty-one vices of 1:29-31), and 1 Timothy (lawless and disobedient persons, ungodly and sinners, unholy and profane persons, patricides and matricides, prostitutes, kidnapers, liars, perjurers, and false teachers).

4.3. In actuality, in the past 2,000 years this hermeneutical principle concerning *totality* and *consistency* has enjoyed only occasional enforcement. For the most part, subjectivity and selectivity have prevailed in how the Bible has been applied ethically. The vices mentioned in this passage were differently weighted by different readers in different situations. Some vices were considered more serious than others. Some were categorized as "mortal" sins (incest, idolatry), others as "venial" (theft, reviling). Adultery just a generation ago was grounds for exclusion from Holy Communion and legal grounds for divorce. This is no longer the case today when excommunication no longer "works," no fault divorce has become a reality, and divorce no longer disqualifies from the Holy Ministry. Curiously and inconsistently, being *malakoi* and *arsenokoitai*—anachronistically understood as referring to "homosexuals" (male and female) who engage in same-sex sexual relations—is allowed to disqualify from ministry in several modern denominations, while divorce, which the Lord himself prohibited (Mark 10:2-12), raises nary an eyebrow, let alone protest.

4.4. On the other hand, the ancient revulsion against emasculation, effeminacy, and males assuming, or forced into, the passive role of females is far less pervasive today. The effeminization of males that was seen by the biblical communities as a violation of nature and God's will is no longer an issue of moral or legal consequence--at least in cultures of the modern western hemisphere. Furthermore, rare are the religious bodies today that exclude thieves or greedy persons, or drunkards or revilers or robbers or even adulterers or prostitutes, or idolaters from the kingdom of God and the precincts of the sanctuary. By what criterium then are exceptions made in regard to *malakoi* and *arsenokoitai?* The only criterium that seems to be evident *in practice* is that of personal dislike or fear--what translators or commentators or church officials or self-appointed posses of the morality squad have as their pet peeve or phobia. It may be that a thorough study of this subject must include an examination of such phobias and peeves in order to ascertain why the issue of homosexuality has become such a focus of attention in the first place and why gay, lesbian, bi-sexual and transgender persons are so high today on many peoples' phobia and hate lists.

4.5. If 1 Cor 6:9-10 is explored for ethical significance today, all terms of the list must be related today to the issue of *justice/injustice*, as they were by Paul. Being *malakoi* and *arsenokoitai*, like being any other of the persons listed, will be viewed as wrong today for the same reason this was declared wrong by Paul—because of the *injustice* in which these persons, like all the persons listed, were involved. This hermeneutical principle of *interpretive fidelity* (fidelity to the point and rhetorical thrust of the original argument) also is often violated in the rush for ethical application. If it had been observed in the hunt for homosexuals, persons wishing to apply this text today would be asking how modern-day *malakoi* and *arsenokoitai* are *acting unjustly*.

5. Another hermeneutical constraint on the contemporary use of this text involves *historical, social and cultural differences* separating Paul's society and cultural horizons from those of the modern, post-Enlightenment, western, industrialized world of most contemporary Bible readers. These differences in contexts, conceptual constructs, and horizons of meaning must be acknowledged and allowed to guide any theological and ethical use of the Bible today. Failure to do so results in reading *into* the text what should be derived *from* the text, eisegesis instead of exegesis, and imposition of modern concepts, constructs, and vocabulary instead of exposition of ancient ones. The ultimate consequence is a distorted and misleading reading of the text, an abuse rather than sound use of the Bible for theological and ethical purpose.

5.1. The specific modes, expressions, and implications of male-male sexual relations and their possible ethical evaluation in 1 Corinthians or elsewhere in the Bible in general are conditioned by their own historical, social, cultural and religious contexts. These contextual factors may be, and in most cases are, different from those shaping current understanding and evaluation of the nature and practice of homosexuality. As in all cases where the Bible is used as a norm for modern ethical reflection, these differences must be taken seriously. Failure to do so has resulted and will continue to result in a distorted anachronistic and ethnocentric reading of biblical texts, a disregard and denial of the historicity of the word of God and the doctrine of the incarnation, and a mess of rules rendered implausible and impracticable because isolated from their original contexts of meaning.

5.2. The difference in social structures and cultural horizons between Paul's world and the present makes it difficult, if not impossible, to directly apply Paul's exhortation and mode of argumentation in 1 Cor 5-6 to today's scene in the USA. This is not only due to the unclarity of certain of Paul's terms, like *malakoi* and *arsenokoitai* or *pornos*, *pornê* and *porneia*. It is also because the social and cultural premises informing Paul's thought are no longer those of most Americans. Excommunication no longer is effective and no longer practiced as an ecclesial disciplinary tactic (1 Cor 5:1-13) because the social premise on which it was based is no longer shared by today's post-Enlightenment. western industrialized world. A theory of rugged individualism, personal independence, and appeal to a putative "interiorized" sense of morality or "conscience" has today replaced the group orientation, dyadic personality, and group-centered morality typical of Jesus and Paul's world. Consequently, excluding persons from the community does not make sense and does not "work" and so it is no longer practiced in the western Church. Or it is effective only in those situations or cultures (like those of the Mediterranean or Middle East or traditional face-to-face groups) where the group orientation of Paul's culture and ethos is still in evidence.

On the other hand, nothing in 1 Corinthians, or for that matter in any other biblBical writing, speaks directly of the biological or psychological *condition* of homosexuality or homosexual "orientation" as this is understood today and as it concerns believing Christian gay persons intent on worshipping and serving God.

5.3. This interpretive hermeneutical problem applies to all of 1 Cor 5:1-6:20, all of 1 Corinthians, and all of the Bible in general. Paul's ethical requirements and proscriptions, like those throughout the NT, presume a constellation of specific social-economic arrangements, religious perspectives, and cultural scripts. The plausibility and persuasive power of these ethical injunctions required that his hearers shared this complex of arrangements and scripts. The meaning of *malakoi* and *arsenokoitai,* the cultural and social practices Paul assumed these terms to have reflected, and the nature and rhetorical thrust of Paul's exhortation were all fundamentally shaped by the cultural world Paul inhabited.

5.4. In regard to the theological and ethical use of this text, this means that this passage and Paul's argument will be plausible and persuasive only in those situations today where similar social and cultural conditions prevail. This will be in very few places around the modern world. It will certainly not be the case in the United States and modern industrialized and democratized cultures in general. From this vantage point also, this text will have little relevance for US religious denominations examining the issue of homosexuality and its theological and ethical ramifications. Theological doctrines and ethical rules cannot be based on biblical texts whose rationales and plausibility are based on cultural perceptions, values and worldviews no longer held or considered valid.

5.5. Put in more general terms, modern use of, and appeal to, biblical ethical *rules* (prescriptions and proscriptions) today will have little plausibility or persuasive power if modern readers do not also accept the premises and perceptions and scripts underlying these ancient injunctions. This is a hermeneutical observation that pertains to the use today of any verse or passage of Scripture for ethical or theological purposes. On the other hand, *principles* drawn from biblical passages can better weather the passage from antiquity to the present (e.g. such principles as: "that act is forbidden that is inconsistent with the gospel as proclaimed by Jesus and the NT authors;" or "that act is allowed that builds up the body of Christ").

6. Today we study the biological, psychological, and psychosomatic dimensions of sexuality and homosexuality, dimensions unimagined or differently conceived by Paul and his contemporaries. We speak of "X" and "Y" chromosomes and speculate about genes as determinative of gender and orientation—factors as alien to Paul and Jesus as the computer and saran wrap. Today some researchers and church bodies accept the distinction between sexual orientation and sexual conduct, a distinction also unknown to Paul and the ancients. Some today regard a homosexual orientation, like a heterosexual or bisexual orientation, as something conveyed in the genes and transmitted by nature and/or given by God. In this case, it is not one's "sexual "orientation" that is "immoral" but *the acting out* of that supposedly God-given orientation. This is the official position of the Evangelical Lutheran Church in America, which therefore requires sexual abstention from sexual intercourse on the part of all ordained clergy with an admitted homosexual orientation. In theory, church officials and congregations are eager to have homosexuals declare their orientation and abstain from sexual activity. In actuality, church practice emulates that of the military and whispers "don't ask, don't tell". The position of the ELCA concerning the sexual activity of *lay* homosexuals is less clear and perhaps for this reason less enforced. Other Protestant bodies seem to swim in similar types of murky theological and ethical soup. The Roman Catholic official position is that homosexuals are in their natures "disordered," a position informed more by natural law theory than by the Bible.[45] A merit of this position is that it avoids the problem of viewing the Creator as the source of a "condition" or "orientation" of which the church forbids a sexual expression. Presumably the thought is that "disordered" conditions can be "healed" and rightly "ordered," experience to the contrary notwithstanding. Theoretically, the issue is irrelevant to the orientation and activity of Roman Catholic clergy, however, since celibacy is required of all, heterosexuals and homosexuals alike. At the same time, the view of homosexuals as "disordered" in their sexuality also includes the clergy under the "disordered" umbrella. So not much consistency here either. In sum, confusion continues to prevail in the churches, with honesty, transparency of policy, and courage to confront the issues directly all too often sacrificed on the altar of institutional expediency and fear of reversing earlier unenlightened positions.

---

45 The *Letter to the Bishops of the Catholic Church on the Pastoral Care of Homosexual Persons"* issued by the Congregation for the Doctrine of the Faith on October 31, 1986, the Festival of the Reformation (!), states that "Although the particular inclination of the homosexual person is not a sin, it is a more or less strong tendency ordered toward an intrinsic moral evil; and thus the inclination itself must be seen as an objective disorder" (Paragraph 3). The text of the Letter is printed in full in Gramick and Furey 1988:1-10. The remainder of the volume contains informative analyses and critiques.

7. As in 1 Corinthians, so in the Bible as a whole, the available evidence concerning male-male sexual relationships is simply too sparse, too ambiguous, and conditioned by cultural perceptions and behavioral patterns too alien to those of modern time to provide an adequate basis for a contemporary ethic of homosexuality as homosexuality is currently understood. Conversely, the gender constructs, sexual norms, and rationales involved in the biblical texts that are thought relvevant to the issue of homosexuality are inconsistent with current scientific data and thinking concerning gender, sexuality, sexual identity, sexual choice, and ethical practice of the present. A case for or against the morality of homosexuality as it is understood today will have to be made on evidence other than the six biblical passages (including 1 Cor 6:9-10) customarily cited. The silver lining in this dark exegetical cloud is that this may direct researchers to other scriptural sources more appropriate for viewing sexuality in creational, evangelical, redemptive, and spiritual terms and particularly within the Pauline framework of crucifixion and resurrection.

Works Cited

Boswell, John. *Christianity, Social Tolerance, and Homosexuality*. Chicago: University of Chicago Press, 1980.

Brawley, Robert L., ed. *Biblical Ethics and Homosexuality: Listening to Scripture*. Louisville: Westminster-John Knox, 1996.

Cartledge, P. "The Politics of Spartan Pederasty." *Proceedings of the Cambridge Philosophical Society* n.s. 27 (1981): 17-36; reprinted in Siems, pp. 385-412, with addendum, 413-415.

Countryman, L. W. *Dirt, Greed, and Sex: Sexual Ethics in the New Testament and Their Implications for Today*. Minneapolis: Fortress, 1988.

Dean-Jones, Lesley. "The Cultural Construct of the Female Body in Classical Greek Science." In *Women's History and Ancient History*. Ed. S. B. Pomeroy. Chapel Hill: University of North Carolina Press, 1991. Pp. 111-137.

Delaney, Carol. "Seeds of Honors, Fields of Shame." In *Honor and Shame and the Unity of the Mediterranean*. Ed. David D. Gilmore. Washington: American Anthropologist Association, 1987.

Douglas, Mary Tew. *Purity and Danger. An Analysis of Concepts of Pollution and Taboo*. London: Routledge & Kegan Paul; New York: F. A. Praeger, 1966.

Douglas, Mary Tew. *Natural Symbols: Explorations in Cosmology*. London/Boston: Routledge & Kegan Paul, 1970.

Douglas, Mary Tew. *Implicit Meanings. Essays in Anthropology*. London/Boston: Routledge & Kegan Paul, 1975.

Dover, K. J. *Greek Homosexuality*. Cambridge, MA: Harvard University Press, 1978; reprinted, 1989.

Elliott, John H. *I Peter*. Anchor Bible 37B. New York: Doubleday, 2000.

Grammick, Jeannine and Furey, Pat, eds. *The Vatican and Homosexuality. Reactions to the "Letter to the Bishops of the Catholic Church on the Pastoral Care of Homosexual Persons."* New York: Crossroad, 1988.

Greenberg, David F. *The Construction of Homosexuality.* Chicago: University of Chicago, 1988.

Halperin, David M. *One Hundred Years of Homosexuality and Other Essays on Greek Love.* New York: Routledge, 1990.

Halperin, David M.; Winkler, John J.; and Zeitlin, Froma, I., eds. *Before Sexuality: The Construction of Erotic Experience in the Ancient Greek World.* Princeton: Princeton University Press, 1990.

Herter, H. "Effeminatus." *RAC* 4 (1959): cols. 620-650.

Hoheisel, Karl. "Homosexualität." *RAC* 16 (1992): 289-364.

Hupperts, C. A. M. *Greek Love, Homosexuality or Paederasty? Greek Love in Black-figure Vase-painting.* Proceedings of the 3rd Symposium on Ancient Greek and Related Pottery. Copenhagen, 1988.

Jordan, Mark G. The Invention of Sodomy in Christian Theology. Chicago: University of Chicago Press, 1997.

Kamlah, E. *Die Form der katalogischen Paränese im Neuen Testament.* WUNT, 7. Tübingen: Mohr (Siebeck), 1964.

Koch-Harnack, Gundel. *Knabenliebe und Tiergeschenke:Ihre Bedeutung im päderastischen Erziehungssystem Athens.* Berlin, 1983.

Krenkel, W. A. "Männliche Prostitution in der Antike." *Altertum* 24 (1978): 49-55.

Lilja, Saara. *Homosexuality in Republican and Augustan Rome.* Commentationes Humanarum Litterarum 74. Helsinki, 1983.

Lewis, Thomas S. W. "The Brothers of Ganymede." In *Homosexuality: Sacrilege, Vision, Politics.* Saratoga Springs: Skidmore College, 1983. Pp. 147-165.

Malina, Bruce J. *The New Testament World. Insights from Cultural Anthropology.* 3d revised and expanded ed. Louisville:Westminster John Knox, 2001.

---------."Interpreting the Bible with Anthropology: The Case of the Poor and the Rich." *Listening* 21/2 (1986): 148-1959.

---------."Limited Good and the Social World of Early Christianity." *Biblical Theology Bulletin* 8 (1979): 162-176.

-------- "Mary—Woman of the Mediterranean: Mother and Son." *Biblical Theology Bulletin* 20 (1990): 54-64.

Malina, Bruce J. and Neyrey, Jerome H. "Honor and Shame in Luke-Acts: Pivotal Values of the Mediterranean World." In *The Social World of Luke-Acts: Models for Interpretation.* Peabody, MA: Hendrickson Publishers, 1991. Pp. 25-65.

Marrou, H. I. "Pederasty in Classical Education." Ch. 3 in *A History of Education in Antiquity*. Trans. G. Lamb. New York: The New American Library-Mentor, 1964. Pp. 50-62, 479-82.

Nissinen, M. *Homoeroticism in the Biblical World. A Historical Perspective*. Trans. by K. Stjerna of *Homoerotiikka Raamatun maailmassa*, Helsinki, 1994. Minneapolis: Fortress, 1998.

Patzer, Harald. *Die Griechische Knabenliebe*. Sitzungsberichte der wissenschaftlichen Gesellschaft an der Johann Wolfgang Goethe-Universität Frankfurt am Main 19,1. Frankfurt, 1982.

Percy, William Armstrong III. *Pederasty and Pedagogy in Archaic Greece*. Champaign, IL: University of Illinois Press, 1996.

Petersen, William L. "Can arsenokoitai Be Translated by 'Homosexuals'?" (1 Cor.6:9, 1 Tim 1:10)." *Vigiliae Christianae* 40 (1986): 187-191.

Petersen, William L. "On the Study of `Homosexuality' in Patristic Sources." *Studia Patristica* 20. Ed. E.A. Livingstone. Louvain: Peeters, 1989. Pp. 283-288.

Scroggs, Robin. *The New Testament and Homosexuality. Contextual Background for Contemporary Debate*. Philadelphia: Fortress, 1983.

Siems, A. K., ed. *Sexualität und Erotik in der Antike*. Wege der Forschung 605. Darmstadt: Wissenschaftliche Buchgesellschaft, 1981.

Stegemann, Wolfgang. :Homosexualität—ein modernes Konzept." *Zeitschrift für Neues Testament* 2 (1998): 61-68. (Cited as 1998a)

Stegemann, Wolfgang. "Keine ewige Wahrheit. Die Beurteilung der Homosexualität bei Paulus." In *Diskussionsbeiträge zu Homosexualität und Kirche*. Ed. Barbara Kittelberger, Wolfgang Schrüger and Wolfgang Heilig-Achneck. Munich: Claudius Verlag, 1993. Pp. 262-85. (Cited as 1993a)

Stegemann, Wolfgang. "Paul and the Sexual Mentality of His World." *Biblical Theology Bulletin* 23/4 (1993): 161-66. (Cited as 1993b)

Stuhlmann, Hasitschka, M, and Stegemann, W. "Homosexualität im Neuen Testament. Ein kulturelles oder ein theologisches Problem?" *ZeitNT* (1998): 53-68. (Cited as 1998b)

Vögtle, A. *Die Tugend- und Lasterkataloge im Neuen Testament, exegetisch, religions- und formgeschichtlich untersucht*. NTAbh 16, 4/5. Münster: Aschendorff, 1936.

Waetjen, Herman C. "Same-Sex Sexual Relations in Antiquity and Sexuality and Sexual Identity in Contemporary American Society." In Brawley, Robert L., ed. *Biblical Ethics and Homosexuality: Listening to Scripture*. Louisville: Westminster-John Knox, 1996. Pp. 103-116.

Wibbing, S. *Die Tugend- und Lasterkataloge im Neuen Testament und ihre Traditionsgeschichte unter besonderer Berücksichtigung der Qumran-Texte*.

BZNW 25. Berlin: Töpelmann, 1959.

Williams, Craig A. *Roman Homosexuality: Ideologies of Masculinity in Classical Antiquity*. New York: Oxford University Press, 1999.

Winkler, John J. *The Constraints of Desire: The Anthropology of Sex and Gender in Ancient Greece*. New York: Routledge, 1990.

Wright, David F. "Homosexuals or Prostitutes: The Meaning of ARSENOKOITAI (1 Cor. 6:9, 1 Tim 1:10)." *Vigiliae Christianae* 38 (1984): 125-153.

Zaas, P. S. "Catalogues and Context. 1 Corinthians 5 and 6." *New Testament Studies* 34 (1988): 622-629.

Action Situates

Douglas R. McGaughey

This paper was originally read at the Pacific Northwest AAR/SBL Regional Meeting in Eugene, Oregon, on May 5, 2002. It is dedicated here to the celebration of the work in liberating theology by Herman Waetjen.

The paper reaches the following conclusions: 1) The core issue for humanity is not a Manichaean choice between good and evil, where we are obviously on the side of the good, but the issue of the interplay in experience between necessity and freedom. The route to the good is not by eliminating evil but by responding to and acting in our individual and corporate "life-world" where good and evil are ambiguous and yet where we may seize possibilities for the good within the ambiguity of our situation. 2) On the one hand, necessity has to do with the inescapable, hence necessary, conditions of possibility of experience and not with determinism or predestination. 3) On the other hand, freedom is not concerned with escaping the material conditions of life by merely rising into the spirit. Rather, freedom is concerned with "self-transcendence" (i.e., the paradoxical necessity of seizing upon the possibilities of our actual, ambiguous situation as we seek to inhabit the world in healing and just ways). 4) The path for re-thinking the relationship between necessity and freedom (action and experience) is not the actual but the possible. The emphasis is on an affirmation of ambiguity while nevertheless affirming responsibility and accountability.

Introduction

A cornerstone of the "postmodern condition" is Jean-François Lyotard's observation of the postmodern world's incredulity and antipathy toward "meta-narratives".[1]   What the postmodern condition rejects in meta-narratives is not only any and all absolute explanations of experience and history either a priori[2] or a posteriori[3] but also all absolutes whether of "substance" or "being".   Nonetheless, given the pervasiveness and necessity of our dependence upon narrativity as history or fiction,[4] given the role of "sociological" paradigms[5] for understanding who we are, and given our inability to

---

1   See Jean-François Lyotard, *A Postmodern Condition: A Report on Knowledge*, translated by Geoff Bennington and Brian Massumi (Minneapolis, MN: University of Minnesota Press, 1985), xxiii.

2   An example meta-narrative of an absolute a priori explanation of history would be the narrative of Christianity critiqued by Nietzsche as "Platonism for the masses" or Hegel's grand narrative of the "cunning of reason". For the dismissal of "Platonism for the masses", see Friedrich Nietzsche, "Jenseits von Gut und Böse," in *Nietzsches Werke* (Leipzig: Alfred Kröner Verlag, 1910), 5. For a discussion of Hegel's "cunning of reason", see Paul Ricoeur, "Should We Renounce Hegel?" in *Time and Narrative*, vol. 3, edited by Kathleen Blamey and David Pellauer (Chicago: The University of Chicago Press, 1988), 193–206.

3   An a posteriori explanation of experience is one that would emerge out of our ability to obtain absolute knowledge of events, but this is denied by Heisenberg's uncertainty principles. See the following two articles: Albert Einstein, et.al., "Can Quantum-Mechanical Description of Physical Reality be Considered Complete?" *The Physical Review* 47, Second Series (May 1935): 777–80 and Niels Bohr, "Can Quantum-Mechanical Description of Physical Reality be Considered Complete?" *The Physical Review* 48, Second Series (October 1935): 696–702.

4   See Paul Ricoeur, *Time and Narrative*, 3 vols, translated by Kathleen Blamey and David Pellauer (Chicago: The University of Chicago Press, 1984–85), particularly vol. 3: 18, 158, 186, and especially190.

5   Thomas Kuhn distinguishes between "sociological" and "exemplary past achievement" paradigms. Sociological paradigms are corporate mental models embraced by a discipline or a society for representing and processing "reality" since we do not have direct and immediate access to the world

absolutely adjudicate truth claims among narratives, the suspicion towards meta-narratives must not turn into a rejection of all narrative as if narrativity was merely self-referential[6] or an endless folding over on itself[7], neither expressive or illuminating of experience. In practical theology, living by narratives is equivalent to living by faith. Yet, meta-narratives in particular are as much if not more important for their ability to evoke possibilities for individuals and communities than they are valuable as exhaustive descriptions or absolute systematic explanations of life.

As an exercise in practical theology, the focus of this paper is the first-order[8] experience and action that leads to the creation of narratives. The way the paper enters into its discussion of first-order experience and action is to suggest that a crucial dimension has been overlooked in our usual understanding of both experience and action. Hence, the paper is structured by "problematizing" experience and action.

The strategy of the paper is to investigate the relationship between body and spirit through the lens of our inability not to act. In the beginning was the act, but the act presupposes a structure that makes it possible. It is this interaction between action and structure that informs practical theology. What is the significance of the indubitable truth not of Descartes' *cogito ergo sum*, which is always right, but of the inescapability and necessity of our action, which is always ambiguous? The inescapability and necessity of our action allows a shift of focus from the merely actual to the complexity of manifest actuality and concealed possibilities with all of its ambiguity while it simultaneously announces our accountability and responsibility to our individual and corporate concrete situations. For practical theology the issue is not am I and/or my community right, but what are the possibilities of what I/we take to be right? Are the possibilities transforming and healing or crippling and debilitating? Of course, even these alternatives can be perplexingly ambiguous.

Jean Baudrillard and WWIV

In a recent interview with the German weekly news magazine, *Der Spiegel*,[9] the French social critic Jean Baudrillard described our post-September 11th situation as "WWIV". For Baudrillard, WWIII is the war of globalization that is steam rolling advanced and indigenous cultures with internet commerce and consumerism. WWIII periodically erupts in hot wars in various regions of the world disguised, for example, as "religious conflict" in India, Northern Ireland, Palestine, or the Philippines, as a "war against drugs" in Columbia, or as a war to push back "tyranny and terrorism" as

---

"as it is". Exemplary past achievement paradigms are patterns (e.g., grammatical paradigms) that we learn and reapply in ever new circumstances. See the Postscript of Thomas S. Kuhn, *The Structure of Scientific Revolutions: Foundations of the Unity of Science*, 2d ed. (Chicago: University of Chicago Press, 1970).

6   Ferdinand de Saussure speaks of the self-referential character of linguistic systems (hence, also narratives) in Ferdinand de Saussure, *Course in General Linguistics*, eds Charles Bally and Albert Sechehaye, translated by Wade Baskin (New York: McGraw-Hill, 1966), 114, 118.

7   Jacques Derrida speaks of the text (hence, narrative) as an endless folding over on itself in "The Double Session" in Jacques Derrida, *Dissemination*, translated by Barbara Johnson (Chicago: University of Chicago Press, 1981), 270.

8   For the distinction between "first-order experience" and "second-order reflection" see Mortimer J. Adler, *How to Read a Book: The Art of Getting a Liberal Education* (New York: Simon and Schuster, 1940), 276.

9   See Jean Baudrillard, "Spiegel Gespräch. Das ist der vierte Weltkrieg," *Der Spiegel* 3 (2002): 178–81.

in the case of the Gulf War and the War in Afghanistan. To be sure, WWIII is more often a silent war in which the developed nations exploit the world's reserve of poor labor in sweat shops so that the first world can wear its designer clothes as an expression of "sign-value" or "coded difference[10]" in order to distinguish the wearer in a "value hierarchy," or WWIII is the silent war of the rape of the environment as in the case of the metal coltan,[11] necessary for every computer, cell phone, and palm pilot, found exclusively in the largest natural preserve in Africa. Coltan is being mined to the devastating destruction both of humans and of the flora and fauna of this nature preserve. However, if globalization is WWIII, what is WWIV?

Baudrillard answers, "There is no front and no lines of demarcation; the enemy sits in the heart of the very culture that is fighting it. That is, if you will, WWIV: no longer between peoples, countries, systems and ideologies, but the human species against itself.[12]"

The human species has long succumbed to the facile judgment that the world is divided (externally) into good and evil with the good on "our" side. "We" are good; our "enemy" is evil. However, Baudrillard describes the human condition as an incessant internal struggle, as the struggle within ourselves with good and evil. He quotes the 16th century, French essayist Michel de Montaigne: "'Were one able to remove evil from humanity, one would destroy the very condition of possibility for life.'[13]" Baudrillard adds that the pressing question is "[n]ot why is there evil ... Evil is what is always there, entirely naturally. Why is there good? That is the real miracle.[14]" Baudrillard views WWIV, then, not as an external dualistic struggle between peoples, countries, systems, and ideologies, but as an internal dualistic struggle that recognizes humanity's inability to escape from the evil lurking within each and every one of us. Baudrillard calls his view of the human condition "Manichaean[15]" and compares his view with the French Cathars (or Albigensiens) of the12th and 13th centuries brutally liquidated by the Roman Catholic Cathar crusade between 1209 and 1229 CE.

What Baudrillard finds attractive in the Cathars is their rejection of "... the material world as evil even as they trusted in God for salvation and the possibility of perfection.[16]" Baudrillard adds: "That is a far more radical view than the one that sees evil as only the falling, fading, and disintegrating satellite of the good.[17]" Baudrillard challenges our perception of ourselves as good and our confident belief in the gradual but certain elimination of evil from the world. What remains unclear (perhaps it is on the interviewing editor's cutting room floor) is the meaning of the aside to the God of salvation and perfection. Without question, however, his concluding remarks are a challenge to our materialist world of consumerism. How strange it sounds to us materialists that we might have embraced and continue to embrace unadulterated evil

---

10 Richard J. Lane, *Jean Baudrillard* (London: Routledge, 2000), 75.
11 See Blaine Harden, "The Dirt in the New Machine," *The New York Times*, 12 August 2001*The New York Times Magazine*.
12 Lane, *Jean Baudrillard*, 181.
13 Lane, *Jean Baudrillard*, 181.
14 Lane, *Jean Baudrillard*, 181.
15 Lane, *Jean Baudrillard*, 181.
16 Lane, *Jean Baudrillard*, 181.
17 Lane, *Jean Baudrillard*, 181.

as our very criterion of reality. For as materialists, what is not verifiable or falsifiable in the senses is by definition not real. The "reality" of Globalization, the reality of WWIII, is materialist. The "reality" of WWIV is invisible.

A central conviction of Western culture and particularly of Christianity has been the belief that with or more likely without divine aid we can be victorious over evil. Baudrillard proposes, however, that we have confused "bad luck" for "evil". "Bad luck" is the accidental nature of evil as a consequence of family, physical causality, and economic system. We can do something about "bad luck" because by definition it did not necessarily have to occur. However, evil, Baudrillard proposes, is permanent: "Evil is the world as it is and was. Bad luck is the world as it didn't have to be. The transformation of evil into bad luck is the most profitable industry of the 20th century.[18]" This most profitable industry is the military-industrial complex that exploits the fears and the self-righteousness of the privileged over against the under-privileged.

Baudrillard seems to be calling us to the Christianity based upon humanity's "total depravity". However, if evil is inescapable not as the consequence of any "Fall" but as constitutive of the nature of reality, then why would humanity be condemned for what it must be and could not not do? If evil is at the core of our very being and we can never be sovereign over it, then perhaps WWIV is a war that can never be won even with divine aid. Is reality fundamentally dualistic (Manichaean)? Does Christianity invoke a monism merely as a convenient way of avoiding our responsibility for the irresolvable conflict between good and evil within each of us as individuals and as communities?

Problematizing Experience

Action is more than mere experience. Action is a physical activity that grounds us in a particular situation. On the one hand, there is a necessity to action. The necessity is not with respect to "what" we must do but with respect to our having to do something. Experience, on the other hand, is passive, but, more importantly and contrary to all too common belief, the notion of "experience" in and of itself is not sufficient even as it is necessary to determine a truth claim. Simply because we experience something is no confirmation that what we are experiencing is "true". In short, *experience is a necessary but not a sufficient criterion for truth*.

Experience is not sufficient as a criterion for truth because we cannot know with absolute certainty any substance (οὐσία) either mental or physical in "reality" or in "experience". Yet the loss of substance does not mean loss of certitude.[19] What we

---

18 Lane, *Jean Baudrillard*, 181.

19 Although this is precisely what Kant's opponents accused him of doing (i.e., of eliminating the certitude of metaphysics eroding the status of substance). In this context one finds the emergence of the "new" meaning of the word "nihilism" at the end of the 18th century. In other words, nihilism in the sense of loss of certitude based on metaphysical substance neither originates with Nietzsche, nor with Turgenjew's novel *Father and Sons*, nor in Jacobi's open letter to Fichte in 1799. In 1796 Daniel Jenisch published *Ueber Grund und Werth der Entdeckungen des Herrn Professor Kant in der Metaphysik, Moral und Aesthetik Nebst einen Sendschreiben des Verfassers an Herrn Professor Kant über die bisherigen günstigen und ungünstigen Einflusse der kritischen Philosophie* in which he critiqued Kant for having eliminated such metaphysical certitude. Otto Pöggeler, however, does not want to attribute to Janisch the honor of first using the term "nihilism" in this sense. Pöggeler suggests

can do is describe "how" we can experience as we do even if we cannot determine with absolute certainty any "what" or content of experience or reality beyond the immediate present of self-consciousness. The human condition does not allow for certain knowledge of essences either abstract or concrete.

Obviously, we would not have to search for understanding if we were not finite. Our finitude is confirmed not simply because we are not able to ignore the physical world over which we have little or no control but also by the inaccessibility of "objects" in the world and even our very "selves".[20] We experience the physical world and our own selves as they appear to us and not as they are in themselves. Our project in search of understanding to inform our action is a project rooted in our finitude.

The minimalist conclusion to be drawn from our finitude and from our condition as a project of understanding is that knowledge is always incomplete. The maximalist conclusion proposes that, by limiting our focus for what constitutes reality and experience to what is "factual" and/or "actual", we make our focus far too narrow. For the maximalist, any proper encounter with the human condition as a project of finite understanding (not knowledge) must think beyond "essences" (either abstract or concrete). In other words, it must think beyond "substances" and the correctness of our judgments about them. To be sure in our everyday world, we have given up any real sense of absolute truth. Short of absolutes, we approach the indefinite nature of experience in terms of predictable actual alternatives. In other words, we turn the indefinite into calculable probabilities. However, for the maximalist, we must learn to think beyond "calculable probability" to engage the aporetic interplay of concealed possibilities in any and all understanding of actualities and probabilities.

Far from providing an indubitable criterion for truth, experience is the source of the raw materials of ambiguous actuality and possibility that demands our understanding. Experience is not certain but equivocal.

The Linguistic Institution Presupposes Experience

One strategy for overcoming the indeterminacy of scientific realism is to elevate linguistic systems to an a priori status. Such a strategy subordinates experience to linguistic systems. One becomes a scientist, for example, by learning the "language game" of a scientific discipline just as one becomes a Christian by learning the "language game" of a Christian community. However, George Lindbeck reverses the order of things when he proposes that linguistic formulation precedes experiential

---

that "several indicators" point to France as the origin. See Otto Pöggeler, "Hegel und die Anfänge der Nihilismus-Diskussion," *Man and World An International Philosophical Review* 3, no. 3 (September 1970): 186–87, 198–99, n. 6. See as well, Otto Pöggeler, "'Nihilist' und 'Nihilismus,'" *Archiv Für Begriffsgeschichte* XIX (1965): 197–210 (Bonn: Bouvier Verlag Herbert Grundmann, 1965).

20 Immanuel Kant stresses the inaccessibility to us of the "thing-in-itself" as he underscores the individual's inability to gain access to her/his "real self". See Immanuel Kant, *Critique of Pure Reason*, translated by Norman Kemp Smith (New York: St. Martin's Press, 1965), B152–53: "This is a suitable place for explaining the paradox which must have been obvious to everyone in our exposition of the form of inner sense (§6): namely, that this sense represents to consciousness even our own selves only as we appear to ourselves, not as we are in ourselves. For we intuit ourselves only as we are inwardly *affected*, and this would seem to be contradictory, since, we should then have to be in a passive relation [of active affection] to ourselves."

conviction.[21]   Whereas it is unequivocally the case that "language is the great institution that precedes us all,[22]" the power of language is its ability to illuminate and be confirmed by experience.   It is simply not the case that one must always first encounter the teaching (the language game of science or the kerygma of the community) and then seek out the experiential basis for embracing the teaching.   There is no question that in some circumstances that is the case, but the reverse is also the case.   One has (an) experience and seeks out the language (i.e., the scientific language or the kerygmatic doctrine) to articulate that experience.   Hence, *neither the objective world of substances alone nor the subjective world of language alone provide an explanation for experience.*

Understanding (Experience) as the Ambiguous Projection of Possibilities

In *Truth and Method* Hans-Georg Gadamer describes the process of understanding in experience as an interactive encounter between "text" and the presuppositions of the "reader".[23]   Gadamer reminds us that "... the goal of all communication and understanding is agreement concerning the object."[24]   However, neither the path to agreement is the same for every reader nor is any particular agreement exhaustive of the meaning of the text.

> Not occasionally only, but always, the meaning of a text goes beyond its author. That is why understanding is not merely a reproductive, (sic) but always a productive attitude as well.   Perhaps it is not correct to refer to this productive element in understanding as 'superior understanding'... Understanding is not, in fact, superior understanding, neither in the sense of superior knowledge of the subject because of clearer ideas, nor in the sense of fundamental superiority that the conscious has over the unconscious nature of creation.   It is enough to say that we understand in a different way, if we understand at all.[25]

Gadamer proceeds to point out that "... the true meaning of a text or a work of art is never finished; it is in fact an infinite process."[26]   What gives a reading "authority" is not that it is exhaustive and absolute but because it "... has a wider view or is better informed ..."[27]   The route to this "wider" and "better informed" view is not through

---

21 See George A. Lindbeck, *The Nature of Doctrine: Religion and Theology in a Post-Liberal Age* (Philadelphia: Westminster Press, 1984).

22 Paul Ricoeur, *Time and Narrative*, vol. 3, translated by Kathleen Blamey and David Pellauer (Chicago: The University of Chicago Press, 1988), 221.

23 . See Hans-Georg Gadamer, *Truth and Method*, translated by Garret Barden and John Cumming (New York: Seabury Press, Continuum, 1975), 235–78. Gadamer uses "reader" and "text" as metaphors for any encounter between an "observer" and an "object"/"event". Hence, one can substitute event for text without violation.
    For the discussion that follows, I am offering an expanded reading of Gadamer's discussion of Heidegger's "fore-structure" as well as of Gadamer's own analysis of understanding in terms of "prejudices" (Vorurteile). Gadamer begins this section of *Time and Method* (235-274) by evoking Heidegger's analysis of the "fore-structure of the understanding".

24 Gadamer, *Truth and Method*, 261.

25 Gadamer, *Truth and Method*, 264.

26 Gadamer, *Truth and Method*, 265.

27 Gadamer, *Truth and Method*, 248 Paul Ricoeur warns, as well, against the belief of an exhaustive mastering of the meaning of a text by acknowledging the limits to meaning as a consequence of the "mystery of time". However, Ricoeur does not view the mystery of time as a limit that shuts down

more comprehensive *actual* (!) knowledge but, rather, through the conscious engagement of the *"prejudices"* or *presuppositions* that always and already inform any "reading" of a "text".   It is precisely the reader's need to engage her/his own presuppositions and not merely the objective, actual meaning of the text that opens the text's possibilities in an open ended process of understanding that rewards every new reading. Possibilities change with situations. Hence, re-newed readings open up new possibilities of understanding.

However, experience here is not a foundation or ground that automatically legitimizes our reading or establishes the truth of our understanding. In "fact", experience here involves more than the merely actual to include the unique horizon of possibilities that enables the interface between the individual and her/his actual situation. What Gadamer calls our "prejudices" or presuppositions include not only the public possibilities of one's situation but also those distinctive possibilities unique to the individual within the confines of her/his (now to be viewed as an historical) situation. Gadamer's term "prejudice" (Vorurteil) although literally "prejudice" (pre-judgment) is more appropriately to be translated here as "possibilities" because Gadamer explicitly ties his discussion to Heidegger's analysis of the "fore-structure" of the understanding in *Being and Time*[28] where understanding means the projection of possibilities.[29] The encounter with the text (experience) is an interplay of public and private possibilities (Vorurteile, prejudices) within the horizon of an actual historical situation.

Gadamer's highlighting of "experience" as an open-ended dynamic of manifest actuality and concealed possibilities' exemplified by the encounter between a "reader" and "text" is a far more profound description of experience than that offered by Robert H. Sharf.[30]   Sharf seeks to problematize experience as a valid foundation for adjudicating (religious) experience by proposing that experience is just too ambiguous a notion to justify the weight placed upon it to serve as a criterion for truth.[31] However, his alternative to capricious "subjective" experience is a naive "objective" realism.

> The word 'experience, insofar as it refers to that which is given to us in the immediacy of perception, signifies that which by definition is nonobjective, that which resists all signification. In other words, the term experience cannot make ostensible a *something*

---

shared meaning: "It ought not to be said that our eulogy to narrative unthinkingly has given life again to the claims of the constituting subject to master all meaning. On the contrary, it is fitting that every mode of thought should verify the validity of its employment in the domain assigned to it, by taking an exact measure of the limits to its employment ... The mystery of time is not equivalent to a prohibition directed against language. Rather it gives rise to the exigence to think more and to speak differently." Ricoeur, *Time and Narrative, Vol. 3*, 274.

28 See Gadamer, *Truth and Method*, 235. Although Gadamer speaks of the "fore-structure of the understanding", his actual citation is not to that discussion in *Being and Time*, 191, but to the hermeneutical circle that involves the "fore-structure of the understanding", 194-195.

29 Heidegger says: "... understanding has in itself the existential structure which we call '*projection*' ... [P]rojection, in throwing, throws before itself the possibility as possibility, and lets it *be* as such. As projecting, understanding is the kind of Being of Dasein in which it *is* its possibilities as possibilities." Martin Heidegger, *Being and Time*, translated by John Macquarrie and Edward Robinson (New York: Harper and Row, 1962), 184–85.

30 See Robert H. Sharf, "Experience," in *Critical Terms for Religious Studies*, edited by Mark C. Taylor (Chicago: The University of Chicago Press, 1998), 94–116.

31 See Robert H. Sharf, "Experience," 99, 113.

that exists in the world. The salient characteristic of private experience that distinguishes it from 'objective reality' is thus its unremitting indeterminacy ... The category experience is, in essence, a mere placeholder that entails a substantive if indeterminate terminus for the relentless deferral of meaning. And (sic) this is precisely what makes the term experience so amenable to ideological appropriation.[32]

Sharf does not deny subjective experience, but he complains that it is too indefinite to carry any epistemological or alethic weight.

... [W]hile experience--construed as that which is 'immediately present'--may indeed be both irrefutable and indubitable, we must remember that whatever epistemological certainty experience may offer is gained only at the expense of any possible discursive meaning or signification.[33]

Sharf limits epistemological claims to what is verifiable or falsifiable in the senses. However, what Sharf overlooks is that "public actuality" is problematic not only because whatever certitude it has is "grounded" not in the perceptible but in the imperceptible (mathematics and law, see below) but also because it involves the perspectival nature of experience that can never know either things "as they are in themselves" or the entire concealed dimension of possibilities.[34] In this sense, his presupposition of the truth claims of the natural sciences as providing the standard for any and all truth claims is a mis-understanding of the mathematical sciences themselves, which are concerned with quantifiable relation (i.e., mathematical expression of law) inaccessible to the senses and not with verifiable judgments confirmed by objective things/substances.

Rather than a grasp of the objectively verifiable or falsifiable, understanding is the projecting of possibilities we already possess and dis-cover in our "reading" of experience in an attempt to make sense of our present and to anticipate our future.

Science: Relation and Not Substance

The nature of the "factual" and "actual" has been dramatically transformed by the rise of the mathematical or natural sciences. Contrary to Sharf and popular conceptions of science, however, what is either factual or actual is not concerned with knowledge of the substances of "things" either physical or abstract. The alternatives for understanding reality of medieval scholasticism (extreme realism, moderate realism, and nominalism) that were focused on substance (οὐσία) have been replaced by what we may call "relationalism".[35]

---

32 Robert H. Sharf, "Experience," 113.

33 Robert H. Sharf, "Experience," 114.

34 One valuable contribution by Sharf is his documentation of the emergence of the category of "experience" as the key descriptive category of Eastern religion to be a construct of the 20th century East in response to colonialism.

35 The following analysis of the shift from substance to relation is based upon Ernst Cassirer, *Substanzbegriff und Funktionsbegriff* (Berlin: Bruno Cassirer, 1910) and Ernst Cassirer, *Das Erkenntnisproblem in der Philosophie und Wissenschaft der neueren Zeit*, 4 vols., reprint, 1907 (Darmstadt: Wissenschaftliche Buchgesellschaft, 1944). Cassirer's terminological choice is unfortunate for the contemporary ear because we have come to view "function" as a form of reduction. In other words, were we to give a functional explanation of something, we would be describing how a thing is reducible to a state of affairs or a situation other than itself. For example, a functional explanation of religion would be to describe religious phenomena as "illusion" (Freud), as merely

Prior to the rise of the mathematical sciences, reality and knowledge were limited to "universals" and "particulars". Knowledge consisted in grasping the "essence" or universal. Extreme realism understood particulars to be "copies" of the eternal "originals" (i.e., essences). Moderate realism placed essences in particulars and knowledge in the mind where the essence was stripped of its matter. Finally, nominalism denied essences to claim there was only particulars. For nominalism, mental "essences" are merely subjective abstractions created by the individual mind as a consequence of its experience of a set of particulars. Knowledge in this case is our capacity to remember the "names" for particulars, but these names are entirely capricious. All that truly "is" are particulars. Particulars, however, have "substantial" natures according to the nominalist . Although we can only experience particulars in and through their "appearances", there is something substantial about particulars that gives them their independent and distinct status "over against" the observer.

With the mathematical sciences, however, came a conceptual revolution with respect to the nature of substance. The focus of the mathematical sciences is not merely on "extension" (i.e., what is quantifiably measurable in the senses) but on "relation". Extension is a form of "appearance" manifesting what one could conclude is a substance, but relation is concerned with "how" things interact with one another. Interactions can be quantified as a "more" or "less" without any notion of substance. Hence, the attention is no longer on "what" things "are" (their essential nature or substance). Rather, attention is shifted to "how" the elements in any specific set of interacting "things" are related to one another. By paying attention to relationships and the necessities (the laws) manifest by those relationships, one can determine exactly how something "must be" without ever having to prove "what" things as substances (or essences) in reality "are". *Certitude* with regard to our knowledge of eternal universals or the essential natures of particular things has shifted to identification of *necessity* in the relational interaction between and among things.

In other words, if we experience a particular relationship, then we must necessarily have these specific elements. For example, if one has two intersecting lines and connects them by means of a third line, the result is necessarily and always a triangle. Nonetheless, "points" and "lines" do not exist by definition. As soon as one has any extension, the "point" is a "line"; as soon as one has any width, the "line" is a "plane". What is important is not the essence but the relationship among the elements. One can speak about necessary relation (what is universally the case) in experience without ever having to determine what the actual substances are. In short, experience itself is not the criterion for truth. Rather, the structural relationships within experience illuminate a necessary truth to experience. Truth is concerned, then, with "how" elements interact and not merely with "what" we are experiencing.

The structure of consciousness according to the mathematical sciences is neither grounded in ideas as eternal essences (substances) nor in physical objects (substances). Rather, the structure of consciousness sketches the relational elements necessary for us to experience a world of physical phenomena as we necessarily must experience it. In

---

"social" in contrast to the "private" sphere (Durkheim), or as part of the ideological "superstructure" dependent upon an "economic base" (Marxism).

short, there is no transcendental consciousness without a physical world.[36] Kant, who appropriated the insights of the mathematical sciences for understanding the structure of transcendental consciousness, anticipated long before Husserl the notion that "consciousness is always consciousness-of something[37]". Transcendental consciousness, then is inseparable from its world of phenomena. Despite Hegel's portrayal of him as an absolute solipsist,[38] Fichte maintained that the self was necessarily rooted in a world because we cannot not act. At the heart of the Fichtean project is the insight that *"we do not act because we know but we know because we act"*[39].

The revolution of the mathematical sciences is still focussed, however, on actuality and not the more radical dynamic of possibility. The concern with relation is a concern with "how" elements are actually interacting with one another. The necessary certitude of scientific calculation is a certitude with respect to how things actually interact. There is without a doubt a dramatic shift from extreme and moderate realisms' focus on universals and from nominalisms' focus on particular things. This shift is one from substance to relation.

Necessity in the mathematical sciences has to do with the necessary interrelationship (expressed in laws) between the structure of consciousness and the actual world of experience. Hence, necessity for the mathematical sciences does not mean predetermined by the actual (substance) but, rather, is concerned with the necessary interrelationships between and among relational elements which determine "how" the world is and must be. As a consequence, necessity in the mathematical sciences has excluded a third form of necessity: the necessity of our having to eliminate some possibilities in order to actualize others. In short, *the necessity of the mathematical sciences ignores the necessity of action* in which we have no choice but to privilege a range of possibilities over others that must be excluded.

Experience: A Set of Aporiai

The strategy for re-problematizing experience appropriately must move beyond the binary structure of experience as constituted by two "substances." Substance suggests

---

36 Although a "mechanical" or physical explanation is never adequate to account for experience, Kant insists that we must always commence with the mechanical explanation (see Immanuel Kant, *Critique of the Power of Judgment*, translated by Paul Guyer and Eric Matthews, The Cambridge Edition of the Works of Immanuel Kant [Cambridge: Cambridge University Press, 2001], 283–84, 286) and it is precisely our anchoring in the physical world that can correct or rein in the extravagances of spiritual enthusiasm, which would remove us from the physical world (see Immanuel Kant, *Über Pädagogik*, vol. VI of *Immanuel Kant. Werke in Sechs Bänden*, edited by Wilhelm Weischedel [Darmstadt: Wissenschaftliche Buchgesellschaft, 1998], 457–58.)

37 See Edmund Husserl, *Ideas: General Introduction to Pure Phenomenology*, translated by W. R. Boyce Gibson, reprint, 1931 (New York: Collier, 1962), 108: "It belongs as a general feature to the essence of every actual *cogito* to be a consciousness *of* something."

38 See for example, Wilhelm Anz, *Kierkegaard und der deutsche Idealismus* (Tübingen: J.C.B. Mohr (Paul Siebeck), 1956), 16, n. 21.

39 See J.G. Fichte, "Die Bestimmung des Menschen," in *J.G. Fiche-Gesamtausgabe Der Bayerischen Akademie Der Wissenschaften* (Stuttgart-Bad Cannstatt: Friedrich Frommann Verlag (Günther Holzboog), 1981), 264–65, 280, 284. See as well, Cassirer's discussion of Fichte in Ernst Cassirer, *Das Erkenntnisproblem in der Philosophie und Wissenschaft der neueren Zeit*, vol. 3, reprint, 1920 (Darmstadt: Wissenschaftliche Buchgesellschaft, 1994), 126–216.

permanence. The tradition has alternated between conceptions of the permanent and impermanent in its quest for absolutes: permanent substance (οὐσία) was taken to be either mental or physical with the absolute "side" serving as the ultimate ground and explanation of the other. However, our experience of both the mental and physical involves the changing and unchanging. There is a sense in which both the "external" and "internal" dimensions of experience are appropriately described as "that which cannot be other than what it is" as well as "that which can be other than the way it appears to be".

Events are capricious. In any given moment, what is happening can be quite otherwise than the way it appears to be. However, once they have occurred, events are unchangeable. In short, there is an aporia with respect to events: they are changeable and unchangeable.

Consciousness, too, is simultaneously changing and unchanging. The Western tradition has distinguished between "that which can be other than the way it appears to be" from "that which cannot be other than what it is". In Platonism (not Plato[40]), this distinction was used to distinguish between "unchanging" Reality in the sense of extreme realism and the changing world of sense perception. "That which can be other than the way it appears to be" is the transient world of external events since objects are mere "copies" of eternal universals and "composite". For Platonists, in contrast to these changing copies, universals are the necessary presupposition for any and all experience. Universals are precisely that dimension of experience that remains the same yesterday, today, and tomorrow;[41] they cannot be other than what they are. Hence, the realm of sense perception is impermanent; universals are permanent.

However, there is a sense in which all of conscious experience and not merely universals is necessarily what it is since we can in any one moment only be conscious of what we are conscious (i.e., we cannot be conscious of something else at the same time). Nonetheless, there is an ambiguity to consciousness parallel to the ambiguity of transpiring external events: *what consciousness "necessarily" is experiencing can be outright false.*

The aporetic moments of experience can be summarized as follows: Externally in the present moment, things can be other than what they appear to be, but, after the event, events are necessarily what they are. Internally in the present moment, experience is necessarily what it is though it is not necessarily correct, but universals are necessarily what they are since they cannot change.

---

40 To be sure, whereas Plato understood universals to be "hypotheses" (see *Republic* 511b), Platonists (extreme realists) take hypotheses to be metaphysical absolutes. Our inability to define universals upon which all "knowledge" rests is the key to Socratic wisdom in the *Apology*: wisdom consists of knowing that we do not know what we think we know. Wisdom does not mean ignorance of most things that in time and with appropriate diligence and effort we could acquire. Rather, wisdom recognizes that our very epistemological limits mean that any and all knowledge rests upon assumptions (hypotheses), not certain definitions.

Ernst Cassirer describes the role of "hypotheses" in Plato, as well, and concludes that Plato is a "relationist", not an extreme realist. See ~ Ernst Cassirer, *Das Erkenntnisproblem in der Philosophie und Wissenschaft der neueren Zeit*, vol. 2, reprint, 1907 (Darmstadt: Wissenschaftliche Buchgesellschaft, 1944), 175, 181.

41 See, for example, the similes of the sun and the line *Republic* 505-511.

Relationalism shows us that experience consists of the interaction between these two dimensions. With relationalism we arrive at an additional meaning to the notion of "that which cannot be other than what it is": when the structural interrelationship between the particulars and the laws governing our experience of those particulars is necessarily what it is, then we have certitude.

Experience gives us aporetic structural elements that require us to dismiss the temptation to reduce the "real" down to either the "internal" or the "external". Yet, what "connects" the aporetic moments of the internal and the external? What bridges Lessing's "ugly ditch[42]" between mind and body? Heidegger is the most recent philosopher[43] who provides us with a key insight into "how" it is possible to make the connection between this transcendental structure and its world of phenomena. The structure of transcendental consciousness is not the consequence of a mere "accident" that consciousness is next to the world. The "self" is no permanent substrate or transcendental ego "within" from which I "go out" to a world only to withdraw to the self into a region "outside" of the world.[44] Neither is the self merely something actual next to a world of actual things. Rather, the self *is* its world. The self is its world as a project of possibilities concealed by and in the "objective" (actual) world. The self as an open ended project of possibilities is inseparable from its world.[45] Hence, the

---

42 See Gotthold Ephraim Lessing, *Theological Writings*, with an introduction by Henry Chadwick, A Library of Modern Religious Thought (Stanford, California: Stanford University Press, 1957), 53: "*accidental truths of history can never become the proof of necessary truths of reason*".

43 Cassirer's philosophy of symbolic forms sees language as the bridge connecting the gap between the external and the internal. "... [D]urch sie (language) wird weder ein einseitig Subjektives, noch ein einseitig Objektives bezeichnet und zum Ausdruck gebracht, sondern es tritt in ihr eine neue Vermittlung, eine eigentümliche Wechselbestimmung zwischen beiden Faktoren ein. Weder die blosse Entladung des Affekts, noch die Wiederholung objektiver lautlicher Reize stellt demgemäß schon den charakteristischen Sinn und die charakteristische Form der Sprache dar: diese [die charakteristische Form der Sprache] entsteht ... erst dort, wo beide Enden [Subjekt und Objekt] sich in eins Verknüpfen und dadurch eine neue, vorher nicht gegebene Synthese von 'Ich' und 'Welt' geschaffen wird." Ernst Cassirer, *Die Philosophie der symbolischen Formen, Erster Teil: Die Sprache*, reprint, 1928 (Darmstadt: Wissenschaftliche Buchgesellschaft, 1964), 26.

  Heidegger rethinks the meaning of "Being-of beings" and "time" y means of the notion of "possibility" that necessarily finds the self rooted in a world. However, the focus on "possibility" is not new with Heidegger. Already Plato makes "possibility" the key category for understanding both the "Good" (the highest mental principle) and the "chora" (the receptacle in which the physical cosmos occurs). For a discussion of Plato's "Good" (ἀγαθός) as "possibility", see Hans Michael Baumgartner, "Von der Möglichkeit, das Agathon als Prinzip zu denken. Versuch einer transzendentalen Interpretation zu Politeia 509b," in *Parusia. Studien zur Philosophie Platons und zur Problemgeschichte des Platonismus*, Festgabe für Johannes Hirschberger (Frankfurt am Main: Minerva G.m.b.H., 1965), 89–101, and Douglas R. McGaughey, *Christianity for the Third Millennium: Faith in an Age of Fundamentalism and Skepticism* (San Francisco: International Scholars Publications, University Press of America, 1998), 190–93. For a discussion of Plato's "chora" (χώρα) as "possibility", see Thomas Kratzert, *Die Entdeckung des Raums* (Amsterdam: B.R. Grüner, 1998), 109–10.

  In addition, Heinz Happ has shown that Aristotle's notion of "hyle" does not mean mere "physical stuff" because it is applied to the mind as much as to the physical world. Rather, "hyle" means "possibility". See Heinz Happ, *Hyle. Studien zum Aristotelischen Materie-Begriff* (Berlin: Walter de Gruyter, 1971), 696–98, 710. See, as well, Aristotle's Metaphysics 1060a 20: "... [hyle] does not exist in actuality, but exists in potency."

44 See Section 13, "A Founded Mode in which Being-in is Exemplified. Knowing the World" in Heidegger, *Being and Time*, 86–90.

45 In *Being and Time*, Heidegger describes what he calls the "structure of care" (state-of-mind,

necessary relational structure of transcendental consciousness that makes it possible for us to experience the world is "grounded" in a transcendental horizon of possibilities that is the concealed dimension of each and every individual and corporate situation.[46]

Problematizing Action

We cannot not act! Only by denying what we are can we escape evil by retreating into a Cathar or Manichaean dimension of spiritual perfection separate from the world. Further, we may not view the human condition as an inexplicable interface between two kinds of substance, one a "bottled-up" intangible, immaterial (good) consciousness, the other a tangible, material (evil) world. The "fact" that we cannot not act leads us beyond the dichotomy of mental and empirical "facts" to a self rooted in a concrete situation in the world and to a truth of manifest concealment (an ambiguous and inseparable mixture of good and evil) by means of which we, aporetically, are accountable to and responsible for our actions in the world. Action exposes the illusion of any vulgar skepticism.[47] Action unequivocally situates!

Situatedness alone, however, is necessary but not sufficient for determining the truth of experience. For example, Baudrillard describes three kinds of simulation.[48] First-order simulation is where the representation of "the real" is obvious (e.g., an out-dated road map). Second-order simulation blurs the boundaries between reality and representation (i.e., "the 'map' and reality can no longer be discerned, so the map has become as real as the real; e.g., in the absence of a written description, an account of

---

understanding, interpretation, and discourse illuminated by birth, death, guilt, conscience, freedom, and finitude) that establishes our rootedness in a situation that is not static but is temporal precisely because time is possibilities. See Section "IV. Temporality and Everydayness" of Division Two of Heidegger, *Being and Time*, 383–423, "birth": 425-426, 442-443, "death, guilt, conscience, freedom, and finitude": 436-437 and, particularly, Heidegger's discussion of possibility 183.

46 This is the central thesis of *Kant and the Problem of Metaphysics*, James S. Churchill (Bloomington, IN: Indiana University Press, 1968). Heidegger asks: "How can finite human *Dasein* in advance pass beyond (transcend) the essent when not only has it not created this essent but also is dependent on it in order to exist as *Dasein*? Thus, the problem of ontology is the question relative to the essence and the essential ground of the transcendence proper to the precursory comprehension of Being." *Ibid.*, 47. Heidegger answers, 121-122: "... Kant concentrates the entire problem of the essence of the finitude of knowledge in the concise formula of 'the possibility of experience' [A 156ff., B 195ff.]. The term 'experience' denotes the finite, receptive, intuitive knowledge of the essent. The essent must be given to knowledge as the ob-ject. However, the term 'possibility' has in the expression 'possibility of experience' a characteristic ambiguity.

The expression 'possibility of experience' refers ... to that which makes finite experience possible, i.e., experience which is not necessarily but contingently real. The possibility which renders this 'contingent' experience possible is the *possibilitias* of traditional metaphysics and is identical with *essentia* or *realitas* ...

Hence, the 'possibility of experience' denotes primarily the unified totality of that which makes finite knowledge essentially possible ... Consequently, the possibility of experience is identical with transcendence."

47 David Hume distinguishes between "vulgar" and "refined" skepticism in David Hume, *Dialogues Concerning Natural Religion and the Posthumous Essays of the Immortality of the Soul and On Suicide*, edited by Richard H. Popkin (Indianapolis: Hackett Pub., Co., 1982), 5, 12. Vulgar skepticism involves the doubting of the existence of anything and everything independent of consciousness. Refined skepticism involves proportioning our assent to the degree of the evidence.

48 See Lane, *Jean Baudrillard*, 86.

the ritual, the "map", that would account for a set of archaeological artifacts; or where the written description, the "map", is taken to be historical as in the case of biblical literalism). Third-order simulation involves "'... the generation by models of a real without origin or reality ...'[49]" Third-order simulation is perhaps most readily exemplified by the region of "hyperreality" that we call virtual reality. The boundary between the real and the unreal becomes apparently meaningless in the third-order simulation of hyperreality.

Action, however, illuminates the limits of hyperreality. Yet, if action does draw us "back" to the "real" world by exposing the simulacrum, nonetheless, second- and third-order simulation do properly problematize the strategy of action as the route to a world/reality to which we are accountable and responsible.

Baudrillard: Not Mere Simulation but Situations and Possibilities

The response of action to the simulacrum is not a response of naive "naturalism". In other words, acting does not serve as a strategy for exposing first-, second-, or third-order simulation in the simplistic belief that acting places us in the "real" world. Rather, action illuminates a situation and a horizon of possibilities. The difference between hyperreality and reality is a difference between situations and possibilities.

The simulacrum of appearance Baudrillard describes is grounded in and continues the philosophical focus on "substance". Baudrillard's simulacrum defines appearance as the absence of "substance". However, the Copernican turn to the subject by the mathematical sciences and transcendental idealism overcomes the debilitating obsession with substance and its dubitable truth claims by shifting to "relation" rather than "substance" as the basis for judgment. The issue can no longer be "what" is "real" but "how" can and do we experience and "understand" anything? In short, the issue is not: what do I know?; but how does what I (assume to) know empower me to act?

Relation is inseparable from situation, and situation is more than mere actuality. A situation includes a horizon of possibilities. Possibilities, however, are not free floating. Possibilities are inseparable from actual situations. Hence, the range of possibility is necessarily dependent upon the situation in which one acts. It is precisely the range of possibilities that distinguishes between hyperreality's virtual reality and the "real" world of responsibility and accountability.

Freedom and Necessity

The individual is necessarily grounded in a world of concealed possibilities as a consequence of action. We do not have conscious sovereignty over all of those possibilities. Nonetheless, we must and cannot not act. We act on the basis of our understanding of the possibilities as well as the actualities of our situation, but it is precisely because of those possibilities that we can become other than what we now actually are and, since we are not entirely sovereign over our possibilities, that we can be (sometimes dangerously) surprised.

Action involves necessarily choosing among projected possibilities decided upon on the basis of our understanding of the possibilities of our situation. Having made

---

49 Lane, *Jean Baudrillard*, 86.

our choice, we necessarily negate some possibilities as we actualize others. Hence, our "freedom" is not the mere freedom of "spirit" elevated above "matter".[50] Freedom is the ability to actualize possibilities that simultaneously involves the negation (but never the complete annihilation) of alternative possibilities.[51] Yet this process of actualization, the exercising of freedom as self-transcendence, is inseparable from necessity. We must necessarily act. We must necessarily act in a specific situation. Yet, we can never be fully conscious of all of the possibilities of our situation. We must necessarily choose, but, since we are not entirely sovereign over our possibilities, there is a sense in which our possibilities choose us.[52] Freedom is inescapably "grounded" in the ambiguity of necessity and negativity as a consequence of human finitude (as a consequence of our situatedness).

---

50 This classical notion of freedom as a capacity higher than matter, is found in Descartes, Kant, and Hegel. Alois Emanuel Biedermann and Otto Pfleiderer, in contrast, speak of freedom in the sense of this paper: spirit in the world; consciousness in situation. For example, Biedermann wrote: "Religion is not a fantasizing out of this world into the next world or out of this time into an after-life, but it is the actual spiritual interaction with the eternal divine heaven in every moment and at every location of our creaturely existence. If this is not its real kernel, then it is a dream without any kernel." Alois Emanuel Biedermann, "Die Zeitstimmen vor dem Richterstuhl der evangelischen Allianz," *Zeitstimmen aus der reformierten Kirche der Schweiz* 4 (1862): 196. Further, "All truly religious interest concentrates itself with respect to how humanity, during its temporal life, comes to an actual adoption of the eternal as its personal possession in life. What humanity thereby has for its temporal life ... is what we want to describe, and nothing else, as a process of the elevation of humanity out of its natural life of the flesh to its truly spiritual life ..." Biedermann, "Die Zeitstimmen," 197. Otto Pfleiderer distinguishes between conditional freedom and conditional dependence as he emphasizes the elevation of the human in freedom (in spirit) "above" yet "in" the world. See Emanuel Hirsch, *Geschichte der neuern evangelischen Theologie*, vol. 5 (Gütersloh: C. Bertelsmann Verlag, 1954), 565–66.

51 Here we encounter the notion of freedom as "self-transcendence" similar to that formulated by David Tracy. See David Tracy, *The Analogical Imagination: Christian Theology and the Culture of Pluralism* (New York: Crossroads, 1989), 120, 129, 130. The necessity of our choosing among and hence negating possibilities Heidegger calls the "negativity" (die Nichtigkeit) of life. See Heidegger, *Being and Time*, 329–31.

52 This is precisely what Heidegger means by the hermeneutical circle. "... a 'circle', belongs to the essence and to the distinctive character of understanding ... When it is objected that the existential Interpretation is 'circular', it is said that we have 'presupposed' the idea of existence and of Being in general, and that Dasein gets Interpreted 'accordingly', so that the idea of Being may be obtained from it. But (sic) what does 'presupposition' signify? In positing the idea of existence, do we also posit some proposition from which we deduce further propositions about the Being of Dasein, in accordance with formal rules of consistency? Or (sic) does this pre-supposing have the character of an understanding projection, in such a manner indeed that the Interpretation by which such an understanding gets developed, will let that which is to be interpreted *put itself into words for the very first time, so that it may decide of its own accord whether, as the entity which it is, it has that state of Being for which it has been disclosed in the projection with regard to its formal aspects?* ... Because it is primordially constituted by care, any Dasein is already ahead of itself. As being, it has in every case already projected itself upon definite possibilities of its existence; and in such existentiell projections it has, in a pre-ontological manner, also projected something like existence and Being ...

When one talks of the 'circle' in understanding, one expresses a failure to recognize two things; (1) that understanding as such makes up a basic kind of Dasein's Being, and (2) that this Being is constituted as care. To deny the circle, to make a secret of it, or even to want to overcome it, means finally to reinforce this failure. We must rather endeavour to leap into the 'circle', primordially and wholly, so that even at the start of the analysis of Dasein we make sure that we have a full view of Dasein's circular Being." Heidegger, *Being and Time*, 362–63.

Freedom and Transformation

Nonetheless, the crucial benefit of our viewing our situation in terms not only of manifest actuality but also of concealed possibilities is that, whereas we cannot change the actual, we can recover alternative possibilities concealed in both the past and the present. Here is where the true nature of freedom as self-transcendence is to be won and where our reflections return to practical theology.

We cannot change the actual of an historical event or the actual of a universal. Nonetheless, we can tease out other possibilities concealed by and in an historical event or a set of universals.[53] Past events as well as universals preserve concealed possibilities.

If it is not possible for us to change what is actually the case or what actually happened in the past, we can revisit what actually happened to affirm and even recover negated possibilities preserved by what actually was or is the case. In this sense, not only is understanding open ended since the possibilities of a text for a new context are never exhausted, but also history is open ended since we can yet recover negated and concealed possibilities out of the past to inform our action in the present for an anticipated future. The dynamic of possibilities is precisely the nature of time itself.

For example, whatever healing that can occur from the atrocities of history is precisely feasible because of the open ended process of projecting possibilities out of unalterable actualities. Our capacity as individuals and communities to return to the past to retrieve alternative possibilities does not in any way ignore the suffering of the past or forget that the possibilities we retrieve from the events of past generations are ours and not the possibilities of the ones who actually suffered. Nonetheless, our search for alternative possibilities empowers us to avoid the destructive actions of the past as we remember the suffering of those who have gone before us. Our lives are inseparable from our world and others. The "project" of life is a search for understanding that involves precisely the projecting of possibilities for a shared world we may all yet inhabit. Paul Ricoeur describes the ethics of such a project as remembering the deeds and suffering of those who have gone before us as we seek to make our personal and corporate decisions to create just institutions. We make those decisions on the basis of our understanding, that is, by the projecting of imaginative variations of possibilities among which we choose for a world we may yet inhabit.[54]

Conclusion

The postmodern world challenges us to move beyond substance but postmodernism has neglected the necessity (the certitude) of relation. Furthermore, contrary to postmodernism we cannot ignore narratives be they meta-narratives, cultural narratives, familial narratives, or individual narratives. The challenge of narrativity is neither to reject all meta-narratives nor to discover the "true" narrative. The twentieth century has taught the lesson: clinging to "true" narratives, particularly religious

---

53 Cassirer reminds us that a crucial insight by John Locke is that ideas (universals) are always systems. They are never in isolation. See Cassirer, *Das Erkenntnisproblem, vol. 2*, 255, 257.
54 See the Seventh Study and the Eighth Study of Paul Ricoeur, *Oneself as Another*, translated by Kathleen Blamey (Chicago: The University of Chicago Press, 1992), 169–239, and especially 330, 352.

narratives whether adhered to out of "religiousness" or "religious mindedness"[55], has led to the treating of a particular narrative as absolute and to the destruction of the conditions of life for others (even for ourselves) in the name of the absolute narrative. It is the abuse of narrative that has led erroneously the postmodern world to reject meta-narratives.

Absolute narratives are comforting because they conveniently ignore or eradicate evil from ourselves while attaching all evil to others. Hence, the lesson drawn from Baudrillard is not his critique of the simulacrum but his challenge to us to confront the evil within every narrative and to seize new transforming and healing possibilities out of that evil. Hence, in contrast to Baudrillard, we must move beyond the polarity of good and evil (beyond Manichaeism) to search out those renewing possibilities confirmed by our need to act and by the open-endedness of all situations as we seek to create a corporate world in which we all can live in just institutions. When we are able to identify the evil that is in us not as an actual state of "total depravity" (original sin) but as the risk involved in the exercising of our freedom of self-transcendence, we have established one aspect of a practical theology that illuminates the concealed possibilities of any and all situations to bring about just institutions. The second aspect of practical theology emphasizes the spiritual nature of the entire enterprise since "reality" is a mental (i.e., non-tangible) construct dependent upon the relational structure of transcendental consciousness with the world in which it must act. These two aspects, the possible and the spiritual, constitute the central focus of practical theology and remind us that action means situation. Action establishes our rootedness in an ambiguous, yet lived world of manifest actuality and concealed possibilities.

There are three kinds of necessity. One, determinism/predestination, is incompatible with freedom. The second, relationalism, identifies the necessary conditions that make our experience possible. The third is concerned with action. We must act, and we must choose among possibilities (i.e., actualize some and negate others) in our action. It is the last two forms of necessity that make understanding possible. Our challenge is to learn to discern the insightful, healing, and transforming possibilities for our concrete situation.

Two central takes on the nature of experience have shaped the Christian tradition. The Latin tradition has focused on sin and separation from God. There is no experience more obvious to the Western Christian tradition than human sin. However, the Greek tradition is rooted in an equally compelling experiential insight. There is no experience more obvious to the Greek and Eastern Christian tradition than intangible consciousness (spirit) that roots humanity in the eternal already in this transient life. Given the untenability of the metaphysics informing both of these traditions, perhaps a take on experience as illuminated by practical theology offers an equally compelling experiential insight: life is an open horizon of possibilities arising out of and inseparable from concrete historical situations to which we are responsible and accountable.

---

55 This distinction between "religiousness" and "religious mindedness" is taken from Clifford Geertz, *Islam Observed: Religious Development in Morocco and Indonesia* (Chicago: University of Chicago Press, 1971), 61, 111. The difference consists of "being held by religious convictions" (religiousness) without equivocation and merely "holding" religious convictions in spite of one's doubt.

Works Cited

Adler, Mortimer J. *How to Read a Book: The Art of Getting a Liberal Education*. New York: Simon and Schuster, 1940.

Anz, Wilhelm. *Kierkegaard und der deutsche Idealismus*. Tübingen: J.C.B. Mohr (Paul Siebeck), 1956.

Baudrillard, Jean. "Spiegel Gespräch. Das ist der vierte Weltkrieg." *Der Spiegel* 3 (2002): 178–81.

Baumgartner, Hans Michael. "Von der Möglichkeit, das Agathon als Prinzip zu denken. Versuch einer transzendentalen Interpretation zu Politeia 509b." In *Parusia. Studien zur Philosophie Platons und zur Problemgeschichte des Platonismus*, Festgabe für Johannes Hirschberger, 89–101. Frankfurt am Main: Minerva G.m.b.H., 1965.

Biedermann, Alois Emanuel. "Die Zeitstimmen vor dem Richterstuhl der evangelischen Allianz." *Zeitstimmen aus der reformierten Kirche der Schweiz* 4 (1862): 40–44, 63–68, 69–81, 85–101, 109–23, 129–43, 149–64, 173–88, 193–203, 213–26, 229–43, 249–64.

Bohr, Niels. "Can Quantum-Mechanical Description of Physical Reality be Considered Complete?" *The Physical Review* 48, Second Series (October 1935): 696–702.

Cassirer, Ernst. *Das Erkenntnisproblem in der Philosophie und Wissenschaft der neueren Zeit*. Vol. 2. 1907. Darmstadt: Wissenschaftliche Buchgesellschaft, 1944.

_____. *Das Erkenntnisproblem in der Philosophie und Wissenschaft der neueren Zeit*. Vol. 3. 1920. Darmstadt: Wissenschaftliche Buchgesellschaft, 1994.

_____. *Die Philosophie der symbolischen Formen, Erster Teil: Die Sprache*. 1928. Darmstadt: Wissenschaftliche Buchgesellschaft, 1964.

_____. *Substanzbegriff und Funktionsbegriff*. Berlin: Bruno Cassirer, 1910.

de Saussure, Ferdinand. *Course in General Linguistics*. Eds Charles Bally and Albert Sechehaye. Translated by Wade Baskin. New York: McGraw-Hill, 1966.

Derrida, Jacques. *Dissemination*. Translated by Barbara Johnson. Chicago: University of Chicago Press, 1981.

Einstein, Albert, et.al. "Can Quantum-Mechanical Description of Physical Reality be Considered Complete?" *The Physical Review* 47, Second Series (May 1935): 777–80.

Fichte, J.G. "Die Bestimmung des Menschen." In *J.G. Fiche-Gesamtausgabe der Bayerischen Akademie der Wissenschaften*, 148–311. Stuttgart-Bad Cannstatt: Friedrich Frommann Verlag (Günther Holzboog), 1981.

Gadamer, Hans-Georg. *Truth and Method*. Translated by Garret Barden and John Cumming. New York: Seabury Press, Continuum, 1975.

Geertz, Clifford. *Islam Observed: Religious Development in Morocco and Indonesia*.

Chicago: University of Chicago Press, 1971.

Happ, Heinz. *Hyle. Studien zum Aristotelischen Materie-Begriff.* Berlin: Walter de Gruyter, 1971.

Harden, Blaine. "The Dirt in the New Machine." *The New York Times*, 12 August 2001*The New York Times Magazine.*

Heidegger, Martin. *Being and Time.* Translated by John Macquarrie and Edward Robinson. New York: Harper and Row, 1962.

_____. *Kant and the Problem of Metaphysics.* James S. Churchill. Bloomington, IN: Indiana University Press, 1968.

Hirsch, Emanuel. *Geschichte der neuern evangelischen Theologie.* Vol. 5. Gütersloh: C. Bertelsmann Verlag, 1954.

Hume, David. *Dialogues Concerning Natural Religion and the Posthumous Essays of the Immortality of the Soul and On Suicide.* Edited by Richard H. Popkin. Indianapolis: Hackett Pub., Co., 1982.

Husserl, Edmund. *Ideas: General Introduction to Pure Phenomenology.* Translated by W. R. Boyce Gibson. 1931. New York: Collier, 1962.

Kant, Immanuel. *Critique of Pure Reason.* Translated by Norman Kemp Smith. New York: St. Martin's Press, 1965.

_____. *Critique of the Power of Judgment.* Translated by Paul Guyer and Eric Matthews. The Cambridge Edition of the Works of Immanuel Kant. Cambridge: Cambridge University Press, 2001.

_____. *Über Pädagogik* in *Werke in Sechs Bänden.* Vol. VI. Edited by Wilhelm Weischedel, 691–761. Darmstadt: Wissenschaftliche Buchgesellschaft, 1998.

Kratzert, Thomas. *Die Entdeckung des Raums.* Amsterdam: B.R. Grüner, 1998.

Kuhn, Thomas S. *The Structure of Scientific Revolutions: Foundations of the Unity of Science.* 2d ed. Chicago: University of Chicago Press, 1970.

Lane, Richard J. *Jean Baudrillard.* London: Routledge, 2000.

Lessing, Gotthold Ephraim. *Theological Writings.* With an introduction by Henry Chadwick. A Library of Modern Religious Thought. Stanford, California: Stanford University Press, 1957.

Lindbeck, George A. *The Nature of Doctrine: Religion and Theology in a Post-Liberal Age.* Philadelphia: Westminster Press, 1984.

Lyotard, Jean-François. *A Postmodern Condition: A Report on Knowledge.* Translated by Geoff Bennington and Brian Massumi. Minneapolis, MN: University of Minnesota Press, 1985.

McGaughey, Douglas R. *Christianity for the Third Millennium: Faith in an Age of Fundamentalism and Skepticism.* San Francisco: International Scholars

Publications, University Press of America, 1998.

Nietzsche, Friedrich. "Jenseits von Gut und Böse." In *Nietzsches Werke*. Leipzig: Alfred Kröner Verlag, 1910.

Pöggeler, Otto. "Hegel und die Anfänge der Nihilismus-Diskussion." *Man and World An International Philosophical Review* 3, no. 3 (September 1970): 163–99.

_____. "'Nihilist' und 'Nihilismus.'" *Archiv Für Begriffsgeschichte* XIX (1965): 197–210. Bonn: Bouvier Verlag Herbert Grundmann.

Ricoeur, Paul. *Oneself as Another*. Translated by Kathleen Blamey. Chicago: The University of Chicago Press, 1992.

_____. "Should We Renounce Hegel?" In *Time and Narrative*, vol. 3, edited by Kathleen Blamey and David Pellauer, 193–206. Chicago: The University of Chicago Press, 1988.

_____. *Time and Narrative*. Vol. 3. Translated by Kathleen Blamey and David Pellauer. Chicago: The University of Chicago Press, 1988.

Robert H. Sharf. "Experience." In *Critical Terms for Religious Studies*, edited by Mark C. Taylor, 94–116. Chicago: The University of Chicago Press, 1998.

Tracy, David. *The Analogical Imagination: Christian Theology and the Culture of Pluralism*. New York: Crossroads, 1989.

Hermeneutics of Integration
A Proposal for a Model of Biblical Interpretation

Eung Chun Park

This article surveys the history of the three major hermeneutical models and their applications to biblical interpretation. Then it proposes a model of biblical hermeneutics that would benefit from the positive insights from the already developed models and yet take into account some of the special features of biblical interpretation in the postmodern era, such as the historical dimension of the bible, multilayered traditions behind the finalized texts, the role of faith, and ethics of interpretation.

Preamble

The last century of the second millennium witnessed a paradigm shift with regard to the way human beings perceive and construe reality. The firm belief that there are objectively definable norms and standards that have universal validity was seriously challenged and the premise that reality is something out there as given was forcefully contested. The monolithic foundation for essentialism that epitomized the ethos of modernity began to crumble in the advent of constructionism of postmodernity, which has a self-consciously pluralistic outlook. Postmodernity observes that there is no such thing as "universal validity" or "pure objectivity." Postmodernity declares that reality is a construct, socially and culturally conditioned. If I may take the liberty of coining a new word in contribution to the so-called pomo-babble phenomenon, *construal*ity replaces *real*ity in the realm of human perception. In postmodernity, no construct is inherently more authentic than any other. The age of absolutism is gone; the new era of relativity has come.

Even though the word "postmodernity" as *terminus technicus* was first applied in architecture,[1] no discipline is more affected by what the term embodies than literary criticism and hermeneutics, both of which have immediate relevance to biblical interpretation. For the last few decades postmodernity has made a strong imprint in biblical studies. The influence of secular hermeneutics on biblical criticism is no new phenomenon. In fact, the history of modern biblical interpretation runs parallel to the history of hermeneutics with the result that various biblical exegetical methods embody different hermeneutical principles. The purpose of this article is to survey the history of the development of the three hermeneutical models and their relations with biblical interpretation and to propose what I call hermeneutics of integration as one of

---

1 David Harvey, *The Condition of Postmodernity: An Inquiry into the Origin of Cultural Change* (Cambridge & Oxford: Blackwell Publisher, 1990), 38-9, "With respect to architecture, for example, Charles Jencks dates the symbolic end of modernism and the passage to the postmodern as 3.32 pm on 15 July 1972, when the Pruitt-Igoe housing development in St Louis (a prize winning version of Le Corbusier's 'machine for modern living') was dynamited as an uninhabitable environment for the low-income people it housed." Since then, Harvey says, the ideas of "high modernism" gave way to an onslaught of diverse possibilities that deviated from the abstract, theoretical, and doctrinaire ideals of the previous period.

the possible paradigms of biblical interpretation that does justice to the general as well as special natures of the bible as a collection of written texts.

Three hermeneutical models and their implications on biblical interpretation

A human being is *homo interpretans*. Interpretation is a basic modus vivendi in human existence. The object of interpretation can be anything that signifies something. However, hermeneutics as an academic discipline is primarily, if not exclusively, interested in the interpretation of linguistic communication in the form of written text. Communication through written language involves three basic elements: the author, the text, and the reader.[2] The history of hermeneutics and that of literary critical theory, which are closely related with one another, reflect the shift of focus among these three elements.

Author-Oriented Hermeneutics

When someone writes a text, s/he *intends* to communicate something. This intention of the author is first conceptualized as a communicable idea and then it is translated into linguistic form in his/her mind before it is actually written down. Therefore, it can be said that the meaning of a text comes into being in the mental process of the author even before it takes shape as a text. From this perspective, the meaning of a text is identical with the intention of the author. In that vein, Friedrich Schleiermacher, who is called the progenitor of modern hermeneutics, regards hermeneutics as an art of understanding, and he identifies understanding as an act of re-experiencing the mental process of the author of the text.[3] In other words, interpretation takes place when the reader penetrates into the structure of the sentences, reverses the mental process of the author, and arrives at the original meaning that the author had in mind at the time of composition.[4] This interpretative process is analyzed by Schleiermacher as consisting of two parts: the grammatical interpretation, which deciphers the language of the text, and the psychological interpretation, which seeks to reconstruct the thought that the linguistic text contains. The former is governed by general and objective rules, but the latter inquires the subjective side of the author and therefore it requires a certain degree of empathy with the author.

By formulating the principles of general hermeneutics in this way, Schleiermacher obviates the distinction between *hermeneutica sacra* and *hermeneutica profana*, arguing that the process of human understanding is the same whether it is for a sacred text or a secular one. This methodological principle and the emphasis on the author in Schleiermacher's hermeneutics had the effect of affirming the validity of historical

---

2   Cf. Roman Jakobson, "Closing Statement: Linguistics and Poetics" in Thomas Sebeok, ed., *A Style in Language* (Cambridge: MIT Press, 1960), 350-77. Here Jakobson presents a communication model with the sender, the message, and the addressee, the context, the contact, and the code as the basic elements in verbal communication. Umberto Eco, *The Role of the Reader: Explorations in the Semiotics of Texts* (Indiana University Press, 1979), 10, uses only the first three: the sender, the message, and the addressee.

3   Richard E. Palmer, *Hermeneutics: Interpretation Theory in Schleiermacher, Dilthey, Heidegger, and Gadamer* (Evanston: Northwestern University Press, 1969), 86.

4   Schleierrmach's hermeneutics is called Romantic hermeneutics because of his optimistic belief in the interpreter's ability to re-experience the mind of the author.

criticism in biblical interpretation.[5] The authors of the biblical books and the historical circumstances that shaped their thought world naturally became the primary subjects of biblical studies.

Historical criticism based on author-oriented hermeneutics was also promoted by the so-called historical positivism, which dominated the field of history as academic discipline in the 19th century. Leopold von Ranke, who is the leading theoretician of historical positivism, believed that history could accurately represent the realities of human life in the past and that it is the task of the historian to reconstruct the *bruta facta* of the past "as it actually was (*wie es eigentlich gewesen*)"[6] and to comprehend the intentions of human actors of the past events in order to construct a coherent history.[7] The most important concept in historical positivism is "objectivity". It was believed that historiography should be free of presuppositions of the historians and be "purely objective" and "value-neutral" in perspective.

Author-oriented hermeneutics also finds a close parallel in the traditional literary criticism, which identifies the meaning of a literary work with the authorial intention. According to the so-called "Great Man Theory of Literature," great literature is the product of great literary figures and the chief value of literature is to provide intimate access to the souls of the authors.[8] In order to understand the meaning of a poem, for example, one needs biographical information of the poet as well as the social, cultural, and political circumstances of the time of composition, since all these extra-textual factors must have influenced the authorial intention.

Many of the current biblical exegetical methods embody this author-oriented hermeneutics with varying degrees of acceptance of the Rankean historical positivism. For example, redaction criticism, which is still indispensable both in Old and New Testament scholarship, is an endeavor to go back to the minds of the authors of biblical writings and to their historical circumstances. Even the more recent social-scientific criticism and the cultural-anthropological approach to the bible can be said to belong here in the sense that their practitioners try to reconstruct the social and cultural history of the past as closely as possible to what they were really like at that time.[9] Even though the historical positivism of the 19th century with its extravagant claims on objectivity has become a thing of the past, its basic premises are still in the foreground and background of current biblical scholarship.

Text-Oriented Hermeneutics

The first serious revolt against the sway that the author had over the control of the meaning of the text was launched by the English poet and literary critic, T. S. Eliot. In

---

5   Edgar Krentz, *The Historical-Critical Method* (Philadelphia: Fortress Press, 1975), 24

6   Leopold von Ranke, *Geschichten der romanischen und germanischen Völker*, preface to the 1st edition (Werke, Leipzig, 1874, vol. xxxiii-xxxiv, p. vii). This reference is quoted from R. G. Collingwood, *The Idea of History* (Oxford: Clarendon Press, 1946), 130; See also Ernst Breisach, *Historiography: Ancient, Medieval, and Modern* (The University of Chicago Press, 1983), 233.

7   Georg G. Iggers, *Historiography in the Twentieth Century: From Scientific Objectivity to the Postmodern Challenge* (Wesleyan University Press, 1997), 3.

8   Terry Eagleton, *Literary Theory: An Introduction*, 2nd ed. (University of Minnesota Press, 1996), 41-2.

9   Cf. Stephen C. Barton, "Historical Criticism and Social-Scientific Perspectives in New Testament Study" in Joel B. Green, ed., *Hearing the New Testament: Strategies for Interpretation* (Grand Rapids: Eerdmans, 1995) 61-89, esp. 67-76.

his influential article, "Tradition and the Individual Talent" (1919), he declared, "Honest criticism and sensitive appreciation are directed not upon the poet but upon the poetry."[10] By diverting the focus from the author to the work of art itself, Eliot became a forerunner of the new literary critical movement in America called New Criticism.[11] K. W. Wimsatt and Monroe Beardsley, who were among the key players of New Criticism in America in the 30s to 50s, reject the literary critical methods that regard either the authorial intention or the emotive effect of literature as the criterion of the meaning of literary art. They call the former approach "the intentional fallacy" and the latter "the affective fallacy,"[12] and argue that the meaning of poetry should be sought in the poetry itself.

New Criticism is a theory of the autonomy of the literary text as the exclusive locus of meaning. According to this theory, once a literary text is published, it has its own autonomous life independent of its author, and its meaning is intrinsic to the text itself. Therefore, the literary critic should not look for extra-textual information such as biography of the author or the historical circumstances of its composition in order to understand the meaning of a literary work. Instead, "close reading" is the best way of appreciating literature. Even though this hermeneutical model is a radical departure from the author-oriented theory, the two models share a fundamental premise on methodology, that is, the belief in objectivity in interpretation. Whether the primary object is the author or the text, interpretation should be done by disinterested readers with self-conscious detachment.

In fact, the field of hermeneutics per se was largely unaffected by New Criticism, probably because the latter was largely confined in the realm of literary criticism, especially in the interpretation of poetry, and also because it was short-lived. However, the shift of focus from the author to the text warrants the designation "Text-Oriented Hermeneutics" for the kind of interpretative model that New Criticism represents. Put in this perspective, Russian Formalism as well as French Structuralism can also be said to belong to text-oriented hermeneutics to the degree that they also rely on the inner dynamic of the text itself for the meaning of a literary work. The impact of New Criticism on biblical interpretation was also minimal. Part of the reason is that New Criticism, since it was primarily concerned about poems and its analytical tools were designed for aesthetic dynamics of the text, had only limited applicability on biblical interpretation.

Reader-Oriented Hermeneutics

Generally speaking, both the first and the second hermeneutical models are based on ontological realism on the one hand and epistemological positivism on the other. The former presupposes that objects exist out there in the external world independently of our perception, and the latter that we as subjects can have objective knowledge about the existing objects. These premises reflect the optimism of the Enlightenment concerning the power of human rationality.

---

10 M. H. Abrams, et al. eds., *The Norton Anthology of English Literature*, vol.2 (Norton, 1974), 2201.

11 In his essay Eliot uses the term "aesthetic criticism" for his own proposal in contrast to the traditional "historical criticism." The name, "New Criticism" was first given by John Crowe Ransom.

12 W. K. Wimsatt, *The Verbal Icon: Studies in the Meaning of Poetry* (University of Kentucky Press, 1954), 4-18, & 21-39.

Edmund Husserl, who is called the founder of Phenomenology, denies ontological realism and says that all realities are only *phenomena*, that is, things that only appear to exist.[13] But he maintains epistemological positivism, at least, concerning our absolute knowledge of the phenomena.[14] His notion of "transcendental subject" implies that the traditional subject-object dichotomy is still operative here. Martin Heidegger rejects Husserl's idea of "transcendental subject" and stresses the fundamentally historical nature of human understanding.[15] Since human existence cannot transcend history to attain the Archimedian vantage point, understanding is unavoidably conditioned by the existential realities of the one who tries to understand. Therefore, interpretation can never be "purely objective" without presuppositions of the interpreter.[16] It goes without saying that this interpretive stance of Heidegger greatly influenced the existential hermeneutics of his Marburg colleague and friend Rudolf Bultmann.

Hans-Georg Gadamer continues the notion of historicality of understanding and denies the possibility of "objectively valid knowledge" of Dilthey. According to Gadamer, understanding is never neutral; it is always perspectival. Gadamer even talks about "prejudices as conditions of understanding."[17] In a well-known passage in his magnum opus, *Truth and Method*, Gadamer discusses "the horizon of the past" and "the horizon of the present." He says that these horizons are not fixed but they are constantly changing.[18] These two horizons are inherently connected with each other in spite of the temporal gap between them. Gadamer says, "Hence the horizon of the present cannot be formed without the past. There is no more an isolated horizon of the present in itself than there are historical horizons which have to be acquired. *Rather, understanding is always the fusion of these horizons supposedly existing by themselves*." (Italics original)[19]

This growing emphasis of phenomenological hermeneutics on the existential dimension of the interpreter as a determining factor of interpretation became the theoretical foundation for the third interpretive model that centers on the role of the reader in construing the meaning of the text. That is why these phenomenological hermeneuticians are called forerunners of postmodernism.

Postmodern critics are not the first to recognize the role of the reader in the realm of literature. The whole tradition of ancient Greek rhetoric greatly concerned about the effect of orations on the part of the audience. Also, as early as the third century CE, a Greek philosopher by the name of Longinus Cassius (213–273) wrote a famous literary critical treatise, *On the Sublime*, in which he recognized the importance of the emotive effect of literature on the reader and argued that the value of a literary work

---

13 The name "Phenomenology" is derived from the Greek word, *phainomenon*, which is a present middle/passive participle neuter singular of *phaino* (to show). In Platonic dualism, *to phainomenon* refers to "what only appears to be" in contrast to *to on*, which is a present active participle neuter singular of *eimi* (to be), meaning "what really exists." The term "Phenomenology" was first used by Edmund Husserl.

14 Eagleton, *Literary Theory*, 57.

15 Josef Bleicher, *Contemporary Hermeneutics: Hermeneutics as Method, Philosophy and Critique* (Routledge, 1980), 98.

16 Palmer, *Hermeneutics*, 135-37

17 Hans-Georg Gadamer, *Truth and Method* (2nd ed. New York: Continuum, 1995), 277.

18 Gadamer, *Truth and Method*, 304.

19 Gadamer, *Truth and Method*, 306.

should be assessed by the sublimity it creates in the mind of the reader. Thus Longinus is said to have produced the first affective theory of literature.[20] However, his notion of the role of the reader in literature is still a passive one. It is only in the twentieth century that an active role of the reader in hermeneutics began to be acknowledged.[21]

The movement toward reader-oriented hermeneutics in literary criticism began with what is called "reception aesthetics" in Germany. As a theory of interpretation, reception aesthetics was heavily influenced by phenomenological hermeneutics but it was more interested in the role of the reader in the literary text as a concrete entity rather than such abstract notion as Dasein as the subject of interpretation. In his phenomenological analysis of the reading process, Wolfgang Iser, who is called the founder of the German reception aesthetics, points to the polysemantic nature of text and the indeterminacy of its meaning.[22] In the process of reading, Iser observes, this polysemantic possibilities of the text are encountered by the active imagination of the reader, which functions as the arbitrator, and then a configurative meaning, which he calls "Gestalt," is being construed. In that sense, the reader is not a passive receiver of a ready-made meaning but an active contributor in the production of meaning of the text. By the same token, reading is not a passive act but a "re-creative" process, without which no meaning is construed.[23]

Stanley Fish, who is a prominent reader-response critic in America, redefines the concept of "meaning" in literature. That is, meaning is not an entity that is embedded in the text waiting to be extracted, but it is an *event* that the reader experiences in the process of reading. In other words, the reader's response is the meaning.[24] With this new notion of meaning, he goes further to say, "Interpretation is not the art of construing but the art of constructing. Interpreters do not decode poems; they make them."[25] In the same vein Fish even denies that the formal features of the text and the structure of the (authorial) intention exist independently of the reader.[26] In short, the text does not exist until the reader creates it by the act of reading. Thus comes the radical notion that it is not the author but the reader who writes the text.[27]

Another peculiar form of reader-oriented hermeneutics is the so-called deconstruction of the much-discussed French poststructuralist Jacques Derrida. Deconstruction denies the autonomous existence of all existing things and ideas. Following structuralists' claim that there is no ontologically necessary correspondence

---

20 David Daiches, *Critical Approaches to Literature* (Prentice-Hall, 1956), 46-47.
21 The difference between the kind of "affective" theory of Longinus and the twentieth century reader response-criticism is emphasized by Jane P. Tompkins, "The Reader in History: The Changing Shape of Literary Response" in *Reader Response Criticism: From Formalism to Post-Structuralism* (ed. by Jane P. Tompkins, Johns Hopkins University Press, 1980), 201-32. esp. 202-203.
22 Wolfgang Iser, "The Reading Process: A Phenomenological Approach" in *Reader Response Criticism: From Formalism to Post-Structuralism*, 50-69.
23 Iser uses the term "recreative," and the hyphen between "re" and "creative" is mine.
24 Stanley Fish, "Literature in the Reader: Affective Stylistics" in *Reader Response Criticism: From Formalism to Post-Structuralism*, 70-100.
25 Stanley Fish, *Is There A Text In This Class?: The Authority of Interpretive Communities* (Harvard University Press, 1980), 327.
26 Stanley Fish, "Interpreting the Variorum" in *Reader Response Criticism: From Formalism to Post-Structuralism*, 164-84. esp. 177.
27 Jane P. Tompkins, "An Introduction to Reader-Response Criticism" in *Reader Response Criticism: From Formalism to Post-Structuralism*, ix-xxvi. esp.xxii.

between the signifier and the signified, deconstructionists say that nothing exists of itself and every existence is only by virtue of the differences that we make.[28] In deconstructive thinking, realities are not real; they are nothing but constructs, and behind all constructs there are hidden agendas. So deconstruction as a form of literary criticism tries to debunk the socio-politically constructed realities embedded in the text by de-centering and de-constructing the matrix of the textual codes, always turning the table against the grain of the authorial intention, which was woven into the text.[29] That is why it is often called a "negative criticism."

Directly or indirectly, reader-oriented hermeneutics has inspired many different forms of the so-called "advocacy" criticism or ideological criticism, which pushes a particular socio-political agenda with regard to race, gender, ethnicity, sexual orientation, etc. Ideological criticism starts with the accusation that modern historical criticism is fundamentally a bourgeois enterprise in the disguise of "objectivity" or "universal validity," and it tries to raise voices of various marginalized groups of people.[30] Feminist interpretation, black theology, liberation hermeneutics, and postcolonial interpretation are only a few examples. In practice, they may eclectically use various interpretive methods based on the first or second hermeneutical model, but in the sense that they all take seriously the existential realities and the social location of the reader as the hermeneutical vantage point, they belong to the third interpretive model, that is, reader-oriented hermeneutics.

The rise of these various forms of reader-oriented hermeneutics in the twentieth century is certainly a manifestation of the growing influence of postmodernity. By rejecting essentialists' notions of universally valid norms and standards and by endorsing existential particularities as the only thing that matters, postmodernism provided the ideological ground for reader-oriented hermeneutics, which rejects the notion of the one authentic and universally valid interpretation in favor of plurality of meanings. The notion of the indeterminacy of meaning, which is the foundation of the plurality of meaning in reader-oriented hermeneutics, could very well maximize the potential of the text to speak meaningfully to various groups of intended and unintended readers. Even apart from this functional benefit, there is something fundamentally valid about reader-oriented hermeneutics, especially with regard to its explanatory power for the question of what actually happens in the process of reading. In other word, without necessarily discrediting other hermeneutical models, we could acknowledge, to say the least, that reader-response criticism is *descriptively* correct in its phenomenological analysis of reading. Even for this one aspect alone, reader-response criticism should not be overlooked by any student of hermeneutics, biblical or secular, in the future.

Most of those reader-oriented hermeneutical methods mentioned above have been applied to biblical interpretation and have contributed to the discovery of new ways of interpreting the bible. This interpretive diversity is certainly a blessing and it will continue to enrich our understanding the bible. They also have exposed the on-going

---

28 Jacques Derrida, *Margins of Philosophy* (tr. by Alan Bass, The University of Chicago Press, 1982), 5-7.
29 A good example of the application of deconstruction to a biblical passage is found in Stephen D. Moore, *Post-Structuralism and the New Testament: Derrida and Foucault at the Foot of the Cross* (Fortress, 1994), 43-52.
30 A. K. M. Adam, *What is Postmodern Biblical Criticism?* (Fortress, 1995), 51.

history of the misuse of the bible in the name of the putative objective interpretation. On the other hand, though, reader-oriented hermeneutics raises serious methodological questions that have not been adequately addressed.

First of all, there is the problem of the potential hermeneutical anarchy. If the reader's response is the meaning of the text, there will be as many meanings of a text as there are readers, and that would inevitably result in a chaotic state in interpretation. Stanley Fish, unlike some postmodern critics, does not sanction such interpretive anarchy. So he presents two mechanisms that he thinks could ward off invalid interpretations. First, Fish makes it clear that when he says "the reader" he does not mean any reader. In his reader-response criticism, "*the* reader is the *informed* reader," who has linguistic, semantic, and literary competence.[31] In that context, the reader in Fish's version of reader-response criticism is called the ideal or idealized reader.[32] Secondly, Fish resorts to the notion of "interpretive communities," which will set up the boundaries for valid interpretations.[33] These interpretive communities are made up of those who share interpretive strategies. These strategies exist prior to the act of reading and therefore determine the shape of what is to be read. However, Fish does not elaborate on who has the right to set the norms for the interpretive strategies.

For those who want to embrace reader-response criticism without completely rejecting the first hermeneutical model, this notion of the informed reader and the interpretive community can be a great harmonizing point. It is particularly promising for biblical hermeneutics because the majority of the interpretation of the bible has always been done by a community of informed scholars. But on the other hand, Fish's notion of the informed reader and the interpretive communities with common strategies has been criticized by other reader response critics as falling back onto the extra-textual forces for the determination of meaning. If the legitimacy of interpretation is reserved for a selected group of people who are highly educated so that their clique may predetermine the boundaries of possible meanings, interpretation remains at the hands of a few elites with power and privilege.

Secondly, the problem of hermeneutical anarchy is directly connected with the issue of the authority of the interpretation of the bible. Traditionally, both in the first and the second hermeneutical model, valid biblical interpretation was identified with correct exegesis, while eisegesis was anathematized. That is how the authority of the interpretation of the bible was safeguarded. In postmodern hermeneutics, it is the other way around. That is, exegesis, derived from the Greek verb *exhegeomai* meaning "to take something out of," is condemned while eisegesis, from *eishegeomai* meaning "to bring something into," is legitimized. In fact, strictly speaking, in reader-oriented hermeneutics there is no such thing as exegesis but only eisegesis is realistically possible and existentially relevant. Thus the authority of the interpretation of the bible

---

31 Fish, "Literature in the Reader" 86-87. (Italics his)

32 Cf. Umberto Eco, *The Role of the Reader*, 7-11. Here Eco talks about the "Model Reader," who is foreseen by the author as a model for the possible reader. This Model Reader is supposedly able to deal interpretatively with the expressions in the same way as the author deals generatively with them. However, Eco observes, in reality no actual reader is the same as the Model Reader. So the authorial intention is never fully grasped. In that sense, Eco's concept of Model Reader, in contrast to Fish's ideal reader, ends up intensifying the problem of hermeneutical anarchy.

33 Fish, *Is There A Text In This Class?* 171

is radically relativized. This could potentially be a crisis. In reader-oriented hermeneutics, one might say, the bible is in danger of becoming a channel, through which human beings raise their own voices while putting God in silence. It is a danger of *Deus dicens* being replaced by *homo dicens*. Challenged by this potential crisis, the church needs to find a way to critically embrace reader-oriented hermeneutics so that the reader is taken seriously but not too seriously.

A Proposal for the Hermeneutics of Integration

In the arena of human intellect there is no such thing as absolutely valid theory. All the three hermeneutical models mentioned above have varying degrees of validity as well as fallibility. So, it would be meaningless to evaluate them in absolute terms without putting them in proper context. What we need to do as responsible interpreters of the bible is to carefully assess each of them as they are specifically applied to biblical interpretation and then to *integrate* all the positive insights of the three hermeneutical models for a holistic interpretation of the bible. That is to say, our aim is not to make a selection for one hermeneutical theory over against the others but to critically appropriate all of them in order to give the biblical text a full and comprehensive treatment it deserves. Biblical text is complex. It is polysemantic and polysemous. It even has the potential to mean what the original authors did not intend to mean. No single hermeneutical theory could possibly do justice to this multi-faceted nature of the biblical text. That is why a hermeneutics of integration is needed in biblical interpretation.

There are a few characteristics of the bible and its interpretations that we have to take into consideration, when we try to apply the aforementioned hermeneutical theories *integrally* to biblical interpretation.

1. The Judeo-Christian traditions are firmly rooted in history and their scriptures are fundamentally historical in nature. Therefore, any hermeneutical theory that does not take history seriously will run the risk of missing the most important points of the bible. That is why New Criticism and structuralism as such largely failed to take root in biblical criticism.[34] In that sense, the first hermeneutical model will always be an important component of biblical interpretation. Having learned from phenomenological hermeneutics, we should no longer naively assume that "pure objectivity" is possible. However, that should not give us an excuse to become a-historical. As long as the bible tells history of a certain kind, biblical interpretation must include historical investigation and biblical interpreters should conduct it as *objectively as possible*. If, as it is, absolute objectivity is impossible, relative objectivity should still be striven after.[35] This is in no way to privilege the first hermeneutical model over against the other two. Rather, it points to where it needs to begin.

---

34 For a discussion on the limits of formalism in biblical interpretation see Lynn M. Poland, *Literary Criticism and Biblical Hermeneutics: A Critique of Formalist Approaches* (AAR Academy Series 48, Scholars Press, 1985), 65-97.

35 The term "relative objectivity" is taken from Roy Wagner, "The Idea of Culture" in *The Truth about the Truth: De-confusing and Re-constructing the Postmodern World* (ed. by Walter Truett Anderson, New York: Putnam, 1995), 53-57.

2. Many of the interpretive theories developed by literary critics have a single literary work as the object of interpretation. For example, it is in the context of interpreting individual poems that New Criticism talks about the autonomy of the text. In contrast, the bible is a collection of books written and edited by a great variety of known and unknown figures over a long period of history. This even includes numerous anonymous tridents who made their contributions, small as they may be, to the process of the formation of the source materials, oral or written, and fragmentary or coherent. In other words, the "biblical text" as a repository of historical or existential meanings is larger than the sum total of the sentences of the canonical books of the bible. This richness of the text and the intertextuality, represented by the many diverse layers of traditions in the bible, should be recognized and fully appreciated in biblical hermeneutics.

3. The role of faith in the interpretation of the bible both in the past and in the present should be recognized in biblical interpretation. This should not necessarily alter the actual methodology of interpretative theories. In other words, Schleiermacher's principle of general hermeneutics applicable for both *hermeneutica sacra* and *hermeneutica profana* should remain valid. But, at appropriate points in the multi-layered process of biblical interpretation, the religious dimension of the text itself and that of its interpreters should be given a legitimate place. This particular concern may not be addressed adequately when biblical interpretation is engaged in historical criticism based on the first hermeneutical model, but it may find a congenial place in the application of the third hermeneutical model to biblical interpretation, which allows the reader to go beyond the historical dimensions of the text.[36]

4. In the past, biblical interpretation tended to be judged according to the dogmatic criteria set by whatever institutionalized tradition it belonged to. Historical-critical consciousness has contributed to freeing biblical interpretation from dogmatic grip. However, once biblical interpretation embraces reader-oriented hermeneutics, it needs yet another guideline in order to avoid lapsing back to the pre-critical stage or creating a new hermeneutical chaos. Granted that much harm has been done to certain groups of people in the name of the bible throughout the history of biblical interpretation, the new paradigms of biblical interpretation will have to be formulated in such a way that its outcome should enhance rather than undermine the shalom of all the people God created.[37] In other words, biblical interpretation is not a value-neutral business. It has a definite agenda. And the agenda is to envision and advocate the peace and justice among all nations and people in the entire inhabited world.

The above points do not make a concrete, well-defined method of interpretation of the bible. They are preliminary suggestions for a more comprehensive model of biblical

---

36 For a suggestion of how reader-oriented criticism can effectively be applied to biblical interpretation, especially with regard to the issue of integrating faith, see Edgar V. McKnight, *Postmodern Use of the Bible: The Emergence of Reader-Oriented Criticism* (Abingdon, 1988), 217-67.

37 Here I draw on the concept of the "ethics of interpretation" in Elizabeth Schüssler Fiorenza, "Defending the Center, Trivializing the Margins" in Heikki Räisänen et al, *Reading the Bible in the Global Village* (Atlanta: Society of Biblical Literature, 2000), 29-48. See esp. 43-48.

interpretation. I call it a "hermeneutics of integration" in the sense that it is in dialogue with all the three different hermeneutical models in search for a creative appropriation of them. Surely, some aspects of these different hermeneutical models can be mutually exclusive. But that does not necessarily invalidate the hermeneutics of integration, since the ambiguities of our existential realities make the biblical text malleable even to mutually contradicting theories. Integration supersedes contradictions among theories, when it renders the text meaning*ful* and *full* of meaning, since we believe that God continues to speak through the bible in spite of all the unresolved contradictions of our interpretations.

Works Cited

Abrams, M. H., et al. eds., *The Norton Anthology of English Literature*, Vol.2. Norton, 1974

Adam, A. K. M., *What is Postmodern Biblical Criticism?* Fortress, 1995

Barton, Stephen C., "Historical Criticism and Social-Scientific Perspectives in New Testament Study" in Joel B. Green, ed., *Hearing the New Testament: Strategies for Interpretation*. Grand Rapids: Eerdmans, 1995, 61-89

Bleicher, Josef, *Contemporary Hermeneutics: Hermeneutics as Method, Philosophy and Critique*. Routledge, 1980

Breisach, Ernst, *Historiography: Ancient, Medieval, and Modern*. The University of Chicago Press, 1983

Collingwood, R. G., *The Idea of History*. Oxford: Clarendon Press, 1946

Daiches, David, *Critical Approaches to Literature*. Prentice-Hall, 1956

Derrida, Jacques, *Margins of Philosophy*. tr. by Alan Bass. The University of Chicago Press, 1982

Eagleton, Terry, *Literary Theory: An Introduction*, 2nd ed. University of Minnesota Press, 1996

Eco, Umberto, *The Role of the Reader: Explorations in the Semiotics of Texts*. Indiana University Press, 1979

Fiorenza, Elizabeth Schüssler, "Defending the Center, Trivializing the Margins" in Heikki Räisänen et al, *Reading the Bible in the Global Village*. Atlanta: Society of Biblical Literature, 2000, 29-48.

Fish, Stanley, "Interpreting the Variorum" in Jane P. Tompkins, ed., *Reader Response Criticism: From Formalism to Post-Structuralism*, Johns Hopkins University Press, 1980, 164-84

Fish, Stanley, "Literature in the Reader: Affective Stylistics" in Jane P. Tompkins, ed., *Reader Response Criticism: From Formalism to Post-Structuralism*, 70-100

Fish, Stanley, *Is There A Text In This Class?: The Authority of Interpretive Communities*. Harvard University Press, 1980

Gadamer, Hans-Georg, *Truth and Method* 2nd ed. New York: Continuum, 1995

Harvey, David, *The Condition of Postmodernity: An Inquiry into the Origin of Cultural Change*. Cambridge & Oxford: Blackwell Publisher, 1990

Iggers, Georg G., *Historiography in the Twentieth Century: From Scientific Objectivity to the Postmodern Challenge*. Wesleyan University Press, 1997

Iser, Wolfgang, "The Reading Process: A Phenomenological Approach" in Jane P. Tompkins, ed., *Reader Response Criticism: From Formalism to Post-Structuralism*, 50-69

Jakobson, Roman, "Closing Statement: Linguistics and Poetics" in Thomas Sebeok, ed., A *Style in Language*. Cambridge: MIT Press, 1960, 350-77

Krentz, Edgar, *The Historical-Critical Method*. Philadelphia: Fortress Press, 1975

McKnight, Edgar V., *Postmodern Use of the Bible: The Emergence of Reader-Oriented Criticism*. Abingdon, 1988

Moore, Stephen D., *Post-Structuralism and the New Testament: Derrida and Foucault at the Foot of the Cross*. Fortress, 1994

Palmer, Richard E., *Hermeneutics: Interpretation Theory in Schleiermacher, Dilthey, Heidegger, and Gadamer*. Evanston: Northwestern University Press, 1969

Poland, Lynn M., *Literary Criticism and Biblical Hermeneutics: A Critique of Formalist Approaches*. AAR Academy Series 48, Scholars Press, 1985

Tompkins, Jane P., "An Introduction to Reader-Response Criticism" in idem, ed., *Reader Response Criticism: From Formalism to Post-Structuralism*, ix-xxvi. esp.xxii.

Tompkins, Jane P., "The Reader in History: The Changing Shape of Literary Response" in idem ed., *Reader Response Criticism: From Formalism to Post-Structuralism*. 201-32

Wagner, Roy, "The Idea of Culture" in Walter Truett Anderson, ed., *The Truth about the Truth: De-confusing and Re-constructing the Postmodern World*. New York: Putnam, 1995

Wimsatt, W. K., *The Verbal Icon: Studies in the Meaning of Poetry*. University of Kentucky Press, 1954

Critical Interpretations

These articles contain interpretations of Biblical passages and issues that arise out of the early Christian movement and remain important for Christians to this day.

Psalm 19

Heavenly Law and Order

Robert B. Coote

Psalm 19 is a unity and concerns obedience to the divine command. This is as true of the first half as it is of the second: the heavenly bodies declare God's honor by adhering to their heavenly courses laid down by God. The sun is the great exemplar; the planets are presumptuous deviants. Positing the conventional correspondence between heavenly order and social regulation, the psalm extols not law in the abstract, but automatic obedience to God's surrogates, the Jerusalemite magistracy that introduced it into the Psalter.

I grew up with Addison's radiant version of the first half of this psalm, written in 1712 and later set to the tune for the same verses in Haydn's oratorio *The Creation*—"The spacious firmament on high, with all the blue ethereal sky, and spangled heavens, a shining frame, their great Original proclaim.... In reason's ear [not aloud] they all rejoice, and utter forth a glorious voice, forever singing, as they shine, 'The hand that made us is divine.'" The editors of the *Presbyterian Hymnal* (1990) chose to leave out this stately hymn, in favor of a pair of paraphrases composed by Christopher Webber in 1986.[1] As often observed, Psalm 19 appears to have two distinct halves, one on creation and the other on the law, and not surprisingly this bifurcation occurs in hymnody. Addison rendered only the first half of the psalm, and Webber divided the two halves between two hymns. Until about 30 years ago, most critical commentators analyzed Psalm 19 as two distinct psalms combined into one. I phoned Webber to find out what made him split the psalm in two. An Anglican, he said he simply followed the 1979 *Episcopal Prayer Book*, which followed the Common Lectionary. The Lectionary assigns the two parts of the psalm to two different weeks—whether for scholarly reasons I don't know. Happily it also appoints the entire psalm for a third week, so that periodically churchgoers hear both parts together, and wonder perhaps what the two parts have to do with each other. Recent commentators have eschewed analyzing Psalm 19 as a mere combination—a distasteful idea these days—and have found in the psalm an obvious unity and coherence, whether as originally composed or combined from parts. It is a mistake, they intone, to take apart what the Bible puts together.

The psalm's unity may appear obvious to most readers and hearers, who in any case may be more prone to put together than take apart. But what exactly makes for its unity? This is not a new question: even those who have thought the psalm is a mere combination have asked why the combination was made. The answers remain various and include the following. The psalm, it is said, reflects the ancient Near Eastern commonplace of a relationship between the sun and justice.[2] The sun and the law are

---

1 Hymns 166 and 167.

2 David J. A. Clines, "The Tree of Knowledge and the Law of Yahweh (Ps. XIX)," *Vetus Testamentum* 24 (1974) 12, n. 4, traced this observation, from the start dependent on the recovery of ancient Near Eastern texts, to L. Dürr, "Zur Frage nach der Einheit von Ps. 19," in *Sellin-Festschrift: Beiträge zur Religionsgeschichte und Archäologie Palästinas*, ed. William F. Albright (Leipzig: A. Deichert, 1927), 37-48. A. H. van Zyl, "Psalm 19," in *Biblical Essays: Proceedings of the Ninth Meeting of Die Ou-*

equally glorious gifts from the creator to his creatures. As the sun illuminates the world, so the law instructs humans—an analogy suggested by the luminary qualities of the law praised by the psalm. As nothing is hidden from the sun, nothing escapes the law.[3] The celebration of Torah supplies a lack in the celebration of creation: "the cosmos celebrates God's glory, but it does not teach his will."[4] Even more vaguely, "in the completed Psalm the creation is the matrix in which the specificity of the Torah is situated, so that the two together lead to an affirmation that obedience to Torah is the way in which Israel receives the gift of life from the creator."[5] The juxtaposition has a polemical purpose: the psalm opposes sun worship during the reign of Josiah by trumping a hymn to the sun with a hymn to Israelite Torah.[6] Similarly, since the terminology describing the law is reminiscent of the tree of knowledge in Genesis 2-3, the psalm pits the Torah against the discredited tree of knowledge, and the hymn to creation corresponds to Genesis 1.[7] While a polemical purpose might have shaped the psalm, it could not, in the view of one renowned expert on inner-Scriptural resonances, explain its continued use as a prayer. What about the concluding petition, this expert asks, in which the psalmist, anxious over hidden errors, unwitting faults, and willful offenses, pleads that these not "coerce" (*yimš^elû*) him and that his words and thoughts find favor before God? In this view, the psalm is to be divided into three parts instead of two and the whole interpreted in terms of the last third, which "provides the religious-psychological motivation for the entire prayer."[8]

For the last twenty years, interpretations of Psalm 19 have by and large followed this threefold division, along with the interest in theological psychology that almost inevitably goes with it. In this division, in the words of one interpreter, the third part is a prayer for God's help, in which "the psalmist acknowledges that he cannot be righteous through *torah* alone."[9] In the same vein, another interpreter has proposed that "the created order has proclaimed God's sovereignty [part 1], and it is the

Testamentiese Werkgemeenskap in Suid-Afrika (Stellenbosch: 1966), 150, traced it back to Schroeder, "Zu Psalm 19," *Zeitschrift für die alttestamentliche Wissenschaft* 34 (1914) 69-70. Schroeder: "...since a primary activity of the sun god [in the ancient Near East] is juridical, we find ourselves in v. 8ff. as well in the sphere of the [now extant] hymns to the sun." The sun, however, plays no overt role in judgment in Psalm 19.

3   For the latter three ideas, see Sigmund Mowinckel, *The Psalms in Israel's Worship*, vol. 1 (Oxford: Blackwell, 1962), 90-91.

4   Hans-Joachim Kraus, *Psalms 1-59: A Commentary* (Minneapolis: Augsburg, 1988; German orig. 1961), 275.

5   Walter Brueggemann, *Reverberations of Faith: A Theological Handbook of Old Testament Themes* (Louisville: Westminster John Knox, 2002), 68 (s.v. "Ethics").

6   Nahum Sarna, "Psalm XIX and the Near Eastern Sun-God Literature," in *Proceedings of the IV World Congress of Jewish Studies*, Vol. 1 (Jerusalem: World Union of Jewish Studies, 1967), 171-75; *Songs of the Heart* (New York: Schocken, 1993), 74.

7   Clines, "Tree of Knowledge," 12-13. Kraus, *Psalms 1-59*, 274: "hardly convincing."

8   Michael Fishbane, *Text and Texture: Close Readings of Selected Biblical Texts* (New York: Schocken Books, 1979), 84-90 (chap. 6 "Psalm 19/Creation, Torah, and Hope"), quotes on p. 86. "Rather than parts 1 and 2 serving polemical functions for the psalmist, a holistic view of the received psalm shows these subsections to provide both the prologue and the counterpoint to his request [part 3]. His desire to be forgiven for covenantal transgressions is set within a larger praise of God as lawgiver and creator" (86). Earlier interpreters also recognized the obvious break in meter and thought within the second half of the psalm, which might be divided into a hymn to the law and a prayer for pardon and guidance.

9   James Luther Mays, *Psalms* (Louisville: Westminster John Knox, 1994), 99-100.

privilege and responsibility of a sovereign to provide…guidance and instruction for the servants [part 2]."[10] But this is not all that matters. In this Protestant interpretation, the third part indicates that the *torah* is "something other than a static system of reward/punishment… In the final analysis, even God's personal instruction to humanity is not sufficient to ensure that human behavior will be in harmony with God and God's ordering of the world." Only by the grace of God can the psalmist "live in humble dependence on God."[11] A third interpreter, influenced by the recent burgeoning of studies of solar worship in Israel and the temple, has revived the earlier accent on ancient Near Eastern resonances in the psalm and in a synthesis of older and newer approaches, including the threefold division, interpreted the psalm in terms of the pervasive imagery of the sun. In this view, the treatment of the sun is not polemical but serenely affirmative: "through the juxtaposition of sun and *tôrâ*, solarized worship of God is wrapped in the scroll of *tôrâ*-piety…. The psalmist boldly transfers a powerful cosmic image associated with temple worship and lodges it squarely within the ethos of *tôrâ*."[12]

This latest treatment is particularly welcome because of its wide-ranging attention to the ancient Near Eastern matrix. Moreover, almost in passing the author puts his finger on an important neglected theme in the psalm. "As *tôrâ* is solarized…so the sun is 'torasized,' that is, recast as an object of moral reflection and a figure of righteousness. The…moral language used to describe *tôrâ* as 'upright' or 'straight' and 'righteous' is cosmically illustrated in the prescribed movement of the sun across the heavens. Figuratively, the sun models the path ordained by God that all are to follow…. The sun not only evokes the ethos and efficacy of *tôrâ*; it also embodies and models *tôrâ*-piety."[13] This important insight is consistent with the method adopted of reading the whole psalm through the prism of both sun and law; but it is overwhelmed by an accumulation of less germane solar comparisons, stated without reference to previous treatments of the same insight, and weakened by the suggestion that such a view of the sun depends uniquely on this psalm (the sun is "recast," italics mine).[14] It

---

10   J. Clinton McCann, Jr., "The Book of Psalms: Introduction, Commentary, and Reflections," in *The New Interpreter's Bible*, Vol. IV, ed. Leander E. Keck (Nashville: Abingdon, 1996), 752. On the relationship of parts 1 and 2 from this perspective, see Mays, *Psalms*, 98.

11   McCann, "The Book of Psalms," 751-53. McCann summarizes: "The love that motivated God to create…is the same love manifested…in the life of the psalmist (vv. 11-14)…. Love is the basic reality of the [created] universe" (754).

12   William P. Brown, *Seeing the Psalms: A Theology of Metaphor* (Louisville: Westminster John Knox, 2002), 81-103 (chap. 4 "The Sun of Righteousness: Psalm 19 and the Joy of *Lex*"), quote on p. 99. More doubtfully: "No harsh polemic is at work, as some have tried to claim" (99).

13   Brown, *Seeing the Psalms*, 97. For the sun on the righteous way, Brown appositely compares Ps 119:3, 15, 32, 37

14   For earlier treatments of the notion of a law-obedient sun in this psalm, see Sverre Aalen, *Die Begriffe "Licht" und "Finsternis" im Alten Testament, im Spätjudentum und in Rabbinismus* (Oslo: Norske Videnskaps-akademi i Oslo1951), 27-28; Van Zyl, "Psalm 19," 150 (a reported view—"The redactor who united the two independent poems wished to stress the idea that Yahweh's will and Torah are the foundation stones of justice and order"); A. A. Anderson, *The Book of Psalms*, Vol. 1 (London: Oliphants, 1972), 167 ("Both parts speak of the divine: nature is not only created by God but it is also ordered and maintained by him, and therefore it truly proclaims the glory of God"). Neither Van Zyl nor Anderson refers to Aalen. P. A. H. de Boer explained *qaw* in Ps 19 as the ordinances established by rather than kept by the celestial bodies, the orderly progression of days, nights, months, and seasons: "Étude sur le sens de la racine QWH," *Oudtestamentiesche Studiën* 10 (1954) 225-46, esp.

also focuses unduly on the sun alone, since in this interpretation the sun is the sole relevant representative of "the heavens."

As Aalen, however, pointed out over 50 years ago, there is more in the sky than the sun, and the notion that the sun might represent obedience goes well beyond this particular psalm. It is lamentable that scholars who have recognized the analogy of the law-obedient sun have not taken Aalen's view seriously, since he comprehended spot-on the meaning of Psalm 19—that the sun, moon, and stars proclaim God's honor through their conformity with the commands of God, in parallel with human beings—and he did so with just the right tone of supposition, though without addressing exegetical particulars.[15] Aalen concluded by referring to 1 Enoch 2-5, whose opening analogy expresses the same view of the heavens: "Examine all the activities which take place in the sky and how they do not alter their ways, (and examine) the luminaries of heaven, how each one of them rises and sets; each one is systematic according to its respective season; and they do not divert from their appointed order."[16]   By endeavoring to look again at the sky the way the psalmist and the writer of 1 Enoch saw it, we may come to a more accurate understanding of this psalm, and one that for us is less vague, I believe, and more defensible than those recently proposed.

245-46. It is surprising that De Boer treated *qaw* in Psalm 19 under the heading of the root *qwy/w*—as does Brown-Driver-Briggs—since the lengthened *w* clearly indicates a root *qww*. Note however the III-*y/w* byform *miqwâ*, "cord," in Josh 2:18, 21, and the ostensible analogy of *s aw* from the root *s wy/w*. Kraus took *qaw* in Isa 28:11to mean "strange sound" and understood the term here to refer to a "hymnic—and at the same time overwhelmingly instructive—'sound'" (*Psalms 1-59*, 271-72). The comparison of *qaw* with Arabic *qawwah* (second form), "shout," in e.g. *The Tanakh: A New Translation of the Holy Scriptures According to the Traditional Hebrew Text* (Philadelphia: The Jewish Publication Society, 1985), 1126, founders on the fact that the third root consonant *h* is consonantal.

15   "So wie Gott einen Bund mit Israel geschlossen hat, so auch mit Tag und Nacht (Jer 33,25, vgl. 31,35f). Für den Lauf der Natur gelten Gesetze (*h uqqot*...oder *h uqqim*...), die nicht übertreten werden dürfen, auch nicht von Tag und Nacht oder von den Himmelskörpern (ebd. und Ps 148,3-6), genau so wie Israel solche Gesetze hat.... So wie Israel Gott kennt und auf seinen Willen acht gibt, so 'kennt die Sonne ihren Niedergang,' d.i. die von Gott bestimmte Untergangszeit (Ps 104,19). Gott bietet dem Morgen zu kommen (Hiob 38,12). Durch ihren Gehorsam gegen Gottes *h uqqim*, d.h. durch die Erfüllung der ihnen aufgelegten Gesetzmäßigkeit preisen Sonne und Mond und Sterne Gott als ihren Schöpfer (Ps 148,3ff), verkünden seine Ehre und Schöpfermacht (Ps 19,2ff). Wir unterstreichen, daß dies der Gedanke im letztgenannten Psalm ist. Hier ist das ganze Schema deutlich greifbar, der Wechsel von Tag und Nacht, V. 3, das Gesetzmäßige an den Bewegungen der Gestirne, exemplifiziert auf die Sonne, V. 5ff, der Parallelismus der Naturgesetze mit den Israel gegebenen Gesetzen, V. 8ff. Damit sollte das Kompositionsproblem dieses Psalms gelöst sein.... ...diese Theorie [the parallel of sun and law] erklärt nicht die ersten Verse des Psalms.... ...der gesuchte Parallelismus zwischen den beiden Teilen [des Psalms] muß im Gehorsam der Gestirne sowohl als auch der Menschen gegenüber dem Gesetz liegen. In den Ausdrücken 'Himmel' und 'seiner Hände Werke' sind Mond und Sterne einbegriffen, vgl. Ps. 8,4; sie nehmen am Lobpreis Gottes teil, vgl. Ps 148. Wie die Gestirne des Nachthimmels und das Gestirn des Taghimmels im Rahmen des Wechsels von Tag und Nacht ihrem Gesetz gehorchen (Teil 1), so sind auch die Menschen dem Gesetz gehorsam (Teil 2).... Der Parallelismus bezieht sich im übrigen nicht nur auf den Gehorsam, sondern auch auf den Lobpreis, die Worte, die Tag und Nacht, der Himmel und seine Gestirne wie auch der Mensch, V. 15, aussprechen." Aalen, *Die Begriffe*, 27-28.

16   The Ethiopic for the last phrase is "their appointed commandments." See Ephraim Isaac, "1 (Ethiopic Apocalypse of) Enoch: A New Translation and Introduction," in *The Old Testament Pseudepigrapha. Vol. 1 Apocalyptic Literature and Testaments*, ed. James H. Charlesworth (Garden City: Doubleday & Company, 1983), 14; cf. George W. E. Nickelsburg and James C. VanderKam, *1 Enoch: A New Translation* (Minneapolis: Fortress, 2004), 21.

To begin with, it is necessary to revert to the twofold rather than threefold analysis of the structure of Psalm 19.

> The heavens recount respect for God,
>> as the firmament discloses his handiwork.
>
> Day by day it pours forth utterance,
>> and night by night it declares acknowledgment.[17]
>
> But there is no utterance, there are no words:
>> their sound is not to be heard.
>
> Yet through all the world their cord/chord[18] goes forth,
>> and to the ends of the earth[19] their vocables.
>
> **With them**[20] is set[21] a canopy for the sun,[22]
>> and he like a bridegroom emerges from his bower,
>> like a mighty man[23] joys to run the course:

---

17 The usual translation of this bicolon takes day and night as the subjects of the verbs: day speaks to day and night to night. Consistent with the opening lines of the psalm, it is not day and night that "speak"—day and night are times, not entities—but sky and firmament, both of which "speak" both night and day. "Speech" emanates from God's "handiwork"—firmament, sun, moon, and stars—hence the singular verbs. The correct grammar is recognized by Samuel Terrien, *The Psalms: Strophic Structure and Theological Commentary* (Grand Rapids: Eerdmans, 2003), 205-6: "Day by day he utters speech,/And night by night he imparts knowledge"; however, Terrien takes the quietness of these opening lines to signify meditation, and he does not say who the "he" is.

18 Numerous emendations of *qaw* have been proposed. The most common by far is *qôl*, "voice, sound"; but as Charles Briggs and his daughter Emilie Grace Briggs pointed out, in the LXX the usual rendering of this term is *phōnē*, while the LXX (*phthongos*), Jerome (*sonus*), and Symmachus (*ēchos*) all suggest instead a noise or musical sound—though such renderings might have been guesswork (*A Critical and Exegetical Commentary on the Book of Psalms*, vol. 1 [Edinburgh: T. & T. Clark, 1906], 172). In modern treatments this idea is found already in commentaries by, among others, Ewald (1880), Delitzsch (1883), and Gunkel (1926)—for the latter see below—and is implied by Brown-Driver-Briggs ("chord, music") without proviso (p. 876a). But the idea has not been generally accepted because "there is no usage to justify this meaning" (Briggs, 172, endorsed by e.g. Van Zyl, "Psalm 19," 154, n. 8). For the plain sense "cord," see Beyse in *Theologisches Wörterbuch zum Alten Testament*, vol. VI, ed. George W. Anderson and others (Stuttgart: W. Kohlhammer, 1989), 1223-24; for "chord," see below. Terrien recognizes that *qaw*, v. 5, "sometimes designates a musical string" (*The Psalms*, 210, n. 9), though the passages he cites do not directly support this meaning, as just noted; he translates the word "melody."

19 In Fishbane's adroit rendering—though once more in anachronistic terms—"Their words reach the rim of space."

20 The phrase "in/with them" is usually understood to mean "in the sky." However, the correspondence between this phrase and the same phrase in the equivalent pivotal position in the second stanza ("*with them* is your servant too illumined/warned") suggests that the meanings of both phrases correspond as well: "with them," i.e. with the inaudible utterances, words, and c(h)ords parallel to the words of the law, or with the c(h)ords only, seen as constituting, enmeshing, or supporting the sun's canopy.

21 Most translators assume that God is the subject of the active verb *śām*. Within the context of the psalm as understood here, the phrase may alternatively be viewed as impersonal.

22 Anderson, *Psalms*, 169: "[In the ancient Near East] the sun has a 'tent' and not a 'palace'…. The tent is, apparently, the place where the sun 'spends' the night (cf. *ANET*, p. 391a)." As noted by Brown, this feature was first pointed out by Gunkel: *Seeing the Psalms*, 97.

23 A near consensus has seen the two figures of the similes in this stanza—bridegroom and "strong man" or "athlete"—as distinct. More likely the figure is a single one: the joyous warrior as bridegroom.

From the ends of the heavens he comes forth,
  and his circuit is to their further ends—
  there is nothing hid from his blaze.

The law of Yahweh is perfect—restoring life;[24]
  The stipulations of Yahweh are sure—making wise the simple.

The precepts of Yahweh are straight—gladdening the mind;
  The commandment of Yahweh is pure—brightening the eyes.

The fear of Yahweh is clean—lasting forever;
  The judgments of Yahweh are true—altogether right.

They are more to be desired than gold—even much fine gold,
  and sweeter than honey—even dripping from the comb.

With them your servant too[25] is illumined/warned;
  in keeping them is much gain.

Wanderings who can perceive? From hidden (deviations) clear me.
  And from presumptions restrain your servant—
  then shall I be blameless, and clear of great transgression.

Let the utterances of my mouth
  and the reflections of my mind meet your acceptance,
  O Yahweh, my rock and my redeemer.

The current penchant for dividing the psalm into three stanzas rather than two is a diversion. The supposed three stanzas have no consistent length or pattern.[26] The change of meter to so-called *qînâ* lines and the ostensible change of subject appear at first to set the lines about the law off from the rest of what both precedes and follows.

---

24 The *qînâ* line (combining a long and a short phrase) is taken here as a complete line in itself rather than as bicolon because the semantic pattern aa¹bb¹ is more expected than the pattern aba¹b¹. The two examples of the latter given by Adele Berlin in her landmark study of biblical parallelism both involve lexical rather than semantic patterning (Ps 33:10-11, Isa 51:6): *The Dynamics of Biblical Parallelism* (Bloomington: Indiana University Press, 1985), 84. The one example of complete aba¹b¹ patterning that she points to is Jer 31:16b-17 (p. 86). In commenting on Isa 40:9, a group of lines with the same structure as those in Ps 19:8-11, she arranges the lines in an aa¹-bb¹ pattern (p. 90). A fine example of an aa¹bb¹ "*qînâ*" pattern in Isaiah appears in Isa 1:18-20. For a similar typographical arrangement of Ps 19:8-11, cf. e.g. Briggs, *The Book of Psalms*, 163, and J. van der Ploeg, "Psalm XIX and Some of Its Problems," *Jaarbericht van het Vooraziatisch-Egyptisch Genootschap Ex Oriente Lux* 17 (1963) 193. In one of the latest datings of Psalm 19, Hans-Peter Mathys, "Das Alte Testament—ein hellenistisches Buch," in *Kein Land für sich allein: Studien zum Kulturkontakt in Kanaan, Israel/Palästina und Ebirnâri für Manfred Weippert zum 65. Geburtstag*, ed. Ulrich Hübner and Ernst Axel Knauf (Freiburg: Universitätsverlag/Göttingen: Vandenhoeck & Ruprecht, 2002), 278-93, suggests that the phrase "restoring life" points to the Hellenistic concept of the library as the "sanatorium of the soul" (290) and hence a Hellenistic dating. However, the dates of Psalm 19 and of its inclusion in the developing corpus of the "psalms" of the house of David remain moot.

25 Translations usually ignore this *gam*; a few relate it to the value of the law: RSV/NRSV "moreover," Brown "indeed." In fact, it refers back to the first stanza and means that not only the sun and the rest of the heavens fall under God's command, but the psalmist also.

26 The recent strophic analysis of Terrien, *The Psalms*, 205-214—three strophes, each with two groups of three bicola, followed by a final wrap-up verse—is unconvincing. This arrangement quite improbably separates v. 5ab from what precedes and makes v. 11 the beginning of the third strophe rather than the end of the second.

These two features—change of meter and subject—indeed signal the beginning of a new stanza, but not one that ends with the comparison with comb drippings, unless at the same time a line is drawn through the middle of the first stanza like the second, to create four parts instead of two.[27] As translated above, the two stanzas consist each of nearly matching sets of four bicola and two tricola. The one departure from this pattern is the bicolon following the *qînâ* riff on the law: "With them your servant too...." The reason for this anomaly is not clear. This bicolon marks an important turn in the argument of the psalm; is its structural deviance an ironic marker of the psalm's theme? In any case, the change of meter and subject should not be overstated. As long recognized, Hebrew poetry slips easily from one "meter" to another, often within a single composition.[28] No significance inheres in the *qînâ* section of Psalm 19 by virtue of its meter alone. More importantly, though the subject of Psalm 19 shifts with the *qînâ* section from sky to law, the sequitur—the heavens obey and so ought we —which is our theme makes this shift as much a link as a break.

The psalm's two stanzas deal with the heavens and humanity; and, as often in the ancient world, it is assumed that the heavens serve as an ideal for humanity. What the stars and sun do people ought to do.[29] At first it looks like the stars praise God for his majestic and awesome works: that's the apparent emphasis of the first half, nicely captured in Addison's verse. There may be something to this view. Calvin held it. Citing both Psalm 19 and Romans 1, he stated the theological truism, so widely believed, as McNeill points out, that it scarcely needed repeating, that "wherever you cast your eyes, there is no spot in the universe wherein you cannot discern at least some sparks of God's glory. You cannot in one glance survey this most vast and beautiful system of the universe...without being completely overwhelmed by the boundless force of its brightness" (*Institutes*, 1.5.1). Calvin went on: innumerable evidences in heaven and on earth declare God's wisdom, "thrusting themselves upon

---

27 Michael O'Connor labels such commonly occurring groups of typically five to eight lines "batches": *Hebrew Verse Structure* (Winona Lake: Eisenbrauns, 1980), 529-33. Psalm 19 as a composition consists of not the merger of two sources or the secondary coopting of a more original text (vv. 1-4), but instead the inclusion of a distinctive type of material—which may or may not be an independent source—in a larger whole. In Psalm 19, a litany on the "law," of a type found in baroque form in Psalm 119, is included as a step in a larger argument. Other examples of such incorporated material might include poetic women's songs and series of blessings in the prose narrative in Genesis, Exodus, and Numbers, the song of the prophet Elisha in 2 Kings 3, etc.

28 See e.g. Norman K. Gottwald, "Hebrew Poetry," in *Interpreter's Dictionary of the Bible*, Vol. 3, ed. George A. Buttrick (Nashville: Abingdon, 1962), 834; David L. Petersen and Kent Harold Richards, *Interpreting Hebrew Poetry* (Minneapolis: Fortress, 1992), 45-47; Adele Berlin, "Introduction to Hebrew Poetry," in *The New Interpreter's Bible*, vol. IV, 308-309.

29 The practice and theory of astrology, or casting horoscopes, similarly presupposed a correspondence between the positions of stars and the fortunes of people, but played no discernible role in the composition of Psalm 19. Although divinatory antecedents went back to the Old Babylonian period, horoscopes did not become common in Mesopotamia before the late first millennium BCE, under Hellenistic influence, and even then tended to be skeletal by modern standards. The earliest Greek horoscopes, also brief, date from the late first century BCE. See Walter Farber, "Witchcraft, Magic, and Divination in Ancient Mesopotamia," in *Civilizations of the Ancient Near East*, ed. Jack Sasson (New York: Scribner, 1995), vol. 3, 1907-08; Francesca Rochberg, "Heaven and Earth: Divine-Human Relations in Mesopotamian Celestial Divination," in *Prayer, Magic, and the Stars in the Ancient and Late Antique World*, ed. Scott Noegel, Joel Walker, and Brannon Wheeler (University Park: Pennsylvania State University Press, 2003), 169-85.

the sight of even the most untutored and ignorant persons, so that they cannot open their eyes without being compelled to witness them" (1.5.2). In his commentary on Psalm 19, Calvin speaks of "the splendor of the heavens preaching the glory of God like a teacher in a seminary of learning"[30]—I'm not sure whether that comparison implies an exalted view of seminary education or a comedown for the sun, moon, and stars. Either way, no one denies the main point, which can be enlarged no end: "the heavens are the book from which the whole world can derive its knowledge of God!"[31] On the other hand, as pointed out above, with respect to Psalm 19 something is missing from this interpretation. The hymn by Webber follows the first half of the psalm much more closely than Addison's, and it is not surprising that by itself it makes no particular point. The second half of the psalm is about obedience to and conformity with God's law and appears to have little to do with praise apart from obedience.

If the second half is not about praise except through obedience, could the first half be about obedience and conformity? Indeed, there is more here than meets most modern eyes, with their value-free view of the vast night sky.[32] In fact, I am not sure that the first half has much at all to do with God's praise per se, besides the honor that accrues to God because the heavenly myriad comply with his command. In any case, there can be no doubt that, as Aalen pointed out, it has mainly to do with the stars' and the sun's obedience to God's law and conformity with God's decree, and that is what the two parts of the psalm have in common.[33] The correspondence is made clear by the forms of the two stanzas, which mirror each other, and by the phrase *bāhem*, "with them"[34] that marks the turning point in each half with corresponding meanings ("with the silent chords that reflect God's command," "with the judgments that reflect God's command"). The subjects of the second "batch" of each stanza, the sun and the servant, correspond to each other, a tie confirmed by the pun *nizhār*, "warned,

---

30 John T. McNeill, ed., *Calvin: Institutes of the Christian Religion*, vol. 1 (Philadelphia: Westminster, 1960), 53, n.5.

31 Artur Weiser, *The Psalms* (Philadelphia: Westminster, 1962), 199.

32 Fishbane, for example, saw an intense contrast between creation and revelation in his parts 1 and 2. In part 1, "nature is presented neutrally—it just 'is.' The didacticism of part 2, by contrast, is tendentious and purposeful. With the Revelation…[in part 2], value enters and transforms the world of nature [part 1]"; Fishbane, *Text and Texture*, 87-88. The temptation to regard the subject of Ps 19:2-7 as "nature" may be hard to resist. It appears often, as in the rubric beneath which Peter Craigie considers the psalm: "Nature and Law" (*Psalms 1-50* [Waco: Word, 1983], 177). In the biblical world, the conceptualization of the created order was *never* "neutral."

33 Recognized by many, but still a minority view appealing to a variety of explanations. Cf. Weiser, *Psalms*, 201: "the two parts of Psalm 19…were united in one psalm for use in public worship, the idea of the divine order constituting the spiritual bond which linked the two parts together (cf. the term 'law' in v. 4)." The parenthesis referred to his interpretation of *qaw* as "gauge" on p. 199: "The knowledge of the world's divine ordering (literally plumb-line or canon) penetrates into every country, because the laws of Nature [sic] can be inferred everywhere and directly from the orbits [sic] of the celestial bodies and from the change of day and night." Van Zyl, "Psalm 19," 150, copying Weiser: "The idea of the divine order constituted the spiritual bond which linked the two parts together"; Van Zyl regarded the idea as "relevant" but not exhausting the meaning of the psalm's unity. My view is that the divine order is celebrated not by and through the particular and varying motions of the celestial bodies but, as entailed in the alternation of day and night, by and through their sheer common and rectilinear regularity.

34 I.e. with words in different forms and manifestations. The first *bāhem* appears not to be represented in the LXX. It is possible, however, that the translator combined the *l-* before *šemeš* with the *b-* of *bāhem* to produce the translation *en tō hēliō*.

illumined." But even these are secondary indications. In antiquity, the psalm's correspondences were universally known and could be virtually assumed.[35] To the psalmist, heavenly harmonies (audible or not) that paid honor to God entailed heavenly law and order, and the psalmist was only expressing what everyone already thought. When reading the Psalms it is always important to see the concrete picture the psalmist sees. This is the great value of recent treatments that make broad use of ancient Near Eastern iconography and conceptuality for perspective on the Psalms. What these treatments have missed, however, is that in Psalm 19 many heavenly beings besides the sun play a role. To grasp this point, we have to go outdoors and look at the sky, during the night as well as the day,[36] with the eyes of ancient poets and psalm receivers.

The nighttime sky is strewn with tiny lights, which in the biblical view are the animate creatures of God who make up God's heavenly court and military. As animate beings, they put on an amazing spectacle. Watch the stars for more than a few minutes, long enough to observe them moving, the proof of their animate nature. After an hour or two, they have all shifted position, but the remarkable thing—and this is what the psalmist thinks most important by far—is that they have all shifted together, in order, in formation, like an extremely well disciplined army, which of course is what "hosts" means in the expression "Lord of Hosts."[37] The stars are the Lord's host, God's battalions. If you watch them marching across the sky all night long, you should find yourself impressed that despite their vast numbers and heavenly rank they show not a trace of unruliness, but have remained in exactly the same formation from dusk to dawn. You would think that floating individually in the

---

35 In the usual fashion for a Jerusalem temple psalm, Psalm 19 brings all under the dominion of Yahweh, thus confining celestial and earthly correspondences to a defined channel. For the ancient Near Eastern milieu, see N. M. Swerdlow, ed., *Ancient Astronomy and Celestial Divination* (Cambridge, MIT Press, 1999). In Mesopotamia the search for omens in celestial change included even the fixed stars: for numerous examples, see Erica Reiner in collaboration with David Pingree, *Baylonian Planetary Omens: Part Two, Enuma Anu Enlil, Tablets 50-51* (Malibu: Undena Publications, 1981), passim.

36 Already in its second pair of lines the psalm parallels day and night, a clear indication that more than the daytime sun is the subject of the first stanza. Since the sun dominates the second "batch" of the stanza, it is a fair assumption that the nighttime sky dominates the first and that the plentiful beings of the nighttime sky, the moon and especially the stars, are the antecedents of the plural suffixes in the third and fourth pair of lines: "their sound…their c(h)ord…their vocables." In the priestly conception apparently shared by Psalm 19, nighttime precedes the creation of the day, as in Genesis 1. On the shift of reckoning the beginning of the day from morning to evening, apparently the result of replacing an Egyptian practice with a Babylonian practice, see Jan A. Wagenaar, "Passover and the First Day of the Festival of Unleavened Bread in the Priestly Festival Calendar," *VT* 54 (2004) 262-66.

37 In parade if not on the march. March by rank and file was not typical of pre-industrial armies. "The concept of discipline has become so much a part of our idea of military life that it is hard for us to realize what a new phenomenon it was in European warfare in the seventeenth century": Michael Howard, *War in European History* (New York: Oxford University Press, 1976), 56. Evidence for the existence of military formation in pre-Roman times includes two Egyptian wooden models of companies of Middle Kingdom Nubian soldiers, apparently on the march (James B. Pritchard, *The Ancient Near East: An Anthology of Texts and Pictures* [Princeton: Princeton University Press, 1958], illus. no. 42); the Greek phalanx (see Hans Delbrück, *Warfare in Antiquity* [Lincoln: University of Nebraska Press, 1990; Germ. orig. 1900; Eng. trans. 1975], 53-62, 67-70); the ranks of thousands of terra-cotta warriors from the third and second centuries BCE found at Xian and Weishan in China (see Zhang Wenli, *The Qin Terracotta Army: Treasures of Lintong* [Florence: Scala Books, 1996]); and the foursquare formation of Israel encamped described in Numbers.

spacious expanse of the nighttime sky these high and mighty warriors would show some individual initiative, or periodically regroup, or strike out on their own to prove their mettle against some exceptional challenge. But they don't. The next night, as darkness falls, the great sidereal march continues, and night after night, month after month, year after year they march, round and round, with no deviation, no alteration, no detour, no retreat, no backtracking, no failure of discipline, no disobedience. The stars, battalions continuously on the move, stay in line, forever holding to their decreed courses.[38] It is an awe-inspiring sight.

What keeps the stars in line? Obedience and conformity to the word of God. The heavenly order conforms to God's ordinances with a fixed regularity, as though they were bound together by invisible bonds or cords.[39] As God says to Job, in an important parallel to Psalm 19, "Can you bind the bonds[40] of the Pleiades, or loose the cords of Orion? Can you lead forth the [unknown asterism][41] in their season, or guide the Bear[42] with its children? Do you know the ordinances of the heavens? Can you establish their rule on the earth?" (38:31-33).[43] The relationship between God's

---

38 For the psalm as a whole, the meaning of "tell the glory (honor) of/recount respect for" God is clear from the description of the sun, joyous to *run his course*; the stars are celebrated for doing the same.

39 Brown takes *qaw*, "c(h)ord," to refer "to the designated paths…that the celestial bodies follow…or, more likely, to beams or rays emanating from the astral bodies themselves, particularly the sun…." (*Seeing the Psalms*, 82, 237, nn. 2, 3). The first, doubtful though it is, is the likelier of the two meanings. The second, which Brown prefers and elaborates on, is untenable. The evidence for the iconographic representation of rays from heavenly bodies besides the sun is sparse at best. Where rays are pictured on the sun or stars, they are shaped like narrow triangles that look nothing like cords: see Ernst Weidner, *Gestirn-Darstellungen auf babylonischen Tontafeln* (Wien: Österreichische Akademie der Wissenschaft, 1967), tables 1, 2, 5, 6, 9, 10. More important, the singular of *qaw* can hardly refer to the sun's multiple rays (Brown arbitrarily translates the singular with "lines"). For the meaning "cord" as "commanded course," as I suggest, a plural form of *qaw* might be preferable; however, the singular can be construed as distributive—each body's individual path: "their cord/chord, the commanded course of each of them." The significance of the rectangular projections with parallel spaghetti-like wavy lines oblique to the sun's rays on Neo-Assyrian and earlier depictions of the sun is uncertain. This feature of the stylized portrayal of the sun goes back to Old Babylonian times at least. In the well-known picture of Shamash shown by Brown (*Seeing the Psalms*, 96, Fig. 13), for example, the sun's light rays are portrayed with the usual straight triangles, the wavy bands appear to emerge on a different plane behind the main subject, and similar wavy lines are used to portray water waves and a flounced garment, so that the interpretation of the wavy lines as "rays" seems dubious. It is possible that they represent the heat of the sun: lines (sometimes straight, sometimes wavy) emanating from the earliest cuneiform signs for "fire, torch" and "anger" may suggest the use of such lines for heat waves in Mesopotamian depictions.

40 This translation assumes metathesis of *dalet* and *nun* to produce a form of the root *'nd*. For a typical justification of this widely accepted emendation, see Marvin H. Pope, *Job: Introduction, Translation, and Notes* (Anchor Bible; Garden City: Doubleday, 1965), 254.

41 "Typically, in [Job] 38:32, *mazzārōt* is also no longer understood as a variant on *mazzālōt*, constellations, scholars agreeing that a single star or constellation must be the point": Baruch Halpern, "Assyrian and Pre-Socratic Astronomies and the Location of the Book of Job," in *Kein Land für Sich*, ed. Hübner and Knauf, 259. The identification of the supposed asterism is uncertain.

42 Halpern interprets the constellation *'ayiš* instead as Leo: "Assyrian and Pre-Socratic Astronomies," 260.

43 The unusual word for "rule" here (*mišt ār*) has a Babylonian cognate that was used to describe the tracks of the stars as though they were ruled lines for writing. The implications of this parallel for interpreting Psalm 19 go back at least as far as N. H. Torczyner (Tur Sinai), "*šitir šamê*, die Himmelschrift," *Archiv orientální* 17 (1949), who related these ruled and written lines to the praise of the torah in the second stanza of the psalm. For the latest treatment of this passage, see Halpern,

statutes regulating the heavenly creatures and acknowledgment by those creatures is made clear in Ps 148: "Praise Yahweh from the heavens, praise him in the heights! Praise him, all his court officers, praise him, all his host! Praise him, sun and moon, praise him, all you shining stars! Praise him, you highest heavens, and you waters above the heavens! Let them praise the name of Yahweh, for he commanded and they were created. He stationed them in place for ever and ever; a statute he laid down, which cannot be transgressed."[44] The concept of the heavenly regulatory decree was far from unique to the Bible. It was shared with the great Babylonian account of the creation of the world by Marduk (*Enuma eliš*, written long before Psalm 19), who installed the stars as follows: "He fashioned the stations (=constellations) for the great gods/ Stars, their counterparts, as images he installed therein/ The year he defined, drew the borderline/ For each of the twelve months set up stars./ After he had drawn the demarcations for the year,/ he fixed the stand of the Pole Star to define their bounds/ And that none should err or be remiss/ he established with the Pole Star the stations of the gods Enlil and Ea" (5.1-8).[45]

"Assyrian and Pre-Socratic Astronomies," 255-64. Halpern discusses the gradual depersonalizing of the stars, the waning of the view that the stars were "bodies possessed of their own volition (255)" during the seventh and sixth centuries BCE, positing an "international" cosmological discussion to this end. If there was such a discussion, it is not certain that the writer of Psalm 19, its Pythagorean resonances notwithstanding, participated in it.

44 The RSV and NRSV ("bounds") unhelpfully relegate the translation "law" for "statute" (*h ōq*) to a footnote; the KJV got it right: "he hath made a decree which shall not pass."

45 Alexander Heidel, *The Babylonian Genesis* (Chicago: University of Chicago Press, 1942), 44-45, 116-17, translation slightly modified; for Nebiru, see also *Enuma eliš* 7.124-34, Heidel, *Babylonian Genesis*, 59. For an alternative translation of the passage, see Benjamin R. Foster, *Before the Muses: An Anthology of Akkadian Literature* (Bethesda: CDL Press, 1993), 378: "He made the position(s) for the great gods,/ He established (in) constellations the stars, their counterparts./ He marked the year, described its boundaries,/ He set up twelve months of three stars each./ After he had patterned the days of the year,/ He fixed the position of Nebiru to mark the (stars') relationships./ Lest any make an error or go astray,/ He established the position(s) of Enlil and Ea in relation to it." Foster unpersuasively takes Nebiru as Mercury rather than the Pole Star. For an even more recent alternative, see Wayne Horowitz, *Mesopotamian Cosmic Geography* (Winona Lake: Eisenbrauns, 1998), 114-16: "He fashioned the stations for the great gods./ The stars, their likeness he set up, the constellations./ He fixed the year, drew the boundary-lines./ Set up three stars for each of the 12 months./ After he drew up the designs of the year,/ He set fast the station of Neberu to fix their bands./ So that none would transgress or be neglectful at all,/ he set the station of Enlil and Ea with it." For an earlier, still useful treatment, Benno Landsberger and J. V. Kinnier Wilson, "The Fifth Tablet of *Enuma Eliš*," *Journal of Near Eastern Studies* 20 (1961) 154-79 ad loc. Cf. also the colophon to Enuma Anu Enlil (given here as a composite of several texts): "When Anu Enlil and Ea, the great gods, created heaven and earth and made manifest the celestial signs, they fixed the stations and established the positions of the gods of the night...they divided the courses of the stars and drew the constellations as their likenesses. They created night, day...month and year...": Francesca Rochberg-Halton, *Aspects of Babylonian Celestial Divination: The Lunar Eclipse Tablets of Enūma Anu Enlil* (Archiv für Orientforschung Beiheft 22; Horn: Verlag Ferdinand Berger u. Söhne, 1988), 270-71. In Mesopotamia, the sky was divided into three bands parallel to the ecliptic, assigned respectively north to south to Enlil, Anu, and Ea. These bands defined the straight paths of the celestial bodies. As Horowitz suggests, these bands are probably defined by the "borderlines" or "boundaries" set up by Marduk in *Enuma eliš* 5.1-8; cf. *Cosmic Geography*, 252-56. In Horowitz's interpretation, the same is true of the "bounds" or "bands" mentioned in the sixth line: "No text explains in detail how the stars, Sun, Moon, and planets move through the sky" (*Cosmic Geography*, 258), while references in Mesopotamian texts to cosmic "bonds" (though not those in *Enuma eliš* 5.1-8) apply mainly to even mightier cords that "secure the heavens in place" (*Cosmic Geography*, 265).

The cords representing God's ordinances are both metaphorical and real. As real cords, stretched taut and held fast, they resonate (in English "cord" and "chord" are etymologically the same and throughout their histories overlap in meaning), producing what after Pythagoras in the sixth century BCE was called the "harmony of the spheres."[46] Pythagoras originated the notion that the planetary spheres were spaced according to musical intervals; but, the planets apart—we will come to them in a moment—the underlying idea, that the heavenly orders were numerical in their regularity and resonated through their regularizing bonds, was probably a commonplace from ancient to early modern times, and there is little reason to wonder whether Pythagoras, who according to legend sojourned in both Egypt and Babylon, or the psalmist thought of it first, and no reason to wonder at the continuity of the idea through the ages. *The Merchant of Venice* (no later than 1597) is representative. Lorenzo enthuses to Jessica as they sit together in the moonlight, "Look how the floor of heaven/ Is thick inlaid with patens [plates, disks] of bright gold./ There's not the smallest orb which thou behold'st/ But in his motion like an angel sings,/ Still quiring to the young-eyed [eternally keen-sighted] cherubins:/ Such harmony is in immortal souls;/ But, whilst this muddy vesture of decay/ Doth grossly close it in, we cannot hear it" (5.1.58-65).[47] It was also evident that although the heavenly chords resonated, they could not be heard by humans. Many reasons were given; the most famous was Aristotle's, who argued that since the harmonies have surrounded us since the day we were born, they are the ultimate in white noise: from day one we quickly get so used to them that they blend imperceptibly into the background.

The musical correspondence between the heavenly and human realms found in Psalm 19 likewise became a commonplace of the ages. It appeared often in Greek thought, and was fully expounded in the late fourth century CE by Gregory of Nyssa, with reference to Psalm 19 itself.[48] In the Renaissance it was given consummate

---

46 Gunkel accepted the Pythagorean parallel to the psalm's image of silent celestial utterances—even though it had already been rejected by Delitzsch in his commentary—and declined to speculate whether the notion originated in Greece or the Near East: "Was soll es anders sein als die Anschauung, die der von den griechischen Gelehrten so genannten 'Harmonie der Sphären'... zugrunde liegt, wonach die Himmel schwingend gewaltige Töne von sich geben" (*Die Psalmen*, 75). For Gunkel this parallel was evident from the image as a whole, not from the term *qaw*, which he derived, quite implausibly, from the root *qy/w'*, "spew, disgorge," and translated "surge, torrent" (of words). The Pythagorean interpretation of Psalm 19 has found few followers, among them the habitually unconventional Julius Morgenstern, *Hebrew Union College Annual* 19 (1945) 509. Swayed by notions of the Bible's uniqueness and its interest in "Nature," Weiser categorically rejected the Pythagorean affiliation: "The mention of day and night (v. 2) makes it impossible to regard these personifications as reminiscences of the former deification of the heaven and the stars or to deduce from them the notion of the harmony of the spheres—which is not to be found in the Old Testament. Our poet holds a view on these matters which is entirely his own" (*The Psalms*, 198). Halpern locates "an almost Pythagorean chorus of the heavens" in Isa 44:23 and 49:13: "Astronomies," 256. In the Greek-speaking world, the connection between law and music was already made in the use of *nomos*, "norm, custom, convention," to refer to an air for lyre, melody, or strain. This connection sprang from the not surprising notion that music was governed, from earliest times, by fixed or canonical norms. See Bruno Gentili, *Poetry and Its Public in Ancient Greece: From Homer to the Fifth Century* (Baltimore: Johns Hopkins University Press, 1988; Italian orig. 1985), 24-26, 36-37.

47 Cited by Gunkel, *Die Psalmen*, 75. The text and glosses are from *The Riverside Shakespeare* (Boston: Houghton Mifflin, 1974), 280.

48 In the middle of the first book of his treatise on the Psalmic inscriptions, Gregory begins by considering "how the Psalter has made its teaching about the virtuous life desirable. He first gives

expression, again by Shakespeare, in the speech of Ulysses early in *Troilus and Cressida* (by 1603) as he explains why his fellow Greeks have failed to make any headway against the Trojans: "The specialty of rule [the prerogative of command which belongs to the ruler] hath been neglected.... Take but degree [rank, hierarchy] away, untune that string,/ And hark what discord follows" (1.3.78-110). With cosmic string untuned, "Each thing melts (meets)[49]/In mere oppugnancy: the bounded waters/ Should lift their bosoms higher than the shores,/ And make a sop of all this solid globe;/...And the rude son should strike his father dead;/ Force should be right, or rather, right and wrong/...Should lose their names, and so should justice too!/...The general's disdain'd/ By him one step below, he by the next,/ That next by him beneath...." (110-31).[50] The sea floods the land, right and wrong lose their meaning, and, to top all, the hierarchy of military command dissolves: this is the state of affairs that Psalm 19 opposes.

Of course not every star in the sky falls dutifully into line, as is well known. There *are* deviants in the sky, and not insignificant ones: chiefly the sun, moon, and planets. The psalmist is aware of this and, leaving the moon aside, incorporates the sun and planets in the scheme. The sun, marching to a slightly different regular beat, is deftly made the ideal of enhanced obedience, the planets of wayward and arrogant disobedience. The sun and the planets are contrasted in the corresponding second batch of each stanza, the parts beginning "With them."

Amidst, and perhaps by means of, the inaudible chords and vocables of the stars, the sun is assigned his course. The sun moves steadily across the sky just like a star, but each day shifts backwards, losing his place, or propelling his stellar minions ahead, by about four minutes in time each day. As you can imagine if you haven't witnessed it for yourself, this is very conspicuous, and since the earliest astronomical records the annual course of the sun through the stars (the "Zodiac") has been noted. But still the

---

what he considers to be an obvious answer to this question. It is the music of the psalms that make their teachings desirable. They are sung, so he asserts, by everyone in all circumstances of life. Without rejecting this as an answer, he turns to a less obvious reason.... This involves the philosophic view that man [*sic*] is a miniature cosmos and, therefore, reflects the arrangement of the cosmos itself. Gregory describes the latter by a musical analogy of melody derived from variety, and harmony produced from opposites. This accord with one another of all things in the universe is the archetypal music. The music which is within man, produced by the strings of his life being neither too tight nor too loose, resonates with the music of the cosmos as a whole. It is this corresponding underlying structure of man with the cosmos that makes the music of the psalms so desirable, Gregory suggests, and not the simple fact that singing is a pleasurable activity": Ronald E. Heine, *Gregory of Nyssa's Treatise on the Inscriptions of the Psalms: Introduction, Translation, and Notes* (Oxford: Clarendon Press, 1995), 12-13. For the treatise itself, see pp. 87-92, where Gregory refers to Psalm 19: "...the composition of the universe in the diversity of the things which are observed individually in the cosmos plucks itself by means of some structured and unchanging rhythm, producing the harmony of the parts in relation to the whole, and sings this polyphonic tune in everything. It is this tune which the mind hears without the use of our sense of hearing. It listens to the singing of the heavens by transcending and being above the faculties of sense-perception that belong to our flesh. This, it seems to me, is also how the great David was listening when he heard the heavens describing the glory of the God who effects these things in them by observing their systematic and all-wise movement" (89). Heine describes the idea that the human being is a miniature cosmos as "rather common among the Greeks...first attested in the presocratic philosopher Democritus" (88-89, n. 12).

49 Quarto (1609) "melts"; Folio (1623) "meets."

50 *Riverside Shakespeare*, 455.

sun maintains a sturdy regularity. Despite his migration, by God's command he returns to exactly (as far as anyone before the second century BCE knew) the same spot in the sky at the same time each year. But what most impresses the psalmist is the straightness—the rectitude—of the sun's path.[51] As the sun appears each morning, he is like a bridegroom emerging from his abode and setting his path straight in the direction of his bride with one thing only on his mind. And, obviously a mighty heavenly warrior indeed, he is like a human warrior who knows he is stronger, fitter, and faster than anyone else and is more than happy to course straight from bower to bride, outperforming any and all companions. The sun is not an ordinary member of God's hosts, but he is a loyal member. He is the general among the hosts, privileged to move among the troops while far outshining them all. Yet despite his extraordinary distinction, he maintains a steady, straightedge course, adhering strictly to God's orders and in this discipline accomplishing his assigned task of illuminating—and ruling—all. He is God's obedient and obeisant servant, not one of the liberated, enlightened, and blissful "brothers" celebrated by an exhilarated Schiller in his "Ode to Joy" and Beethoven in his Ninth Symphony, brothers who, like individual suns "flying (at will) through Heaven's glorious expanse," are charged to "run your course, joyous, like a hero to victory."

The sun illustrates an ideal for all humans, which brings us to the second half of the psalm. A person's conformity may not match that of the stars, as the psalmist believes everyone's should, but it can match the sun's: purposeful, obedient departure from the uniform norm.[52] Thus the statutes and judgments of God—for this psalmist temple ordinances and judicial precedents to be adhered to, but perhaps also a written fount of wisdom to be read and pondered "day and night," much as in Psalms 1 and 119—represent the command of God to humans just as the acknowledgments of the stars represent the command of God to the sun. "With them your servant is illumined and admonished."

The contrast, the foil, the hazard, is to be like the planets. The planets are guilty of what the stars are so astonishingly innocent of: periodically brighter than other stars, they fluctuate in brilliance, always trying and failing to blaze like the sun and imitate the sun's path among the fixed stars. The planets are presumptuous upstarts, would-be suns who don't even come close. They wander, as the Greeks said, and deviate, and vacillate, and detour, and retreat, and backtrack, and unlike the sun show little consistency from one day or one year to the next. They lack discipline, and are manifestly possessed of a troublesome mind and will. They have an attitude. They are out of tune. God save me, the psalmist prays, from becoming like a planet: "Wanderings[53] who can perceive? From hidden (deviations) clear me, and from

---

51 The sun's straight path varies in height above the horizon, between the extremes of the solstices; of this variation the psalmist takes no note.

52 Though he arrives at something like this theme by a different route, Brown states it well: the sun is "a figure of righteousness. ...the sun's 'trek' or 'path'...can connote moral, faithful conduct. Figuratively, the sun models the path ordained by God that all are to follow.... The sun...embodies and models *tôrâ*-piety"(97). Van Zyl makes an incisive comparison with Prov 4:18: "the way of the righteous is like the light of dawn, which shines brighter and brighter until full day"("Psalm 19," 151).

53 For this translation of *šegî'ôt*, "meanderings, errors, swervings, swayings," cf. *Enūma eliš* 5.7, "...that none should err." The verb in Babylonian, *egû*, "tire, become careless, err" (cognate with Hebrew *yaga'*, "tire, grow weary"), is synonymous with Hebrew *šāga'*.

presumptions restrain your servant." Fortunately for world order, there are few planets in the sky—the psalmist could have seen only four or five of them[54]—a lamentable minority manifestly rebelling against the hierarchical, authoritarian, patriarchal, and conformist command of God. God help me hold my position in the straightedge line of march that in obedience makes known God's commanding glory.

As indicated, in the Greek world as well as elsewhere in antiquity, the tendency was to integrate the planets into the orderly scheme of the heavens, which should after all manifest uniformity. The cardinal principle of planetary order for most elite remained for two millennia the Pythagorean discovery of the real numerical basis of musical intervals, as applied speciously to the relations of the planets.[55] Whether the planets were deviants, as for Psalm 19 and the popular mind, or the supreme expression of heavenly regularity, as for the Pythagoreans, the Platonists, and most of European intellectual humanity until the seventeenth century and later, the meaning was the same: the loyal, obedient, servile regularities of the heavens were the model for social order on earth, and that order was a "cosmos" insofar as it conveyed an agreeable sense and feeling of what was fitting and just.[56] From this perspective, it is hard to imagine a headline more incongruous than that for a recent review of a biography of a famed jazz artist: "Music of the Spheres."[57]

---

54 Depending on whether he saw Mercury.
55 The Babylonian scribal observers of the nighttime sky, who eventually were able to calculate the true mathematical regularities of the planets, were the exception: "...the scribes of Enuma Anu Enlil developed a mathematical and scientific interest in the intricacies of lunar and planetary phenomena that went far beyond their application as omens, for which goal-year prediction alone would be adequate with no need for mathematical astronomy.... From the earliest omen texts and Diaries to the latest almanacs and ephemerides, for century after century, generations of teachers and students observed, calculated, and also pondered deeply how these irregular but periodic phenomena were to be described, reduced to precise rules, and computed for the past, present, and future. They have left no record of their theoretical analyses and discussions, but to judge from the works they have left us, the Diaries and ephemerides, the goal-year texts and almanacs, the discussions of two Scribes of Enuma Anu Enlil contained more rigorous science than the speculations of twenty philosophers speaking Greek, not even Aristotle excepted. I say this seriously, not as a provocation, and further, I believe it is due precisely to the scientific and technical character of Babylonian astronomy that most historians and philosophers remain without comprehension of it, still preferring to dote upon childish fables and Delphic fragments of Pre-Socratics, requiring no knowledge of mathematics and less taxing to the intellect"; N. M. Swerdlow, *The Babylonian Theory of the Planets* (Princeton: Princeton University Press, 1998), 181. Cf. John M. Steele and Annette Imhausen, eds., *Under One Sky: Astronomy and Mathematics in the Ancient Near East* (Winona Lake: Eisenbrauns, 2004).
56 At the San Francisco Theological Seminary, where the honoree of this volume and I taught and worshiped together for over twenty years, the Montgomery Memorial chapel is adorned with exquisite stained-glass windows featuring quasi-Masonic themes from Hebrew and Pythagorean lore, with labels. The paired windows labeled "Law" (showing the Ten Commandments) and "Testimonies" (showing a scroll of Scripture) and the paired windows labeled "Music" (showing ancient Greek instruments) and "Song" (showing the music of a Protestant hymn)—the latter pair a reflex of the celestial chords and their "music of the spheres"—are juxtaposed. See Robert B. Coote and John S. Hadsell, *San Francisco Theological Seminary: The Shaping of a Western School of the Church, 1871-1998* (San Anselmo: First Presbyterian Church, 1999), 286.
57 Review by Brent Staples of *Space is the Place: The Lives and Times of Sun Ra*, in *The New York Times Book Review*, Aug. 17. 1997, p. 9. Musician Herman Poole Blount (1914-93), alias Sun Ra, "Sonny" to his friends, dedicated all his compositions to the Creator and claimed to have come from the planet Saturn.

The stars—at least from the vantage of a human lifetime—are not into jazz, its regularities notwithstanding; and, if they were, both the Pythagoreans and the psalmist would have regarded it as an appalling disaster, nothing short of chaos. A few short years after Shakespeare composed Ulysses' speech, where just this conviction was laid out, the German astronomer Johannes Kepler demonstrated that the regularities of the planets—he remained a committed Pythagorean—had nothing to do with the perfection of circular motion or the exactitude of simple arithmetic intervals,[58] and the Italian natural philosopher Galileo showed that the heavenly sun and moon were both blemished. Ulysses' worst fear had come true: "that string"—the psalmist's c(h)ord—was now "untuned." The upholders of the patriarchal social order were devastated, finding their voice in among others the dean of the cathedral of London and a favorite at the court of James I, John Donne: "And new Philosophy," he wrote in 1611, "calls all in doubt,/ The Element of fire is quite put out;/ The Sun is lost, and th'earth, and no mans wit/ Can well direct him where to looke for it./ And freely men confesse that this world's spent,/ When in the Planets, and the Firmament/ They seeke so many new; then see that this/ Is crumbled out againe to his Atomies./ 'Tis all in peeces, all cohaerence gone;/ All just supply, and all Relation:/ Prince, Subject, Father, Sonne, are things forgot."[59] Things cannot get worse than that. Once Newton, another confirmed Pythagorean as well as Christian (albeit with "Arian" tendencies), had redefined the basis of the mathematical correspondence between earth and heaven by discovering that heavenly bodies and earthly bodies obey *the same laws* of motion, in 1687, and once property had begun to replace command as the foundation of social order, the door was open for Addison to make Ps 19:1-6 into an affirmation of "reason's" recognition of God in the heavenly phenomena without any reference whatever to social order, or to God's precious and sweet law.[60]

---

58 Johannes Kepler, *The Harmony of the World*, ed. by E. J. Aiton and others (Philadelphia: American Philosophical Society, 1997); Bruce Stephenson, *The Music of the Heavens: Kepler's Harmonic Astronomy* (Princeton: Princeton University Press, 1994).

59 "Anatomie of the World—The First Awakening," 205-16.

60 Of course the connection between heavenly order and the moral order was far from lost. Newton himself was obsessed with the realization that the obedience of heavenly bodies to laws made possible the quantification of biblical prophecy and the construction of the timetable of God's judgment of sinful humanity, past and future. Music also continued to play a vital role in natural philosophy, not least for Newton: see Penelope Gouk, *Music, Science and Natural Magic in Seventeenth-Century England* (New Haven: Yale University Press, 1999). Immanuel Kant's most famous autobiographical statement, made at age 64 at the conclusion of his *Critique of Practical Reason* (1788), pairs the heavenly and moral orders as prelude to a splendid evocation of human worth: "Two things fill the mind with ever new and increasing admiration and awe, the oftener and more steadily we reflect on them: the starry heavens above me"—which Kant had studied systematically from as early as 1751 —"and the moral law within me"; *Critique of Practical Reason*, trans. Lewis White Beck (New York: Bobbs-Merrill, 1956), 166 ("Zwei Dinge erfüllen das Gemüt mit immer neuer und zunehmender Bewunderung und Ehrfurcht, je öfter und anhaltender sich das Nachdenken damit beschäftigt: der besternte Himmel über mir und das moralische Gesetz in mir"). The failure of the notion that God's law was archetypically located in the sky contributed to the theological crisis of the seventeenth and eighteenth centuries: see e.g. William C. Placher, *The Domestication of Transcendence: How Modern Thinking about God Went Wrong* (Louisville: Westminster John Knox, 1996, 132-35. The investigation of heavenly order and disorder—together seen as reflecting and shaping human existence —has been a constant of religious imagination and scientific investigation alike from pre-biblical antiquity to the present: Marcelo Gleiser, *The Prophet and the Astronomer* (New York: W. W. Norton, 2002).

This was a distortion of a psalm that names God's law five times over in six lines, six if you count "the fear of Yahweh." In one sense this naming is quite abstract. Psalm 119 pays similar tribute to God's law by treating it as wisdom and referring to it with eight synonyms, each repeated 22 times, once for each letter of the Hebrew alphabet: law, stipulations, precepts, commandment, judgments, utterance, word, and statute. ("Wisdom" in the ancient world was scarcely distinguishable from one court to another, but law often was different, so such terms were used to suggest the elite author's social distinction.[61]) Psalm 19 uses the first five of these terms. Why not "utterance" or "word"? Because "there is no utterance, there are no words"—as line five in the psalm's opening batch states. That still leaves six terms available. Why not "statute"? Apparently because "statute" is what Psalm 148, Job, Jeremiah, and others call God's commands regulating the heavenly creatures, so that can be considered redundant with the heavenly "utterances" and "words," which "are not." In place of "statute," the poet refers to the "fear" of Yahweh, *yir'at*, a pun, as often observed, on "brightening" the eyes, *me'îrat*, in the line before.

In another sense, however, "law" is far from abstract and means just what it says. The eight-line iteration of the value of this law is more than a literary or theological flourish. It bespeaks a resolute opposition—by an unspecified party—to the threat of lawlessness. Law, as stated above, means the ordinances of Jerusalem and the temple. Calvin the lawyer loved these lines. The Reformation "second use" of the law, to restrain social evil, is never to be belittled. Social order according to law is a social good, provided justice is not violated; anyone who doubts as much might want to consult people today in Colombia, Rwanda, Congo, Algeria, Sudan, Afghanistan, Iraq, or any of the other locations of the 23 "emergencies" recently responded to by the UN —to say nothing of social disorder in the United States. There may even be something to say for "revolutionary discipline" in uprisings of the weak. Calvin, attempting to help legislate in the absence of king and bishop, the linchpins of early modern social order in Europe, affirmed the importance of the second use in the work of the Consistory, whose members monitored the behavior of the people of Geneva, including refugees, in their neighborhoods and summoned them for correction if found deviant. Typically upwards of ten percent of the populace were summoned for correction in a given year. Reformation historian and Presbyterian elder Robert Kingdon once characterized the proceedings of the Consistory, a sort of bourgeois Star Chamber, as a "moral reign of terror," though he later nuanced this judgment.[62] Calvinists have always promoted the social utility of religion. In San Francisco in 1851, white Anglo-Saxon Presbyterians, in character, took unflinching notice of the

---

61 Some have interpreted the first half of Psalm 19 in terms of what they see as the "wisdom" behind Genesis 1-3: Odil Hannes Steck, "Bemerkungen zur thematische Einheit von Psalm 19,2-7," in *Werden und Wirken des Alten Testaments: Festschrift für Claus Westermann zum 70. Geburtstag*, ed. Reiner Albertz and others (Göttingen: Vandenhoeck & Ruprecht, 1980), 318-24; Craigie, *Psalms 1-50*, 178-81.
62 "Calvin and the Family," *Pacific Theological Review* 17:3 (Spring 1984) 5-18, esp. p. 7, where he had already moderated his description. See also Robert M. Kingdon, *Adultery and Divorce in Calvin's Geneva* (Cambridge: Harvard University Press, 1995); Kingdon, ed., *Registers of the Consistory of Geneva in the Time of Calvin, Vol. 1: 1542-1544* (Grand Rapids: Eerdmans/H. H. Meeter Center for Calvin Studies, 2000; French orig. 1996); and William G. Naphy, *Calvin and the Consolidation of the Genevan Reformation*, with new Preface (Louisville: Westminster John Knox, 2003 [orig. 1994]).

evil men were capable of, beginning with themselves and expressing themselves in the racist rhetoric of the times, and the remedy provided by religion:

> It cannot be too often affirmed that religion is the best guaranty of social order.... Without religion, without moral restraints, without sacred influences thrown around every member of society, we are and must be insecure. Pride of birth, country, privilege, can not save us, can not withhold men from evil. There are in the world no more adroit thieves, more enterprising freebooters, more daring villains, more ruthless assassins, than those in whose veins flows our boasted Anglo-Saxon blood. They are not weak, they are not contemptible, they are not ignorant.... They are intelligent, quick, often educated, physically courageous, unwearied, spirited, indomitable in purpose. Fond of power, wanting in benevolence, unscrupulous about measures, greedy of possession, and black at heart, they have become what they are, the very terror-kings of mischief. Against such men none but moral forces can be lasting and effecting.[63]

In the face of such a prevalent reality, it may well seem that moral conformity, morals legislation, strict execution of tough laws, and enforcement of the straight and narrow provide the best defense. In some contexts, who is to gainsay this reaction? Let the blackguards fall in line—like the stars in the sky.

However, it is Calvin's third use of the law that set him apart from Luther and charged him most with excitement. Here lies one of the great distinctives of the Reformed tradition, the law seen as positive, as the essential follow-on of the gospel, instructing the faithful how to live ever more righteously. Not law and gospel as opposites, but gospel and law as complements of each other. This is what gives Reformed churches their distinctive sense of responsibility toward the political order, and what makes the Old Testament supposedly a living Testament in Reformed churches more than in any other. It is at this critical juncture, in laying out the great third use in the *Institutes*, that Calvin cites Psalm 19, "The law of the Lord is perfect, restoring the soul, the precepts of the Lord are straight, gladdening the heart, etc." (2.7.12). And more brusquely in his own words: "The law is to the flesh like a whip to an idle and balky ass, to arouse it to work." Such a law must seem a little less attractive than much fine gold and fresh honey—except for God's grace.[64]

---

63 Quoted from the Congregationalist/New School Presbyterian *The Pacific*, 1 August, 1851, by William Muhler, *Religion and Social Problems in Gold Rush California, 1849-1869*, GTU diss., 1989, 137-38. A 2002 survey found that only a little over one out of three adults in the United States believes that it is necessary to believe in God to be moral; in Canada the figure was two out of three (*New York Times*, December 2, 2003, p. A16).

64 The Spirit is essential to Calvin's understanding: "The third and principle use...finds its place among believers in whose hearts the Spirit of God already lives and reigns." The chastising, judgment-with-grace reading of Psalm 19 in our national history is perhaps best, if most extremely, exemplified by Lincoln's understanding of the "mighty scourge of war" as measure-for-measure retribution for the "wrong" of slavery, sealing his Second Inaugural argument that "a solidarity in sin made the punishment communal, uniting the nation in the sufferings it had brought upon itself" (Garry Wills, "With God on His Side," *New York Times Sunday Magazine*, March 30, 2003, 26-29, quote on p. 28): "The judgments of the Lord are true and righteous altogether." See also Garry Wills, "Lincoln's Greatest Speech?" *The Atlantic Monthly*, Sept. 1999, 69; Ronald C. White, Jr., *Lincoln's Greatest Speech: The Second Inaugural* (New York: Simon & Schuster, 2002), 158-59. Extracting the line from its context and focusing as always on what unified the nation, Lincoln took "judgments" to refer to the war, or chastisement itself rather than the monitory basis of chastisement.

The writers of the Westminster Confession (1646) expressed the pre-modern understanding of the law it shared with Psalm 19 in such a way that there could be no doubt about the prescribed rectitude and conformity required by the church they thought they were putting in place during the social, political, and military turmoil of England in the 1640s. According to the Confession, "Christian liberty" means not "slavish fear"—the uses of the law "do sweetly comply" with the gospel—but "a childlike love and a willing mind," the next best thing to regimented stars reflecting their marching orders back in resonant chords of acknowledgment. "God alone is lord of the conscience" means not that anyone can think what they like, but that the conscience is free from "doctrines and commandments of men [imposed from without] which are in any thing contrary to his Word, or beside it, in matters of faith or worship," as defined by the official church. However, "they who, upon pretense of Christian liberty, shall oppose any lawful [i.e. sanctioned by the Confession and its terms] power, or the lawful exercise of it, whether it be civil or ecclesiastical, resist the ordinance of God. And for their publishing of such opinions, or maintaining of such practices, as are contrary to the light of nature; or to the known principles of Christianity, whether concerning faith, worship, or conversation... they may lawfully be called to account and proceeded against by the censures of the Church and"—the following phrase had to be removed from the American version of the Confession to conform with the First Amendment—"by the power of the Civil Magistrate" (chaps. 19-20). So much for freedom of speech and freedom of the press, or freedom in any modern political sense. It is hardly necessary to point out that just thirty years later, when the other name British "Presbyterians" went by was "Nonconformists" and Charles II strove to force them into conformity, many Presbyterians in Britain died martyrs to the cause of freedom, thanks to the evil that the Confession's concept of law and liberty represented. To return to the world of Psalm 19 and the Calvinist conformist morality it bolstered would be to bring back the world of religious tyranny, blasphemy charges, and fatwas against deviance that in many parts of the world have happily been left behind.[65]

It would also be to return to the world of Psalm 19 in a still more basic sense. Given its celestial scope, Psalm 19 is often read as a universal statement of the congruence of God's law with natural law, as though as an ordinary magistrate's prayer it might ingenuously invoke cosmic endorsement for the most ordinary of local rulings in tune with universal right. On the contrary, in all likelihood Psalm 19 was introduced into the "Davidic" temple book of prayer and praise to reinforce the notion of the monarch as the blameless paragon for the subjects under his sovereignty.[66] Its world is

---

65 "[Archbishop of Canterbury] Rowan Williams...peddles the modish notion that secularism is disguised tyranny. He warns of 'the unspoken violence of the anything but neutral secular sphere.' And he insists that the 'claim of religious truth over and against [secularism] is not, as the anxious contemporary unbeliever assumes it must be, a bid for control.' As an anxious believer, I find this complacent. Is there no attempt by the papacy, or the Ayatollah, or indeed the Anglican Evangelicals, to control social morality? He concludes: 'The Church is therefore neither an amiable commentator on the margins of public life, superfluous and ceremonial...nor a theocratic bully.' Alas, the evidence suggests that it is the former when it is prevented (by secularism) from being the latter." Theo Hobson in *Times Literary Supplement*, July 11, 2003, 17.

66 Cf. Leslie C. Allen, "David as Exemplar of Spirituality: The Redactional Function of Psalm 19," *Biblica* 67 (1986) 544-46, noting the connection with Ps 18:20-30 and 21:7.

not the world of the humble magistrate but, as with much of the Hebrew Scriptures, of the elite faction desiring to muster political support for its rule in Jerusalem—whether the monarchy was royal or, by the fifth century BCE, priestly. The method compares with that of the sixteenth- and seventeenth-century European "nationalists" described by Anthony Marx, the method of political and social exclusion through cultic, or "religious," conflict.[67] The world of Calvin and the Westminster Confession is the same as the world of Psalm 19 not only by the analogy of obedience to divine law, but also by analogy of the political use of that obedience.

The point of Psalm 19 should be obvious by now: what keeps the stars in line, God's ordinance, keeps the political subject in line, too—at least by the psalmist's intent. I have left the following turn till last: the opening vision of the psalm focuses of course less on God's command than on the stars' response. The entire psalm is thus controlled by the perspective of willing creatures, both heavenly and human, who readily respond, in a Gramschian mode, with reverence and respect.[68] It is the words of response (albeit silent, wordless) rather than God's commands that give substance to the cords that bind the stars in lockstep order, such substance as they have: the cords are invisible, the chords inaudible, and hence the bonds ethereal, like Addison's "sky," and mystical in their speechlessness.[69] Given the hierarchical, authoritarian, conformist, regimented, militaristic,[70] and proleptically chauvinist standpoint of the

---

67 Anthony W. Marx, *Faith in Nation: Exclusionary Origins of Nationalism* (New York: Oxford University Press, 2003). Marx defines nationalism as "a collective sentiment or identity, bounding and binding together those individuals who share a sense of large-scale political solidarity aimed at creating, legitimating, or challenging states" (6). In the words of Stanley Hoffman in *Foreign Affairs*, Sept. Oct. 2003, 179, "[Marx's] interest lies in the efforts of states, struggling with divisions and conflicts, to obtain a social cohesion that is fragile or absent, and in looking for the origins of nationalism in political actions by the states and by masses [subjects] whose 'allegiance to centralized authority could not be taken for granted'…. The central point of the book is that nationalism results from a process of exclusion (most other writers have stressed inclusion), and particularly from internal discord over religion." It would be a mistake to assume that this way of understanding nationalism does not apply to the entire agrarian era, not just to pre-industrial Europe. Marx's book is not so much a refutation of the common contemporary understanding of nationalism (as in Anderson, Gellner, Hobsbawm, etc.) as a treatment of a different—though very much related—and more ancient phenomenon. The same is true of another recent and critical work, Adrian Hastings, *The Construction of Nationhood* (New York: Cambridge University Press, 1997).

68 To which a "thanksgiving hymn" from Qumran that quotes *qaw* from Psalm 19 seems to add a somewhat abject submissiveness: the suppliant contemplates confessing his profound sin (he is "a counsel of shame, and a source of pollution, a melting-pot of wickedness, and an edifice of sin") but hesitates to say anything, because God is the creator of all speech before a word is uttered. "You [God] have determined words with a measuring-cord (*qaw*)…you bring forth sounds according to their mysteries…to make known your glory, and recount your wonders…"; see William L. Holladay, *The Psalms through Three Thousand Years: Prayerbook of a Cloud of Witnesses* (Minneapolis: Fortress, 1993), 109-10. The hymn in the *Presbyterian Hymnal* that best expresses the point of Psalm 19 is Hymn 554, "Let all things now living a song of thanksgiving to God our creator triumphantly raise." The second stanza begins, "By law God enforces. The stars in their courses, the sun in its orbit obediently shine…. We, too, should be voicing our love and rejoicing…."

69 Like Kraus, many commentators have tried to make sense of *qaw* in Psalm 19 in relation to the notoriously uncertain phrase *qaw leqaw* parallel to *s aw les aw* in Isa 28:10, 13. Clearly a few verses on, in Isa 28:17, *qaw* has the meaning "cord." Whatever the meaning of *qaw* in vv. 10 and 13, its parallelism there with *s aw*, "command," is in striking agreement with the implication of cord embodying or reflecting command in Psalm 19.

70 The exemplar of rectitude is the sun as *gibbôr*, "warrior." For a reader-response exploration of the

psalm, it could well be wondered whether the notion of keen conformity exemplified by the sun is not more reflective of mind-control and domineering morals police than of piety.

Perhaps the closest biblical parallel to the grand factional pretensions in the face of social and political uncertainty represented by Psalm 19 is the vision in Jer 31:31-40, which unfolds as follows: Yahweh will reconstitute a subject people by unilaterally inscribing a new covenant law directly onto the hearts (*scil.* minds, wills) of Israel and Judah, making them not only incapable of violating the law, but also insensible of any need to as much as verbalize the law. These *h uqqîm*, "statutes" (NRSV "fixed order"), are as fixed as the statutes that govern the sun, moon, and stars and keep the sea at bay, in a world beyond measurement. A new Jerusalem, however, will indeed be measured out, as a center for both Israel and Judah (the undying Davidic irredentist posture), with a "measuring line" (*qaw hammiddâ*) that will, like the cord in Psalm 19, "go out, proceed forth," until the whole of Jerusalem is marked off as sacred to Yahweh and never again to be overthrown.[71]

In light of the contemporary affirmation of individual worth, cultural difference, and positive toleration, to say nothing of the ideal of modern democratic republicanism widely and rightly avowed by Christian faithful, we probably need to revisit Psalm 19 with a less sentimental eye. We need to read it as other than the Romantic literary artifact posited by questionable estimations like "the greatest poem in the Psalter and one of the greatest lyrics in the world"[72] And we need to discern how other parts of Scripture instead lead us to value the diversity of human courses through life in response to God's word, in the restricted world of most of us, a world that in places may only look as though it has been largely spared the turmoil and agony of state-induced or state-sanctioned moral violence.

---

ambiguity of the psalmic ideology that "victory in war"—as fulfilled in God's control over the cosmos and judicial process alike—"is glorious," see David J. A. Clines, "A World Established on Water [Psalm 24]: Reader-Response, Deconstruction and Bespoke Interpretation" in *Interested Parties: The Ideology of Writers and Readers of the Hebrew Bible* (Sheffield: Sheffield Academic Press, 1995), 172-86.

71 Aalen, *Die Begriffe*, 27. This passage belongs to the quasi-Deuteronomistic strand of the book of Jeremiah, and its totalitarian disposition is consistent with the political program represented in Deuteronomy. Whether or in what way the passage derives from the prophet Jeremiah, whose relationship to the Deuteronomistic reform is still debated, is uncertain. In the Bible there exist much subtler and more nuanced and unassuming treatments of the ideological problems of political restoration, which however also take for granted the worldwide glorification of the city of David. These include the book of Isaiah and, not least, the "Levitical" Psalter as a whole, comprising more or less Psalms 2-89, of which Psalm 19 may have been a part. The importance of the stellar order for priestly hegemony is explored by Jacco Dieleman, "Stars and the Egyptian Priesthood in the Graeco-Roman Period," in *Magic in History: Prayer, Magic, and the Stars in the Ancient and Late Antique World*, ed. Scott Noegel, Joel Walker, and Brannon Wheeler (University Park: Pennsylvania State University Press, 2003), 137-53. For the New Testament, Bruce Malina lays out the importance of the stars for the reconstitution of the cosmos in *On the Genre and Message of Revelation: Star Visions and Sky Journeys* (Peabody: Hendrickson, 1995).

72 C. S. Lewis, *Reflections on the Psalms* (New York: Harcourt, Brace, and Company, 1986), 63, cited by Craigie, *Psalms 1-50*, 183; McCann, "The Book of Psalms," 753; and others. Cf. Weiser, *The Psalms*, 198, on the "author" of Ps 19:1-6 [Heb 2-7]: "His insight, the result of great concentration, combines with his powerful metaphorical language to raise him to the status of a great poet who has stimulated the creative work of such eminent men as Goethe [Schiller?], Haydn, and Beethoven."

The Reign of Christ as the Inbreaking Rule of the One and the Many

A Reading of 1 Corinthians 15:20-28

Cornelia Cyss Crocker

For Herman C. Waetjen, whose suggestion that one might understand Christology as eschatologized anthropology was faith-enriching and life-transforming, in deep gratitude for years of profound teaching and inspired mentoring. I am truly thankful for the many conversations we shared about 1 Corinthians. He is the one who pointed me in the direction of this reading, and his penetrating insights and vast learning are reflected throughout this article.

In the tradition of the Christian church, 1 Corinthians 15:20-28 has been interpreted in a variety of ways. Since the earliest times, this passage has given rise to great debates about the Trinitarian question and the issue of the son's subordination,[1] it has been viewed as hinting at an apocalyptic plan and order for the end of time,[2] and it has been perceived as implying the coming of a millennium or interregnum.[3] In contrast, the present reading takes its cue from the fact that this text connects the reign of God to Christ, to those in Christ, to those of Christ. This notion that Christ, or the Christ, is intimately linked to the reign of God and is actually exercising the rule of God will be the focal point of this reading. Such an interpretation makes sense particularly when this pericope is interpreted in light of the broader argument that Paul is making in chapter 15 about the reality of the resurrection and the resulting call for an eschatological orientation of people's lives.[4] In fact, these verses underscore the close link that exists in Paul's thinking between Christology, anthropology, and eschatology. Precisely such theological presuppositions allow Paul to envision the reign of Christ as the One and the many ruling on behalf of God.

---

1   This is especially the case in orthodox Christianity. See Brother Casimir, O.C.S.O., "When (the Father) Will Subject All Things to (the Son), Then (the Son) Himself Will Be Subjected to Him (the Father) Who Subjects All Things to Him (the Son) – A Treatise on First Corinthians 15.28 by Saint Gregory of Nyssa." *The Greek Orthodox Theological Review* 28 (1983). 1-11. Similar interpretations of this passage by some of the other church fathers are discussed by Joseph T. Lienhard, "The Exegesis of 1 Corinthians 15, 24-28 from Marcellus of Ancyra to Theodoret of Cyrus." *Vigiliae Christianae* 37 (1983). 340-359. But see W. Larry Richards, "*Hypotagesetai* in 1 Corinthians 15:28b." *Andrews University Seminary Studies* 38 (2000). 203-206.

2   Johannes Weiss argues that in this passage, Paul lays out the "geschichtlich-apokalyptischen Plan der Dinge." *Der Erste Korintherbrief.* (Goettingen: Vandenhoeck & Ruprecht, 1910). 362. Similarly, Hans Conzelmann maintains that "apocalyptic order" is the theme of this pericope. *1 Corinthians.* (Philadelphia: Fortress Press, 1975). 269.

3   Whether Paul's theology does indeed imply the idea of a millennium and an interregnum is discussed in a recent article by Wolfgang Schrage, "Das messianische Zwischenreich bei Paulus." In *Eschatologie und Schoepfung. Festschrift fur Erich Graesser zum siebzigsten Geburtstag.* Edited by Martin Evang, Helmut Merklein, and Michael Wolter. (Berlin, New York: Walter de Gruyter, 1997).

4   While many scholars have argued that especially verses 23-38 have little to do with the broader argument Paul is making in chapter 15, I maintain that they are central to Paul's thinking about the resurrection. See also William Dykstra, "1 Corinthians 15:20-28, an Essential Part of Paul's Argument Against Those Who Deny the Resurrection." *Calvin Theological Journal.* 4 (1969). 195-211.

Affirming the Resurrection a Third Time: The Typological Argument of 15:20-22

After Paul has recalled to the Corinthians the good news "which I proclaimed to you, which you also received, in which you also stand, through which you are also being saved" (15:1-2),[5] he goes on to list a series of reminders and "proofs" that would underscore the validity of his proclamation.[6] The first such statement can be found in 15:3b-8. It contains a traditional confessional formula that Paul himself may have introduced to the Corinthian church and that the Corinthians may very well have been using as part of their worship service; and it also contains some additions, most likely verse 6 about the more than 500 eyewitnesses and most certainly verse 8 where Paul recounts his own experience of encountering the risen Christ.[7] The second argument that Paul constructs in support of the reality of the resurrection occurs in 15:12-19. This one is logical in nature[8] and tries to lead the logic of saying "there is no resurrection of the dead" *ad absurdum* by basing this entire line of reasoning on the premise "God ... raised Christ" (15:15b) – and that reality can neither be lied about (15a) nor undone (15c).   As a third way of underscoring the validity of proclaiming the resurrection, Paul uses typological reasoning (15:20-22) to emphasize again that "Christ has been raised" (15:20) and that hence there is a resurrection of the dead.[9] After reflecting on the kind of reign and rule that ought to, and will, result from Christ being raised (15:23-28), Paul goes on to talk about the continuing reality of the resurrection in yet another way.   He points out that the Corinthians already live as though they did believe his message, since one way in which their new faith and way of life are made manifest is through their striking practice of being baptized on behalf of the dead (15:29).[10] Finally, Paul reminds the Corinthians that his own ministry puts his life in danger "every hour" (15:30), that he "die[s] every day" (15:31), and that he had to "fight with wild beasts in Ephesus" (15:32).   Like the Corinthians' baptismal

---

5   All translations from the Greek New Testament are my own.

6   In this section, I employ the notion of "proof" in a lose sense. It is not meant to refer to any kind of scientific proof; instead, it is meant to indicate that Paul is trying to make a point and "prove" that he is right through the type of argument and the kind of rhetoric he employs.

7   For a thorough discussion of the extent of the confessional formula that begins at 1 Corinthians 15:3b and Paul's own additions see Conzelmann, *1 Corinthians*. 251-254. Also Wolfgang Schrage, *Der Erste Brief an die Korinther*. (Duesseldorf and Neukirchen-Vluyn: Benzinger Verlag und Neukirchener Verlag, 2001). Vol. 4. 18-26. Similar Pauline affirmations of the resurrection of Jesus Christ can be found in 9:1, in Galatians 1:15-18 and in Romans 1:4.

8   What was said about the notion of "proof" holds true for the term "logic" as well: it must not be understood in a strictly modern-scientific sense, but rather in terms of the ancient art of argumentation and persuasion.

9   This is to counter the Corinthians' reported speech in 15:12 and 16.

10   Such early Christian baptism on behalf of the dead emerged in the context of a variety of death-related rituals practiced in the Greco-Roman world. "Justin, the second-century Christian apologist, refers to the practice of pagan 'magic' at tombs, the calling forth of departed spirits (*Apology* I 18). From a Roman point of view, the spirits of one's ancestors, in particular the *genius* of the *paterfamilias*, were especially important and even part of daily family religion in the home and sometimes at tombs. . . Among other practices were the sacrifices offered on behalf of the dead and the famous *taurobolium*, baptism in bull's blood for the welfare of the emperor." Ben Witherington, *Conflict and Community in Corinth. A Social-Rhetorical Commentary on 1 and 2 Corinthians*. (Grand Rapids, MI and Carlisle: William B. Eerdmans Publishing Company and The Paternoster Press, 1995). 293-294.

practice, Paul's own actions are quite literally death-defying, so that death is neither a barrier to being incorporated into the body of Christ through baptism (15:29) nor is death a threat in the dangerous life that Paul has to confront every hour (15:30-32) as he fulfills his obligation to proclaim the gospel (9:16). Thus in all five arguments that Paul composes in 15:3b through 15:34, he emphasizes things that the Corinthians already seem to confess and know, that they appear to say and do and that actually contradict their own slogan that "there is no resurrection of the dead" (15:12, 16).[11]

Hence within the larger passage of 15:4b-34, verses 20-28 contain the third and central argument in the list of five "proofs" that Paul enumerates in order to underscore the reality and validity of his proclamation that Christ was raised and that there is a resurrection of the dead. In this third argument, he uses typological reasoning to make his point (15:20-22) and then develops it in the two steps. First, Paul emphasizes the parallel between the human being Adam and the human being Christ; the Greek *anthropos* is used to describe each of these two figures (15:21).[12] At the same time, there is a fundamental reversal in spite of this parallel, since through one human being, Adam, came death while through the other human being, Christ, came resurrection from the dead (15:21).[13] Thus the Adam-Christ pattern functions for Paul as a reversed parallel. But there is second important aspect to this argument, since Paul maintains that what is true for the One who is the first fruit (15:20, 23) or the firstborn (Rom 8:29) or the type is also true for the Many. These Many who come later, who follow, who are "in Adam" and "in Christ", are like their typological forbearers, so that in Paul's reasoning, "Adam" and "Christ" each function like a paradigm.[14] People bear the image of the human being of dust and of the human being of heaven (15:49), and thus they die in Adam and will be made alive in Christ (15:22). Hence in the typological argument of 15:20-22, Paul constructs Adam and Christ as reversed parallels that each function paradigmatically as "the type of the one who was to come" (Rom 5:14).

Such use of typological argumentation can also found elsewhere in 1 Corinthians, specifically in 12:12-27, where Paul refers to the "one" and the "many" in verses 12, 14, and 20 as he explores how the followers of Jesus Christ might work together as an integrated and loving community that is one body with many members.[15] In 2 Corinthians 5:14-15, the events of death-and-resurrection are understood in terms of "one" and "all", and the same holds true for the old-into-new statement of verse 17. The one-and-many reasoning also occurs in Romans 5:12-21, where Paul refers to the "one" Adam and to "all" of humanity and then speaks very explicitly of "the one and the many" (5:15, 19) as he transfers this kind of logic to the relationship he perceives

---

11 It is interesting to note that, throughout this entire section, Paul makes no reference to those passages from the late Old Testament and the intertestamental period that may hint at the resurrection of the dead, such as Daniel 12:2-3, 2 Maccabees 7:23, 28-29, and 4 Maccabees 16:25.

12 Christ is referred to as *anthropos* (human being) also in Romans 5:15, 17, and 19.

13 This reversed parallel is picked up again in 15:45-49.

14 The Greek work is *typos*. The paradigmatic aspect of typos is most evident in Rom 5:14, while the sense of *typos* as "example" can be perceived in 1 Corinthians 10:6, Philippians 1 3:17 and in 1 Thessalonians 1:7. Only in Rom 6:17 does Paul use *typos* in the sense of "type" or "kind".

15 John A. T. Robinson discusses Paul's notion of the one and the many in his monograph, The Body. *A Study in Pauline Theology*. (London: SCM Press, 1961). See especially 58-67.

between Jesus and all who are part of the new humanity, of the new creation.[16] Finally, in his discussion of Hagar and Sarah in Galatians 4:21-5:1, Paul treats these two women as typifying not only two different kinds of marriage relationships with Abraham but also as exemplifying allegorically two different types of covenants that make manifest two different ways of life in two kinds of "Jerusalem".[17]

Further typological reasoning can be found within the larger cultural-religious context that surrounds Paul's letter writing: it occurs in several of the Jewish apocryphal texts of the intertestamental period and in the work of Philo. In those passages, it is primarily Adam who is regarded as typifying humanity as such, though not necessarily as signifying human beings in their fallenness and brokenness but rather as exemplifying their connection to the divine, as emphasizing their bearing the image of God.[18] Adam as wise and glorious and also Enoch and Noah as well as Moses and Jacob/Israel were all prominent Scriptural figures that were treated as ancestors of the human race, either in its original creation or in a new form, as a new humanity.[19]

> The fact that all men [!] are derived from one ancestor Adam means that in him all men are one. There is a real unity of men in him; all belong to each and each belongs to all. . . Adam, then, stands for the real unity of mankind in virtue of his creation.[20]

Thus it is in the intertestamental setting of Judaism that the close conceptual link between the one and the many emerges.[21] Hence the motifs of the con-substantiality of

---

16 Paul's typological argument in Romans 5 is explored in more detail by Francis Watson, "Is There a Story in These Texts?" In Bruce W. Longenecker, ed., *Narrative Dynamics in Paul. A Critical Assessment.* (Louisville: Westminster John Knox Press, 2002). Later in the letter, in Romans 9:7, a similar train of thought concerning the one and the many is perceptible with respect to Abraham's offspring. Paul quotes Gen 21:12 where God promises Abraham, "in Isaac, descendents shall be named for you." The one son Isaac becomes the first-born of Abraham's many descendents who are related through being "in" Isaac.

17 When Paul talks about Hagar and Sarah, the two wives of Abraham, and treats them and their sons as each typifying a different kind of life and a different kind of covenant relationship with God, he himself employs the term "allegory" (Gal 4:24).

18 Sirach 49:16, Ezra 28:12, and Wisdom of Solomon 10:1f all emphasize the extraordinary size, glory, and wisdom of Adam. In Philo, statements about Adam as an ideal and idealized figure can be found in Op. *Mund.* 136-139, *Conf. Ling.* 146, and *Quaest. Gn.* 1:21, 53. For a more comprehensive discussion of Adam in the intertestamental literature, see Eduard Schweizer, "Die Kirche als Leib Christi in den Paulinischen Homologumena." In his *Neotestamentica. German and English Essays* 1951-1963. (Zurich, Stuttgart: Zwingli Verlag, 1963). 272-292. This article is available in English in a collection of essays by Schweizer, *The Church as the Body of Christ.* (Richmond, VA, 1964).

19 Schweitzer writes, "Ein neuer Stammvater beginnt ein neues Geschlecht des Heils. Von Henoch wird erwartet, dass er sein Volk verherrliche und Erloeser ihrer Suenden sei. An Noah knuepfen sich Hoffnungen bei Philo. Er ist Ende des verdammten Geschlechtes und Beginn eines schuldlosen . . . Als Anfaenger der zweiten Schoepfung ist er gerechter Koenig aller irdischen Kreatur . . . Auch Moses nimmt eine aehnliche Stellung ein. "Die Kirche als Leib Christi." 280.

20 W. D. Davies, *Paul and Messianic Judaism.* (London: SPCK, 1958). 53, 55.

21 The social-scientific analysis of Kenelm Burrigdge explores the theme of the One and the Many in terms of the sociology of millennialism. It appears that late Judaism exhibited some conditions that would foster millennial movements, such as the general populations' growing awareness of being disenfranchised and the resulting "externalization of thoughts and activities" about new social, political, and economic possibilities. See his *New Heaven, New Earth. A Study of Millenarian Activities.* (New York: Schocken Books, 1969). 116. The rise of messianic figures, both before and after the life, death, and resurrection of Jesus Christ, attests to such conditions and movements. In all

the ancestor and the rest of humanity, of the common fate between the new ancestor/savior and the saved, and of the savior as the head of a new "tribe" that will follow him can all be found prior to the letters of Paul.[22] However, thinking in terms of two typologies, of Adam and of Christ, and constructing a contrast between them seems to be a Pauline development. For while Adam and Christ each function as representatives of the entire human race, there is no indication that the reversed parallel that Paul constructs in 1 Corinthians 15:20-22 and elsewhere existed in earlier texts.[23]

Paul's typological thinking enables him to emphasize a close relationship between both Adam and human beings and Christ and human beings, so that "the respective relationships [allow] for the actions of these individual figures to become constitutive for others."[24] Because of such typological thinking, Paul can conceive of a "union or solidarity between Christ and his people";[25] he can think in terms of human beings being incorporated into Christ;[26] he can even understand "the Christ" as a corporate entity.[27] Based on such patterns of typological reasoning, Paul can therefore state conclusively that the resurrection, which was true for the one human being Jesus Christ, is also true for the many human beings who are in Christ, who belong to him. Hence Paul's typological argument, where Christ functions as the first fruit (15:20) or model or paradigm that exemplifies what is to happen to those who share in his typology, represents a well-established line of reasoning that would render null and void any claim that there is no resurrection of the dead.[28]

---

of them, the many understood themselves as tightly linked to the one prophet or messiah whom they followed. See Richard A. Horsley, *Bandits, Prophets and Messiahs. Popular Movements in the Time of Jesus.* Harrisburg: Trinity Press International, 1999).

22 Schweizer, "Die Kirche als Leib Christi". See 274. This type of thinking is also reflected in images such as the vine and the branches (John 15:1ff, see also Ps 80:8-16) and the building of which Christ is the headstone (Eph 2:20-22).

23 Andreas Lindemann writes, "Die Adam-Christus-Typologie ist vor Paulus nicht belegt; man kann deshalb fragen, ob womoeglich der Apostel selber als ihr Schoepfer anzusehen ist." In "Die Auferstehung der Toten. Adam und Christus nach 1 Kor 15." In *Eschatologie und Schoepfung. Festschrift fur Erich Graesser zum siebzigsten Geburtstag.* Edited by Martin Evang, Helmut Merklein, and Michael Wolter. (Berlin, New York: Walter de Gruyter, 1997). 156. In any case, "Adam und Christus [sind] jeweils Representanten der ganzen Menschheit." Ibid. 154, see also 166.

24 C. E. Hill, "Paul's Understanding of Christ's Kingdom in 1 Corinthians 15:20-28." *Novum Testamentum* XXX, 4 (1988). 305.

25 Ibid. See 303.

26 Ibid. See 307.

27 Dale Martin argues that Paul "firmly assumes that identity is constructed upon participation . . [that there is] a connection between the Christian's body and Christ's body." *The Corinthian Body.* (New Haven and London: Yale University Press, 1995). 130. Paul's discussion in 1 Corinthians 12 makes that very clear, with 12:12 as the prime example of such participation. For a discussion of contemporary philosophies that treat the issues of One, Many, Other and Difference in the thoughts of Whitehead, Levinas, Derrida and others, see Joseph A. Bracken, *The One in the Many. A Contemporary Reconstruction of the God-World Relationship.* (Grand Rapids and Cambridge: William B. Eerdmans Publishing Company, 2001).

28 Johan Vos examines in detail just what the Corinthian Christians may have denied, whether it was the resurrection in general, or the future resurrection -- so that Paul would be arguing against a completely realized eschatology--, or the resurrection of the body -- so that Paul would have taken a stance against anthropological dualism. "Argumentation und Situation in 1 Kor. 15." *Novum Testamentum* 41 (1999). 311-333. There is also the important question about the scope of the resurrection, whether it includes all of humanity or only those in Christ, which is a matter of great relevance in contemporary inter-faith

Tension, Motion, and Union: Eschatological Implications of 15:23-24a and 27b-28

While the close link that Paul perceives between the One and the Many, between Christology and anthropology renders much of his Christological thinking corporate and participatory[29], there is nevertheless a distinction to be made between the one Jesus Christ and the many human beings who are in Christ. This distinction becomes apparent in verses 23-24a and 27b-28 as Paul writes about *tagma* and *parousia*. The first term can signify not only the sequence of events but also the proper ordering of relationships; and so *tagma* is often used to denote ranks and troop divisions within the Greco-Roman military context.[30]   The second concept originally refers to the coming of an important figure and can mean a visit from a distant ruler and perhaps even indicate the presence - *"par-ousia"*- of the emperor himself.[31] Thus Paul uses common military-political terms in these verses but shifts their meaning as he employs them in a religious-eschatological sense during his discussion about the resurrection of the dead. This underscores that Paul's beliefs concerning the resurrection are guided by strong eschatological expectation; in fact eschatology is central to Paul's entire theological thinking.[32] Paul's eschatology can be characterized as tensive, in motion, and oriented towards union with God, and that has important implications for how Paul conceives of the resurrection of the dead in the future and of the reign of Christ now.

The tensive aspect of Paul's eschatological thinking emerges from several statements he makes in his letters. On the one hand, there are repeated references to the future and to future events that Paul expects to happen at the end of the ages. Thus every time that *parousia* is liked with the person of Jesus Christ in Paul's writings, it is implied and understood that the coming of Christ lies firmly in the future.[33] Used that way, this term can be found not only here in 1 Corinthians 15:23 but also four times in 1 Thessalonians (2:19, 3:13, 4:15, 5:23).[34]   In addition, there are hints at, and

---

dialogue.

29 The notion of participation as a foundational trajectory of Pauline theology is emphasized by Udo Schnelle in his "Transformation und Partizipation als Grundgedanken paulinischer Theologie." *New Testament Studies* 47 (2001). 58-75.

30 *Tagma* is defined as "that which is ordered", as "division, group, class" and also as "order, turn, arrangement". Walter Bauer, William F. Arndt, and F. Wilbur Gingrich, *A Greek-English Lexicon of the New Testament and Other Early Christian Literature*. (Chicago and London: University of Chicago Press, 1979). 802-803. The term is often used in a military context but can also occur without any military connotation.

31 *Parousia* indicates the coming and the presence of important people, though in the New Testament, the term is used specifically to denote Christ's coming again at the end of human history. Bauer, Gingrich, Danker, *Greek-English Lexicon*. 629-30

32 That view was first advanced by Albert Schweitzer in his *The Mysticism of Paul the Apostle*. (Baltimore and London: Johns Hopkins University Press, 1998.) The notion of eschatology is itself a concept with layers of meaning and has been defined in three ways: as the teaching of the last and final things, as the future hopes of Christians in a changing world now, and even as that which challenges and changes theological thinking in its foundational assumptions. Gerhard Sauter, *Einfuehrung in die Eschatologie*. (Darmstadt: Wissenschaftliche Buchgesellschaft, 1995.) See 2-3.

33 Witherington reads *parousia* it in the context of "imperial eschatology" which the Corinthians may have shared and which may have caused too great a focus on their present political order; so that Paul's eschatological future-orientation might be a response and correction to such a stance. *Conflict and Community in Corinth*. 295-98.

34 At other times, Paul employs the term *parousia* in an every-day human context, namely to speak about

descriptions of, the kind of things that Paul expects at that future coming of Jesus Christ; and in 1 Thessalonians 4:13-18 and in 1 Corinthians 15:51-55 he uses auditory and visual metaphors to speak of the resurrection of the dead and their union with the Lord that one can anticipate at that future time. On the other hand, there are indications in those same Pauline letters that his eschatological expectations have already been fulfilled or are very close to being fulfilled. This emphasis on the present as the time of God's coming is most strongly evident in 2 Corinthians 6:2, where Paul quotes Isaiah 49:8 about the time of the Lord's favor and the day of salvation and then states "See, now is the acceptable time; see, now is the day of salvation."[35] In 1 Corinthians, Paul speaks of the impending crisis (1 Corinthians 7:26) and notes that time is short (7:29) and that the present form of the world is passing away (7:31). In his letter to the Romans, Paul urges his readers to repentance before the coming of God's righteous judgment (Romans 2:4b-5) and emphasizes that the whole creation is waiting with eager longing for deliverance (8:18-23) and that "salvation is nearer to us now than when we first became believers" (13:11-14). This sense of the nearness of God's kingdom and of the urgency to transform human hearts, minds, and social structures right now stands in tension with Paul's expectations of a future *parousia* of Jesus Christ. For while God's promised deliverance has been realized in the death and resurrection of Jesus Christ, the rulers and rules of "this present age" continue to exist and to exert power over human beings.[36] This paradox of a partly realized and partly future-oriented eschatology finds striking expression in 1 Corinthians 16:22, where Paul uses the Aramaic formula *Maranatha*. Since there were no spaces between words in ancient writing, this terms can be read as either *maran atha* and then means "our Lord has come" and signifies an event already in the past, or it can be interpreted as *marana tha* which means "our Lord, come!" and points to something that still lies in the future.[37] Perhaps Paul selected this formula precisely for its fine ambiguity; it certainly underscores the tensive nature of his eschatological thinking.

Secondly, Paul's eschatology needs to be understood as being in motion. A sense of movement is clearly evident in this passage, since Paul employs the words *aparche*, *epeita* and *eita* to speak about Christ as the first fruit of being made alive by God (15:23, 22) and indicates that then the ones of Christ will rise at his *parousia* and that then the end will come.[38] Because of these concepts, phrases, and particles, readers throughout the centuries have looked to 1 Corinthians 15:20-28 for indications about the stages of development as human history moves toward its conclusion, they have

---

an upcoming visit of Stephanas (1 Cor 16: 17) and of Titus (2 Cor 7:6-7) and of his own presence with the Corinthians (2 Cor 10:10) and Philippians (Phil 1:26, 2:12).

35 In this context, Conzelmann notes that Paul "transposes the kingdom into the present." *1 Corinthians.* 270

36 It needs to be remembered that Paul is operating with two different notions of time. On the one hand, there is human linear time with past, present and future (1:5-8, 26-28; 3:1-3, 11-16; 14:20), on the other hand, there is the apocalyptic-eschatological sense that perceives time in two ways as "this age"(1:20; 2:6 and 8; 3:18) and the age to come. These two notions of time exist side by side as time is understood in both human and divine terms.

37 For a discussion of *Maranatha* see Conzelman, *1 Corinthians.* 300-301. Also Schrage, *Der Erste Brief an die Korinther.* Vol 4. 472-3, especially note 274.

38 While there is a distinction in this passage between Jesus' resurrection and the general resurrection at his *parousia*, those two events are linked in Matthew 27:50-53.

searched this passage for hints about an orderly and predictable sequence of events, they have examined it for clues about the specific timing of what is to occur at the end of time. What has emerged from this discussion is a focus on the reign of Christ as an interim time, as a millennial rule that will arise between Christ's *parousia* and the end of time which will bring God's and/or Christ's final judgment.[39] What such an *interregnum* or *Zwischenreich* will be like has been the subject of much speculation,[40] as have questions about how long it will last and whether it will ever come to an end.[41] However, there is no indication in this text that Paul is thinking in terms of discreet stages of development or of a clear sequence of occurrences or of a specific timing of events. All that can be said is that things are in motion, that there is fluidity as human history unfolds, that there is an overlap between the "already" and the "not yet". And while it is not possible to make firm predictions about the *parousia* and the end of time, it is clear that God's future determines the present, just as events form the past have meaning for us now.[42] More importantly, instead of locating the reign of Christ solely at the end of time in a celestial setting, Paul's eschatology needs to be understood as situating the reign of Christ primarily in the present time and as perceiving it essentially as a terrestrial reality.[43] For only such an interpretation would preserve the tensive nature of Paul's eschatology and make it clear that Christ's reign has already commenced now, even as it unfolds ever more fully into the future as human history moves towards completion.

Finally, verses 27b-28 convey in many ways Paul's most profound insight about *tagma* at the end of time because they focus on the ultimate relationship between God the Father (24, 28) and the son.[44] Since "son" may be understood collectively as the

---

39 Rudolf Bultmann observes, "Bei Paulus erscheint bald Gott als Weltrichter (Rom 14,10; 1 Thess 3,13 usw), bald Christus (1 Thess 2,19; 1 Kor 4,5; 2 Kor 5,10)." *Der Zweite Brief an die Korinther* (Goettingen: Vandenhoeck & Ruprecht, 1976). 145.

40 Schrage writes that Christ's kingdom is "mit Ostern begrundet" and speaks of "ein eschatologischer Ueberwindungsprozess zwischen Ostern und Parousie." Hence, "Insofern ist eher von einer Zwischenherrschaft als einem Zwischenreich zu sprechen." Schrage, "Das messianische Zwischenreich bei Paulus." 349.

41 The phrase "whose kingdom shall have no end" was inserted into the Nicene Creed based on Luke 1:33, precisely because of 1 Corinthians 15:23-28 and the possibility of arguing that Christ's kingdom would end when God would be all in all (15:28). John F. Jansen compares three positions on this question, one from the patristic age, one from the reformation period, and one from the present time in "1 Corinthians 15:24-28 and the Future of Jesus Christ." In W. Eugene March, ed. *Texts and Testaments. Critical Essays on the Bible and Early Church Fathers.* (San Antonio: Trinity University Press, 1980). 173-97. Conzelmann maintains that "the kingdom of Christ is temporally limited. This view is bound up historically with the Jewish view of the temporal limitation of the messiah's kingdom." *1 Corinthians.* 272, note 88.

42 Examples in Paul's letters are figures from the past like Adam in this passage, Abraham (Gal 3:6-4:10), and Moses (1 Cor 10:1-13). But most importantly, what was true for the One Jesus Christ in the past will also be true for the many who are in Christ as the future unfolds towards which all humanity is moving now.

43 This is a major focus in Herman Waetjen's teaching and ministry. Following Paul's thinking in Romans 6:1-11, he emphasizes throughout his work that, by being in Christ, human beings have entered into death and resurrection with Christ and are called to labor in Christ's kingdom now. See especially his article "The Actualization of Christ's Achievement in our Historical Existence: Breaking out of the New Babylonian Captivity." *The Princeton Seminary Bulletin.* XVII, 3 (1996): 291-309.

44 Here *tagma* refers to a different kind of "ordering": it is used not with respect to time but to denote a

One and the Many, based on Paul's earlier line of reasoning and also on his use of two quotes from Scripture that speak paradigmatically about humanity at its best (Psalm 8:7 and 110:1),[45] this would indicate that for Paul, the end and goal of all human history are union with God.[46] Paul's sense that God will be intimately connected with all creation, that God will be all in all (15:28) is evident not only in this passage but is also hinted at in 8:6 and in Romans 9:5 and 11:36.[47] Surprisingly, what emerges in 1 Corinthians 15:28 as Paul reads Psalms eight and 110 in light of his experience of the risen Christ (see 9:1; Galatians 1:13, 16) is a sense of *tagma*, of ordering that is not hierarchical in nature but horizontal. Even though horizontal does not need to mean equal, it is clear that for Paul God is not conceived of as above all but as all in all and in all things. A survey of the literature of the ancient world shows that this notion of all-in-all is used elsewhere "to describe personal relations of love, devotion, friendship, need fulfillment and popular leadership" and thus gives a sense of just how the Creator might be related to the creation at the end of time. [48] In light of this, any discussions among Biblical scholars about the relationship between God and Christ, about the Trinitarian issue, and about the final subordination of the son[49] need to be careful not to construct too sharp a distinction between Theo-logy and Christology.[50] Instead, Paul's firm conviction that human history is moving towards union with God as its ultimate goal should be read as a rejection of all thinking in terms of opposites, dualisms, and divisions and as a final subversion of all hierarchies.

---

relational quality between persons.

45 I read "the human being" and "the son of the human being" in Psalm 8 and also "my [earthly] lord" in Psalm 110 (109 in LXX) typologically/paradigmatically and as indicating again the relationship between the One and the Many.

46 Regarding union with God the Creator, Douglas McGaughey writes, "Surveying the Christian tradition for the perspective of its spiritual and material metaphysical options, we can identify two fundamental models of faith: unification and separation. . . The model of separation maintains that humanity is separated from God because of original and personal sin. . . [In] the model of unification the emphasis is upon the always and already accomplished, if only partial, union of the individual Christian with God in spirit." *Strangers and Pilgrims*. (Berlin, New York: Walter de Gruyter, 1997). 476-9.

47 Conzelmann links the idea that God will be all in all things with Sirach 43:27-28, verses that also suggests that God is greater even than all that God created. *1 Corinthians*. 274-5.

48 David Fredrickson, "God, Christ, and All Things in 1 Corinthians 15:28." *Word and World* 18, 3 (1998). 260. The relational aspect of *panta en pasin* is examined throughout his essay.

49 Some interesting suggestions have emerged in recent scholarship about the meaning of *hypotasso*, the term that indicates subordination. W. Larry Richards argues that it might be read as middle voice in 15:28b and would then mean that the son subordinates himself. "*Hypotagesetai* in 1 Corinthians 15:28b." *Andrews University Seminary Studies* 38 (2000). 203-206. Fredrickson maintains that *hypotasso* implies not so much subjection as personal identity through participation. "God, Christ and All Things in 1 Corinthians 15:28." 260-62.

50 Uta Weil believes that 1 Corinthians 15:23-28 is very theocentric, noting that this passage starts with the divine passive ("was raised") and ends with God being all things in all things. "Theo-logische Interpretation von 1 Kor 15,23-28." *Zeitschrift fuer die neutestamentliche Wissenschaft* 84 (1993). 27-35. J. Lambrecht insists on a Christocentric interpretation of 24c-27a, but points out that "the end is decidedly theocentric." "Paul's Christological Use of Scripture in 1 Cor 15:20-28." *New Testament Studies* 28 (1982). 511. Jansen argues in favor of a Trinitarian interpretations, "1 Corinthians 15:24-28 and the Future of Jesus Christ." See especially 187, 192. This issue of a theocentric versus a Christocentric or even Trinitarian interpretation of this periscope continues to be an important one for many Christian readers.

The Reign of Christ as the One and the Many Ruling in Life on Behalf of God (24b-27a)

Both Paul's sense of the resurrection as a reality for the one and the many as well as his notion of eschatology as tensive, in motion and moving towards union with God form the conceptual framework for 15:24b-27a. In these verses, Paul refers to the kingdom that Christ will hand over to God the Father and then states what he regards as the tasks of this kingdom and reign of Christ. He does this briefly and almost in passing, after he has mentioned a set of events that he expects at the end of time (23-24a), so that verses 24b through 27a can be regarded as Paul's recapitulation of a crucial happening that is central to these events. But while it is clear that the emphasis in these verses is on the kingdom, the *basileia*, several questions emerge for the reader that are raised by Paul but are not elaborated in this passage. Therefore I will explore in more detail three interconnected matters: how the term *basileia* and the related verb *basileuo* are to be understood, who it is that exercises such reign and rule, and what the tasks are which this reign of Christ is charged to fulfill.

The terms *basileia* and *basileuo* that Paul uses in verses 24 and 25 may be translated as kingdom and being king, as reign and reigning, or as rule and ruling. It is a divine kingdom that Paul refers to here, and it is clearly linked to the prophecy in Daniel 2:44, "in the days of those kings the God of heaven will set up a kingdom that shall never be destroyed, nor shall this kingdom be left to another people. It shall crush all these kingdoms and bring them to an end, and it shall stand forever."[51] This divine kingdom, in contrast to the kingdoms of "this world" or "this age", is at the center of 15:20-28 and even of the larger argument that Paul construct in 15:3b-34. The statements that Paul makes in his letters about the divine kingdom are primarily negative in character, which means that he emphasizes primarily what the kingdom of God is not and who will not be among those who inherit it.[52] Speaking positively, Paul reminds his readers that God does call us into God's own kingdom and glory (1 Thessalonians 2:12), and he also indicates that the kingdom and reign of God is at the same time the reign of Christ which Christ will hand back over to God in the end (1 Corinthians 15:24).[53] Exercising this reign, this *basileia* by the grace and authority of

---

51 This prophecy is uttered by Daniel as he interprets King Nebuchadnezzar's dream about the great statue fashioned from different kinds of material that was struck and destroyed by a stone not made by human hands. Thus both the notion of a kingdom set up in accordance with God's plan and of putting an end to all earthly kingdoms are taken from Hebrew Scripture and reiterated here in 15:24.

52 Paul writes about the divine kingdom, "the kingdom of God is not food and drink but righteousness and peace and joy" (Romans 14:17), it is "not word/speech but power [*dynamis*]" (1 Corinthians 4:20), "the unrighteous will not inherit" it (1 Corinthians 6:9), "thieves will not inherit" it (1 Corinthians 6:10), and "flesh and blood will not inherit" it (1 Corinthians 15:50). Based on these statements it would appear that some of the earliest Christians had made assumptions about the kingdom of God and Christ that Paul is seeking to correct.

53 Karl Ludwig Schmidt observes, "Diese *basileia* Jesu Christi ist zugleich die *basileia* Gottes. . .So stehen Gott und Christus nebeneinander, wobei bald Gott, bald Christus zuerst genannt ist. . . Am Ende der Tage gibt Christus, der in dieser Weise die basileia vom Vater empfangen hat, diese an ihn zurueck 1 K15,24; er kann Gott nur geben, was diesem schon eigen ist." *Theologisches Woerterbuch zum Neuen Testament*. I, 581-2. Based on Schmidt's thorough survey of how the reign of God and the reign of Christ are understood in the New Testament, creating a binary opposition between a Christocentric and a Theocentric interpretation of 1 Corinthians 15:20-28 does not make much sense.

God means ruling or reigning in life, *basileuo*, through the one Jesus Christ (Romans 5:17).

Linked to this question about the meaning of *basileia* is the issue of how one is to understand "Christ" in this passage, since it is Christ who has the kingdom and rules at this time. Much research has been done on how Paul's employs the notions of Christ, Jesus Christ, Christ Jesus, being in Christ and Christ being in us (Romans 8:10) in his various letters, and it is not always clear whether Paul is referring in any given text to the human being Jesus Christ, the risen Lord, or the church as Christ's resurrected body on earth.[54] Yet based on Paul's typological reasoning in this passage and on his metaphor of the church as a body earlier in the letter (12:12-27, see also Romans 12:4-5), it makes sense to understand the implied "Christ" of 15:24-28 and the "son" of 15:28 as collective terms. For while the 3rd person singular is used in several verbs throughout this pericope, this grammatical singular ties in with Paul's reference to the paradigmatic human being, the typological mortal one from Psalm eight and again signifies both the One and the Many. Likewise I read *auton* in verse 25 as referring to the quote from Psalm 110, "he must reign until he has put all things under his feet,"[55] and as designating the people of God as a whole. Hence even though the grammar of this passage would imply a singular person as "Christ", the intertexts of Psalms 8 and 110 as well as Paul's earlier thinking in terms of the One and the Many suggest that he is in fact referring to a collective, to all the ones who are in Christ.[56] This notion of a collective body of people who are in Christ and who participate in the work of Christ would render Paul's Christology of the One and the Many an eschatologized anthropology,[57] since it charges human beings to become ever more Christlike in their living and in their doing. This interpretation coheres well with Paul's theology as it emerges throughout his letters, most notably his sense of dying and rising with Christ (Romans 6:3-8) and the resulting call to be alive to God (6:11) as we rule in life (5:17). What is amazing is the fact that for Paul, those who are in Christ are indeed able to exercise together the reign and rule of God, precisely because "it is God who establishes us … in Christ and has christened us by putting his seal on us and giving us his Spirit in our hearts as a first installment."[58]

The final question is how Paul's sense of exercising God's reign and of ruling in life can best be understood. The history of the church has shown that, if being in Christ and exercising Christ's reign is interpreted primarily in soteriological terms, it may come to be regarded as an exclusive way of approaching God and even as the sole way of being in relationship with God. There are countless examples of such an interpretation throughout the centuries which have led not only to the church's

---

54 For Paul's notion of being "in Christ" see Fritz Neugebauer, "Das Paulinische 'In Christo'." *New Testament Studies* IV (1957-58). 124-138. Also William B. Barcley, *"Christ in You." A Study in Paul's Theology and Ethics.* (Lanham, New York, Oxford: University Press of America, 1999).

55 I owe this insight to Herman C. Waetjen. Most other interpreters understand *auton* as referring back to *Christos* in verse 23.

56 This movement from the One to the Many is also evident in Daniel 7 where the one who appears before the Ancient of Days (7:13-14) turns out to be the people of the holy ones the Most High (7:27).

57 This central teaching of Herman C. Waetjen has profoundly influenced my own understanding of Pauline theology.

58 This is a literal translation of 2 Corinthians 1:21-22 where Paul employs the same verb *chrio* to talk about both Christ/ the anointed one and the ones who were christened/ anointed "into him".

applying Christ's rule in an authoritarian manner among Christians but also to forceful missionizing and to the colonialization of peoples of other faith traditions. On the other hand, if exercising the reign of Christ is understood also, and even primarily, in terms of service, then a different scenario emerges. Then the focus can be on just how urgent a task it is for the Christ to be at work in transforming human social constructs, so that they would correspond more and more to the kind of relationships that will exist in the reign of God.[59] Such active <u>trans</u>formation of power structures among human beings, in contrast to being <u>con</u>formed to them (see Romans 12:2), means collaborating with God to put an end to every rule and authority and power (1 Corinthians 15:24) as they now exist.[60] Paul uses the powerful verbs *hypotasso* (subordinate, subjugate) six times and *katargeo* (to render void, to abolish) twice in just four verses (15:24-28) to convey a sense of the "crushing" and "bringing to an end" that echo from his reference to Daniel 2:44, while "putting under his feet" is an image derived from Psalms 8:7 and 110:1.[61] Every rule and authority and power needs to be subverted and neutralized through the actions of real human beings now, so that God is more and more able to be all things in all things. The fact that Paul includes in the list of agents to be subjugated even death as the last enemy has led to the assumption among many Christian readers that the principalities and powers mentioned here are to be understood in a cosmic manner.[62] However, reading "every rule and authority and power" in only a cosmic sense may lead to a quietist and millennial understanding of this passage that could tempt those in Christ to withdraw from the prevailing social structures and the political realm.[63] But instead, any non-participation in the values of "this age" needs to make manifest the values and virtues of the reign of Christ in an

---

59 I use "the Christ" here in the same way in which Paul uses it in 1 Corinthians 12:12.

60 Walter Wink surveys the use of *arche* (ruler), *exousia* (authority), and *dynamis* (power) in the LXX and other contemporary Jewish writings in *Naming the Powers. The Language of Power in the New Testament.* (Philadelphia: Fortress Press, 1984). 151-63. See also Romans 8:38, where a similar list appears that mentions not only rulers and powers but also death, life, angels, things present, things to come, and height and depth.

61 Interestingly, in Philippians 3:21 Paul mentions "the Lord Jesus Christ" as the one who has "the power that enables him to make all things subject to himself." This stands in contrast to the notion of God putting powers and rulers under the feet of God's chosen ones in Psalms eight and 110. Schrage writes, "Sachlich ist es aber durchaus zutreffend, dass Gott und Christus in ihrem Wirken hier sehr eng aneinanderruecken und nicht gegeneinander ausgespielt werden, zumal auch sonst dieselben Taetigkeiten bei Paulus auf Gott und Christus zurueckgefuehrt werden koennen. Von dem eindeutigen *hypotaxantos* her wird man dabei ihr Verhaeltnis so zu bestimmen haben, dass Christus der von Gott deligierte Statthalter und Repraesentant der Herrschaft Gottes ist. Wie sehr Paulus beide tatsaechlich zusammendenkt, ergibt sich auch daraus, dass Paulus hier das *hypotassein* auf Gott, in Phil 3,21 aber auf Christus zurueckfuehrt." "Das messianische Zwischenreich bei Paulus." 353.

62 Such an interpretation would cohere better with the theology of Ephesians and Colossians than with the authentic Pauline letters. This connection between 1 Corinthians 15:20-28 and Ephesians 1:20-23 and even 1 Peter 3:21b-22 and Hebrews 1:3 and 2:8 is examined by Martinus C. De Boer, "Paul's Use of a Resurrection Tradition in 1 Cor 15,20-28." In *The Corinthian Correspondence.* Edited by Reimund Bieringer. (Leuven: University Press, 1996). 639-651. See also Schrage, *Der Erste Brief an die Korinther.* Vol. 4, 212.

63 This is especially true if Romans 13 is not interpreted as a time-bound manual for Christian survival under the oppressive Roman occupation but as a time-less call to live in a 'quietist' fashion obedient to the ruling authorities – which would be the exact opposite of what Paul is advocating in 1 Corinthians 15:20-28!

active manner,[64] so that the new way of being a community in Christ would have a transformative effect on the larger society.[65] For the newness of life that becomes available through participating in the death-and-resurrection of Jesus Christ and the freedom that results from it not only mandate but also enable those in Christ to transform the suffering of the world into greater wholeness,[66] so that the reign of God can be glimpsed at least in part in every new generation.[67]

---

64 The virtue and vice lists that appear in the authentic Pauline letters, in the Gospels, and in the work of the Pauline school are not uniquely Christian, but they do seek to prescribe how the reign of Christ is to be exhibited by human beings even in "this age" and at the present time. See "Virtue/Vice Lists." *Anchor Bible Dictionary.* VI, 857-59.

65 Examples for such transformative praxis can be found in Paul's own letters, especially in Philemon with respect to slavery, in 1 Corinthians concerning marriage and singleness (chapter 7), about how to deal with food issues and idol worship (chapters 8-11), and about how to live in a diverse community (chapter 12, 14). In all instances, Paul advocates change, even reversal of the prevalent values of the day, specifically in relation to slavery, gender hierarchies, theological disagreements, economic inequalities, and spiritual diversity. For Paul, being in Christ implies a commitment to mutuality and to fostering horizontal relationships among all human beings!

66 Such a sense of greater wholeness would have different meanings at different times and locations and could include the struggle for the rights of the poor, of children, of women, of racial-ethnic minorities, of people of various sexual orientations, of the aged, of immigrants and aliens, etc. Eduard Schweizer cautions, though, that "the presence of the kingdom of God, according to one of the most shocking words of the New Testament, is the presence of suffering and failure (Matt. 11:12)." In *Saved by Hope. Essays in Honor of Richard C. Oudersluys.* Edited by James I. Cook (Grand Rapids: Eerdmans, 1978). It would seem that the task of those in Christ is an arduous one and that the reign of Christ is only present in small increments even 2000 years after the life, ministry, death and resurrection of Jesus Christ.

67 The language of Walter Wink is helpful and suggestive. He writes, "The reign of God is not 'built' but sampled. We have a foretaste, an appetizer, an aperitif, a down payment (Rom. 8:23, 2 Cor 1:2, 5:5; Eph 1:14) We 'have tasted the goodness of the word of God and the powers of the age to come' (Heb. 6:5)." *Engaging the Powers. Discernment and Resistance in a World of Domination.* (Minneapolis: Fortress Press, 1992). 70. I would add that human beings won't have a foretaste of God's reign unless they actively help out in God's kitchen!

Works Cited

Barcley, William B. *"Christ in You." A Study in Paul's Theology and Ethics*. Lanham, New York, Oxford: University Press of America, 1999.

Bauer, Walter, F. Wilbur Gingrich, and Frederick W. Danker. *A Greek-English Lexicon of the New Testament and Other Early Christian Literature*. Chicago and London: University of Chicago Press, 1979.

Bracken, Joseph A. *The One in the Many. A Contemporary Reconstruction of the God-World Relationship*. Grand Rapids and Cambridge: William B. Eerdmans Publishing Company, 2001.

Brother Casimir, O.C.S.O. "When (the Father) Will Subject All Things to (the Son), Then (the Son) Himself Will Be Subjected to Him (the Father) Who Subjects All Things to Him (the Son) – A Treatise on First Corinthians 15.28 by Saint Gregory of Nyssa." *The Greek Orthodox Theological Review* 28 (1983). 1-11.

Bultmann, Rudolf. *Der Zweite Brief an die Korinther*. Goettingen: Vandenhoeck & Ruprecht, 1976.

Kenelm, Burridge. *New Heaven, New Earth. A Study of Millenarian Activities*. New York: Schocken Books, 1969.

Conzelmann, Hans. *1 Corinthians*. Philadelphia: Fortress Press, 1975.

Davies, W. D. *Paul and Messianic Judaism*. London: SPCK, 1958.

De Boer, Martinus C. "Paul's Use of a Resurrection Tradition in 1 Cor 15,20-28." *The Corinthian Correspondence*. Edited by Reimund Bieringer. Leuven: University Press, 1996. 639-651.

Dykstra, William. "1 Corinthians 15:20-28, an Essential Part of Paul's Argument Against Those Who Deny the Resurrection." *Calvin Theological Journal* 4 (1969). 195-211.

Fitzgerald, John T. "Virtue/Vice Lists." *Anchor Bible Dictionary*. VI. 857-59.

Fredrickson, David. "God, Christ, and All Things in 1 Corinthians 15:28." *Word and World* 18, 3 (1998).

Hill, C. E. "Paul's Understanding of Christ's Kingdom in 1 Corinthians 15:20-28." *Novum Testamentum* XXX, 4 (1988).

Horsley, Richard A. *Bandits, Prophets and Messiahs. Popular Movements in the Time of Jesus*. Harrisburg: Trinity Press International, 1999.

Jansen, John F. "1 Corinthians 15:24-28 and the Future of Jesus Christ." In *Texts and Testaments. Critical Essays on the Bible and Early Church Fathers*. Edited by W. Eugene March. San Antonio: Trinity University Press, 1980. 173-97.

Lambrecht, Jan. "Paul's Christological Use of Scripture in 1 Cor 15:20-28." *New Testament Studies* 28 (1982).

Lienhard, Joseph T. "The Exegesis of 1 Corinthians 15, 24-28 From Marcellus of Ancyra to Theodoret of Cyrus." *Vigiliae Christianae* 37 (1983). 340-359

Lindemann, Andreas. "Die Auferstehung der Toten. Adam und Christus nach 1 Kor 15." In *Eschatologie und Schoepfung. Festschrift fur Erich Grasser zum siebzigsten Geburtstag.* Edited by Martin Evang, Helmut Merklein, and Michael Wolter. Berlin, New York: Walter de Gruyter, 1997.

Martin, Dale. *The Corinthian Body.* New Haven and London: Yale University Press, 1995.

McGaughey, Douglas. *Strangers and Pilgrims.* Berlin, New York: Walter de Gruyter, 1997.

Neugebauer, Fritz. "Das Paulinische 'In Christo'." *New Testament Studies* IV (1957-58). 124-138

Philo of Alexandria. *De Opificio Mundi, De Confusione Linguarum, Quaestiones et Solutiones in Genesin.*

Richards, W. Larry. "*Hypotagesetai* in 1 Corinthians 15:28b." *Andrews University Seminary Studies* 38 (2000).

Robinson, John A. T. *The Body. A Study in Pauline Theology.* London: SCM Press, 1961.

Sauter, Gerhard. *Einfuehrung in die Eschatologie.* Darmstadt: Wissenschaftliche Buchgesellschaft, 1995.

Schmidt, Karl Ludwig. "Basileia" *Theologisches Woerterbuch zum Neuen Testament.* I, 581-2.

Schnelle, Udo. "Transformation und Partizipation als Grundgedanken paulinischer Theologie." *New Testament Studies* 47 (2001).

Schrage, Wolfgang,. "Das messianische Zwischenreich bei Paulus." In *Eschatologie und Schoepfung. Festschrift fur Erich Graesser zum siebzigsten Geburtstag.* Edited by Martin Evang, Helmut Merklein, and Michael Wolter. Berlin, New York: Walter de Gruyter, 1997.

_____. *Der Erste Brief an die Korinther.* Duesseldorf and Neukirchen-Vluyn: Benzinger Verlag und Neukirchener Verlag, 2001.

Schweitzer, Albert. *The Mysticism of Paul the Apostle.* Baltimore and London: Johns Hopkins University Press, 1998.

Schweizer, Eduard. "Die Kirche als Leib Christi in den Paulinischen Homologumena." In his *Neotestamentica. German and English Essays 1951-1963.* Zurich, Stuttgart: Zwingli Verlag, 1963. 274-277.

_____. "1 Corinthians 15:20-28 as Evidence of Pauline Eschatology and its Relations to the Preaching of Jesus." In *Saved by Hope. Essays in Honor of Richard C. Oudersluys.* Edited by James I. Cook. Grand Rapids: Eerdmans, 1978.

Vos, Johan. "Argumentation und Situation in 1 Kor. 15." *Novum Testamentum* 41 (1999). 311-333

Waetjen, Herman. "The Actualization of Christ's Achievement in our Historical Existence: Breaking out of the New Babylonian Captivity." *The Princeton Seminary Bulletin.* XVII, 3 (1996): 291-309.

Watson, Francis. "Is There a Story in These Texts?" In *Narrative Dynamics in Paul. A Critical Assessment.* Edited by Bruce W. Longenecker. Louisville: Westminster John Knox Press, 2002.

Weil, Uta. "Theo-logische Interpretation von 1 Kor 15,23-28." *Zeitschrift fuer die neutestamentliche Wissenschaft* 84 (1993). 27-35.

Weiss, Johannes. *Der Erste Korintherbrief.* Goettingen: Vandenhoeck & Ruprecht, 1910.

Wink, Walter. *Naming the Powers. The Language of Power in the New Testament.* Philadelphia: Fortress Press, 1984.

_____. *Engaging the Powers. Discernment and Resistance in a World of Domination.* Minneapolis: Fortress Press, 1992.

Witherington, Ben. *Conflict and Community in Corinth. A Social-Rhetorical Commentary on 1 and 2 Corinthians.* Grand Rapids, MI and Carlisle: William B. Eerdmans Publishing Company and The Paternoster Press, 1995.

Not "Cleansing" but "Closing Down"

A Narrative-critical and Political Interpretation of the so-called "Cleansing of the Temple" in Mark 11:11-25

Joseph Kang

She lives in a small apartment in the outskirts of St. Petersburg.
She is handicapped, suffering from a serious spine disease.
   Her pension is meager.
When her money runs out, she begs at a supermarket entrance
   For young shoppers to give her a little to buy bread . . .
The lady's name is Tatyana Andreyevna Vysogorets-Dostoyevsky,
   and she is the directly descended great-grand daughter of
      Fyodor Mikhailovich Dostoyevsky,
the world-known author whose books are busily published in many
   languages and sold and read throughout the world.

(From unpublished article by Marina Shishova, "*Christianity, Poverty and Wealth in the 21 Century: Russian Story*," The Orthodox Institute of Missiology, Ecumenism and New Religious Movements: PIMEN)

Introduction

The story of the so-called Jesus' "cleansing" of the Jerusalem temple appears in all four gospels (Matt 21:12-17, Mk 11:15-19, Lk 19:45-48, Jn 2:14-22). The difference between the Synoptic Gospels and the Fourth Gospel is, however, striking. In the Synoptic Gospels the incident happens near the end of Jesus' ministry, seemingly as both a climax and summary of his activity, while the Fourth Gospel presents the incident at the outset of Jesus' ministry. Differences can also be observed in the details of Jesus' action. The description of Jesus' action against the temple is more dramatic in the Fourth Gospel than in the Synoptic Gospels. The conversation between Jesus and the Jews in the Fourth Gospel following Jesus' outrageous action against the temple is not found in the Synoptic Gospels, although the question about Jesus' authority from the Jewish leaders and Jesus' response to the question appear later in a different context in the Synoptic Gospels (Mk 11:27f., par.).

Even in the Synoptic Gospels, which may have shared the same tradition, we also notice significant differences. While Matthew and Mark connect the story of Jesus' action against the temple to the story of Jesus' cursing of the fig tree, Luke omits the story of the fig tree, and makes the story of Jesus' action against the temple very brief. Between Mark and Matthew the difference is also obvious. Matthew "consolidates both into a single episode. As a result the wilting of the fig tree, which must of course be instantaneous, becomes a more impressive basis for Jesus' teaching on faith."[1] In

---

1   Waetjen, H. C., *The Origin and Destiny of Humanness* (San Rafael: Crystal Press, 1976), p. 205.

the meantime the story of Jesus' cursing of the fig tree is separated into two parts in Mark, making a narrative frame for the story of Jesus' attack on the temple.

Form-critical approach to this story focuses on its original *form,* and concludes that the story of Jesus' cursing of fig tree and the story of Jesus' "cleansing" of the temple are originally different *forms.* According to the form-critics, the story of the fig tree is classified as *a miracle story* or *legend* while the story of the temple cleansing is taken as *biographical apophthegm* or *paradigm.*[2] In his analysis of the story of the temple cleansing, Bultmann claims that only Mk 11:15b-17 would probably be considered *apophthegm* although v.17 may be a secondary interpretation of the scene in vv.15ff. that belonged to the original tradition. Of course, he considers that the first sentence of v.15 (καὶ ἔρχονται εἰς Ἱεροσόλυμα) and vv.18ff. are the result of editorial work. The hermeneutic problems caused by this historical-critical approach have long been observed in New Testament scholarship, and we don't need to go into its details here.

Redaction-criticism seems to have somehow overcome the mishaps of the form-criticism as it focuses on the *theology* of each gospel by paying attention to its editorial works. In his redaction-critical study of the story of Jesus' "cleansing" of the temple, Kelber concludes as follows:

> Time and again 11:15-19 has been approached with the objective of extracting a historical reconstruction of the "cleansing" event. But one need only ask the vital *historical* questions to recognize that the text is not calculated to deal with them . . . While the text in its *present form* is unlikely to have recorded from the perspective of Jesus' history, it assumes a vital role in the theological program of Mark and is ultimately designed to answer Mark's historical question.[3]

In many aspects, Kelber's reading of the story is very analytical and quite penetrating. He makes a critical and relevant assessment of Mark's editorial technique in the interpolation of the "cleansing of the temple" (11:15-19) into the story of the fig tree fatality (11:12-14, 20-21). Kelber explains that by this means of interpolation Mark communicates a possible interrelationship between fig tree and temple, withering and "cleansing", which is obviously an integral part in the story. He also makes a convincing explanation of Jesus' expulsion of the trades-people and their sacrificial birds in terms of an attack directed against the temple as a whole. Finally, he quite correctly concludes: "In the view of Mark, therefore, Jesus not only puts an end to the temple's business operation, but also suspends the practice of cult and ritual. At this point the temple no longer operates. It is shut down in all its functions."[4]

In my view, while he remains in his hermeneutic camp of redaction-criticism as far as his first writing *The Kingdom in Mark* is concerned, Kelber has still paved a good way toward *narrative criticism* which then allows for a political reading of the story.

During the last twenty years or so, remarkable achievements have been made in the narrative criticism and political reading of Mark's Gospel, and it is not a coincidence that we find Kelber's subsequent writings done according to this discipline.[5] The

2   Bultmann, R., *History of the Synoptic Tradition* (New York: Harper & Row, 1963), 3rd. ed., pp. 36, 218; Dibelius, M., *From Tradition to Gospel* (New York: Charles Scribners' Sons, 1935.), p. 106.

3   Kelber, W., *The Kingdom in Mark: A New Place and a New Time* (Philadelphia: Fortress Press, 1974), pp. 98-9.

4   Kelber, *Ibid.*, p. 101.

5   Kelber W., *Mark as Story of Jesus* (Philadelphia: Fortress Press, 1979). This narrative-critical

narrative-critical interpretation considers each gospel as integral writing, not merely as an editor's or a theologian's work. And it approaches the biblical stories not as a historical source for something that lies behind the text but as a literary text that can be analyzed in its literary plot, characterization, point of view, etc. Narrative criticism tries to view the biblical story as an interactive whole, with harmonies and tensions that develop in the course of narration.[6] As Powell explains, "The narrative criticism that is currently practiced in NT studies is an eclectic discipline that borrows from a number of areas, including rhetorical criticism, structuralism, and reader-response criticism. The method is still undergoing development..."[7]

"Since the picture of Jesus that is offered by the Gospel is conditioned by the realities of [social] context that permeates the author's stock of material, its comprehension requires some knowledge of Mark's 'extra-textual' world."[8] This would be accomplished by looking into the sociopolitical context of the story. Along with sociological interpretation, a political reading of the Gospel is believed to help us understand the narrative world in more concrete ways. In this short article I would not dare to go beyond what has been achieved by these hermeneutic disciplines. If I could, however, I would attempt to make a little more elaboration on the previous interpretations.

Jesus, in Solidarity with the Starved

"Journey" provides a thematic structure to the Markan narrative of Jesus. Mark begins the story of Jesus with the phrase, "the beginning of the good news of Jesus Christ" (1:1), which is followed by the presumably conflated citation from two or three Septuagint texts of the Hebrew Scripture (Isa. 40:3, Mal 3:1 or Exod 23:20) about "construction of the way" (1:2-3).[9] This "way" motif appears most often in the middle section of the Gospel in description of Jesus' journey to Jerusalem, which begins on the way to the villages around Caesaria Philippi in gentile territory (8:27).[10] The journey moves back through Galilee (9:30) to Capernaum (9:33), then to the region of

---

interpretation of Mark was produced five years after his first redaction-critical interpretation, *The Kingdom in Mark*. Later more publications have been made by the same discipline. See, Rhoads, D., and Michie, D., *Mark as Story. An Introduction to the Narrative of a Gospel* (Philadelphia: Fortress Press, 1982); Malbon, E. S., *Narrative Space and Mythic Meaning in Mark* (San Francisco: Harper & Row, 1986); Kingsbury, J.D., *Conflict in Mark: Jesus, Authorities, Disciples* (Minneapolis: Fortress Press, 1989); Camery-Hoggatt, J., *Irony in Mark's Gospel: Text and Subtext*, SNTSMS 72 (Cambridge: Cambridge Univ, 1992); In the area of political reading we may include Belo, F., *A Material Reading of the Gospel of Mark* (Maryknoll, N.Y: Orbis Books, 1981); Almost at the same time two books were published with the subtitles, "Political or Socio-political reading." See, Myers, C., *Binding the Strong Man: A Political Reading of Mark's Story of Jesus* (Maryknoll: Orbis Books, 1988); and Waetjen, H. C., *A Reordering of Power: A Socio-Political Reading of Mark's Gospel* (Minneapolis: Fortress Press, 1989).

6   See, Tannenhill, R., "Narrative Criticism," Coggins, R.J., and Houlden, J. L. ed., *A Dictionary of Biblical Interpretation* (London: SCM Press; Philadelphia: Trinity Press International, 1990), p. 488.

7   Powell, M. A., "Narrative Criticism," Green, J.B., ed., *Hearing the New Testament. Strategies for Interpretation* (Grand Rapids: Eerdmans, 1995), p. 240.

8   Waetjen, H. C., *Reordering*, p.4

9   So, was the title, *The Beginning of the Gospel - Construction of the Way*, [in Korean], (Seoul: Korean Institute of Theological Studies, 1991) was given by Kang, J. for his writing on Mark's Gospel.

10 In this section the word, "way" (ὁ ὁδός) occurs eight times. For more detailed discussion, see Rhoads and Michie, *Mark as Story*, p. 64; See also Waetjen, *op. cit.*, pp. 171f.

Judea and beyond the Jordan (10:1). Finally, as Mk 10:32 describes: "They were on the **way**, going up to Jerusalem, and Jesus was walking ahead of them." Jesus' journey is going to end in confrontation and death in Jerusalem.

Approaching Jerusalem, Jesus encamps at Bethphage and Bethany, near the Mount of Olives (11:1). This must refer to Zech 14:2-4:

> For I will gather all the nations against Jerusalem to battle,
>   and the city shall be taken and the houses looted and the women raped;
> Half the city shall go into exile. . .

> Then the Lord will go forth and fight against those nations
>   as when he fights on a day of battle.
> On that day his feet shall stand on the Mount of Olives,
>   which lies before Jerusalem on the east . . .

From Bethany where Mount Olive stands, Jesus enters Jerusalem as "*the one who comes in the name of the Lord*" (11:1-10, esp. v.9). In the city he comes to the temple "*to look around at everything*," and "only to vacate it at nightfall and to depart from the city altogether" (v.11).[11] The expression, περιβλεψάμενος does not denote a tourist's look[12] but a critical or even judgmental look by Jesus.[13] He enters, subjects the entire *cosmic pillar* or *the cosmic egg*[14] of the Jewish world in his critical eyes, and leaves. "The entry and exit motifs are tightly contracted in this episode. As it had formerly been his habit to enter and leave a house, a boat, a synagogue, a town, so does he now go in and out of the temple. In this manner the centrality of the temple is passed over and the center of life is relativized to a mere transitional stage on Jesus' way. The temple is devoid of a sense of fulfillment and finality . . ."[15]

On the following day (τῇ ἐπαύριον) Jesus comes to Jerusalem again. Yet, just coming out of Bethany he feels hungry (v.12b). Seeing a fig tree full of leaves in the distance Jesus approaches it so that he might get some figs. But he doesn't find any of the fruit he hoped for. Apparently because he was so disappointed, Jesus curses the tree: "*From now on may no one ever eat fruit from you!*" (vv.13-14).

Here in this episode we can find at least two expressions unreasonable or even absurd: "*he was hungry*"; and "*he found nothing but leaves, for it was not the season for figs*." First, the expression that Jesus was hungry doesn't make good sense as he is just coming out of Bethany, probably soon after breakfast in the morning. Two phrases, ". . . *As it was already late, he went out to Bethany with the twelve*" in v.11b, and the opening phrase of v.12, "*On the following day*" imply that Jesus' journey from Bethany to Jerusalem should have taken place in the morning.[16] Although the Hebrew name of the town 'Bethany' means "*house of the poor*," we don't have any indication in the text that Jesus and his disciples did not have any meal there.

---

11 Kelber, *Kingdom*, p. 98
12 Cf. Nineham, D. E., *The Gospel of St. Mark* (Baltimore: Penguin Books, 1964), p. 294.
13 Cf. The same expressions appear in 3:5,34, 5:32, and 10:23.
14 Eliade, M., *The Sacred and the Profane: The Nature of Religion* (Harvard Books, 1959), pp. 176-77.
15 Kelber, *ibid*.
16 So does Waetjen write, "On the following morning . . ." in *Reordering*, p. 181

Finding the expression, *"he was hungry"* (ἐπείνασεν) problematic, New Testament commentators either simply ignore it or explain it as "an explanation that was added later, since the disappointment of a hungry person is not sufficient provocation for a curse like this. Such a curse can be understood only as a sign of judgment upon Israel."[17] We may not find any convincing answer for our historical questions concerning all the details in the story. However, we can perhaps see the implication the author may have intended in this narrative. In my view, the phrase, *"he was hungry"* becomes the core of the matter that makes what comes next significantly explicit. In fact it effectively sets the tone of the entire story. If we accept the close relationship between the two stories of Jesus' cursing of the fig tree and the story of Jesus' so-called "cleansing" of the temple, and take Jesus' cursing of fig tree as a symbolic gesture for his judgmental negation of the temple, as we will explore more in detail later, the phrase, *"he was hungry"* must also be explained in the same line of symbolism. Thus, in its symbolic line, Jesus' hunger would best be understood as his **shared hunger** with the impoverished Jewish ὄχλος and ἔθνος. In other words, we can explain Jesus' hunger in terms of his identification or solidarity with the mass number of people (cf. v. 17),[18] who have been suffering poverty and hunger in the midst of affluence[19] provided and controlled by the temple economy. As he feels hungry, Jesus is feeling nothing else but the quest for basic human need.

We also find the second unreasonable expression in v.13*b*, *"When he came to it, he found nothing but leaves, for it was not the season for figs."* Out of his own hunger Jesus seeks figs from the tree: *"(as) if he could find anything on it!"* The Greek expression, τι εὑρήσει ἐν αὐτῇ should be understood as Jesus' query for fruits, as the beginning phrase of v.14, καὶ ἀποκριθεὶς εἶπεν αὐτῇ indicates. At any rate, he finds no figs but leaves since *"it is out of season."* What was expected of the tree, particularly considering that it was out of season, seems to be unreasonable, and this expectation is not fulfilled. This outcome has a surprising and extremely unreasonable verdict on the tree: *"May no one ever eat fruit from you again!"* The tree itself has not done anything wrong. Absolutely not! What is wrong is Jesus' ridiculous cursing of it! The fig tree must be doing just fine, as demonstrated by the fact that it is full of green leaves promising bountiful fruits in due season. "Certainly Jesus, who has lived in Palestine all his life, is aware of this. A tree that participates in the orderly cycles of nature can only produce its fruit in season."[20] How can we then explain this awkward sentence? The historical-critical explanation, i.e., that this remark was not a part of the original story, but was added later when the story was included in the events before the Passover, is not at all convincing.

---

17 Schweizer,E., *The Good News According to Mark* (Atlanta: John Knox Press, 1976), p. 232; See also, Kelber, *ibid*.

18 Jesus' solidarity with the poor is well attested by the expression, "he saw a large crowd (ὄχλος), and he was moved with compassion (ἐσπλαγχνίσθη) . . ." in Mk 6:34. See, also Mk 8:2 where his compassion for the ὄχλος who have nothing to eat is illustrated.

19 For the great luxury in the houses of the high-priestly families, see Jeremias, J., *Jerusalem in the Time of Jesus* (Philadelphia: Fortress Press, 1969), pp. 95f.

20 Waetjen, *Ibid*.

It may be true that "no one has been able to explain the strange statements to the satisfaction of other commentators."[21] In my view, however, Kelber makes a plausible theological explanation of this problem in the framework of Markan eschatology:

> ὁ γὰρ καιρὸς οὐκ ἦν σύκων the very clause which disrupts the logic of the story, is one of Mark's gar clauses which invite the reader to understand the context in the light of something outside the data explicitly presented to us.... Mark's mentioning of *kairos* points outside the immediate fig tree plot to the principle affirmation of the arrival of the *kairos* in 1:15 . . . In a general sense, the fig tree disaster demonstrates the abortion of the *kairos* and the frustration of the arrival of the Kingdom. The *kairos* is fulfilled in Galilee, but unfulfilled in Jerusalem.[22]

Moreover, by taking illustrations in the Hebrew prophets (Jer 8:13, Is 28:3f., Hos 9:10,16, Mi 7:1, Jl 1:7, 12) and several other supplementary texts Telford makes a helpful description of the symbolic significance of the fig tree or fig:

> The fig tree was an emblem of peace, security, and prosperity and is prominent when descriptions of the Golden Ages of Israel's history, past, present, and future, are given —the Garden of Eden, the Exodus, the Wilderness, the Promised Land, the reigns of Solomon and Simon Maccabaeus, and the coming Messianic Age. It figures predominantly in the prophetic books and very often in passages with an *eschatological* import . . .

> The blossoming of the fig-tree and its *giving of its fruits* is a descriptive element in passages which depict Yahweh's visiting his people with *blessing*, while the *withering of the fig tree*, the destruction or withholding of its fruit, figures in imagery describing *Yahweh's judgment* upon his people or their enemies. The theme of judgment is, if anything, more pronounced in the prophetic books. Very often the reason given . . . is cultic aberration...*a corrupt Temple cult and sacrificial system*. In some cases, indeed, the fig or fig-tree . . . can be used expressly as a symbol for *the nation itself* . . . Who could doubt, then, the extraordinary impact that Jesus' cursing of the fig-tree would have produced upon the Markan reader, schooled to recognize symbolism wherever it occurred.[23]

Telford's explanation allows us to read the story in a more concrete and integrated way in its narrative context. Jesus' irrational and malicious verdict on the tree, therefore, can be understood better in light of what he does to the temple in the following story. That is, the cursing of the fig tree foreshadows Jesus' negation of the temple. This may be the reason why the outcome of Jesus' curse is postponed until after his outrageous action against the temple in vv.15-17. By cursing the barren tree, Jesus shares the disillusionment and evaporated hope of the common people living in the midst of incredible wealth generated by the priestly-run temple economy, which is symbolized by the fact that the tree is *full of leaves*. As Myers explains, "the symbolic action of Jesus' cursing of the fig tree is Mark's own little haggadic tale, as well as a midrash on Hosea 9:16. Its narrative function is to begin Jesus' ideological project of

---

21 Juel, D. H., Mark. Augusburg *Commentary on the New Testament* (Minneapolis: Augusburg, 1990), p. 156.

22 Kelber, *Kingdom*, pp. 99-100. He refers to Schreiber, J., *Theologie des Vertrauens* (Hamburg: Furche-Verlag, 1967).

23 Telford, W., *The Barren Temple and the Withered Tree*. JSNT Supplementary Series I, (Sheffield: JSOT Press, 1980), pp. 161ff.

subverting the temple-centered social order. The reappearance of the fig tree in the apocalyptic parable (13:28-32) at the conclusion to this section confirms this. In the second sermon, the leafy (i.e., fruitless) fig tree is offered as a sign of the 'end time'. The world that is coming to an end is the world of the temple-based state."[24]

Not Cleansing, but Closing Down!

The story of Jesus' action against the temple (vv. 15-19) can be divided into three parts:

1. Coming upon Jerusalem. Jesus enters *into* the temple taking actions against it (vv.15-16);

2. Teaching (v.17); and

3. Reaction of the Jewish authority toward Jesus (vv. 18-19).

The first part of the story begins with the phrase, *"Coming [into] Jerusalem"* (v.15a). By this expression, Jesus' outrageous verdict on the fig tree is implicitly connected to this old capital city. A further elaboration is made by the phrase, καὶ εἰσελθὼν εἰς τὸ ἱερὸν. The purpose of Jesus' coming to Jerusalem is depicted by the phrase, *"entering [into] the temple."* So, another extended link is made between the fig tree and the temple itself. Two aorist verbs and one imperfect verb are used to describe what the purposeful entry of Jesus into the temple was: *"Began to throw out . . .," "overturned . . .,"* and *"was not letting anyone carry utensils . . ."* All of these actions are taking place *"[in] the temple"* after Jesus enters *[into]* the temple. It is noteworthy that the word, "temple," (εἰς τὸ ἱερὸν ἐν τῷ ἱερῷ διὰ τοῦ ἱεροῦ) is used three times without indicating the Court of Gentiles.[25] Many New Testament commentators take the temple only as a religious institution, which leads to religious/theological reductionism. The temple was, however, "the basis of a whole political-economic-religious system headed by the priestly aristocracy."[26] Moreover, the temple was functioning as an instrument for the Roman imperial legitimation and its control over a subjected people. Jesus' action can be thus understood as his attack *"inside the sacred precinct"*[27] against the temple itself.

First, Jesus launches an exorcising expulsion (v.15b: *began to throw out)* of the business people.[28] He drives out those who are trading *(selling and buying)* [in the

---

24 Myers, *Binding*, p. 299.

25 See, Schweizer, *Mark*, p. 233. He explains, "This is Mark's indication that Jesus is thinking of Israel when he utters the curse—that Israel which does not open its temple to him, thus keeping it closed to all nations. There is no other reason for disturbing the moneychangers and merchants. For they were situated in the Court of the Gentiles, which was not sacred although it was not totally secular." He fails to see Mark's literary plot by paying too much attention to the historical facts which the implied author of Mark has no concern. Cf. Also, Kee, H. C., *Community of the New Age. Studies in Mark's Gospel* (Philadelphia: The Westminster Press, 1977), pp. 114f.

26 Horsley, R. A., *Jesus and the Spiral of Violence: Popular Jewish Resistance in Roman Palestine* (San Francisco: Harper & Row, 1987), p. 287.

27 Waetjen, *Reordering*, p. 181.

28 Here we can see the correlation between two of Jesus' exorcisms in Capernaum in a synagogue (1:21ff.) and in Gerasene (5:1-20). This is not fully elaborated but just hinted in Kelber, *Kingdom in Mark,* p.100; and Myers, *Binding the Strong Man*, p. 305.

temple]. It is not explicitly expressed what is being sold and bought, although it can easily be imagined in the light of Jeremias' explanation:

> On the Mount of Olives were two cedars, under one of which were "four shops belonging to sellers of things necessary for sacrifices of purification," which suggests especially doves, lambs, sheep, oil and meal . . . The position of *Migdal Sebo'ayya*, which means Tower of the Dyers, is uncertain. Here were allegedly three hundred shops for the sale of clean animals for sacrifice, and eighty for fine woolen fabrics . . .
>
> According to j. Bets. ii.4, 61c.13, R. Baba b. Buta (a contemporary of Herod the Great) had three thousand head of small livestock brought to the Temple hill to be sold for whole burnt-offerings and peace-offerings. . . These shops apparently belonged to the high-priestly family . . . So we are forced to conclude that in the Court of the Gentiles, in spite of the sanctity of the Temple area, there could have been a flourishing trade in animals for sacrifice, perhaps supported by the powerful high-priestly family of Annas.[29]

Jesus also overturns the tables of money changers, who must be seen as street level representatives of banking interests of considerable power.[30] These money changers are quite suitable symbols of oppressive financial institutions. Doves were sold primarily for the purification of women (Lev 12:6, Lk 2:22-24), the cleansing of lepers (Lev 14:22) and other purposes (Lev 15:14,29). In other words, they were used for sacrificial offerings, mainly from the poor.

Jesus' action in the temple thus should be understood "as an attack directed against the temple as a whole. His disruption of the business transactions wrecks the center of life."[31] His action calls for an end to the entire economic and political system, symbolized by his "overturning" (κατέστρεψεν, which can also mean to "destroy") of the stations used by these two groups. Viewed with "the worm's eyes,"[32] they are none other than representatives of the concrete mechanism of oppression within a political economy that doubly exploit the poor and unclean.

The third and final action denotes that the ultimate goal of these disruptive steps was to shut down the temple's cultic operations altogether (v.16). He "*was not letting anyone carry any utensils* [σκεῦος, here meaning any vessel or item needed for the cult] *through the temple.*" Jesus not only calls an end to the economic and political operation of the temple, but he also suspends the temple's cultic and ritual practice. Waetjen makes an eloquent explanation:

> This is not an act of *reformation* intended to eliminate business activities from the observance of the cult or to separate trade and commerce from the worship of God. Jesus is not "*cleansing the temple.*" As "the one who comes in the name of the Lord," he is *closing it down* . . . Ending the payment of the temple tax and the sale of doves and terminating all activity in the sacred precinct signify the end of the cult and its hierocracy and the tributary mode of distribution which both maintain.[33]

---

29 Jeremias, *Jerusalem in the Time of Jesus*, pp. 48-49.

30 Myers, *Binding.*, p. 301.

31 Kelber, *Kingdom*, p.100; See also Horsley, *op. cit.*, p. 300; cf., Achtemeier, P., *Mark*. Proclamation Commentaries (Philadelphia: Fortress Press, 1975), p. 24.

32 Hill, C., *The World Turned Upside Down* (Penguin Books, 1972). p.14.

33 Waetjen, *Reordering*, p. 182. *Italics* are mine. Therefore, the question whether or not Jesus attempted to take over the temple is not valid in the narrative world of this story. See Horsley, *ibid.*, p. 299 for the

At this point, Jesus makes a justification for his apparently violent and blasphemous action of closing down of the temple, the most important *point of reference* for the Jewish people: "Is it not written, 'My house shall be called a house of prayer for all nations'? But you have made it a den of bandits!" (v.17) Jesus here cites the two great prophets, Isaiah (56:7) and Jeremiah (7:11). In 56:1-8, (the so-called "Third Isaiah") the prophet Isaiah narrates Yahweh's promise to the foreigner and the socially marginal:

> And the foreigners who join
>   themselves to the Lord,
> to minister to him, to love the name of the Lord. . .
> These I will bring to my holy mountain,
>   and make them joyful in my
>   house of prayer;
> For my house shall be called a
>   house of prayer
> for all peoples. (vv. 6-7)

The "house of prayer" on the "holy mountain" (Isa 56:7) should be a place of joy for all who are dispossessed (Isa 56:8). The reality of the temple, however, is far from the divine will expressed in the Scripture: "But you have made it a den of robbers!" The metaphor "den of robbers" is taken from Jeremiah 7:11 (LXX). Jeremiah insists that Yahweh's dwelling with Israel in the "Lord's house" and "in the land" will take place only insofar as justice toward the alien, the fatherless, the widow, and the innocent is maintained (Jer 7:5-7). If stealing, murder, idolatry and exploitation flourish, however, the temple will be destroyed, as was the first shrine at Shiloh (Jer 7:9-15). Thus the expression, "You have made it a den of robbers" becomes the sole ground of Jesus' closing down of the temple itself.

Just as Jesus' disciples *"were hearing"* his cursing of the fig tree (v.14), the Jewish authorities, represented by the chief priests and the scribes *"heard"* his words/action, and *"sought a way to destroy him"* (v.18). The plot to kill Jesus made by the Pharisees and Herodians in Galilee (3:6) is now extended to Jerusalem, this time by the highest national leadership. While the Jewish leadership is determined once again to kill Jesus, *"the whole crowd"* is spellbound. Throughout the Jerusalem narrative the arrest/death attempt denotes the political maneuvering by the Jewish authorities against Jesus (cf. 12:12, 14:1, 11, 55). When they find their national security and entire debt system in threat by this Galilean Jesus, embodying the eschatologically expected New Human Being,[34] the high priests and Scribes have no alternatives but to exterminate him. The dark age is still at work, although it is in extreme fear itself. Paradoxically fear becomes the reason behind their attempt to kill Jesus. The phrase, *"For they were afraid of him . . ."* seems to modify both the previous sentence and the following one as well. His death is now just a matter of time. Jesus himself knows what lies before him as he predicted on his way to Jerusalem (cf. 8:31, 9:31, and 10:33-34). Later the high priest will pronounce the death sentence onto Jesus charging him of *"his blasphemy"* (15:64; cf. 2:7). But when Jesus dies on the cross, the curtain of *"the temple"* is to be

---

discussion on that issue.

34 This expression is based on Waetjen's interpretation of Jesus' baptism in *Reordering*, pp. 68-74.

torn apart from top to bottom (15:38). In the meantime the story of Jesus' closing down of the temple operation comes to its end with the expression: *"And when evening came, they went out of the city"* (v.19).

"Have *the Faith of God!*"

When Jesus and his disciples pass by the next morning, they witness the effect of the curse on the fig tree. They find the fig tree dried up *from* its roots (v.20). The perfect passive participle form of verb, εξηραμμενην depicts that the tree has been dried up from the moment Jesus cursed it. "It is impossible to determine whether the tree withered from the roots upward or from the branches downward. Obviously this detail is oriented toward the temple which the fig tree symbolizes and conveys the finality of its rejection. There is no hope for renewal or revitalization, for the roots are dead; and it is only a matter of time before the rest of the tree reveals this terminal condition."[35]

As Myers correctly notices,[36] the conflation of the temple action and the fig tree curse prompts us to use both the Malachi and Hosea tradition as hermeneutic keys. The "whole nation" is implicated in "robbing" Yahweh through the corruption of the temple sacrifice and tithing system (Mal 3:9), which makes the "disobedient princes" rich (Hos 9:15). Israel is challenged to repent—that is, to restore economic justice—in order to receive "blessing" (Mal 3:10-12). If it does not, Yahweh will "send Elijah the prophet" (Mal 4:5) to issue one last call to repentance: "So that I will not come and smite the land with a curse" (Mal 4:6*b*). But it is this curse that has been enacted: "Ephraim is stricken, their root is dried up, and they shall bear no fruit . . ." (Hos 9:16).

Peter, the spokesperson of the Twelve, recalls the curse Jesus previously made and exclaims, "Rabbi, look! The fig tree which you cursed is dried up!" (v.21) Jesus now turns to his disciples to convince them not only that the temple-based social order can be overturned, but also that they should reconstruct their collective symbolic life apart from the old order. So then Jesus says, "**Have the faith of God!**" (v.22, Έχετε πίστιν θεοῦ). Regarding this extraordinary phrase Waetjen gives a unique but relevant explanation:

> Although his exhortation is generally translated into English as "Have faith in God!" the preposition 'in' does not occur in the Greek text. A genitive construction is employed which is usually identified as an "objective genitive." That is, the word in the genitive case, "God," is considered to be the object of the word it modifies, in this case "faith." But there is no other instance of an objective genitive in Mark's Gospel. Moreover, such a translation would seem to be out of place in view of Jesus' entry into a reordering of power and the resulting horizontal relationship he enjoys with the Creator. As the New Human Being, he displays that "the confidence of God" is like by stilling the storm and walking on the Sea of Galilee. It is the capacity to exercise divine sovereignty over chaos and the creative capability of ordering a world that is no longer determined by fixed boundaries between the sacred and the profane.[37]

This explanation certainly fits the plot of Mark's story of Jesus. On the basis of such an understanding of Jesus' exhortation, we may say that only when one risks the same

---

35 Waetjen, *Reordering*, p. 184.
36 Myers, *Binding*, p. 304.
37 Waetjen, *Reordering*, pp. 184-5.

faith of God (cf. 4:40), he/she could say to *"this mountain,"* "Be raised up and thrown into the sea!" (v.23). In the narrative context of Mark, the expression "this mountain" can only refer to the temple Mount—Mt. Zion.[38] The command to be cast into the sea also recalls the identical symbolic action narrated in the story of the Gerasene demoniac (5:1-20). By exercising such absolute confidence of God one enters into a horizontal relationship with the Creator, as demonstrated by Jesus' closing down of the *axis mundi* of the old age, symbolized by his cursing of the fig tree. It is what prayer is all about: "So, I tell you, whatever you ask for in prayer, believe that you received it, and it will be yours!" (v.24)

So does Jesus conclude, "When you stand praying, forgive if you have anything against anyone; so that your Father in heaven also forgives you your trespasses!" (v.25) Most New Testament commentators find this saying of Jesus on prayer a secondary addition as with v.26 (*omitted in RSV and NRSV texts*) allegedly because of "the rule of forgiving."[39] However, in the light of the same theme of prayer introduced by Jesus' citation of Isa 11:17 in v.17, there is no doubt about its narrative coherence. The same theme is also attested in v. 24 following Jesus' exhortation to the disciples to have "the faith of God."

The fifth petition of the Lord's Prayer must be the background here, where the expression, "debt" (ὀφειλήματα) in Matthew should be preferred to the expression, "sin" (ἁμαρτίας) in Luke.[40] In Mark the term, παραπτώματα, translated in English as "trespasses," is used. In Matthew these two expressions, "debts" and "trespasses" are interchangeably used, while the expressions "sins" and "debts" are used in the same manner in Luke. In Mark's narrative context, παραπτώματα have more economic and political implications than religious. We have seen how Jesus symbolically canceled the Jewish debt system that the Jerusalem temple was embodying. The temple symbolized by the barren fig tree only full of green leaves was characterized as *"a den of robbers"* by Jesus. We may explain it in terms of the temple's *unforgiving* nature, thus only *binding, enslaving and exploiting* (cf. Mk 12:38f.). Subverting the *unforgiving* house of prayer, Jesus now invites those who join in the *"faith of God"* to exercise such faith in *praxis* by the cancellation of all kinds of indebtedness so that everyone experiences nothing but total freedom. The *praxis* of forgiveness by the community of New Human Being (implied by *"you"* in the plural form) becomes the replacement of the old redemptive/debt system represented by the temple. This new community of faith becomes **"the house of prayer for all nations"** as inequality in all its forms is prevented by the inclusiveness, the *praxis* of reconciliation and the renunciation of power and privilege!

---

38 Cf. Waetjen, *ibid.*; Myers, *Binding.*, p. 305; Telford, *Barren Temple*, pp. 118f; and Kelber, *Kingdom*, p. 103.

39 Schweizer, *Mark*, p. 235.

40 Cf. Jeremias, J., *The Prayers of Jesus* (London, 1967) p. 92; See also, Waetjen, *Praying the Lord's Prayer. An Ageless Prayer for Today* (Harrisburg: Trinity Press, 1999), pp. 82f.

Poetics of Trust in God
A Feminist Perspective on the Eschatology of Jesus

Luise Schottroff

This essay deals with basic hermeneutical questions concerning the eschatology of Jesus: the relevance of mythical language, the critique of traditional Christian dualism, the presupposition of linear time, and the impact of Christian anti-Judaism. On this background the second part of the paper presents exegeses of eschatological texts in the Synoptic tradition, especially those which speak about the messianic banquet. (please correct mistakes in my English).

Hermeneutical Foundations

The Future from God's Hand

Whose Hope? The Social Historical Question

"The question whether and under what conditions an apocalyptic frame of mind connects the expectation of world destruction with horror or with hope (or whether that is a false alternative), is a historical and at the same time a practical-political question. It is the same with the question whether the avowal of apocalypticism leads to world flight and resignation or to criticism and opposition. The apocalyptic conviction that the world will not continue on as it is draws a different response depending on whether one profits from the situation or is its victim ."[1] The same is true of the expectation of the kingdom of God: What need do I have of the expectation of the kingdom when everything is well with me and when I can only hope that everything remains as it is, that everything continues as it has until now? Thus, the following investigation of the eschatology of Jesus will be directed throughout to people who speak or dream of world destruction or who envision the kingdom of God only as a future reality. Yet if we neglect the realities of life now, every hope, every statement about the future or about God is ambiguous. That means that reflection about the eschatology of Jesus must deal with both: the realities of life that stand behind historical texts and also with the contemporary social realities of interpreters or prophets in the present time.

Why do I ask about the eschatology of Jesus? My present reality is determined by a far-reaching social resignation. The destruction of the natural foundations of life through the pressures of the market and of profit-making has been driven out of the social agenda. Those who are threatened by joblessness and poverty still attempt to seize a scrap of the vanishing prosperity. Nothing can be changed, everything can only become worse.

I live in a world in which 80% poor and supposedly superfluous stand over and against a prosperous 20%. While in Germany the gap is not so wide, many sense a menacing future. Why do I ask about the eschatology of Jesus? In the Jesus tradition I hear the language of hope, a poetics of trust in God, from which I want to learn. This

---

1   Jürgen Ebach, *Apokalypse. Zum Ursprung einer Stimmung*, in: *Einwürfe* 2, München 1985, (5-61) 6.

language of hope opens up new horizons to me and others. Before I clarify the concept "poetics," let me state clearly that the methodological basis for the present engagement with the eschatology of Jesus is that I proceed from social-historical questions about the people who come to expression in this tradition. And I ask at the same time about the contemporary life world and the social context of the interpreters. It should be an essential component of scholarly method to reflect on one's own hermeneutic in an engagement with history. The social-historical question is correspondingly relevant for the historical material. Even though I use the Western exegetical tradition of interpretation, it is the exception when this tradition asks about the social realities which stand behind the eschatological tradition of the Synoptic gospels. In this tradition the social-historical question seldom influences the interpretation of texts, even if it surfaces at the margins.[2]

Demythologizing and the Relevance of Myth

Rudolf Bultmann's demythologizing program of 1941[3] brought liberation from fundamentalist pressure to several generations of Christians. According to Bultmann, the eschatological texts of the NT do not have be taken literally. They are not to be read as God's timetable for the future. For Bultmann, it was an anachronism to accept and to repristinate[4] concepts of mythical eschatology, as, for example, the existence of demons; that is, to accept these concepts literally and interpret them as compulsory for believers and exert pressure and fear with them. This aspect of the demythologizing program-which can only be noted briefly here-has lost nothing of its liberating power. However, I must criticize two other central aspects of this program: 1) the anti-Jewish distinction between Christian eschatology and its opposite pole, Jewish Apocalyptic, which was evaluated negatively by Bultmann; and 2) the reduction of myth to a supposedly obsolete "mythical world-view," an assumption which is expressed by the very word "demythologizing." Bultmann himself interpreted the resurrection of Christ "existential", but in self-contradiction to his program he did not really demythologize it. There "is a mythological remainder"[5] in Bultmann's own work.

At this point the scholarly discussion has gone further. To be sure, the gospels do not narrate an eschatological myth as a continuous end-time drama fit for recital, but they speak in the language of myth. From the point of view of the history of religion, the promise that the *praeis*/meek will inherit the earth (Mt 5:5) is just as mythical as a narrative of a primeval time of creation. My interest in the use of the word "myth" relates to Bultmann's demythologizing program. All the conceptions of the NT which

---

2   The social historical investigation of Luzia Sutter Rehmann offers an exception to this rule; see *"Geh, frage die Gebärerin . . .": Feministisch-befreiungstheologische Untersuchungen zum Gebärmotiv in der Apokalyptik, Gütersloh*: Chr. Kaiser, 1995. For the social history of apocalyptic expectation Alfred Bertholet, *Daniel und die griechische Gefahr*, Tübingen: J. C. B. Mohr (Paul Siebeck), 1907, is still methodologically relevant.

3   Rudolf Bultmann, *Neues Testament und Mythologie. Das Problem der Entmythologisierung der neutestamentlichen Verkündigung*, München: Chr. Kaiser, 1941, 27-69. (ET: "New Testament and Mythology: The Problem of Demythologizing," in *New Testament and Mythology and Other Basic Writings*, ed. and trans. Schubert Ogden, Philadelphia: Fortress Press, 1984, 14-43).

4   Rudolf Bultmann, loc. cit. 15f.

5   Rudolf Bultmann, loc. cit., 41. Bultmann formulates here a question in the conviction that no "mythological remainder" is left over. I answer the question differently than he with a "Yes, there is and has to be a mythological remainder."

he calls mythical I regard as mythical too. However, I do not agree in all cases with Bultmann's project of demythologizing. Some myths express a truth that cannot be said differently. Without mythical speech it is impossible to speak of God. Occasionally there are attempts to distinguish between a non-Christian myth and a Christian "myth" in order to find a place for Christian dogmatics which is independent of mythical suspicion. The apologetic distinction between a non-Christian myth as untrue and objectifying and a Christian myth which is really myth in a completely different sense is an expression of a pretentious Christian claim to the sole religious truth over against other religions. The eschatology of the NT is mythology which -- viewed from the perspective of the academic study of religion-- belongs to the many-voiced choir of human religion, the truth of which I can understand without taking it literally as fundamentalists do.

I want to value the mythical eschatology of the evangelists, however, precisely in its poetic power. Mythical speech does not--as would also be conceivable--serve the contemporary lore of natural history, to describe heaven and earth. Its images arise from the First Testament tradition of lament, of divine praise, and of promise, and they rank with the best in poetic world literature. I deliberately do not therefore "define" "myth" and "poetry/poetics" systematically, but rather pragmatically -- and referring to historical material. The eschatology of Jesus should be understood, therefore, as myth and as poetry. The language of this myth and this poetry is directly comprehensible even to contemporary people, precisely because it is mythical and poetic.

Dualistic Eschatology or the Unity of Heaven and Earth

In the Christian interpretation of the eschatological Jesus tradition, dualistic interpretative paradigms are dominant: "this world" (*Diesseits*) and "the other world" (*Jenseits*), history and the kingdom of God, earth and heaven are radically distinguished. According to this paradigm, in the eschatology of Jesus history is conceived as a continuous, linear occurrence that rushes to a radical end. "This world," the earth, is a place of divine remoteness and of transitoriness; only "the other world," the kingdom of God, brings true salvation and redemption. This dualism in the Christian understanding of eschatology has been criticized especially sharply by Rosemary Radford Ruether,[6] and I gladly take over her critique without reservation. Ruether criticizes the conception of an ultimate future, an end of history, and a linear plan of salvation as Christian imperialism. She criticizes the conception of the separation of the body from salvation in the individualistic concept of death as an anti-feminine and anti-bodily androcentrism and egoism.[7]

One must ask (with Ruether) whether the eschatology of Jesus is grasped correctly with a dualistic concept. This historical question is allied, however, with the hermeneutical decision against or for a dualistic conception of history and the future. If the traditional dualistic meaning of the texts were adequate, for me the theological

---

6   Rosemary R. Ruether, *Sexismus und die Rede von Gott*, Gütersloh 1985, Kapitel 10. (Ruether), "Eschatology and Feminism," *Sexism and God-Talk: Toward a Feminist Theology*, Boston: Beacon Press, 1983, 235*58).

7   Cf. also Theodor W. Adorno, *Negative Dialektik*, Frankfurt 1966, 362 for criticism on the egoism of the hope for immortality. (ET: *Negative Dialectics*, trans. by E. B. Ashton, New York: Continuum, 1983, 371).

option for a redemptive way of being on the earth and with the earth would take precedence. In this case, I would be compelled to carry out a radical criticism of the Jesus tradition. From a methodological point of view, it follows that the concepts of "this world" and "the other world," which all interpreters of this religious tradition bring with them, must be reflected upon and laid open. Only then are they capable of revision. For the most part, however, such concepts are not hermeneutically tested.

The question of the concepts of "this world" and "the other world," is closely bound up with parable theory. Since the greatest number of texts of the eschatological Jesus tradition occur in the form of parables, it is important to reflect upon the parable theory with which these texts are read. The parables speak of this world, of the world of people and plants. They are the language of revelation which implicitly speaks of God "in parables" and reveals God in parables. The question of the relationship of God to the world of people and plants is central for parable interpretation. For the Jülicher-Bultmann line of parable theory, the world, the image-side of the parable was a "neutral" situation[8] by which the subject matter of the parable, and, therefore, God, was clarified and interpreted. Yet with regard to the contents of the parable, according to this theory, no connection exists between the image and the subject matter. For the newer parable theory derived from the work of Paul Ricoeur,[9] the deformations of the "image" (for instance, the payment of a full day's wage to those who worked in the vineyard for a short time, Mt 20:9) are the points of departure for interpreting the "image" itself as a revelatory event.[10] Although this approach is an attempt to undo the dualism of image and subject matter, in these theories the worlds of the unemployed day laborers, the women baking bread, and the male and female slaves are still not placed in relation to God. Overcoming this dualism happens, in my opinion, where the hands of the women baking bread are grasped as a place of revelation. I regard the parables as revelatory speech which understands the world of people and plants itself as a place of divine action. God has looked upon the suffering of the unemployed day-laborers and revealed God's self where human beings break through the logic of this suffering. The earth itself is a place of divine action and of transformation on the way to the kingdom of God. The everyday world is transparent to God's wrath and God's grace. This transparency holds good not only for the deformations of the "image" taken from the everyday, rather, it holds good for the parable as a whole.

Eschatology and Linear Time

In his demythologizing program Bultmann proceeded with the unquestioned assumption that time and history will always continue in hours, days, years, and millennia. He presupposed a linear model of time. "The mythical eschatology of the

---

8   Rudolf Bultmann, *Die Geschichte der synoptischen Tradition*, 4th ed., Göttingen: Vandenhoeck & Ruprecht, 1958, 214. (ET: *The History of the Synoptic Tradition*, trans. John Marsh, Oxford: Basil Blackwell, 1963, 198).

9   Paul Ricoeur, "Stellung und Funktion der Metapher in der biblischen Sprache," in Paul Ricoeur, Eberhard Jüngel, *Methapher. Zur Hermeneutik religiöser Sprache*, in *Evangelische Theologie*, Sonderheft, München: Chr. Kaiser, 1974, 45-70.

10 On this Luise Schottroff, *"Lydias ungeduldige Schwestern,"* Feministische Sozialgeschichte des frühen Christentums, Gütersloh: Chr. Kaiser, 1994, 83f. (ET: *Lydia's Impatient Sisters: A Feminist Social History of Early Christianity*, trans. Barbara and Martin Rumscheidt, Louisville, KY: Westminster John Knox Press, 1995, 51f.).

NT is brought to an end basically by the simple fact that Christ's *parousia* did not take place as soon as the NT expected; rather, contemporary history continued on and--as every responsible person is conviced--will continue on."[11] This concept of time rests on the time of clocks and conquerors. Clocks suggest this conception of time, and it is in the interest of conquerors that everything may continue on as it is. On this linear concept of time rests the scholarly theory that the "near expectation," which anticipated the kingdom of God within a foreseeable time frame, was an error, and the "delay of the parousia" brought with it a new concept of eschatology. The end of history passed into the distance and instead of the kingdom of God the Church arrived.

The critique of such a linear concept of time by philosophy and feminist theory[12] is congruent with liberation theology's new assessments of Christian eschatology. Joao B. Libanio describes the eschatology of the devout in Brazil: "We have already seen how the religious conceptions of the world which are passed down endure, and what significance eschatology has in that process. How, then, do the people experience the core of eschatology? The eschatological is here synonymous with the nearness of God. This nearness can be perceived by the ones who venture in the 'sphere of the sacred.' It offers a double vision: salvation and threat, attraction and fear, fascination and horror. The people experience the ultimate, the eschatological dimension, of human existence in the form of the sacred. Here is encountered the transcendence of a God who saves and judges, forgives and punishes, extends compassion, but also judges unflinchingly."[13] The nearness of God is experienced in a sacred space, but it also opens up the future now: "Only while we live the eschatology which is already being realized does light fall on the eschatology which is still not realized."[14]

Methodologically, that means that the experience of the nearness of God in space and time is not separable from the people who have this experience and share it with one another. Their eschatological hopes interpret and alter their present and their future. Their experience of time is the experience of a time of being terrified and also of joy over God's nearness; it is the experience of a time of waiting and of hope for a future which God grants. Whoever counts on God in the present lives eschatologically, filled by the present and at the same time full of yearning after the future of God. The concept of *basileia tou theou* has a double dimension of space and time. The kingdom of God is expected and one can enter it (Mk 14:43, Lk 2:25; Mk 10:15, etc.; the use of the verbs *eiserchesthai* and *proserchesthai* in this sense). The concept of the kingdom of God means God's activity: as a righteous judge, as a merciful father, in space and time, in the fullness of God's creation. This God is experienced now, and this God will also order and renew heaven and earth in the future. The believers behold the new creation of the Lord "of heaven and earth" (Mt 1:25 par.). A translation of these experiences into the time of clocks and victors is a misunderstanding.[15]

11 Rudolf Bultmann, *Neues Testament und Mythologie. Das Problem der Entmythologisierung der neutestamentlichen Verkündigung*, München 1941, 31. (ET: "New Testament and Mythodology: The Problem of Demythologizing," in *New Testament and Mythology and Other Basic Writings*, ed. and trans. by Schubert Ogden, Philadelphia: Fortress Press, 1984, 14).
12 Walter Benjamin, "Zentralpark," in *Illuminationen. Ausgewählte Schriften*, Frankfurt 1969, 260; Jürgen Ebach, loc. cit.; R. Ruether, loc.cit.
13 Joao B. Libanio/Maria C. Lucchetti Bingemer, *Christliche Eschatologie*, Düsseldorf 1987, 70.
14 Loc. cit., 68.
15 Kurt Erlemann, *Naherwartung und Parusieverzögerung im Neuen Testament. Ein Beitrag zur Frage*

Jesus and Christian Identity

The Authentic Jesus Tradition

The idea of the "historical Jesus" in Western exegetical scholarship is even today still based on the theory that scholarly investigation is able to separate the authentic Jesus tradition from subsequent community formulations by means of definite criteria. The criteria for this separation are the subject of a continuing discussion; yet they are hypotheses --nothing more. These hypotheses are subject to criticism. Above all, their hermeneutical presuppositions have continually to be uncovered and tested. Since I aim at a pragmatic engagement with the problem of an authentic Jesus tradition, this is not the place to analyze individual criteria of authentication. Over against the hypothesis that the authentic and unauthentic texts can be separated, I pose a different concept: What we know about Jesus, we know from texts which were written down one or more generations later from the perspective of believing followers of Jesus. We have the images of Jesus only as the images of Jesus Christ --the Resurrected One. This character of the texts prevents us from making a reliable distinction between an authentic Jesus tradition and later additions.

A further aspect of this problem is that the assessment of the difference between the contents of Jesus' words and community formulations, a difference which is an important basis for the distinction, has changed in the research of the last decades. While Bultmann worked with a type of decadence theory (the community formulations are recognizable over and against the authentic Jesus tradition by their reduction of the radicality of Jesus and by their interests in the community), today we increasingly find the assessment that the images of Jesus which appear in the gospels are not so inferior despite the further development of christology. From a social-historical point of view the more recent theory presupposes a continuity between the Jesus movement at the time of the historical Jesus and the community at the time of the composition of the gospels. The political and social situation of Jewish people and their gentile Christian sympathizers grew worse after 70 CE compared to the time of Jesus, but was not fundamentally altered. The history of the Jewish people in Roman Empire shows that. The community praxis and the hopes of the Jesus movement and the later communities can be assumed to have changed in detail but not fundamentally, not structurally.

Israel and the Church

For all texts of the NT it is the case that their interpretation is dependent upon the historical evaluation of the relationship of the Church and Israel. Is Jesus as a Jew already on the way to a dissociation from Judaism, in the direction toward a (Gentile) Christian Church? How do I assess Jesus' words which are anti-Pharisaic and critical of

---

religiöser Zeiterfahrung, Tübingen und Basel: Frande, 1995 sees this correctly; however, he retains the "abstract, mathematical/ chronometrical concept of time" as formative for the collective consciousness of all people since the rise of modernity and the industrial revolution (424 etc.). He does not take into account the philosophic, feminist and liberation critique of this concept of time and, therefore, does not recognize that even today people have an experience of time of which the experience of time in the Jesus tradition is one form; and that therefore it cannot be a question of somehow translating the "subjective" experience of time into linear time. Rather, one needs to recognize and obstruct the catastrophe of thought about progress. The concept of linear time, of progress, has come almost to the point of destroying humanity completely.

Israel? Do I understand Jesus and early Christianity as a joint voice inside the Judaism of their time, or do I perceive Jesus at the beginning of a path which led more or less rapidly from Israel to a Church which separated itself theologically and fundamentally from Israel? On the one hand, despite acknowledging the Jewishness of Jesus, Christian New Testament study has a clear inclination to place the separation between Israel and the Church as early as possible. On the other hand, the anti-Jewish structures of a Christian theology of this type have thrust themselves more and more into Christian consciousness. Since the commentary work on the NT reacts slowly and clumsily to changes in this discussion, a new reconstruction of the sayings of Jesus apart from the anti-Jewish model is generally an unfinished task. Even with respect to this question, however, my hermeneutical presupposition applies (see above 1.1.3). If my contemporary theological position differs from that of the New Testament, I am prepared to criticize the NT --in this case because of its anti-Jewishness. However, on historical grounds I hold the view that the separation of the Church from Judaism and the development of an anti-Jewish theology first occurred in the middle of the second century CE, and that the New Testament is an unbroken part of the history of Judaism of its time.[16] Theologically, I proceed from the conviction that Christian identity can be lived and expressed without marking oneself off from Judaism in one's view of the Torah and of the God of Judaism, and without christologically objectifying the uniqueness of Jesus.

Poverty and Wealth

The Jesus tradition, especially those texts from which the eschatology of Jesus is derived, contains a clear option for the poor of his day. Since the interpreters of this tradition in Western society are as a rule at home in in the middle class, the Jesus tradition leads to hermeneutical decisions on this question even if the interpreters do not see this and supposedly only investigate objective historical data. The relation of poor and rich may be clarified with the traditional concept of giving to the poor: the rich remain rich, but feel obliged to make gifts and offer help. The generalization of poverty provides another solution to the problem (all are in some sense poor, above all before God), or the theory is proposed that the Jesus movement and Jesus articulated a special ethic for a society where there is no obligation for normal Christians (so, for instance, the concept of "Wanderradikalismus").[17] Precisely in this question the social and hermeneutical presuppositions must be laid open, and the discussion has to be opened up. From my --relatively prosperous-- perspective, the Jesus tradition raises the clear and painful challenge for Christian churches in prosperous countries to develop alternatives --in theory and praxis-- to factual social injustice. The present increasing impoverishment of ever greater regions of the earth and of many people even in the

16 Luise Schottroff, "Gesetzesfreies Heidenchristentum und die Frauen?" in: Luise Schottroff and Marie Theres Wacker, eds., *Von der Wurzel getragen. Christlich-feministische Exegese in Auseinandersetzung mit Antijudaismus*, New York: Brill, 1996, 227-45. ET "Law-free Gentile Christianity" – What about the Women?, forthcoming in: Amy Jill Levine (ed.), A Feminst Companion to Paul, Sheffield/Continuum 2004, 183-194.

17 For a critique of this concept see Luise Schottroff, *Lydias ungeduldige Schwestern. Feministische Sozialgeschichte des frühen Christentums*, Gütersloh: Chr. Kaiser, 1994, chapter 1 A. (ET: *Lydia's Impatient Sisters: A Feminist Social History of Early Christianity*, trans. by Barbara and Martin Rumscheidt, Louisville, Ky.: Westminster John Knox Press, 1995, 3-11).

prosperous countries, as in mine, compels Christians to carry out an unadorned economic analysis and to participation in structural change, even if only small steps are possible.

Preunderstanding and the Dialogue with History

Here I consciously take over the concept "preunderstanding" from the hermeneutic of Rudolf Bultmann. Bultmann distinguished between bias and preunderstanding. For him, exegesis without preunderstanding is not possible; that is, interpreters will be able to deal rightly with the Jesus tradition only if they seek an existential encounter with Jesus: "Then, however, the interrogation of history will lead not to a reporting of a timeless knowledge, but rather to an encounter with history--which itself is a temporal event. That would be a dialogue with history."[18] I refer consciously more than once in this hermeneutical section to Rudolf Bultmann   --in agreement and opposition-- because in mainstream exegesis his hermeneutic still forms an unsurpassed high point.[19] Only liberation theology and feminist hermeneutic have moved this discussion further, through sociological analysis of what Bultmann calls preunderstanding, and through a fundamental critique of the Western exegetical tradition's understanding of time and of the hermeneutic of the poor in the gospel of Jesus. Methodologically, however, Bultmann's assessment of the role of preunderstanding is unsurpassed. It is not possible to strive for a supposedly correct, purely objective representation of timeless historical knowledge--that is a Potemkin's village, a deceptive facade. A disclosure and analysis of the presuppositions of exegesis is the only way to a scholarly encounter with historical materials. Only in this way can a dialogue with history take place.

The Banquet of God: A Feminist Reconstruction of the Eschatology of Jesus

Toward a Feminist Perspective

As has already become clear, a feminist analysis interrogates eschatologies from a stance that is critical of linear chronology and of the dualistic splitting of the body, this world, and everyday life from the kingdom of God. As an example, I choose a thematic area of the synoptic gospels in which the relationship of God to the reality of the human body can be interpreted most clearly: eating and drinking in the kingdom of God.[20] My question is: How does the eschatological expectation of the banquet of

---

18 Rudolf Bultmann, *Jesus*, Tübingen: J. C. B. Mohr (Paul Siebeck), 1951, 14 (ET *Jesus and The Word*, trans. Louise Pettibone Smith and Erminie Huntress Lantero, New York: Charles Scribner's Sons, 1958, 4; cf. "Ist voraussetzungslose Exegese möglich?" in *Glauben und Verstehen* III Tübingen: J. C. B. Mohr (Paul Siebeck), 1960, 142*150 (ET: "Is Presuppositionless Exegesis Possible," in *New Testament and Mythology and Other Basic Writings*, ed. and trans. Schubert Ogden, Philadelphia: Fortress Press, 1984, 289-96).

19 Gerd Theissen and Annette Merz, *Der historische Jesus. Ein Lehrbuch*, Göttingen: Vandenboeck & Ruprecht, 1996, 221-85, provide an outstanding brief overview of mainstream exegesis on this question.

20 On the eschatological banquet in Jewish sources see George F. Moore, *Judaism in the First Centuries of the Christian Era. The Age of the Tannaim*, Volume II. Cambridge: Harvard University Press, 1954, 364f., and J. Priest, "A Note on the Messianic Banquet," in James H. Charlesworth, ed., *The Messiah. Developments in Earliest Judaism and Christianity*, Minneapolis: Fortress Press, 1992, 222*38.

Jesus cohere with the everyday experience of women, men and children? Are the bodies of people given a share in the experience of God and in the expectation of God, or is the banquet of God absolutely transcendent, unconnected with the realities of everyday life? A connection between the feeding miracles of Jesus and the meal occasions in the Jesus movement has already been pointed out by a nmber of Biblical scholars.[21] It has also been shown that the feeding miracles are connected to the hope for a banquet in God's kingdom.[22] These connections will be made explicit here and will also be explored more deeply later. The exegetical tradition that focuses on the historical Jesus divides the eschatology, the miracles, and the meal practices of Jesus into three distinct sections. I will also distinguish these three levels though with a view to clarifying their inter-connection and to discovering the significance of eschatological hope of human beings and their bodily existence now. Then the conception of future time and the experience of time in the Jesus tradition can also be described more clearly.

With regard to a social-historical perspective, I assume that the Jewish people, or the people who chose to be Jewish, who are part of the Jesus tradition belong as Jesus did to the impoverished, often hungry majority population of the Roman Empire, especially in Syria-Palestine. I proceed further from the conviction that women and children are present as a matter of course at the meals of the Jesus movement and that the miracles include women and children, just as the eschatological banquets in the kingdom of God include them.[23] The question who prepares the meals is not discussed in connection with the eschatological tradition. Still it follows from the history of early Christianity and the leading critical texts such as Mk 10:42-45 parr., that even free men participated in the work of preparing the common meals in the Jesus movement.[24] The social-historical hypothesis outlined here need not be established again in detail. The historical traces which these life realites have left behind in the texts that are to be discussed will, however, be noted from time to time.

The Banquet of God in the Jesus Tradition

Mk 14:25 parr.: The Joy of drinking Wine in Community

The Jesus logion that is passed down in connection with the story about the last meal of Jesus with his community of disciples is spoken from the perspective of a dying man; never again will he drink wine until that day in which he drinks it new in the kingdom of God. In the world and in the tradition in which Jesus and his followers live, to drink wine is to experience joy in community.[25] Departure from the body and the community, and a new beginning of joy in human life in the body and in the

21 See Ulrich Luz, *Das Evangelium nach Matthäus*, Zürich/Neukirchen, 1990, II, 397, Note 18.
22 See Gerd Theissen and Annette Merz, loc. cit., 267.
23 See Kathleen E. Corley, *Private Women--Public Meals. Social Conflict in the Synoptic Tradition*, Peabody, MA: Hendrickson Publishers, 1993.
24 Luise Schottroff, *Lydias ungeduldige Schwestern. Feministische Sozialgeschichte des frühen Chrisstentums*, Gütersloh: Chr. Kaiser, 1994, Kapitel IV 2. (ET: *Lydia's Impatient Sisters: A Feminist Social History of Early Christianity*, trans. Barbara and Martin Rumscheidt, Louisville, Ky.: Westminster John Knox Press, 1995, 204-230).
25 Historical material in Gustaf Dalman, *Arbeit und Sitte in Palästina*, Vol. 4 (Gütersloh: C. Bertelsmann, 1935) Reprint Hildesheim 1964, 388f., 397ff.

community are bound together in this logion. The dying Jesus mourns the loss which is placed before him, and he announces in prophetic words a future in which God calls the joy of bodily existence and community newly into life. The logion represents a protest against the removal from the body and the earth. The wine is simply wine, and Jesus expresses proleptic joy about the new community that is centered aroung table fellowship.[26] If one views the logion from a social-historical perspective, then it speaks of an experience of joy within the community of disciples. For them the dying Jesus puts an end to anxiety and flight, and he brings them together anew as a community which stands in bodily relation to one another and to the body of Jesus. I understand the account of the Last Supper, the eating of the body of Jesus, in the sense of a mystical-bodily experience of union with Jesus. Considered from a religious studies perspective, the narrative of the passion of Jesus contains three different notions of the future: Jesus' own resurrection, which he declares again and again; the discipleship community, which proclaims the resurrection (see, for instance, Mk 14:9 par); and the kingdom of God. In the community of believers after Jesus' death all these future hopes are realized and at the same time are still future. The resurrected one is present and still not fully present; the kingdom of God is experienced and at the same time still an object of hope. The community drinks the wine of God's kingdom and hopes for an earth and heaven in which God alone reigns. Future and present are determined by the relation to God. The dying Jesus leaves the joy of the common meal, and he also knows himself safely imbedded in the community of believers and in the future which arises out of this relation to God. After Jesus' death, the community renews Jesus' hope in the joy of the communal meal which can be at the same time a foretaste of future joy. This future can be understood only out of the relationship to God. The bodily reality of eating and drinking wine in the community of saints is the birthplace of the certainty that the dead are present in this community with their bodies, and it provides hope for a future communal meal in the name of God. In terms of the social-historical meaning, the eschatology of Jesus derives its perspective on the future from the present and from the experience of God by those who proclaim texts or transmit them.

Mt 8:11 par.: Struggle for the Banquet of the Nations!

In this Q logion, as in Isa 25:6-12, the salvific conception of a banquet of God is connected to the concept of pilgrimage to Zion. In the tradition common to Matthew and Luke, the patriarchs as representatives of Israel and people from all over the world participate in the eschatological banquet. Next to the banquet hall is a place of punishment. The "evildoers" (so Lk 13:27 = Ps 6:9) look from the place of punishment into the banquet hall (Lk) or they are cast out of the hall (Mt). The guests of the banquet are represented as a joyful and great assembly in which women and men, Jewish people of past and present, and people from all races of the whole world take part. This metaphor is an inducement to enter through the narrow gate (Mt 7:13; Lk 13:24--even if Mt transmits this Q logion in a different connection, it can be included according to its subject matter as in Lk). At the same time, however, this metaphor is a threat to the evildoer (Lk 13:27) and even to the sons of the kingdom of God (Mt

---

26 Even if the community is only explicitly named in the Matthean parallel, it is implicitly present also in Mk 14:25. That Jesus will drink wine "anew" means the eschatological renewal of heaven and earth in the sense, e.g., of Apoc 21:1.

8:12). The persons addressed so menacingly in both versions are characterized as people who consider themselves to be near to the kingdom of God in their life; "Have we not eaten and drunk together with you (*enopion sou*) and have you not taught in our streets." Similarly the "sons of the *basileia*" (Mt) appeal to their life as the reason why they expect to enter into the banquet hall. The judgment of God (or of the Son of man/Jesus, Lk) falls on them because they have not lived according to God's will, the Torah --despite their participation in the expectation of the kingdom of God. It is clear from the contents that the threat affects people who are comparable to the ones referred to in Mt 7:21 and Lk 6:46 --followers of Jesus who have not acted according to Jesus' teaching and according to the will of God.

The logion Mt 8:11f., par., has been interpreted almost exclusively as anti-Jewish, most likely because of the identification of "sons of the *basileia*" with "Israel" in Mt 8:10. Neverthelss, this anti-Jewish interpretation is unfounded in view of the role of the patriarchs and in view of the Lukan version.

The logion connects the hope for the banquet of God with a consistent life praxis based on the Torah and on the teaching of Jesus as an effective interpretation of the Torah. Righteousness and community among all peoples of the world is greatly desired, and this manner of life is yearned for and demanded without compromise. Here it is not a question of a Gentile mission, but rather a revival of the hope for a community among all people as expressed in Isa 25:6-12 and elsewhere. A different metaphor for the community of people over which only God reigns is found in Mk 4:32 parr., in the conclusion of the parable of the mustard seed. The birds of heaven can live under the branches (or in the shade--Mk) of the cosmic tree in the kingly dominion of God. Here an old oriental metaphor for world dominion is taken up and transformed (see Dan 4:9-18). The birds of heaven were originally metaphors for the people who were conquered by a great kingdom. Now there is no great kingdom any more --only God and the people,without distinctions of rank, safe in God's kingdom.

The experience of time which is expressed in Mt 8:11f --from the perspective of those who are addressed in their present time and situation-- is that of fear as they wait for God's judgment but also long for the banquet of the nations. The physical experience of solidarity across peoples' boundaries is possible and is experienced and, at the same time, it is still anticipated as God's future.

Mt 22:1-14 par.: The Banquet of the Homeless

The parable of the feast should be read from the background of comparable rabbinic parables.[27] They place the guests of the banquet in the center of the parable in a manner similar to Mt 8:11f par. The first persons invited reject the invitation in both versions on materialistic grounds. Even the marriage introduced in Lk 14:20 is, in the context of the other excuses, a rejection on materialistic grounds as it corresponds to the patriarchal social order where marriage is first of all an institution for the procurement of possessions.

The substitute guests are grabbed from the streets (in both versions). The parable should be read like Mt 8:11f. par., as both threat and invitation and not as an eschatological festival script bolstering the status quo. It is not yet clear how the first

---

27 On this see Luise Schottroff, "Das Gleichnis vom grossen Gastmahl in der Logienquelle," *Evangelische Theologie* 47 (1987) 192*211.

group of invited guests are to be_interpreted; and the street people, the homeless, do not portray a (Gentile) Church completely in opposition to Israel. The first invited guests, who cling to possessions, receive through this parable a new chance, and the homeless (whom no one would permit in a well-cared-for house) are the invited guests of God. It appears to be the vision of a banquet in which the possessors give up their possessions and divide their bread and their life with the street people. At God's banquet, they are invited without conditions. That the hungry and homeless alone fill the banquet hall in the parable's conclusion does not mean that the first group of invited guests could not also come in. The parable warns them with exclusion; however, it is not fixed who will be the excluded. Everything is still open. In Lk 13:30 a floating prophetic logion of Jesus is attached to the saying about the banquet of the nations. "Indeed, some are last who will be first, and some are first who will be last" (cf., Mt 1:16, Mk 10:31 par., however, see also Mt 22:14). This perspective also informs the parable in Mt 22:14 par. From the perspective of the present time of the ones who_are addressed, the parable issues a demand without compromise that the possessors turn from possessions since these destroy the heart and the relation to God. For homeless women and men, it means an invitation to the mealtimes of the disciple community of Jesus where they experience and live to see the joy of eating and being filled in community and where they come to know that they have a future which comes from God's hand.

Mt 5:3-12 par.: Laugh and Dance!

The common vocabulary of the beatitudes in Mt and Lk draws its conception of the *basileia tou theou* from the tradition of the eschatological banquet of God. Ultimately, the hungry will be satisfied, the weeping people of God will be comforted (Mt) or laugh in the joy of the banquet (Lk). Those suffering in the present under persecution will be filled with joy. Luke even says "dance" (6:23), evoking images of skipping water or leaping lambs. Mt 5:5 introduces still a different metaphor of salvation: to inhabit the earth. [With this translation I attempt to avoid the inappropriate association of *kleronomein* with "possession" or "inheritance."] Mt does not depict here how the people of God will inhabit the earth. Doubtlessly, he conceives of an earth upon which all humanity and all peoples live with one another in community (cf. Mt 8:11f.). This community of human beings was pictured earlier in the prophets as a community of peace and social justice ("they shall all sit under their own vines and under their own fig trees, and no one shall make them afraid;" Micah 4:4). It is the kingdom of God which represents the future for the earth and all its peoples.

Yet even as people long for the eschatological banquet they experience their present situation as a time of gloom. People are poor[28] and hungry. They mourn or weep over the suffering of the people. They are persecuted for the sake of Jesus/the Son of man. They stand, however, in the tradition of the people of God, where their persecution mirrors the persecution of the prophets, where their sorrow stands in the tradition of

---

28 Even Mt 5:3 should be related, like the Lukan parallels, to material poverty. That the poor (to *pneumati*) are poor means that they are in misery physically and spiritually--in their relation to God. They are hungry and can not praise God. On the linguistic grounds of this meaning see Luise Schottroff, "Das geschundene Volk und die Arbeiter in der Ernte Gottes nach dem Matthäusevangelium," in Luise und Willy Schottroff, eds., Mitarbeiter der Schöpfung. *Bibel und Arbeitswelt*, München: C. Kaiser, 1983, 162-66.

grief surrounding the Babylonian exile (Ps 136). Mt expands on this further when he writes that people hunger after righteousness and are peacemakers who deal with power differently than the arrogant lords (*praeis*, Mt 5:5).

The exegetical dispute about whether the Beatitudes speak of social or ethical conditions is not very helpful. The beatitudes speak of the people of God/Israel, the majority of whom suffer under poverty and political oppression. Yet the overriding reality is that the people remain related to God. God has mercy on the poor and on those who mourn. God transforms the people into a community of peacemakers. The persecution of Jesus' disciples shows that they, as representatives of the people of God, are on the way to God's kingdom. The ones addressed by the beatitudes are the disciples and with them conjointly the whole people (see Mt 4:24-5:12; Lk 6:17-20a).

Sickness affects the people who gather themselves around Jesus and the disciples (so probably Q also). The beatitudes connect three levels of meaning with one another: 1) the reality of the people: hunger and sickness; 2) the transformation of the poor into peacemakers (so Mt) and successors of prophetic battles for justice (so already Q); 3) the vision of God's banquet for the poor. The people marked by sickness and hunger are at the same time God's people for whom God has taken part already in Jesus' healing of the sick. In this eschatology bodily reality is not interpreted as irrelevant or provisional. It is the place of transformation by God and the hope for a new earth which will be celebrated in a banquet. Even the conception of time in the beatitudes links together the present and the future. The eschatological joy is already present (Mt 5:12, Lk 6:23, "in that day" --properly an eschatological usage, is related here to the time of persecution). Laugh and dance when you, like the prophets of Israel, are persecuted for Jesus sake, and that means for the sake of Jesus' praxis among people.

Eschatological Abundance of Bread and Wine in Jesus' Nearness

Both the healing miracles of Jesus and his disciples and also the bread-miracles bring the kingdom of God to people in the present. From the rich tradition which describes the eschatological abundance as an experience of people near to Jesus I select just a few examples: The Feeding of the Five Thousand (Mk 6:32-44 par.), the insulting word directed against Jesus (Mt 11:29 par.), and the promise of abundance through the Syrophoenician woman (Mk 7:28 par.). Regarding this material, I will only point out here that it is significant that bread miracles are told repeatedly (it is not only a matter of literary doublets). The abundant catch of fish (Lk 5:1-11; John 21) also belongs to this material, just as the encouragement sayings do (Mt 6:25-34 par.) and the question about fasting (Mk 2: 18-22 par.). In these texts, Jesus is described as Messiah in whose nearness the kingdom of God is already experienced --for there is nourishment in abundance.

Mk 6:32-44 par.: ". . . and all were filled."

The Feeding of the Five Thousand is told in the language of the past and yet contains all the elements of a vision. The people of God are a people without a sense of direction. Jesus has pity on the people as does God (6:34). The organization of the people of God in the wilderness (Ex 18:21-25) is reflected in the arrangement of people in groups of 100 and 50 persons. Mt adds that even women and children are included in these groups (Mt 14:21) [by] which means that the total number of persons would be quite large. That women and children are present, is, however, self-evident.[29] The leadership structure of the Exodus people, though, is altered. Moses delegated the judging to men who presided over the groups of people (Ex 18:21). The disciples, however, are not entrusted with this leadership task; rather, they take the bread and fish to the meal fellowship. This meal fellowship recalls the Jewish Passover meals (6:42).[30] Jesus divides five loaves of bread and two fish for the people "and all ate and were filled." To demonstrate that the people were filled, it is even pointed out that twelve baskets full of bread and fish were left over. All were satisfied (so Lk formulates it). The political claim of this vision is unlimited: the God of Israel is ordering the people through Jesus and is reigning as a good King. Among the people there are no hierarchies. The leadership task is to lay before the people the meal as servants (*paratithenai* Mk 6:41; Lk 9:16). Commands are given only by Jesus (6:39, implicitly also in 6:36).

The political vision of these texts retained its Sitz im Leben only as long as the followers of Jesus understood themselves as part of the Jewish people, since this vision refers not to a "new" people, but rather to the Jewish people who live in the tradition of the Exodus. The vision of these texts depicts, therefore, what *basileia tou theou* means politically. The people of Israel will live in justice, freedom, and with an economic order in which all can be satisfied. This vision criticizes the status quo. The people are now oppressed and have no political direction of their own. They are like sheep without a shepherd (6:34; cf., Num 27:17, etc.). With this the political situation of Israel in the Roman Empire is named. In the Jesus tradition, the Roman rule is criticized as an unjust system (Mk 10:42 par.). Since Jesus was crucified by Rome on political grounds with the charge that he wanted to be King of Israel, this text is to be brought into positive connection with the historical Jesus. "The political rhetoric of Jesus is evident in all four gospels where he is reported as proclaiming the coming kingdom of God and claiming an essential role in its establishment. What is envisioned is not simply a political entity but a means by which the rule of God over creation will be evident and actualized."[31]

The classification of this story as a <u>miracle</u> story focuses too narrowly on the bread miracle and de-emphasizes the political vision. The "miracle story" tells what the eschatological banquet in the kingdom of God looks like and, as this banquet shows, what it means when God is king (the *basileia* of God). Whether Jesus is presented here as the embodiment of Moses or as God's messiah is difficult to determine. Through the linking of the kingdom of God to Jesus and through the past form of the story, it is asserted that in Jesus' nearness the kingdom of God has occurred already. This is not just a foretaste of the banquet, rather God's banquet itself has taken place. The similarities with the Last Supper of Jesus should not be understood in a way that the

---

29 See above note 23.
30 H. L. Strack and P. Billerbeck, *Kommentar zum Neuen Testament aus Talmud und Midrasch*, Vol. 1, München: Beck, 1978, 13.
31 For an excellent brief summary of the political and theological situation of Jesus see Howard Clark Kee, "The Death of Jesus in Light of the Political Options for First Century C.E. Judaism," in American Interfaith Institute/World Alliance of Interfaith Organizations, ed., *Exploration* Vol. 11, No. 3, 1997, 3.

Last Supper forms the fundamental paradigm of these stories; rather, the Last Supper is a further expression of the expectation of God's reign as conveyed in these texts.

It is certainly correct that this vision is grounded in the experience of the disciple community of Jesus.[32] The joyful experience of having enough to eat in community, the experience that shared bread goes farther than one's own is doubtlessly at the root of such visions. They also reflect the fact that a leveling of hierarchical relationships has been attempted in the disciple community. The role of the disciples in this text is the same as that of Mk 10:42-45 par.

Mt 11:19 par: Glutton and Drunkard

Both John the Baptizer and Jesus were rejected by some of their contemporaries. The Baptist was said to have a demon, and Jesus was said to be a glutton, a drunkard, and a friend of tax collectors and sinners. The reproaches against Jesus address precisely his praxis as represented in Mk 2:13-17 par. (Eating with Tax Collectors) and Mk 2:18-22 par. (The Question over Fasting). Mk 11:19 par. (cf. Mk 2:19 par.) confirms the hypothesis that the bread miracle tradition is rooted in the experience of the disciple community of Jesus. Jesus and his followers have placed the banquet of God's kingdom at the center of their praxis. The abundance of bread in the kingdom of God is reflected in the common meals. Precisely this eschatological abundance is reflected in people's critique of Jesus. To be sure, an excess in eating and plentiful wine characterizes Jesus according to these critics, but if one looks past their criticism back to the bread miracles, then it might be conceivable that the bread miracles could be narrated as an expression of the eschatological, concrete abundance of the kingdom of God that was already experienced during the lifetime of Jesus.

Since Jesus and the disciples, like the majority of the Jewish people in the first century, belonged to the poor who had to fight for survival one might ask how it could happen that so much food was gathered and distributed during the communal meals. A response would be that Jesus and his followers have based their mission the solidarity praxis of the Jewish people. They could go into every house as messengers of God and would be thrown out only on rare occasions (Mt 10:14 par.).[33] In Mt 11:19 par., it is to be recognized that the Jesus movement actually succeeded in bringing together an abundance of bread and wine so vast that the hungry recognized in it the kingdom of God, whereas the critics saw the abundance as an indication that Jesus was a glutton.

Mk 7:28 par.: The Promise of Abundance through the Syrophoenician Woman

In Mk 8:14-21 par., the disciples who forgot to take bread with them in the boat were afraid that they would be hungry. Jesus criticizes them as blind and deaf, since they came directly from the experience of the bread miracle. But in Mk 7:28 par., Jesus is the one who fears that the bread may not be sufficient. Traditionally, Mk 7:27f. par. is read as a metaphor which deals with the gospel and not with bread. This way of reading presupposes that this metaphor implies dualistic thinking and the conception of the founding of the Gentile Church (or something like a precursor of the later Gentile

---

32 See above, note 22.

33 Mk 6:10f and Lk 9:4f can be understood in this way. Mt 10:11 is more cautious; see Paul Hoffmann, *Studien zur Theologie der Logienquelle*, Münster: Aschendorff, 1972, 273.

Church) by Jesus. The text, however, does not speak of the spread of the gospel, but rather of the illness of a non-Jewish child whom Jesus does heal. Jesus employs the bread "metaphor" to indicate the material side of his gospel, the healing, and the sharing of bread. Here it is the anonymous mother of the sick child who changes the metaphor from designating a scarcity of bread to indicating that bread is plentiful for all --for children and dogs. In Mk 8:14-21 par., and in Mk 7:28f., par., it is clear that having sufficient bread for the community was always a worry. Jesus' followers even indicate that he himself was once of little courage and thought that it might not be possible to share the bread with non-Jewish people. In this story, it is the Syrophoenician women who holds firmly to the promise of abundance.

The Lord's Supper and Common Meals: Mk 14:22-25 par.; Acts 2:42-47

According to the synoptic Evangelists, the last meal occasion of Jesus in the circle of his disciples was a Passover Meal. That it was characteristic of Jesus and the Jesus movement to arrange common meals has become clear already. My concern in this last section is to emphasize that the expectation of the kingdom of God was rooted in everyday life and in the community of everyday eating. The interpretive tradition often separates: 1) the meal practices of Jesus as an occasions for community with tax collectors and sinners and for the proclamation of his message (e.g., Mk 2:13-17 par.); 2) the Last Supper as a solemn institution of a rite for his followers; 3) the common evening meal of the disciples in later house communities. The tradition distinguishes between the "Lord's Supper" and a "full meal/agape meal",[34] yet the Acts of the Apostles presuppose daily common meal times in house communities (2:46). To be sure, there are exegetical attempts to explain even these verses from the perspective of making a distinction between the Lord's Supper and the evening meal. Still the word *trophe* means the nourishment which is necessary for the human body and not the rite of bread and wine in a "Lords Supper."[35] The summary statement in Acts 2:42-45 shows that the daily common meals united the community that jubilantly expected (*agalliasis*) the kingdom God, and this joyous expectation expressed itself vocally during eating. The evening meal is itself a place for recollecting Jesus' act of "breaking bread" (2:42). The community remembers Jesus' death, and with the words of institution accomplishes again the connection to Jesus' body. That women and children were present at these daily evening meals is not only obvious but even documented.

---

34 Thus, e.g., Gerhard Delling, "Abendmahl II," in TRE I, 1977, 47-58. The often silent presupposition of the separation of various meals forms is visible e.g., in the widespread hypothesis that the "daily serving/*diakonein*" of Acts 6:1 is not identical with the meal celebrations of Acts 2:42-47. Even the few authors who hypothecize for 1 Cor 11:17-34 the sequence: word of institution over the bread, full meal, word of institution over the cup, further distinguish between "everyday eating" and sacramental eating--thus, e.g., Peter Lampe, "Das korinthische Herrenmahl im Schnittpunk hellenistisch-römischer Mahlpraxis und paulinischer Theologia Crucis (1 Kor 11, 17-34)," ZNW 88 (1991) 183-213.

35 So Gerhard Delling, loc. cit.

There was a controversy with, and because of, Hellenistic widows[36] in one such daily meal celebrations (Acts 6:1).

The meal praxis in early Christianity, specifically the daily communal evening meal, was the central place for the formation of the community and for joy over the kingdom of God that was already experienced in the joy of common eating and drinking. Mutual provision for the material realm belongs to the meal praxis of Jesus and of the later house communities as well. Acts describes this as "having possessions in common." The aim was that no one in the community should be in need (Acts 4:34; cf. Deut 15:4). The vision of justice in the kingdom of God inspired early Christians to link the schatological abundance to an experienced reality: in sharing bread and possessions, in songs of praise over the nearness of God, and in eating and drinking together.

---

36 I contest the widespread conception that the hellenistic widows were refused nourishment that was allotted to them as "relief." The controversey was about serving/*diakonein* at the table. The apostles refused to serve the widows. In society at that time, it was demanded of widows more clearly than of other women to serve and to make no demands of any sort. Evidently, the widows in the community appealed to an offensive position and demanded not only to serve, but also to be served--something the apostles did not permit.

"Calling God 'Father' " (Matt 6:9)

Robert H. Smith

The views of Joachim Jeremias concerning Jesus' use of "abba" in addressing God have been endlessly repeated by many and strenuously repudiated by a few. Geza Vermes, Joseph Fitzmyer, James Barr, Mary Rose D'Angelo, and Herman Waetjen have written important essays, examining the argumentation of Jeremias. The current essay reviews their work and shows how they reach conclusions that rely not only on "science" (history and philology) but also on their religious bias or spiritual agendas. This essay develops ideas presented by D'Angelo and Waetjen and argues that the invocation of God as "father" in the Lord's Prayer and elsewhere in Matthew is an invitation to pray against the "fatherhood" of the emperor. Praying the Lord's Prayer continues to be a significant political act.

It was the 8th Sunday after Pentecost, and the preacher took the Lord's Prayer as text. Early in the sermon the preacher focused on the opening address, "Father." He confidently explained that an Aramaic word, *abba*, lies behind that English word "father." And, he continued, *abba* is one of the first words that children in ancient Palestine uttered as infants. *Abba*, said the preacher, is very much like our words "dada" or "daddy" or "papa." It is a word that comes from the warm circle of the family, where children are embraced by loving parents.

This word *abba*, the preacher continued, even though it was at home in the ancient nursery, was deliberately chosen by Jesus to articulate his adult experience and his mature vision of God. The word captures the unique intimacy that Jesus enjoyed with God. And now in the Lord's Prayer he invites all of us, children and adults alike, to draw near and speak with God as directly and trustingly as he himself did.[1]

Joachim Jeremias

Joachim Jeremias is the person chiefly responsible for our contemporary habit of finding the Aramaic word *abba* behind the English and Greek words for "father" in the New Testament and then linking *abba* with a child's address to its earthly father.

---

1   This is not a completely new idea. Even though he did not, the preacher could have called to his side the *Small Catechism* of Martin Luther, where the Reformer comments on the opening address of the prayer: "Here God would encourage us to believe that he is truly our Father and we are truly his children in order that we may approach him boldly and confidently in prayer, even as beloved children approach their dear father."

Also Cyril, bishop of Jerusalem in the mid 300's, in his *Catechetical Lectures* began his exposition of the Lord's Prayer with these words: "We say that prayer which the saviour delivered to his own disciples, with a pure conscience entitling God our Father, and saying, *Our Father, which art in heaven.* O most surpassing loving-kindness of God! On them who revolted from him and were in the very extreme of misery has he bestowed such a complete forgiveness of evil deeds, and so great participation of grace, as that they should even call him Father." (Catechetical Lectures xxiii.11, in *The Nicene and Post-Nicene Fathers*).

Jeremias propounded his views in a series of books and articles over many years.[2] Here are some of the claims made by him concerning Jesus' use of *abba*.

1. Not only do the gospels "agree that Jesus used 'Father' as a form of address; it is their unanimous witness that Jesus used this address in all his prayers" (excepting his quotation of Ps 22 in Mark 15:34 par). Jeremias goes on to say that "we have every reason to suppose that an abba underlies every instance of *pater (mou)* or *ho pater*." in Jesus' prayers.[3]

2. The words *abba* and *imma* (daddy and mommy) were among the first sounds that a child made. At one time, Jeremias admits, he believed that Jesus very simply "adopted the language of a tiny child when he addressed God as 'Father'." This is the form in which I ordinarily encounter the claim and the way it is usually cited. However Jeremias himself says that his further investigations led him to see that "by the time of Jesus, *abba* had long had a wider use than in the talk of small children."[4] He notes that adult children *addressed* their fathers in this way, and *abba* had also become a way of addressing distinguished older people.[5]

Nevertheless Jeremias still believes that "it would have seemed disrespectful, indeed unthinkable, to the sensibilities of Jesus' contemporaries to address God with this familiar word."[6] He writes that "the origin of the word in the language of infants never falls into oblivion."[7] So Jeremias gives and he takes away.

3. Another of Jeremias' claims is that *abba* is never used as a form of address to God in any of the extant ancient Palestinian Jewish prayer literature. He admits that some isolated examples of *pater* as an address to God appear in post-canonical Jewish literature. However, these are found only in Diaspora Judaism, not in Palestinian Judaism. The Diaspora was in this respect speaking under the influence of the Greek world. Jeremias speaks of two prayers from Palestine that address God as *'abinu malkenu* ("our father, our king"). He stresses that these prayers are not personal or individual prayers but formal liturgical prayers. God is being addressed in them as the Father of the community. He notes that the language of the prayers is Hebrew and not Aramaic, and that *'abinu* is used in closest connection with *malkenu*. So the "father" whom the community addresses is being identified as the heavenly king of the people of God. "We look in vain," writes Jeremias, "for the personal address 'my father'."[8]

---

2   Most of the following citations are from Joachim Jeremias, *New Testament Theology I: The Proclamation of Jesus* (New York: Charles Scribner's Sons, 1971). Cited hereafter as *Proclamation*. That work was preceded by a chapter on "Abba" in *The Central Message of the New Testament* (New York: Charles Scribner's Sons, 1965), cited as *Central Message*. Both of the preceding rest on the more detailed work Jeremias offered as chapter 1 in *The Prayers of Jesus,* published in English in 1967 (London: SCM).
3   See *Proclamation,* 62 and 65.
4   *Proclamation*, 66-67.
5   *Proclamation*, 68.
6   *Proclamation*, 67.
7   *Central Message*, 21.
8   *Proclamation*, 63f.

Jeremias cites the well known anecdote about Hanin (or Hanan, grandson of Honi the Circle-Drawer) found in the Talmud (b.Taan. 23b): "When the world needed rain, our teachers used to send school-children to him (to Hanin), who seized the hem of his coat and said to him, '*abba, 'abba, hab lan mitra* ('Daddy, daddy, give us rain!'). He (Hanin) said to Him (God): Master of the world, grant it for the sake of these who are not yet able to distinguish between an *Abba* who has the power to give rain and an *abba* who has not."

Jeremias comments that while Hanin echoes the word '*abba* used by the school-children, he himself addresses God, not as '*abba* but more formally as "Master of the world." More on this below.

4. Jeremias believes that Jesus, by choosing to address God with the word *abba*, expressed the heart of his relationship to God. He spoke to God the way a child addressed its dear father.[9] Jeremias finds in the word *abba* the very identity of the historical Jesus. Jesus knew God as his '*abba*, and we see the grace of God's kingdom in Jesus' invitation to sinners and publicans to repeat "this one word, *Abba, dear Father*."[10]

Jeremias' Goal

Jeremias' goal in his work on the Lord's Prayer, as in his research on the parables of Jesus and the Last Supper, was to recover the exact words spoken by Jesus and so assure modern believers that they are in contact with the authentic, life-giving voice of Jesus.[11]

The central claim of Jeremias can be summarized this way: Jesus' use of the intimate word *abba* in addressing God was something new and therefore uniquely revealing of his self-consciousness and mission. That claim is still widely accepted and cheerfully disseminated.[12] It has, however, been shaken by various criticisms in recent years.

---

9 *Proclamation*, 67.

10 *Central Message*, 30.

11 *The Parables of Jesus,* revised English edition based on the 6th German edition (London: SCM Press, 1963). *The Eucharistic Words of Jesus,* English edition based on the third German edition (New York: Charles Scribner's Sons, 1966).

12 In a profound and beautiful book on prayer in the New Testament, John Koenig writes, citing Jeremias for support, that "*Abba* comes close to our English word 'Daddy.' If Jesus' special name for God was *Abba*, and this seems undeniable in the light of its widespread liturgical use even by Greek-speaking Gentile believers (see Gal 4:6; Rom 8:15), then every time we encounter the word *pater* on Jesus' lips in reference to prayer, we must mentally translate it back to the more intimate term of address. Other teachers in Judaism at the time of Jesus may have used this prayer name for the Holy One of Israel, but as yet we have no evidence that they told their disciples to envision or invoke God in this way." *Rediscovering New Testament Prayer* (Harrisburg: Morehouse Publishing, 1992), 18.

Herman Waetjen, in his splendid commentary called *Praying the Lord's Prayer* (Harrisburg: Trinity Press, 1999), cites Jeremias with approval just as Koenig does. He continues, however, by drawing fresh conclusions: "Because Jesus has adopted children's speech, it might appear that the same hierarchical relationship is to be presupposed that required children to be subordinated to their father in a patriarchically structured society. The Gospel tradition, however, reflects a radically different relationship between Jesus and God. ...[and] the table fellowship that Jesus inaugurates and promotes...is inclusive, / and it is also horizontally structured." 57f More on Herman Waetjen's views below in a separate section.

Geza Vermes

Oxford scholar Geza Vermes believes that Jeremias in his researches did not take sufficient notice of the facts of Jewish history. Vermes writes, for example, that "whereas the customary style of post-biblical [Jewish] prayer is 'Lord of the universe', one of the distinguishing features of ancient Hasidic piety is its habit of alluding to God precisely as 'Father'."[13] Vermes reads the tradition concerning Honi the Circle-Drawer and his grandson Hanan differently from Jeremias. This tradition, says Vermes, shows that it is wrong to assert that addressing God as "Father" would have been "unthinkable" (Jeremias' word) in the prayer language of ancient Palestinian Judaism. And it is therefore wrong to assert that in characterizing God as "Father," Jesus was laying claim to exclusive sonship.[14]

As a Jewish scholar, Vermes is acutely sensitive to the danger in the longstanding Christian habit of separating Jesus from his Jewish roots and making him "unique." Christians have too often adopted the strategy of glorifying Jesus and his teaching by making odious comparisons with the piety and theology of ancient Judaism. Such comparisons typically laud Jesus' teaching as a breath of fresh air, a pure and bracing spiritual zephir, while characterizing contemporary Jewish teaching and practice as stale, crude, legalistic or materialistic.

So the word *abba* has been used by many Christian scholars to support the claim that Jesus had a warm and intimate relationship with God and invited his disciples to share it at a time when all of ancient Judaism spoke and thought of God as distant, remote, stand-offish. See how superior the new religion is?! Vermes wants us to see that such a view does not do justice to the facts of ancient Judaism.[15] Nor does it do justice, says Vermes, to the reality of Jesus.

Vermes' Goal

Biblical interpreters are these days increasingly aware that the subjectivity of the scholar is an important factor in research. It is useful to ask the question, "What is Vermes' goal?" Whereas Jeremias sought to separate Jesus from ancient Judaism by asserting that his experience of God was unique, Vermes aims to bring Jesus home to Judaism. He seeks to demonstrate that pious, charismatic Jewish teachers thought and spoke of God as *abba*. And Vermes numbers Jesus among those great ancient Jewish charismatic figures. For Vermes, Jesus was a pious Jew, attempting to discern and practice the will of God and to set in motion a movement devoted to such obedient hearing.[16]

---

13 *Jesus the Jew* (Philadelphia: Fortress Press, 1973), 210.

14 Joseph Fitzmyer, writing in "Abba and Jesus' Relation to God" in *A Cause de L'Evangile: Melanges offerts a Dom Jacques Dupont* (Editions du Cerf, 1985), pp. 15-38, appeals to studies of G. Schelbert and cautions that the story is found in the fifth century Babylonian Talmud and cannot be taken easily as evidence for first century usage. Schelbert's views are now summarized in his article on "Abba" in RGG.

15 *Jesus and the World of Judaism* (Philadelphia: Fortress Press, 1984) 39-43.

16 It was not the intention of Jesus, says Vermes, "to preach on God's nature and being as later theologians have done and continue to do. He tried to carry out his Father's will, to fall in with what he felt the Father demanded of him. And he taught his followers to devote themselves to the same task, irrespective of its outcome. The focus of his concern was not God as such, but himself, his disciples, and the world, in their relation to the Father in heaven and his kingdom." (*Jesus and the World of*

Joseph Fitzmyer

Priest-scholar Joseph Fitzmyer, like Vermes, is an expert in ancient Aramaic and Hebrew. However, Fitzmyer and Vermes use their scholarship in the service of differing spiritual perspectives and agendas.[17]

Fitzmyer expresses cautious agreement with Jeremias's philological and historical claims: (1) no evidence has surfaced so far in the literature of pre-Christian or first century Palestinian Judaism that *abba* was used as a personal address to God by an individual; (2) the word *abba* used as an address to God "stands a good chance" of being a genuine utterance of Jesus; (3) it is possible that *abba* originated in baby-talk, but we know it was also used by adult sons addressing their fathers and by younger people addressing honored elders, and therefore this word on the lips of Jesus does not prove that Jesus spoke to God like a small child.[18]

For all his agreement with Jeremias, Fitzmyer disagrees with the way Jeremias has attempted to build an entire christology on a single word. If we want to assert and demonstrate that Jesus was conscious of being "son of God" in a unique sense, we must do so not merely by focusing our attention on the word *abba*. We need to cast our net more widely, says Fitzmyer, and make use of such sayings as the one preserved in Luke 10:21-22//Matt 11:25-27.

Fitzmyer's Goal

Fitzmyer wrote both as scholar and as a believing priest partly in order to answer criticisms of Jeremias that had been made by Vermes and others. Fitzmyer offers a magisterial review of the secondary literature and of the philological and historical issues, and he defends most of what Jeremias has written. Unlike Vermes, Fitzmyer shares Jeremias' commitment to a high christology. In fact one of Fitzmyer's goals is to set Jeremias' christological claims on a more secure foundation.

James Barr

James Barr advertises his conclusions in the title of his article, "Abba Isn't 'Daddy'."[19] He notes that he wrote his article before he became aware of the work of his colleague Geza Vermes with whom he finds himself very much in agreement.

As we might expect from the author of *The Semantics of Biblical Language*,[20] Barr takes Jeremias to task for attempting to build a great theological edifice on a single word. He is at pains to point out how better linguistic and philological science could have saved Jeremias from a series of errors. Barr shows that *abba* was not necessarily Aramaic but might just as well have been a Hebrew word. Jeremias wanted it to be Aramaic, because he wanted it to be in Jesus' native tongue. Barr scoffs at Jeremias' arguments about the origins of *abba* in baby-talk or the babbling sounds of infancy.

Judaism, 43).

17 The title of Fitzmyer's essay is given above in note 14.
18 This paragraph summarizes and cites material from pages 28-35 of Fitzmyer's essay.
19 James Barr, "Abba Isn't 'Daddy'" *Journal of Theological Studies* 39 (1988) 28-47. I cite this article below as *Barr.* Vermes, *The Religion of Jesus the Jew* (Minneapolis: Fortress, 1993), in a chapter on "Abba, Father: The God of Jesus," cites Barr's article with approval.
20 James Barr, *The Semantics of Biblical Language* (Oxford University Press, 1961).

He shows how bad philology was at work in Jeremias' thinking, and he blasts Jeremias for "looking upon origins as if they could tell us about contemporary functions."[21]

Barr notes that if the NT writers thought that the Aramaic *abba* meant "daddy", they had Greek words readily available in the culture to signal that fact. The words *papas*, *pappas*, *pappias* and *pappidion* existed as words "somewhat similar in nuance and usage" to our 'daddy'. NT writers could have used these words to render *abba* but chose not to. The nuance they sought was not that of "daddy" but of "father."[22]

Two of Barr's philological conclusions:

1. "It is fair to say that *abba* in Jesus' time belonged to a familiar or colloquial register of language, as distinct from more formal and ceremonious usage, though it would be unwise...to press this too far. But in any case it was not a childish expression comparable with 'Daddy': it was more a solemn, responsible, adult address to a Father."[23]

2. "Although the use of *abba* in address to God may have been first originated by Jesus, it remains difficult to prove how constant and pervasive this element was in his expression of himself."[24]

That leads Barr to a theological or christological conclusion. Whereas Jeremias says that "Jesus regarded *abba* as a sacred word"[25] and that the word has unique power to reveal Jesus' self-consciousness and sense of mission, Barr concludes that it is difficult, indeed impossible, to prove that *abba* can serve as the key to our understanding of Jesus.[26]

Barr's Goal

Barr's primary goal throughout his essay is to call into question the linguistic arguments of Jeremias and to object to the work of any exegetes who, in ignorance of current philological and linguistic science, think they can build great theological structures upon the foundation of single words.

Vermes, Fitzmyer and Barr all express concerns about the efforts of Jeremias to construct a high christology on the basis of Jesus' use or alleged use of the word *abba*. Vermes says that instead of focusing on *abba*, we will do better to look to the Lord's Prayer. It gives us "a reliable insight into Jesus' mind" with its earthiness and emphasis on obedience to God.[27] This is a piety that Vermes can and does affirm. Fitzmyer turns to passages like Luke 10:21-22//Matt 11:25-27 for insight into Jesus' mind and finds a high christology, exactly what Vermes wants to avoid. Barr, in addition to underminding Jeremias' linguistic arguments, wants to warn against the sentimentalizing of the human relationship to God and of human speech concerning God.[28]

---

21 *Barr* 35.
22 *Barr* 37f.
23 *Barr* 46.
24 *Barr* 47.
25 *Barr* 68.
26 *Barr* 47.
27 *Jesus and the World of Judaism*, 43.
28 Barr wrote a second essay in 1988. "Abba, Father and the Familiarity of Jesus' Speech" appeared in

In spite of the spirited conversation among Jeremias, Vermes, Fitzmyer and Barr, many newer works continue to rely cheerfully on Jeremias, making only the slightest modifications of his claims.[29]

Mary Rose D'Angelo

Something fresh with regard to the address "father" was offered by Mary Rose D'Angelo in an article published back in 1992. Her suggestions seem to me not to have received the attention they deserve. At least her suggestions have not yet reached as far as popular literature and the pulpits of our churches.[30]

D'Angelo surpasses Barr in her negative appraisal of Jeremias. She states that the word "'father' as an address to God cannot be shown (1) to originate with Jesus, (2) to be particularly important to his teaching, or even (3) to have been used by him."[31]

So D'Angelo disagrees not only with Jeremias but with any, like Fitzmyer or the members of the Jesus Seminar, who think that *abba* puts us in touch with the historical Jesus. The Jesus seminar is notoriously miserly in assigning the label "authentic" to the recorded words of Jesus. But even the Jesus Seminar accepts the historicity of Jesus' word *abba/father*.[32]

Theology 91 (1988) 173-179. In it he says that Jeremias' interpretation of *abba*, "while emphasizing the divine fatherhood, gave a cosy twist to it." The penultimate sentence of this essay contains the following words: "Above all, the nuance of 'Abba' was not at all the nuance of childish prattle, but the nuance of solemn and responsible adult speech." Hans Dieter Betz in his *The Sermon on the Mount* (Minneapolis: Fortress Press, 1995), in discussing *abba/father* warns of the danger of "sentimentalism" and a "silly naivete." What the analogy of the father-child relationship intends to express, he writes, "is the recognition of the plain fact that we did not put ourselves on this earth but that we find ourselves here as a result of someone else's will and action." 388. Betz does not comment on the political horizon of "father." But he does speak in the near context of the eschatology of the Lord's Prayer as expecting "the kingdom of God to conquer and annex the territory at present inhabited by the rebellious human race." 391.

29 Charlesworth, reviewing recent discussions, concluded that "Abba" represents Jesus' own voice. But at the same time he agrees with Barr that there is no compelling evidence that Jesus used abba in the sense of 'daddy'. The meaning of the word in the mouth of Jesus is "Father."

   Charlesworth distances himself from the conclusions of B.L.Cooke who wrote that "Jesus' awareness of his Abba as faithfully loving and supremely lovable, an awareness that dominated his prayer and his teaching, was the most basic *word* communicated to him about the transcendent." *God's Beloved: Jesus' Experience of the Transcendent* (Philadelphia: Trinity Press, 1992, p.22).

   Charlesworth cites with approval Robert Hamerton-Kelly who writes that that a consensus exists among scholars that Jesus' abba experience is the starting point of christology. (see "God the Father in the Bible" in *God as Father?* Edited by Johannes-Baptist Metz and Edward Schillebeeckx, New York: Seabury, 1981).

   For these references see James Charlesworth, "A Caveat on Textual Transmissin and the Meaning of Abba: A Study of the Lord's Prayer" in *The Lord's Prayer and Other Prayer Texts from the Greco-Roman Era* (Valley Forge: Trinity Press, 1994).

30 Mary Rose D'Angelo, "*Abba* and 'Father': Imperial Theology and the Jesus Traditions," *Journal of Biblical Literature* 111 (1992) 611-630. She is currently working on a book on Roman family values, the use of "father" as a title for God, and early Christian sexual politics. Her essay will be cited below as *D'Angelo*.

31 *D'Angelo* 630.

32 "Jesus undoubtedly employed the term 'Abba' (Aramaic for 'Father') to address God. Among Judeans the name of God was sacred and was not to be pronounced (in the Dead Sea Scrolls community, a person was expelled from the group for pronouncing the name of God, even accidentally). Yet Jesus used a familiar form of address and then asked that the name be regarded as sacred—a paradox that seems characteristic of Jesus' teachings." *The Five Gospels*, by Robert W. Funk, Roy W. Hoover, and

However, what is most interesting to me is another and more positive aspect of D'Angelo's work. She suggests a shift in the entire discussion. D'Angelo raises once again the question of the linguistic home of the words "*abba*" and "father." Is it baby-talk? Is it colloquial and familiar adult language as distinct from more formal usage? Is it the respectful speech of disciples to their masters or of the younger to their revered elders? Is it language characteristic of the prayers of a few especially pious ancient Jewish charismatics as they addressed God? What context best illumines the word "father" in early Christianity?

With many others D'Angelo notes that speaking of God as "father" was increasingly common in the New Testament and in early Christianity as well as in early Judaism.[33] How can we account for that increase? She suggests that the use of the title "father" may very well have been "in the context of spiritual resistance to imperial pretensions."[34]

Many have noted that, beginning with Julius Caesar (d.44 BC) and then especially under Augustus (d. AD 14), Roman rulers were given the title of "father of the nation" (*pater patriae*). This use of *pater* reflects a view of the empire as a vast family in which the emperor functions as head of the household, as *paterfamilias*.[35]

D'Angelo calls attention to the fact that Roman philosophers like Dio Chrysostom (d. after 112) attempted to instruct and influence the conduct of emperors by invoking the name and therefore the qualities of Zeus. Dio and others wrote that the rule of Zeus, commonly called "father" and "king," should serve as model for any earthly sovereigns who desired their rule to be good and virtuous.

Jews and Christians, however, had a different agenda from Roman rulers and Roman philosophers. Christians agreed with Jews in exalting God's reign and in various ways resisting the absolute claims of Roman emperors. Calling God "father," says D'Angelo, implied resistance to Roman imperial claims. Invoking God as "father" was a solemn and subversive confession that God alone is the Head of our household (whether synagogue or church).

So in D'Angelo's view the Roman imperium is the horizon within which early Christians, like their Jewish cousins, used the word "father" in addressing God and in speaking about God. They were making a spiritual-political statement.

---

the Jesus Seminar (Macmillan 1993), p. 149. Jeremias had claimed that Jesus regarded *abba* as a "sacred" word.

33 Statistics are given and the increasing use is examined in Jeremias, *The Prayers of Jesus* (London: SCM Press, 1967) 29-44.

34 D'Angelo 628.

35 John H. Elliott, *A Home for the Homeless: A Sociological Exegesis of 1 Peter* (Philadelphia: Fortress, 1981), offers an excellent introduction to the whole matter of the Roman emperor as pater patriae prompting the Christian confession of God as the head of the household to which the believers belong. See especially pages 175-233. David Sear, *Roman Coins and their Value* (London: Seaby's Numismatic Publications, 1970) notes that *pater patriae* was first bestowed on Augustus in 2 B.C. and was subsequently conferred on most of his successors at the time of their accession along with two other titles: Augustus and Pontifex Maximus. Nero (55), Vespasian (70), Titus (79) and Domitian (81) received the title and stamped their coins accordingly. Nerva received the three titles in 96 and Trajan in 98. Tiberius (14-37) refused the title, and Hadrian (117-138) and Marcus Aurelius (161-180) accepted it only after ruling for many years. Sear, 51.

D'Angelo's Goal

What is her goal? Why does she launch what she herself calls "a frontal assault" on what Jeremias and others call "the Abba experience of Jesus"? It is more than a purely scholarly matter of setting straight the historical record. D'Angelo is responding to the widespread contemporary conviction that Jesus' use of *abba/father* in his address to God privileges masculine language and imagery for the divine to such an extent that all other language and imagery must be regarded not only as second-rate but as unholy.

D'Angelo sees a problem with her own conclusions. When early Christians responded to Roman imperial claims by declaring that God alone is our "father," they fell into the trap of picturing the Christian God as a "father" or "emperor" whose power exceeds that of every other "father." They pictured God in terms of imperial power, and the "kingdom of God" was understood as the infinitely mighty rival of the kingdom of the caesars. D'Angelo laments the way God came to be pictured in terms of domineering patriarchal and imperial power.

In the concluding paragraph of her essay she writes, "Neither Jesus nor the NT can be shown to have used the word "father" in a way that constitutes a transhistorical revelation that is unique and will be irreparably lost if twentieth-century theology and practice choose other imagery for God." She reminds readers that Christianity was born within patriarchal and imperial horizons, and our traditional language for God arose in that particular setting. We need continually to ask, she says, how those horizons and that context have "limited our visions of the divine."[36] I myself wonder how recovery of those horizons and context might contribute to a revitalization of our vision and language. But more on that below.

Herman Waetjen

Herman Waetjen has recently focused his scholarly and spiritual energy on the Lord's Prayer as it has been handed down to us in the gospels of Matthew and Luke. His study, *Praying the Lord's Prayer*, is full of insight and power.[37]

I opened its pages wondering how he would treat the word "father." At first it seemed that he was in complete agreement with Jeremias. In discussing "father," Waetjen cites Jeremias several times, always with approval. The members of the new community who still today gather as brothers and sisters in the table fellowship inaugurated by Jesus invoke God as *abba/father*. When they address God in that way, they are using "children's speech," identifying themselves as members of the household of God, newly reconstituted by God through Jesus. *Abba*, writes Waetjen, is a term of "intimacy, familiarity, and affection."[38]

However, one of Waetjen's explicitly announced goals is to help Christian people see that the Lord's Prayer lifts the eyes of the suppliant beyond "our immediate world of personal affairs and relationships." The horizon of the Lord's Prayer encompasses "larger issues of justice and peace, poverty and homelessness, moral and

---

36 *D'Angelo* 630.
37 Harrisburg: Trinity Press International, 1999. Cited below as *Waetjen.*
38 This paragraph summarizes material in *Waetjen* 55-59, 71, 74, 76f, 83.

environmental crises." The Lord's Prayer envisions "the actualization of God's rule on earth."[39]

Like D'Angelo, Waetjen moves beyond the quest for the historical Jesus. That business of trying to penetrate behind the canonical gospels to the "Jesus of history" was the focus of much of the work of Jeremias, as it still is of the Jesus Seminar and of many other scholars. But in his introduction Waetjen suggests that petitioners should pray the Lord's prayer "on the basis of the foundational self-understanding" that the gospels of Matthew and Luke convey.[40] Waetjen guides readers away from the methods of those who would isolate the word *abba/father* as a sacred word brimming all by itself with powerful significance. He invites us to read and understand that intriguing word in the context of the Lord's Prayer and then to read the Lord's Prayer in the context of Matthew's gospel.

It is noteworthy that Waetjen treats in a single chapter both the invocation ("father") and the first petition of the Lord's Prayer. He writes that "after the Founder of this new household has been addressed intimately and familiarly as Papa or Father, it is appropriate and indeed necessary to acknowledge the wholly otherness and also the loftiness, the supremacy, and the sublimity of the Head of this family."[41]

Waetjen used three nouns to interpret "father": "intimacy, familiarity, affection." Now he offers another set of three nouns and calls these "necessary" for our understanding of God and our life of discipleship: "loftiness, supremacy, sublimity." The "name" of God means the Being of God, "and the reality of that Being is to be reverenced, glorified, and worshiped."[42]

Waetjen continues by interpreting the first three petitions (the name of God, the rule of God, the will of God) as "the initiatives God is pursuing in the world."[43] We are invited to pray these petitions as a form of self-identification as well as commitment to active engagement in the realization of those initiatives.

The following petitions (our bread, our sins, our struggle with evil) give voice, he writes, to the needs that we all share with other members of God's family.

Waetjen then declares the content of the Lord's Prayer to be "complete."[44] He goes on to remind readers that the canonical gospels portray Jesus as engaged in activities like these: "the pursuit of justice and peace, the termination of all forms of retaliation; the transmission of health and wholeness in the world which we inhabit; embodying the love of 1 Corinthians 13; being open, vulnerable and inclusive in our relationships to others; living and acting out the empowerment of God's indwelling Spirit; contributing as liberally as we can to the needs of all our fellow human beings; accepting and fulfilling our servanthood in the freedom and sovereignty we have as members of God's household."[45] By calling all these activities of Jesus to mind, the Lord's Prayer is "complete."

---

39 *Waetjen* xf.
40 *Waetjen* xiii.
41 *Waetjen* 59f.
42 *Waetjen* 62.
43 *Waetjen* 121.
44 *Waetjen* 119.
45 *Waetjen* 119f.

Praying the Lord's Prayer within this horizon of consciousness invests the address "father" with new meaning. It is tempting to say that understanding "father" within this horizon should lead inevitably to a total break with Jeremias' interpretation of "father" within the horizon of the ancient Palestinian family. However, Waetjen affirms both intimacy and familiarity with God on the one hand and the loftiness and supremacy of God over all things on the other.

Waetjen's Goal

In all of this Waetjen is the engaged scholar, revealing his spiritual commitments as well as his exegetical expertise. He seems to recognize that many Christians are moving along a trajectory from the individualistic, pietistic spirituality of their childhood and youth toward a larger and more robust spirituality of the kind that Waetjen so eloquently articulates. One of Waetjen's chief goals as an interpreter of the Lord's Prayer is to invite readers who have not already done so to join him in the journey.

My Goal(s)

One of my chief aims in writing these sentences has been to honor my friend Herman, from whom I have learned so much through many years of friendship. It is good to say "thank you" out loud and in public. My other goal has been to set myself and others thinking about the political horizon of the invocation of God as "father." Mary Rose D'Angelo opened my eyes to this possibility, and I find that I welcome it more warmly than she herself does.

Taking seriously her suggestion of a political horizon helps us to break free from the old habit of viewing NT writers like Matthew and John as struggling primarily to define the new Jesus movement against the contemporary synagogue movement.

The usual paradigm for understanding the agonistic qualities of Matthew's gospel is that of "the church struggling with the synagogue across the street." Matthew is regularly interpreted as presenting the new Jesus movement as anti-synagogue, as if he were saying, "These are our Christian practices and convictions and they are not only different from but also better than those of your synagogue."

But was Matthew writing primarily in response to his community's struggle with the synagogue? For a long time I have been skeptical of that widespread opinion, preferring to think that Matthew was involved in an internal Christian struggle among factions within the emerging Jesus movement.[46]

However, my eyes are beginning to be opened to the fact that Matthew wrestles in his gospel quite self-consciously with the issue of Jesus as agent of God's sovereignty in a world dominated by Roman power.[47]

---

46 See Robert H. Smith, "Matthew's Message for Insiders: Charisma and Commandment in a First-Century Community" in *Interpretation* 46 (1992) 229-239.

47 The most extensive exploration so far of the relationship between Matthew's gospel and the Roman empire has been carried out by Warren Carter in a series of essays collected and expanded in *Matthew and Empire: Initial Explorations* (Harrisburg: Trinity Press International, 2001). Carter does not dismiss as wrong the conventional focus on relations with the synagogue, but he does think that focus has been too narrow. The older traditional way of reading Matthew turns it into "an exclusively religious work, concerned only with religious questions and personal matters." (p. 1). Carter throws light on "the close and vital relationship between Matthew's gospel and the Roman imperial world."

It should have been obvious to me all along. As Matthew's gospel nears its end, for example, Matthew poignantly narrates the way Jesus was crucified by order of Pontius Pilate, the Roman prefect of Judea. Jesus died and was buried, but then the (apparently) Roman guards at Jesus' tomb did not have the power to contain him. Jesus, raised from the dead, appears to his disciples and utters a declaration in the form of an imperial decree. He begins by announcing his possession of "total authority" not simply "in the church" or "in all matters religious" but over the totality of "heaven and earth." And he bids his first followers to "produce disciples" out of "the totality of the nations." The horizon of these accounts is not church-synagogue disputes and is in fact not narrowly "religious" at all.[48]

The invocation of God as "father" in Matthew's gospel is an invitation to pray against the fatherhood of the emperor. Jesus came neither to restore the kingdom of David nor to urge acquiescence to the dynamics of the kingdom of Caesar but to inaugurate the "kingdom" of God. This theme needs to be recovered in our own contemporary struggles with the claims made by shahs and caesars, presidents and prime ministers.

As is the case with all the other authors cited in this essay, I am influenced in ways that I cannot always fully fathom by my own personal and social-political context. I am writing these words in the early weeks of 2003, when the nation's leaders seem bent on war, and when criticism of the administration is regarded in many circles as unpatriotic.

It has been comfortable for me and for many to think and live in agreement with the piety of people like Joachim Jeremias. How late in my life I have begun to see how uncritical of worldly government my inherited piety has been! So this essay honoring my friend turns out to be also a work of self-examination or even a *mea culpa*.

---

(172). One implication of his study, he writes, is that "reading Matthew as a work of resistance to Rome's empire, *trains contemporary readers to be suspicious of the structures and actions of all ruling powers whether national, ethnic, political, economic, social, cultural, or religious."* (173).

48 See the discussion of the form of Matthew 28:18-20 as an "official or royal decree" in R.H.Smith, *Easter Gospels: The Resurrection of Jesus according to the Four Evangelists* (Minneapolis: Augsburg, 1983) 78-91. For my thinking about Matt 28:18-20 as a royal decree I am most indebted to Bruce Malina, "The Literary Structure and Form of Matt 28:16-20" in *New Testament Studies* 17 (1970) 87-103.

Marking the New Humanity

Discourses on the Way

Theodore Louis Trost

I gratefully acknowledge at the outset that this entire essay is so infused with the work of Herman Waetjen that it functions primarily as a footnote to his writing and teaching.

I. "Kingdom"

We live in an age of "might makes right"; an age in which there is only one world superpower—and I'm not referring here to the omnipotent God of Abraham, Isaac, and Jacob, though that God is conjured up for pious display when it serves certain political ends; an age in which the superpower defends its efforts to effect "regime change" abroad under the rubric "because we can, we must"; and so we do. Or to draw upon another fancy turn of phrase, this time from *Zenyatta Mondatta*, the third album by the rock group *The Police*: we live in an age of "too many cameras and not enough food."[1] Much of Africa is consumed by an epidemic of AIDS; you and I, meanwhile, are made witnesses to this crisis for as long as the CNN report lasts between the commercial for cosmetics and the one for the latest Suburban Utility Vehicle hot off the assembly line from Detroit, or Alabama, or Mexico.

The world as we know it is not the kingdom of God. The end of the Cold War did not bring the kingdom of God into being. Y2K (or the start of the third millennium of the Christian Era) did not bring the kingdom of God into being. The events of September 11, 2001, did not bring the kingdom of God into being. The destruction of the Taliban regime in Afghanistan did not bring the kingdom of God into being. And I doubt that the demise of Saddam Hussein's regime or any other holdout cabal in the so-called "Axis of Evil" will bring the kingdom of God into being.

But wait a second: what is the kingdom of God? This is the question that I'd like to explore here with the help of the Gospel of Mark. I have chosen Mark's Gospel as one voice in a conversation about who Jesus Christ is and what his appearance on earth might mean: a conversation that was organized into what Christians call the New Testament; a conversation that has continued in dialogue with that collection of writings down to this very day.

Mark's Gospel is generally agreed to be the oldest of the canonical gospels, written shortly after (and in all likelihood in response to) the destruction of the Temple in Jerusalem: an act of terror committed by the Romans in 70 AD to bring the unruly Judeans to their knees. That strategy of intimidation—enacted by the world's most powerful nation at the time—did not work, by the way.

Mark's Gospel has been called "the surprising gospel" by numerous biblical scholars.[2] It surprises for a variety of reasons. It contains no birth narrative, for one. Mark is apparently indifferent to the matter of Mary's virginity, or, more importantly,

---

1   Sting, "Driven to Tears," *Zenyatta Mondatta* by the Police, A & M Records, 1980.

2   For example Donald Juel, *A Master of Surprise: Mark Interpreted* (Minneapolis: Fortress, 1994).

Jesus' lineage and his birth in Bethlehem. Mark offers neither a genealogical nor a narrative link to the hallowed kingship of David. Thus the bold claim, already enunciated in the first sentence of Mark's Gospel, that Jesus is the Christ—that is, the "anointed one" (the long-anticipated Messiah)—is perplexing. How can this be? Mark's Gospel also contains no appearance of the resurrected Christ after the burial in Jerusalem. Instead, the most ancient manuscripts have a brief account of an encounter in Jesus' tomb between a young man dressed in white and the three women who have come to care for Jesus' dead body. The young man tells the women that Jesus has left Jerusalem and has gone ahead to Galilee; he tells the women to impart this news to the disciples and Peter, but, according to the last line of the Gospel as Mark wrote it (16:8), the women say nothing to anyone because they are afraid. This conclusion was so unsatisfactory that certain second century scribes made additions to Mark's text (verses 9-20) so that it might better conform to the other stories in circulation at the time—including the accounts by Matthew, Luke and John.

We will get to Mark's surprising—Mark's revolutionary—ending in due time. For now, let's begin at the beginning, with the first words Jesus utters in Mark's Gospel. The Gospel of Mark begins with Jesus undergoing a baptism in the waters of the Jordan River. He is immediately driven out into the wilderness among wild beasts, tempted, we are told, by Satan, and ministered to by angels. After forty days—a recapitulation of Israel's forty years in the wilderness—Jesus emerges in the far reaches of the Promised Land, in Galilee "preaching the good news [that is, the gospel, the *euangelion*] of God and saying: The time is fulfilled and the kingdom of God has come near; repent and believe in the good news" (Mark 1:14-15).

This term "kingdom of God" appears fourteen times in Mark's Gospel. In the hands of the other synoptic Gospel writers, who probably composed their texts with Mark's work before them, the term *basilea tou theou*, or "kingdom of God," is used seemingly interchangeably with the term *basilea ton ouranon*, "kingdom of heaven." This mingling of phrases caused biblical scholars from early on in the history of Christianity to assume that both terms really meant the same thing and referred to an extraterrestrial reality: "not of this world, but of the next"; not *in* time, as it were, but beyond time in an eternity that human beings can reach only through death (as one reading—I'd say the wrong one—of John's Gospel might have it). So "the kingdom of God" is often associated with the notion of heavenly reward, of "pie in the sky in the great by and by." Thus in the belief systems of certain contemporary Christian groups Jesus' bold proclamation gets turned into a plea to the sinners or backsliders to get themselves born again as quickly as possible. To paraphrase: "Time is running out and the kingdom of God is at hand; repent and reserve yourself a place in the heavenly kingdom!"

But if we stay in the Gospel of Mark, no such jump to hyperspace is possible because Mark never introduces the term "kingdom of heaven." He uses "kingdom of God" exclusively. He uses it as a description of what is already happening in the world through the life and work of Jesus Christ. He uses it to signal a new orientation in the world, in the aftermath of the Temple's destruction (historically speaking). Mark uses the "kingdom of God" to suggest a new paradigm of relationship; a new way for people to live together in community and in communion with God: a "reordering of power," as Herman Waetjen has called it.[3]

Now in this 21st century one could argue that the term "kingdom of God" is outmoded. On the surface, at least, it seems to represent an effort on the part of the early church to inscribe patriarchy. And indeed, a literal rendering of this phrase can avoid neither the male nor the hierarchical resonances of the term. With this in mind we might reconstruct the term and turn it into something like the "reign of God," or the "realm of God," or even the "regime of God." But note that a totally new and different concept is at work here on the lips of Jesus and, consequently, in the hearts and in the lives of his followers. This phrase is used parabolically in Mark's Gospel to both elicit the hearer's prior notions of kingdom and to undo them. That's the way parable works. It subverts the myth, the socially-constructed reality in which we live. And if it's a really good parable, it doesn't leave hanging the one who experiences it; rather it offers a whole new way to see, to be in, the world.[4] The Roman Catholic biblical scholar John R. Donahue has noted that the Gospel of Mark as a whole might be interpreted as such a parable.[5] And it also contains really good parables.

Although Mark's Gospel begins with the great pronouncement that the kingdom of God is at hand, the term does not appear again until chapter four, when Jesus begins to teach his disciples the "secrets of the kingdom of God." In this context of teaching, Jesus asks:

> To what should we compare the kingdom of God? Or by what parable may we present it? As a mustard seed, which when it is sown on the earth is smaller than all the seeds on the earth. But when it is sown, it grows up and becomes greater than all the shrubs (or vegetables, the Greek word is *laxanon*) and makes large branches so that the birds of the air can make nests in its shade (Mark 4:30-31).

It is instructive to see what Matthew does with the same parable. First of all, Matthew refers to the "kingdom of heaven." The parable then proceeds along the lines that Mark establishes until we get to the part about the vegetables, or the "shrub" according to the New Revised Standard Version's translation. There Matthew includes reference to the shrub but he stumbles over it on his way to turning the mustard plant into something much larger. Matthew writes: "But when it has grown [the mustard seed] is the greatest of shrubs and *becomes a tree*, so that the birds of the air come and make nests in its branches" (Matthew 13:32).

In Matthew's hands, this is a parable of contrast: small seed, big tree. In order to make the contrast work, Matthew has to turn the mustard shrub, or vegetable—or perhaps most accurately, weed—into a tree; for practically speaking, birds don't make their nests among the vegetables or weeds. And so Matthew offers a nice little moral in the tradition of Aesop. We have here the first century equivalent of the truism "tall oaks from tiny acorns grow." When this is played out before the backdrop of eternity, the lesson can turn into something like this: "This life be over soon. Heaven lasts for

---

3   Herman C. Waetjen, *A Reordering of Power: A Socio-Political Reading of Mark's Gospel* (Minneapolis: Fortress, 1990).

4   This understanding of parable comes from John Dominic Crossan, *The Dark Interval: A Theology of Story* (Sonoma, CA: Polerbridge, 1988; orig. 1975).

5   John R. Donahue, S.J., "Jesus as the Parable of God in Mark," *Interpretation* 32 (1978): 369-86.

always." That's what Miss Celie says to her friend Sophia in *The Color Purple* in order to explain why she allows herself and other women to be beaten by men.[6] What happens "on earth" is of little significance. Abuse is irrelevant because those who endure to the end will be rewarded with eternal life.

But that's not the way the parable functions in the Gospel of Mark. Mark insists on that word *laxanon*, vegetable, shrub, weed, and it renders Jesus' parable absurd. Biblical scholars have puzzled over this and botanists have studied the flora of Galilee thoroughly in the hope of finding some evidence of an ancient and mighty mustard weed. One senses the modern scholar's frustration in trying to make sense of the parable. Consider, for example, this entry under "mustard" in the *The Interpreter's Dictionary of the Bible*:

> A sizeable annual plant with very small seeds. The word (*sinapi*) appears only in the sayings of Jesus, in his parable of the mustard seed and in his simile concerning faith [that is: have faith like a mustard seed]. In the parable, the emphasis is on the growth of the kingdom (or the spread of the gospel?) from small beginnings to the large, world-embracing events of the future, similar to the tiny mustard seed which grows so rapidly into a large plant.
>
> Much debate has raged over the literal implications of the parable, which make the common mustard unsuitable for the illustration even though the Greek clearly refers to it. We know now that the orchid seed, not the mustard seed, is the smallest. The mustard does not grow to tree size, for it is an annual plant. Though fast growing, it could not be suitable for nesting birds in the spring.
>
> If the text must be rendered "makes nests in its branches," the exaggeration would be apparent even to the common person. Botanists avoid this problem by insisting that the verb translated "make nests" means only "settle upon," or "light upon," referring only to small birds. The apparent allusion to [certain Old Testament texts] seems to support the translation in which case the only solution is to take the expression as hyperbole.[7]

The references to hyperbole and, in particular, the Old Testament parallels, are useful here. To put it succinctly, the tradition is wrong in calling this the "parable of the mustard seed." The parable isn't about the growth of a small seed that becomes a big weed. The parable instead offers a contrast between two types of plants that symbolize a particular sense of nation, namely: God's nation or, as Jesus calls it in Mark, "the kingdom of God."

The contrast, then, is between the mighty cedar and the lowly mustard plant. Ezekiel was the famous prophet to the elite community of exiled Jews in Babylon. This community witnessed the destruction of Jerusalem in 587 BCE, including the dismantling of the Temple. In the Book of Ezekiel (Ezekiel 17:22-24), God makes a surprising promise that, despite all evidence to the contrary, devastation and despair will not be a permanent condition for the nation of Israel. Instead, God will once again restore the kingdom to a position of world prominence. Once again, Israel will become a superpower, indeed, the world's only superpower:

6   *The Color Purple*, dir. Stephen Spielberg, perf. Whoopi Goldberg, Oprah Winfrey and Danny Glover, Paramount, 1985.

7   J. C. Trever, "Mustard," *The Interpreter's Dictionary of the Bible* 3, George Buttrick, gen. ed. (New York: Abingdon, 1962), 462-463.

> And the trees of the field shall know that I the Lord bring low the high tree and make high the low tree, dry up the green tree and make the dry tree flourish (Ezekiel 17:24).

All the "trees of the field" will know that Israel's God is in charge of world events. All the other nations and peoples of the world will know that Israel is God's chosen instrument for wielding power and authority on earth.

From Ezekiel's perspective among the exiles, the cedar is an appropriate symbol for Israel's former glory and future destiny as a mighty nation. The cedar was praised for its strength and beauty as a hardwood and prized as a luxury good, a key import, during the reign of Solomon. Indeed, the walls of Solomon's Temple were lined with cedar. The tree itself grew to a height of some 130 feet.[8] It was no stretch of the imagination, then, merely a fact, that varieties of beasts dwelled beneath it and "in the shade of its branches birds of every sort built their nests."

This refrain about the birds building their nests in the tree's branches is a recurring one in the Hebrew Bible. It appears on another occasion in Ezekiel (Ezekiel 31:2-6) and Daniel echoes Ezekiel's language with reference to a great tree that connects heaven and earth (Daniel 4:10-12). Indeed, so towering and magnificent is the tree Daniel describes that it "was visible to the end of the whole earth." Thus when Jesus picks up this refrain and attaches it, seemingly absurdly, to the lowly mustard weed, he makes a radical critique of the "dominant paradigm." God's kingdom is not like the tall tree that towers above all others and dominates the horizon. Instead, the reign of God is exercised close to the ground, among the vegetables, the shrubs, and the weeds!

This, then, is the strange new concept of kingdom that Jesus offers his followers. The old way no longer works. It is time for a regime change. The new regime, the kingdom of God as Jesus inaugurates it and proclaims it in the Gospel of Mark, manifests itself in the common, the ordinary; not in the treetops, but in the weeds; not with the arrogant, but with the simple; not among the proud, but among the humble; not among those who have made a name for themselves or have inherited a name (and the legacies attached to it), but among the disinherited and, indeed, the unnamed.

There are grand lessons to be learned here for any nation that would call itself Christian; for any people who would call upon God's blessing and call themselves blessed.

II. "Glory"

In the African American tradition great reverence is expressed for the ancestors. Julie Dash's film *Daughters of the Dust* depicts this relationship visually through the Unborn Child—a character sent from the ancestral realm to guide the Peazant family from the Gullah Islands off the coast of Georgia into a new life somewhere in the North, presumably New York. In this tradition, the ancestors are not located in a remote netherworld; rather, they exist in a world of potentiality; a world of the future as well as of the past; a world that is in constant communication with "this world"; a world that is "next to" (that is, adjacent to and intersecting) "this world," rather than the "next" one temporally—which comes "after" the current life in "this world."[9]

8   J. C. Trever, "Cedar," *The Interpreter's Dictionary of the Bible* 1, George Buttrick, gen. ed. (New York: Abingdon, 1962), 545-546.

9   *Daughters of the Dust*, dir Julie Dash, perf. Cora Lee Day and Alva Rogers, Kino 1991.

Halloween is the closest American popular culture in general comes to embracing an understanding of the permeable borders between what might be called, in the language of John's Gospel, "this world" and the world "above." Halloween is a time to celebrate and to transgress borders. Every homeowner knows that the phrase "trick or treat" contains within it a threat to commit acts of delinquency should inadequate or insufficient treats be provided to the costumed coterie collected outside the front door. When the ghosts and goblins can barely pronounce their "r's," the threat is basically benign, of course. But many of us recall at this season our own years of childhood and youth. Perhaps a certain nostalgia is stirred up, a nostalgia immortalized in the name of that rock group led by Billy Corgan and called "The Smashing Pumpkins." And so I suspect there is a communal sigh of relief across urban and suburban lawns throughout America when the morning of November 1st comes around: the house is still intact; the light in the lamppost still works; and the pumpkins, though they have disappeared, have not been smashed. . . on *my* sidewalk, at least.

Christianly speaking, Halloween is the eve before All Saints Day: a time when the great saints of the Church—the named martyrs and the confessors—are recalled. All Saint's Day is followed, on November 2nd, by All Soul's Day: a day for remembering people who are less obviously heroes of the faith; for example, people who died, as Pope Benedict XV called it, in the "useless slaughter" of war;[10] people known only to a few friends and relatives; people who died in relative anonymity but in the hope of resurrection. The costumes worn on Halloween, then, symbolize and embody another kind of transgression, from a Christian point of view: the living dressed as the dead (as ghosts; or as beings from that other realm) affirm the presence of the dead among the living. Indeed, with respect to the Church calendar, one could say that the period immediately following Halloween is made up of days and nights of the living dead. It is a time for remembering, for bringing back into being, for keeping alive, for continuing the work and the witness of, the saints. All the saints: the famous ones and the ones whose names, if they are known at all, teeter on the edge of obscurity.

All Soul's Day took on a particularly poignant meaning in San Salvador, the capital city of that embattled country El Salvador, during the 1980s. It was a period when armed militia (death squads who obtained their weapons and military training from the United States) attacked and killed humble villagers who refused to cooperate with the savage—though "capitalism-friendly"—regime. Each year, in Archbishop Oscar Romero's church on All Soul's Day, the names of these citizens, killed by their own government, were read aloud during the Mass. And after each name was pronounced by the liturgist, the congregation would say *"Presente!"* That is: "Present!" Here among us! Not forgotten! Remembered: and therefore not dead yet. These services could go on for hours because so many innocents had been slaughtered. Eventually, the Archbishop himself was shot down by a death squad one Sunday while celebrating Mass; and on the ensuing All Soul's Day, his name was added to the list of martyrs.[11]

(In the aftermath of September 11, 2001, when people wonder in disbelief why the rest of the world seems to hate the United States so much, it is necessary to remember

---

10 Joseph Connelly, "All Souls," *The Westminster Dictionary of Worship*, J.G. Davies, ed. (Philadelphia: Westminster, 1972), 3.

11 This account is derived from the testimony of Jorge Lara-Braud who preached and taught at San Francisco Theological Seminary during the 1980s.

the story of that curiously, yet aptly, named country *El Salvador*: for its own sake and as a cipher for many other nations who have—in those poignantly paradoxical words of the rock group *U2*—"run into the arms of America."[12])

But one does not have to be martyred—to be killed, as it were, in the line of Christian duty—in order to be called a saint. The Puritans who came to America in the early part of the 17th century referred to each other as saints—a way of signaling their orientation toward Christ and community in the world. The story of the anonymous woman in Bethany (Mark 14:1-9) gives a marvelous example of a living saint; an example which, as is typical for the Gospel of Mark, is both unsettling and provocative.

It begins in the house of Simon the leper—a casual enough reference, but it is worth noting (in keeping with the boundary transgression theme) that Jesus dines in the house of someone considered unclean by the conventions and the ritual purity laws of his people. Then this curious episode unfolds. A woman pours an expensive ointment over Jesus' head. Others gathered around the table—Jesus' famous disciples among them—are outraged by this action. And for a change it might seem that the disciples have a point.

I say "for a change" because Jesus' named male disciples in the Gospel of Mark are excruciatingly dim-witted. When Jesus tells them the parables, the disciples don't understand them. When Jesus performs the miracle of the loaves and the fishes, again they don't understand what happened. *Twice.* Peter seems finally to be on the right track as the band of disciples passes through the villages of Caesarea Philippi. Jesus asks them, "who do you say that I am?" and Peter replies "You are the Christ." But almost immediately after that Jesus tells the disciples that the "Son of man" must suffer, be rejected, and killed.

Apparently this narrative of declension is not the program Peter thought he was signing up for back in Galilee. Back then the "Son of man" had all sorts of powers: the power to forgive sins (Mark 2:10); the power to be lord of the Sabbath (Mark 2:28); the power to cast out demons, anoint with oil, and heal the sick (Mark 6:13). This mention of suffering is new and unwelcome. And so Peter, in Mark's words "Took [Jesus] aside and began to rebuke him" (8:32). Jesus in turn rebukes this future saint of the Church with the words "Get behind me, Satan! For you are not on the side of God, but of men!" (The masculine language here is worth retaining, particularly in light of subsequent Church history.) Still later, after all the disciples fail miserably in their attempts to heal a youth who writhes in fits and spasms, the disciples get involved in an extended debate about which one among them is the greatest (Mark 9:34-41).

But now, at last, in the house of Simon the leper, some of the disciples appear to have understood the message. They want to do something for others. And while it may seem to be a matter of crying over spilt oil, as it were, after this woman has committed her beautiful act, their argument is nevertheless convincing. Three hundred *denarii* was the equivalent of one year's worth of wages for a day laborer. Imagine the relief such a sum could provide to the homeless of Bethany and the surrounding villages! Or the homeless of contemporary Washington, D.C., or the children of Baghdad, for that matter. In this era of "faith-based initiatives," it seems the disciples

12 Bono, "Bullet the Blue Sky," *The Joshua Tree* by U2, Island Records, 1987.

are on to something: they have found a way to redistribute resources to the needy; with strong religious motives behind them, their philanthropic efforts are bound to get good results—and at a low cost to the average taxpayer.

Jesus' reply, meanwhile, "the poor you will have with you always," seems uncharacteristically harsh. Indeed, perhaps no single saying from the Bible, taken out of its literary context and applied literally, has done more damage to the welfare of human society than this saying. The opulence of popes and princes, the subjugation of slave, peasant, and worker, and the economic theory of trickle-down, have all been justified on the basis of this saying.

So it is very important to understand what Mark's Jesus is saying here. Jesus says: "She has done a beautiful thing to me. You can do good to the poor whenever you will." In other words the call to serve and the opportunity—indeed, the command—to provide for the welfare of others is always present. This is to reaffirm a biblical imperative as recorded in the Book of Deuteronomy: "For the poor will never cease out of the land, therefore I command you, You shall open wide your hand to your brother, to the needy and to the poor, in the land" (Deuteronomy 15:11). Jesus' initial observation about the poor is anchored in *chronos*, chronological time, which is the sense of time the disciples seem to understand. And in chronological time a certain responsibility (for better or for worse) pertains to the needs of the poor: day in and day out, as it were.

"But," Jesus goes on to say, "you will not always have me." This woman is keyed into something the disciples still have not figured out. She embraces the truth that Peter rejected back in chapter eight even while he was calling Jesus "the Christ," namely: that this is no "victory march" into Jerusalem; suffering and death draw near and only afterwards, resurrection! In contrast to Peter, she is on the side of God and not of men. For her, then, this is a moment like no other. This is not a matter of "any time," but a matter of "all time." The unnamed woman recognizes this moment as *kairos*—the time that extends, proleptically and metaphorically speaking, from Friday to Sunday morning, the "crucified, dead, and buried" of a later creed and the rising on the third day. Her deed foreshadows and ordains (perhaps confirms would be a better word) the rest of the "Christ" story. Her gesture of overabounding grace parallels God's gracious work in Christ. Jesus says: "She has anointed my body beforehand for burying." Like a prophet, she has anointed Jesus king. She has understood the message Jesus came out proclaiming in the first chapter of Mark's Gospel: The time is ripe! Or: the *kairos* has been fulfilled! Or: "Time has come today!" in the words of the prophetic 1960s rock-blues-gospel anthem by the Chambers Brothers.[13] "The kingdom of God is at hand! Repent and believe in the gospel!" (Mark 1:15).

We get a sense of the urgency of this particular moment, I think, by the way that Mark has framed this incident. This anointing for burial and for kingship occurs between mention of a conspiracy on the part of certain authorities in verse one: "And the chief priests and the scribes were seeking how to arrest [Jesus] by stealth and kill him"; and Judas's resolve to betray Jesus in verse ten: "Then Judas Iscariot… went to the chief priests in order to betray [Jesus] to them."

---

13 Lester Chambers, "Time Has Come Today," *The Chambers Brothers: The Time Has Come*, Columbia Records, 1967.

Between these ominous verses we encounter this unnamed woman whose deed is so remarkable that, according to Jesus (and here's a statement for literalists to ponder carefully) "wherever the gospel is preached in the whole world, what she has done will be told in memory of her." Certainly what Judas proceeds to do "on the night of [Jesus'] betrayal" has been told time and again in the Church. Indeed, reference to it is incorporated into the celebration of the Eucharist. But what of this woman's unnoticed deed? A deed Jesus links intimately to the central meaning of the gospel?

As noted above, Mark's Gospel begins with the baptism of an adult Jesus into the River Jordan. Unlike Matthew and Luke, there is no birth narrative in Mark, no story to locate an infant Jesus in Bethlehem—the city of David and the town from whence the long-anticipated Messiah was expected to come. This woman's deed, on the one hand, confirms unambiguously (as opposed to Peter's boggled confession in chapter 8) that Jesus *is* "the Christ," that is: "the anointed." But Jesus says that she has anointed his body for burial. Here the other shoe falls. For though Jesus is the Messiah, he does not come as conqueror. His kingdom is ushered in through being, first of all, conquered—through death. This is the part Peter didn't like! Only through death can come resurrection—as Christians subsequently affirm in the ritual of baptism.

This anointing, by the way, renders superfluous the task of anointing Jesus' body for burial on the third day at the tomb. In Mark's Gospel Mary Magdalene, Mary the mother of James, and Salome come to the tomb with the intention of anointing Jesus. They are greeted by a young man who announces that Jesus is not there, he is risen! And so the young man gives the women—and the readers of Mark's Gospel—another task to perform.

For Mark's purposes it is important to note that the woman who anoints Jesus is not Mary Magdalene. For one thing, why would Mary Magdalene—if she had already anointed Jesus (symbolically, at least)—go to the tomb to do it again? For another, it is characteristic of Mark to leave his most auspicious characters unnamed. In Mark's narrative world, the unnamed ones are the people who understand who Jesus is, what he is doing, and where his story (that is to say, his "way" [*hodos*]—which has become their way) is going.

Who, then, is this nameless one? Simply put, she is one of the saints. And who are the "saints" in the Gospel of Mark? They are the ones, as Jesus states elsewhere in Mark, who came not to be served but to serve (Mark 10:45). This is a marvelously subversive statement; one which, like the saying about the mustard weed, undoes prior notions about how God intends to effect regime change on earth. For in Daniel's apocalyptic vision—his vision of "kingdom come"—all the nations gather to serve the "Son of man" (Daniel 7:14) whose existence is intimately linked in a later passage to a holy community called the "people of the *saints* of the Most High" (Daniel 7:27).[14] But Jesus says that the "Son of man" and those who would identify themselves through him—the "New Humanity," as Herman Waetjen calls them—advance the purposes of the kingdom not by being served, but through service. The gospel is more likely contained in the humble deed rather than the grand gesture. The kingdom of God is not a mighty cedar; it is a mustard weed. Greatness in this realm, then, to use another phrase from Mark's Gospel, is a matter of being last of all and servant of all (Mark

14 Waetjen, *A Reordering of Power*, xiii.

10.43-44). And if being last of all and servant of all means losing your name—or better yet, not needing to defend it—so be it. For in just this way, through service, the saints "glorify God" and enjoy God forever.

But that does not mean forgetting the person or the deed. And so it seems to me entirely appropriate, in the African American tradition and in the spirit of the gospel, that we share the story of Jesus' anointing "unto her memory," in memory of her; that we recognize her—along with so many others who have gone before and after her—as beings among us; that we indeed declare each of them *Presente!* and thereby celebrate the glory of God that shines all around us!

III. "Power"

Let me turn for a moment to where we have been with Mark's Gospel in order to prepare the way for where we are going with it. In the first part of this discourse we looked at what the tradition calls the "parable of the mustard seed," but which might more accurately be referred to as the "parable of the mustard weed"—a parable that arose in contrast to the great cedar tree of Ezekiel 17. Both plants stand as symbols for a kind of socio-political and spiritual *power* that is contained in the concept of kingship, or government, or regime. One of these kingdoms is based on physical might and height. Ezekiel offers us the image of a tree that towers above all others; it rises to the top, hierarchically speaking, and dominates the landscape. The phallic implications of this image would be difficult to ignore—particularly in an age of "long range missiles" and "smart bombs." The other kingdom is based on the weak and the common. The mustard weed Jesus conjures up in Mark celebrates horizontality. It is scattered democratically, so to speak, across the Judean countryside. One of these images offers a potent symbol of power as it seems to operate in the 21st century. The other, the one Jesus recommends, is mocked and scorned in today's world of *Realpolitik* and the quest that stands at the heart of every James Bond (and Austin Powers) movie: the quest for world domination. But then again, Christians who are worthy of bearing that name should not be afraid to be mocked and scorned....

In the second section we encountered a fantastic unnamed woman who anoints Jesus with oil in preparation for his burial. So awesome is this deed, from Jesus' point of view, that he makes a rather bold pronouncement: "wherever the gospel is preached throughout the whole world, what this woman did will be preached in memory of her" (Mark 14:9). Even though sermons are preached all the time in memory of Peter, the one who denied Jesus, and a whole rock opera exists—"Jesus Christ Superstar"— which might be called the Gospel According to Judas, one is hard-pressed to find references to this woman (at least as Mark presents her to us) in the homiletic treasury of Western Christendom. Ironically, her obscurity, her anonymity, is a mark of honor in the narrative world of Mark's Gospel. Indeed, I have characterized her as a "saint" in the kingdom of God, a member of that community of the saints of the most high, a representative of the New Humanity: one who came not to be served but to serve (Mark 10:45).[15]

---

15 This reverence for her, precisely because she is unknown, is different from but related to the appreciation articulated by Elizabeth Schussler Fiorenza. See *In Memory of Her* (New York: Crossroad, 1983), xiii.

And now I'd like to turn to another obscure and anonymous saint. The account I have in mind is so bizarre that neither Matthew nor Luke—both of whom incorporated a great deal of Mark into their narratives—bothered to copy it into their gospels. Mark alone offers a brief glimpse of a "young man" (*neaniskos*, in the Greek) who streaks, as it were, into the pages of the Christian canon only to disappear—perhaps forever— after two verses.

That's a big "perhaps." And indeed a small minority of scholars—Herman Waetjen at the forefront of them—has argued that the youth does not disappear but rather reappears at the end of Mark's Gospel to point the way beyond death in the tomb to a new life lived out in the reality of the resurrection.[16] But that's to get ahead of the story. For now, let's consider the moment of Jesus' capture and arrest: the moment of the young man's appearance in the text.

We begin with the words "And they all forsook him and fled" (Mark 14:50). This word "all" (*pantes*) is used on numerous occasions to designate specifically the well-known, named, twelve disciples as they sit, first with Jesus at table celebrating the Passover meal together, and later that evening, as they follow Jesus to the Garden of Gethsemane. Jesus predicts to the twelve, for example, that in the very near future, "*All* of you will fall away... and the sheep will be scattered" (Mark 14:27). Peter, in what is his typical blustering fashion in Mark's Gospel, declares: "Even if *all* fall away, I will not!" (14:29). Jesus goes on to tell how Peter will deny him that very evening, to which Peter announces "with great emphasis": "Even if I have to die for you, there's no way I will deny you." And, Mark records: "they *ALL* said the same" (14:31).

But then, of course, when the moment came, they *ALL* fled. Except this certain (*tis*) strange young man. He follows—actually "continues to accompany" (*suvnakoloutheou*)—Jesus beyond the moment of his abandonment by the twelve. When the crowd with swords and clubs attempt to arrest the youth, he leaves his clothes behind and disappears naked into the night.

The phenomenon of "streaking" is alleged to have begun at the University of South Carolina in late January or early February, 1974. It quickly spread to other campuses. That same year at the University of Maryland, for example, mass streaks occurred, with up to 125 runners flashing across the campus. It may be a mere coincidence that later that year, on August 8th, Richard M Nixon resigned his post as President of the United States.

Mark's Gospel offers a much earlier example of the phenomenon: one filled with far greater meaning for the course of human history. The young man disappears from the scene; but he does not disappear from the text. He is not running away, I would suggest; he is running ahead. On the one hand, his escape from the bonds that would ensnare him foreshadows Jesus' own escape from the bonds of death. Among other

16 Herman Waetjen, "The Ending of Mark and the Gospel's Shift in Eschatology," *Annual of the Swedish Theological Institute* 4 (1965): 114-131. See also, among others, Robin Scroggs and Kent I. Groff, "Baptism in Mark: Dying and Rising with Christ," *Journal of Biblical Literature* 92/5 (1973): 531-548; Thomas E. Boomershine and Gilbert L. Bartholomew, "The Narrative Technique of Mark 16. 8," *Journal of Biblical Literature* 100/2 (1981): 213-223; and Theodore Louis Trost, "A Portrait of the Young Man (*Neaniskos*) as Hero in the Gospel of Mark," MA thesis, Graduate Theological Union, 1989.

things, then, this miraculous "exodus" (as the gospel writer Luke might calls it [compare Luke 9:31]) anticipates Jesus' own resurrection.

But not only the resurrection of Jesus. For, on the other hand, this young man's departure anticipates a return. We meet him again in the tomb, on the morning of the third day. Dressed in a white robe, he announces to the women that Jesus has risen; he tells them to tell the disciples and Peter the news; and he directs them to Galilee—where they are meant to meet up with Jesus, who has, characteristically, gone ahead of them. Shockingly, Mark's Gospel then ends with the ominous sentence: "they said nothing to anyone for they were afraid." This, in any case, is how the most ancient and reliable manuscripts of Mark record it. The additional verses were appended to the Gospel to make it conform to other well known tales, such as Matthew, Luke, and John (all of which contain accounts of a post-resurrection appearance of Jesus), thereby explicitly confirming through reliable witnesses (rather than by faith alone) the Christ's power over death.

Mark confirms this power over death in another way: by an appeal to the hearer's own experience of baptism. Thus the "young man"—who some interpreters suggest is the author Mark himself (after all, who else would make note of such an obscure and embarrassing escapade?)—most significantly symbolizes the baptized Christian, the "New Human Being": the one who bears the name of Christ and is already participating in the power of the resurrection through proclamation and deed.

A number of factors in this story bring me to this assertion. First, the word "young man," *neaniskos* in the Greek, appears on only two occasions in the entire text of Mark, namely these two occasions: the moment of capture in the garden and the moment when resurrection is proclaimed in the tomb. Something singular is signaled by linking those moments with this word. If, as many have claimed, Mark wanted to suggest a heavenly being at the end of his Gospel, he could have used the word "angel."[17] After all, Mark's Gospel begins with Jesus in the company of these extra-terrestrial messengers (the *angeloi* of Mark 1:13) and it would make good literary sense for the Gospel to conclude with a voice from the heavenly realm. But as I have suggested before, Mark is focused on the kingdom of God as a this-worldly possibility —indeed, reality. And so it is crucial that a human messenger proclaims the resurrection at Gospel's end.

Second, the youth's movement from nakedness to being clothed in white is characteristic of the way the ritual of baptism was practiced in the early Church. After casting off the clothing of the old life (the old Adam and Eve, if you will), the initiate, the *catechumen*, entered the baptismal waters—symbolizing death with Christ— reemerging from them to don a white robe, symbolizing participation in a new creation, the resurrected body of Christ.[18] While water is missing from our story, it is significant that the young man disappears, naked, on Maundy Thursday night—which, according to the Jewish measure of time, is Friday, the new day having begun after sunset. His disappearance coincides, then, with the story the Apostles' Creed summarizes: "was crucified, dead, and buried." After his departure on Good Friday,

---

17 See for example Allan K. Jenkins, "Young Man or Angel?" *Expository Times* 94/8 (1983): 237-240.

18 This understanding of baptism is influenced by Oscar Cullman, *Baptism in the New Testament* (Philadelphia: Westminster, 1950) and Wayne Meeks, "The Image of the Androgyn: Some Uses of a Symbol in Earliest Christianity," *History of Religions* 13 (1974): 165-208.

the young man appears again on the third day, having put on new clothing. He rises with Christ. In other words, he embodies the precise narrative that the water comes to symbolize.

Third, to pursue the matter of the absent water for a moment longer, it is important to recall that Mark's Gospel begins with Jesus' baptism in the Jordan River. And by those waters, John the Baptist makes an intriguing prophecy about the one who will come after him. John says: "I baptize you with water, but he—Jesus [among others?] —will baptize you with the Holy Spirit." In Mark, the Holy Spirit is always associated with speaking, with articulation. In this regard Mark seems to understand the work of the Holy Spirit in a way similar to Luke, the author of Acts. Thus on the great day of Pentecost in the second chapter of the Book of Acts, the people gathered in Jerusalem are filled with the Holy Spirit; they begin to speak in tongues; and everyone understands everyone else—even though they do not all share the same native language (Acts 2:6-12). Here at the end of Mark, the young man says quite plainly: "Jesus is risen! Go. Tell!" As in ancient baptismal practice, the ritual "death by water" and putting on the robe of new life are followed by a confession of faith: Jesus is risen!

Fourth, this phrase "Go, tell" is extraordinary in Mark's Gospel. Mark is often referred to as the "hidden" gospel because an air of secrecy hovers over the whole text. The parables, for example, are mysteries that are explained only to the initiated (including those who read or overhear Mark's Gospel)—though Jesus assures his disciple that, ultimately, "nothing is hidden except to be revealed." In fact, Jesus' constant refrain in the Gospel of Mark is the charge to his disciples to "Tell no one" who he is. Even after Peter declares him the Christ, Mark records, Jesus "charged them to tell no one about him" (8:30).

Fifth there is precedent and prolepsis for the experience the young man undergoes and it does include water. The Geresene demoniac of chapter five appears naked in the tombs at the beginning of the story (Mark 5:1). His nakedness is by inference in Mark —an inference Luke made explicit by inserting the word naked into his parallel account (Luke 8:27). By the end of the story he is clothed and in his right mind—a representation of the movement out of death and into new life that baptism ritually enacts. His sins, or his former life of possession [the Legion] are washed away in the watery chaos and then he is told to go and tell what "the Lord" (*Kyrios*) has done for him. He makes the link between "Lord" and Jesus—telling, throughout the Decapolis, everything that Jesus had done for him [5:20]). He is the only person in Mark's Gospel who is told to "go and tell" until the end of the story when that command is delivered by the *neaniskos* to the women at the tomb—and, by implication, to the reader (everyone else is told to say nothing to anyone). Here we have the pattern I am suggesting for the end of Mark's Gospel: unclothed to clothed (out of death [tomb] into life) leading to confession/proclamation. Thus the demoniac prefigures the young man. They participate in the same act of symbolization.

So now, at last, there is the necessity for proclamation. Finally, someone else is told to "go and tell" at the end of Mark's Gospel and, if the Gospel is to be believed, the word is stifled! The women say nothing to anyone because they are afraid! This is good news? To paraphrase the United Airlines rhetoric of a decade or so ago: "Is this any way to end a gospel?"

"You bet it is!" Because if we have been following the story carefully enough we have every reason to believe that the word will get out. Not perhaps through the route that leads from these named women, Mary, Salome, and Mary Magdalene, onward to the disciples and Peter (not, in any case, until the event of Pentecost—which occurs beyond the narrative world of Mark's Gospel). Rather, the word gets out through the community that the young man symbolizes: the ones who, through their own baptisms, bear the name of Christ and, as I suggested earlier, are already participating in the power of the resurrection through proclamation and deed.

We see signs of this community, this kingdom, throughout Mark's Gospel. If the mustard weed is its symbol, it numbers among its members the remembered woman, the one who graciously anointed Jesus with oil. It also includes Peter's mother-in-law, another unnamed woman who, at the very beginning of the Gospel, ministers (the word is *diakoneo* from which comes our word "deacon") to Jesus and his followers (Mark 1:31). It also includes an unnamed Syrophoenician woman. She approaches Jesus asking him to heal her daughter. Jesus rebukes her, saying that it is not right to give the children's bread to the dogs—that is to the Gentiles. She responds by calling Jesus "Lord" (*Kyrie*) and remarking that even the dogs eat the crumbs from the master's table. Jesus is so moved by this saying (But which saying? The one about the crumbs? Or the one, on the tongue of a Greek woman, that recognizes Jesus as Lord?) that he not only heals the woman's daughter, he also redirects his travel plans. Jesus goes to the Gentile villages and towns on the eastern shore of the Sea of Galilee bearing bread (Mark 7:24-30). Folks in this region, by the way, have been prepared ("Prepare the way of the Lord") for Jesus' appearance because the Geresene man, the former demoniac, had "gone ahead" (of Jesus!) proclaiming Jesus' lordship—another forerunner, like John the Baptizer. This kingdom also includes the unnamed exorcist who goes about the region around Capernaum casting out demons in Jesus' name. When the named disciples object, saying that this unnamed one is not "following us," Jesus replies: "Do not forbid him; for no one who does a work of power (*dynamis*) in my name will soon after speak evil of me" (9:38-41).

Power in this kingdom of God is exercised through service, through healing, through proclamation. Although the woman at Bethany's deed of anointing confirms that this is kingly power in the tradition of the Davidic line, the exercise of this power stands in sharp contrast to the way power was exercised in the historical-narrative accounts of Israel's kings.[19] Consider what happens when power is handed down from

---

19 The appeal to the Davidic line and, therefore, the typology of king in the Christology of Mark, is always made in opposition to, or in parabolic relation to, kingship in the Hebrew Bible. Jesus is anointed "for burial," not domination, as noted above, subverting mythic Messianic expectations. Jesus is called "son of David" by Bartimaeus prior to the entry into Jerusalem. But in contrast to David's initial entry into Jerusalem (2 Samuel 5:8) when the lame and blind—the dispossessed—were slaughtered, Jesus heals one of their symbolic descendants and contrary to the ban imposed by David, brings Bartimaeus, the "son of the dispossessed" into the city of David (Mark 10:46-52). While Mark subverts the typology of king, he honors the typology of prophet. The appeal to Jesus as a prophet in the line of Moses and Elijah is apparent throughout Mark. For our purposes, the difference between the way king and prophet function as types is clearest in a contrast between succession moments. Whereas Rehoboam says "My father made your yoke heavy, but I will add to your yoke" etc. (1 Kings

father to son in David's royal court. The story of Solomon and Rehoboam is one such story—a story that sets in motion bad vibrations that reverberate down to this very day (1 Kings 12:1-15).

King Solomon, a true "son of David" (as blind Bartimaeus calls Jesus), has died. Solomon was known for his wisdom, and also for building the great Temple, the destruction of which so plagued Ezekiel during his exile in Babylon. But in order to build the Temple and to maintain the army needed to protect it, certain adjustments needed to be made in the economy of Israel such that those folk living near the poverty line were forced into a kind of slave labor. Not since the time of Pharaoh had the Jews been slaves.

After his death, the power of the kingdom passes on to Solomon's son, Rehoboam. The people come to him asking for relief; they pledge their loyalty to him if he will only lighten their burden. But after consulting with his drinking buddies (perhaps over a few fermented malt beverages and the ancient Near Eastern equivalent of pretzels), Rehoboam comes back to the assembled of his nation, announcing the arrogant soundbites of his new regime. One of them is threatening: "I will add to your yoke." One of them is sadistic: "I will chastise you with scorpions." One of them is down-right obscene (reflecting the royal court's attitude toward the people; in an act of political savvy Rehoboam does not share this bravado with his audience): "My little 'member' (clearly, in the Hebrew, a euphemism) is bigger than my father's thigh." As one commentator has noted: "Rehoboam chooses slogans over wisdom, machismo over servanthood."[20]

In many ways it seems as if the world still operates along the lines Rehoboam delineated close to 3,000 years ago. But against this power to destroy we still see, even in this graceless age, the power to resist; against the power to inflict death, there are those who use power to restore life. The "mother of all wars" will not bring the kingdom of God into being because the kingdom of God is already at hand! God's kingdom has come on earth and it is being actualized through people who share in, who have been baptized into, resurrection.

Go and tell, the young man says at the tomb. It would be possible to name the names of those who have responded to the young man's invitation. But as the presence of the naked young man and his anonymous companions in Mark's Gospel suggests: it is not necessary to do so. They "continue to accompany" Jesus along the way.

Perhaps you know some of these people.

Perhaps you are one of them.

12:14), John the Baptizer says "I have baptized you with water but he will baptize you with Holy Spirit" (Mark 1:8).

20 Richard D. Nelson, *First and Second Kings* (Atlanta: John Knox, 1987), 79.

Who said, "I am the way, the truth and the life. No one comes to the Father but by me" (John 14:6)? A Debate between Church and Academy

Antoinette Clark Wire

Remembering many good talks weighing such matters with Herman Waetjen, I write this piece for him and look forward to his forthcoming commentary on the Fourth Gospel.

The question in my title is pressed as a debate between the church which assumes that Jesus said these words and the academy which does not. The gospel of John does attribute the words to Jesus, but the contexts in which the words appear in the fourth Gospel belie this.

Their context among the "I am" metaphors in the distinctive Johannine discourses of Jesus suggests that they developed in this Christian community as believers were affirming the ways Jesus was the source of their life. These "I am" claims probably functioned in proclamation of Jesus to outsiders and teaching about Jesus to insiders. But their first-person form followed by assurances of inclusion--"I am the bread of life; whoever comes to me will not hunger;" "I am the vine...; whoever remains in me... will bear much fruit"--reflect an origin either in prophecy or in inspired praise where a first-person divine voice speaks through people, as can be demonstrated in other early Christian prophecies and praises.

In the polemical context of the Fourth Gospel the second clause of an "I am" saying could become an assurance of some people's exclusion--"I am the way... no one comes to the father except by me." This does not tell us whether such exclusion was provoked by the community's rejection of other Jews or by others' rejection of them. .

A further context of this saying within the Johannine farewell speeches of Jesus shows that it is part of a composite effort over many years to state Jesus' legacy and how it would be fostered by the Spirit of Truth.

These genres of first-person prophecy, inspired praise, sectarian polemic and valedictory are not likely to have been ways that Jesus of Nazareth spoke. Rather the hearers and readers at the time of the gospel would have recognized that people were speaking here under the inspiration of God's Spirit, believing as they did that the Spirit would speak for Jesus in fresh voices as each time and place required.

The answer to the question in this title is so obvious that no one asks it. Preachers uniformly attribute the words to Jesus of Nazareth. Scholars uniformly do not. The silence between them extends like a fog across the Scriptures. Church outreach and interfaith dialogue founder. We begin to doubt that we can make sense of our tradition today and we keep it well wrapped up and in hiding.

What might happen if we began to raise such basic questions, putting each of them in a stark, even impertinent, way in order to provoke the debate among us and within us? I am wagering that we have everything to gain by hearing each other out, that all sides have something to learn and something to teach. We might even discover how to talk reasonably with others who are weighing the truth of this gospel.

I. The Literary Statement

The first round in the debate about this question falls to the church, which has consistently said that Jesus spoke these words. This is the plain meaning of the story carried in the Fourth Gospel text.

> Thomas said to him, "Lord, we do not know where you are going. How can we know the way?" Jesus said to him, "I am the way and the truth and the life. No one comes to

the Father except through me. If you had known me you would know my Father. And from now on you know him and have seen him" (Jn 14:5-7).

Recent New Testament research has, in fact, increasingly been willing to take the text as a literary statement and restrict questions to what the story wants to talk about, listening to the reverberations among the parts of the whole Gospel as they amplify or quiet each other. At one time this restriction to the text's viewpoint was made on the grounds of the Scripture's authority, whereas now it is more often made on the grounds of literary integrity: a text is recognized to have the right to interpret itself. Questions about its meaning today are kept on our side of the text as we read these textual dynamics in light of our different contexts and perspectives. In this way the Fourth Gospel can be taken as a kind of template for reflecting on relationships then and now, without considering its origins or sources.

But the question in the title does not stay conveniently in the literary box. Its "who said" points us irretrievably in the historical direction, and we want to know whether or not Jesus of Nazareth said these words during the last week of his life. This is a different question than the one about who speaks in the story, and it introduces a second, historical round in the debate.

II. Historical Development

The broadest problem in historical study of the Fourth Gospel is that it attributes to Jesus not only parables and aphorisms that do not appear in the earliest Gospel of Mark--this is also the case with Matthew and Luke, and a different selection might be expected here as well--but the Fourth Gospel shows Jesus teaching in a style and content quite different than is found in the other Gospels or in Paul's letters. It is only in this Gospel that the stories of Jesus meeting suppliants or inquirers are followed by extended dialogues and, finally, monologues in which Jesus talks at length about his own identity. These speeches do incorporate some phrases otherwise attributed to Jesus. When he says to Nicodemus, "Unless one is born anew, one is not able to see God's kingdom" (Jn 3:3), this is clearly another version of what he says to his disciples in Matthew, "Unless you become like children, you will not enter the kingdom of heaven" (Mt 18:3). But when Jesus continues with two long paragraphs in the Fourth Gospel, "No one has gone up to heaven except the one who came down from heaven, the Son of Man..." (Jn 3:13-21; 31-36) something new is happening to the tradition which requires historical explanation.

A generation or two ago, these long meditations of Jesus on himself were explained to most people's satisfaction in one of two ways. Rudolf Bultmann argued that the writer of this Gospel added an existing collection of discourses by a heavenly revealer to Jesus' story in order to show that Jesus was the incarnate Word who revealed God.[1] The style and content of self-predication in this Gospel came from this revelation source while the writer made it fit Jesus. Oscar Cullmann, at the other extreme, argued that the writer was none other than the Beloved Disciple, a Judean disciple of Jesus

---

1   Rudolf Bultmann, The Gospel of John: A Commentary (Philadelphia: Westminster Press, 1971; German, 1964), 6-7 and passim.

who appears only in this Gospel. He had written from memory a separate tradition of Jesus' sayings that was edited and published after his death as the Fourth Gospel.[2]

Yet neither of these views has a wide following today due to the lack of supporting evidence. Bultmann could not produce evidence that any such collection of divine revealer's discourses existed before the late Second and Third Century Gnostic texts. Cullmann could not produce evidence in the Fourth Gospel or elsewhere that Jesus' teaching about himself was kept private. Though the disciples are said to remember certain things only after Jesus' resurrection (Jn 2:17, 22; 12:16), and the "beloved disciple" is presented as a witness in scenes not elsewhere recorded (19:28-30; 20:3-10), the distinctive sayings of Jesus keep provoking his followers and opponents to engage him, pointing not to an intimate teaching circle but to public conflict situations.

In fact, scholars have largely given up the project of finding a single original source of these sayings of Jesus, either in the religious environment or in the memory of an early disciple. Instead historical research has focused on how these discourses attributed to Jesus were shaped over time within a distinctive Jewish-Christian community as it interpreted the traditional stories and sayings of Jesus during the First Century. This assumes that the Gospel was not shaped by the "towering personality" of a disciple as Cullmann put it,[3] nor by Bultmann's well-read theologian, but that it evolved over time as Jesus' story was told and retold in a distinctive Christian community.

My question "Who said, 'I am the way and the truth and the life; no one comes to the Father except through me'?" focuses the historical problem about these discourses on a single passage. If we can see how these lines may have originated and what they meant, we will have a baseline for understanding the Fourth Gospel. Because there is no consensus of scholars on sayings like this, I draw from many people's work and put it together in my own way that is simpler than the specialists would want to risk.

This claim, "Jesus said, 'I am the way...,'" needs to be understood in its own context, first in the context of the "I am..." metaphors of Jesus which are found only in this Gospel, second in the context of the polemic reflected in the second line, "No one comes to the Father except through me", and third, in the context of Jesus' farewell speech to his followers in which these two lines appear (Jn 13-17).

A. "I am the way" among the Fourth Gospel "I am" Metaphors

Jesus says, "I am...," in each of the Gospels simply to mean "I am the one" or "It's me", but it is only in the Fourth Gospel that Jesus uses the phrase metaphorically as in "I am the light of the world." Seven different first-person metaphors appear--bread, light, door, shepherd, resurrection, way, vine--and some of these are amplified and/or repeated with claims about their truth or life, hence, "I am the true vine" (15:1), "I am the bread of life" (6:35) and "I am the way and the truth and the life" (14:6), making in all twelve such sentences. After the self-identification and the metaphor, a second sentence often makes an appropriate invitation and gives a promise[4].

2   Oscar Cullmann, The Johannine Circle: Its place in Judaism, among the disciples of Jesus and in early Christianity (London: SCM Press, 1976; German, 1975), 63-99.
3   Cullmann, Circle, 10.
4   Here I follow the analysis of Christian Cebulj, Ich bin es: Studien zur Identitätsbildung im Johannesevangelium (Stuttgart: Katholisches Bibelwerk BmbH, 2000, 123-26) who draws from O.

I am the bread of life. Whoever comes to me will not hunger, and whoever believes in me will not thirst (6:35).

I am the light of the world. Whoever follows me will not walk in darkness but will have the light of life (8:12).

I am the door. Whoever comes through me will be kept safe and will come in and come out and find pasture (10:9).

I am the resurrection and the life. Whoever believes in me, even though she die, she will live (11:25).[5]

I am the vine. You are the branches. Whoever remains in me and I in him will bear much fruit (15:5).

These metaphors such as bread, light and vine represent the most basic good things in human life. The invitation and promise that follow thus express the great benefit of life in Christ.

Rather than asking the much contested question of where in the ancient world we can find the roots of this first-person metaphorical speech, I will ask how it was used in the community reflected in this Gospel and what it apparently meant here, drawing on parallels in other Jewish and Christian traditions only to illustrate some current options for use.

One possible use of these "I am..." statements in the Fourth Gospel would be in missionary preaching to challenge non-believers to receive the benefits of the gospel. Jesus is depicted speaking of himself in this way to crowds (6:25-40), to his opponents (6:51-51, 8:12), to his disciples (9:5; 9:40-10:21; 14:6; 15:1-11) and to suppliants (9:5; 11:25)--all the major audiences in the Gospel--which at least shows that these words were not considered private teachings. The first person address could make sense in mission as followers told the stories about Jesus to others, interpreting the feeding story with his saying "I am the bread," the healing of the blind with "I am the light of the world," Lazarus' death with "I am the resurrection," and Jesus' leaving his followers behind with "I am the way." The first person metaphors could thus turn the stories that outsiders heard into a challenge from Jesus' mouth to believe and receive his life.[6]

Here the analogy to Wisdom's preaching in Proverbs comes to mind, her first person address in the street and at the crossroads (Prov 1:20-23; 8:1-31), her positive offer of bread and wine (Prov 9:1-6), even her expectation of being rejected (Prov

---

Schwankl, Licht und Finsternis. Ein metaphorisches Paradigma in den johanneischen Schriften (Freiburg and New York: Herder, 1995, 194-203).

5 Since Jesus is speaking here to a woman, I translate the generic third person verbs in the feminine because English requires me to distinguish gender. This assumes that the repeated masculine singular participles in these sentences, here translated whoever..., are generic rather than limited in meaning to males.

6 J.-A. Bühner proposed that the "I am" metaphors reflect the prophetic messenger formula, "I am (name or role)...and I am sent to..." as in "I am Gabriel, the one who stands before the Lord, and I am sent to speak to you and tell you this good news" (Lk 1:19). (Der Gesandte und sein Weg im 4. Evangelium: Die kultur- und religionsgeschichtlichen Grundlagen der johanneischen Sendungschristologie sowie ihre traditionsgeschichtliche Entwicklung, Tübingen: J.C.B. Mohr [Paul Siebeck], 1977, 138-66). Jesus being sent by God is central to the Fourth Gospel, as is his mission to demonstrate God's love to the world. But the "I am" statements do not seem to be derived from this messenger formula since they do not give the messenger's name, role, and the content of a message.

1:24-33).[7] Yet Proverbs is itself not a mission speech but a teaching text. This suggests a somewhat different role of the "I am" sayings, not in mission outreach, but in the community's teaching. The story of a blind man may be taught to new believers as they hear Jesus telling them he is the light of the world. Or the Lazarus' resurrection story may be told or enacted in worship, including Jesus' promise to Martha, "I am the resurrection," and her confession in response.[8] The interest in revealed knowledge throughout this gospel suggests a particular focus of this community's practice on teaching and learning, not of course in the modern sense of passing on information, but in the sense of forming a life. Jesus' first person speech would legitimate this teaching as Jesus' own and show that the content of revealed knowledge is nothing less than Jesus himself who is the bread that fills, the vine that nourishes, the way that is life.

Yet neither the possible mission or teaching functions of the "I am" statements quite explain how a first-person discourse initially came to be attributed to Jesus in the life of this community. When we look at descriptions or incidents of prophetic speech in the early church, we can see that prophecy was expected to evoke the divine presence in worship.

> If all are prophesying and an unbeliever or outsider comes in, he will be convicted by all, he will be called to account by all, the hidden things of his heart will be revealed so that, falling on his face, he will worship God, proclaiming, "Surely God is among you" (1 Cor 14:24-25).

In invoking God's presence a prophet could speak with the voice of God or of Jesus.

> See, I am coming soon....
> I am the Alpha and the Omega,
> the first and the last,
> the beginning and the end (Rev 22:12-13).

> I, Jesus, have sent my angel to you
> to witness these things to you for the churches.
> I am the root and the stock of David,
> the bright and morning star.
> The Spirit and the bride say, "Come."
> And let whoever hears say, "Come."
> And let whoever is thirsty come.
> Let whoever wants take the water of life without cost.
> (Rev 22:16-17).

---

7   That the tradition of God's personified Wisdom was known and used in the Fourth Gospel context has been widely recognized from its prologue which describes the role of God's Word in creation, in giving light and life, and--in spite of rejection--in enlightening those who follow (1:1-18), all with close analogies in Prov 1-9, Wisdom 1-10 and other wisdom texts (C. H. Dodd, The Interpretation of the Fourth Gospel, Cambridge: University Press, 1963, 274-75; Rudolf Bultmann, The Gospel of John, 122-24; Cebulj, Ich bin es, 44-49, 256-67).

8   Eskil Franck argues that the closest analogue of Jesus' "I am" statements is synagogue interpretation. Following the Torah reading in Palestine the meturgaman put the text into Aramaic in a traditional way and could also be responsible to provide an exposition of the text which might lead to midrash-like extensions of the tradition (Revelation Taught: the Paraclete in the Gospel of John. Ph. D. Diss., Uppsala University, 1985, 105-8).

> Neither angel nor envoy
> but I, the Lord God the Father, have come.
> (Montanus, a Second Century Christian prophet, in Epiphanius, (Panarion 48, 11, 9).[9]

We know from Paul's attempt to limit prophecy in Corinth—"let two or three speak....one at a time"—that many people might prophesy, at times simultaneously (1 Cor 14). Such prophetic voices in the Fourth Gospel community could be interpreting the stories about Jesus in first-person challenges by Jesus to respond, even incorporating the previous person's prophecy when adding new words to it.[10]

The metaphorical aspect of such prophecy may come from a fourth Christian practice even more basic than mission preaching, teaching, and prophecy, namely, praise. First-person speech in songs of praise is widely attested, as in Egyptian Isis worship[11] and in hymns preserved with Gnostic texts.[12] First-person praise is also found in a late First or early Second Century collection of hymns called the Odes of Solomon.[13] Here an apparently Jewish-Christian psalmist speaks of him- or herself as inspired to praise:

> As the wind moves through the harp
> And the strings speak
> So the Lord's Spirit speaks through my members
> And I speak through his love (6:1-2)

At other points the psalmist is generally understood to be speaking in the first-person for the Anointed/Messiah/Christ:

> Nothing appeared closed to me
> Because I was the opening of everything.
> And I went toward my bondsmen to loose them
> That I might not leave anyone bound or binding

---

9 This statement is one of the sixteen oracles of the Montanist prophets which Karl Aland considers authentic (Bemerkungen zum Montanismus und zur frühchristlichen Eschatologie, Kirchengeschichtliche Entwürfe, Gütersloh: Gütersloher Verlagshaus, 1960, 143-48). For an English translation see Ronald E. Heine's The Montanist Oracles and Testimonies (Macon, GA: Mercer University Press, 1989, 3), or see David E. Aune's Prophecy in Early Christianity and the Ancient Mediterranean World (Grand Rapids, MI: Eerdmans, 1983, 315).

10 This function of prophecy in the Fourth Gospel is investigated by Eugene Boring in "The Influence of Christian Prophecy on the Johannine Portrayal of the Paraclete and Jesus" (NTS 25 [1979], 113-23) and in The Continuing Voice of Jesus: Christian Prophecy and the Gospel Tradition (Louisville: Westminster/John Knox, 1991, 155-84, 266-68).

11 For the Isis Aretalogy at Kyme which claims to be a copy of an inscription in Memphis see Jan Bergman, Ich bin Isis: Studien zum memphistischen Hintergrund der griechischen Isisaretalogien (Uppsala: University of Uppsala; Stockholm: Almqvist & Wiksell, 1968, 301-03).

12 Thunder: Perfect Mind, The Nag Hammadi Library in English, James M. Robinson, ed., 3rd rev. ed. (San Francisco: HarperSanFrancisco, 1988), 297-303.

13 On the text of the Odes of Solomon and its translation below see James Hamilton Charlesworth's The Odes of Solomon: the Syriac Texts edited with translation and notes (Chico CA: Scholars,1977). For a general introduction see David Aune, Prophecy in Early Christianity, 296-99. See also Michael Lattke, "Zur Bildersprache der Oden Salomos," Die Oden Solomos in ihrer Bedeutung für Neues Testament und Gnosis, Vol. 4 (Freiburg, Switzerland: Universitätsverlag, 1998, 17-36) and Majella Franzmann, The Odes of Solomon. An Analysis of the Poetical Structure and Form (Freiburg, Switzerland: Universitätsverlag; Göttingen: Vandenhoeck & Ruprecht, 1991, 4, 297-310).

Because they became my members
And I was their head (Ode 17:11-13).

I stood undisturbed like a solid rock
Which is continually pounded by columns of waves but endures
And I bore their bitterness because of humility
That I might redeem my nation and instruct it
And that I might not nullify the promises to the patriarchs,
To whom I was promised for the salvation of their offspring
(Ode 31:11-13).

All my persecutors have died,
And they who trusted in me sought me, because I am living.
Then I arose and am with them,
And I will speak by their mouths.
For they have rejected those who persecute them;
And I threw over them the yoke of my love.
Like the arm of the bridegroom over the bride,
So is my yoke over those who know me
(Ode 42:5-8).

The Fourth Gospel phrase, "I am the way," cannot in its present context be a song of praise. But it is possible that a teacher is using words from an inspired singer who had invoked Jesus' guiding presence in first-person praise.

It seems that we cannot limit the Fourth Gospel community to a single way of using these first-person sayings. If songs of praise had a part in cultivating metaphorical speaking for Christ, and the urgency of mission preaching led to an open and invitational mode of speaking, the Gospel's use of these sayings in stories about Jesus shows that prophetic explication and teaching integrated these uses when the tradition was heard in community worship. Here non-believers would also be present to hear, and singers to praise, while prophets expressed Jesus' life as life for them all and teachers preserved and explicated this tradition. At any event, the worshippers' attention was not on any of these mediators among themselves but on Jesus who was revealing himself.

Once the "I am" metaphors in the Fourth Gospel are understood as inspired interpretations of stories about Jesus within a tradition where God's Wisdom offers herself as nourishment for those who seek life, the words, "I am the way, the truth and the life" can be seen in their full positive meaning. The story of Jesus' last meal with his disciples, who are distraught because he is leaving and they cannot follow him, evokes words of Jesus assuring them that they have the true way to life and full access to God through him. This is elaborated in an extended dialogue of Jesus with his disciples about where he is going and how they can find their way to God, but the full answer to their anxieties has already been condensed into this metaphor, "I am the way." The offer is without restriction and whoever chooses to follow can be on the way.

B. "I am the way" within the Fourth Gospel's Polemical Setting

After the words "I am the way," we anticipate a sentence that gives an invitation, such as, "Whoever walks with me comes to the Father." But instead we have the words, "No one comes to the Father except through me." This raises a second inquiry beyond the context of the "I am" sayings into the broader polemical setting of the Fourth Gospel. Apparently the claim of Jesus being the way is contested, causing an inversion of the inclusive "whoever comes" into the exclusive "no one comes...except...." This formulation occurs also in one other metaphor:

> I am the shepherd [other manuscripts read 'door'] of the sheep. All who came before me are thieves and robbers (10:7).[14]

Again the inversion of an inclusive offer into an exclusive claim indicates some conflict that the community is facing.[15]

The polemic in the Fourth Gospel is most explicit in the long controversy stories that have grown up around telling Jesus' two Sabbath healings and his feeding of the 5000 in Chapters 5 to 10. Here Jesus' offer of life from God becomes a claim to be the sole channel of that life in a conflict with the religious leaders. Since we have access to the conflict only through the eyes of this community as it retells Jesus' story, it is not possible to judge if their exclusivism provoked their being rejected or if the official's rejection of this community provoked the exclusive claims they attribute to Jesus. It could have been a vicious circle. But before the Gospel was written down this community has apparently either walked out or been expelled from the local synagogue, which shows they were as much Jews as were those whom they left behind.[16] Because it is clear that exclusion from the synagogue did not happen in Jesus' time, we must assume that its appearance in this Gospel reflects the history of this community. They seem to be calling themselves "excommunicates" in order to claim they are not afraid to be rejected or even killed for Christ's sake (9:22, 35; 12:42-43; 16:2).[17] Their particular defense of Christ as God's exclusive agent is part of their polemic against the synagogue once they are outside it.

When we hear the words, "No one comes to the Father except through me," as a polemical twist on a prophetic claim that Jesus is the way and whoever follows him can find true life in God, we are ready to understand how this community who shaped the Fourth Gospel tells the story of Jesus' last night with his disciples.

C. "I am the way" within the Fourth Gospel's Farewell Speech

After this gospel tells about Jesus' healing, feeding, and raising the dead in extended discourses on Jesus' benefits for those who follow--and losses for those who do not-- the passion story opens with the last meal. Where the other Gospels recount only the institution of the Lord's Supper and the prediction of betrayal in a paragraph or two, the Fourth Gospel provides its final five-chapter discourse (Jn 13-17). The content

---

14 One other metaphor may also be so interpreted, depending on whether one reads it as polemic or community discipline: "I am the vine; my Father is the farmer. Every branch in me not bearing fruit he cuts out..." (15:1).

15 Gnilka notes that the metaphors of "door" and "way" in particular move beyond positive claims toward a dualistic exclusion of other access points or routes, suggesting the possibility that some metaphors may first have been formulated in polemic (Theologie des Neuen Testaments, Freiburg: Herder, 1994, 4/3/a).

16 The question of when a judicial ban against heretics was formally incorporated into synagogue prayers in the Eighteen Benedictions is a separate issue. This may not have occurred until the mid- or late-Second Century.

17 Cebulj speaks here of stigmatizing and self-stigmatizing with the community's I am saying functioning as stigma-management (Ich bin es, 17-18, 95-114).

stretches from the footwashing which replaces the institution of the meal, the prediction of betrayal, the extended dialogues with the disciples and the monologues of Jesus to his long prayer commending his followers to God. The phrase not yet half-way through the speech, "Come on, let's get out of here" (14:31), is a reminder that this final speech was completed more than once but kept expanding as new interpreters expressed what Jesus would have said.

The speech takes the form of a last testament or farewell address. Genesis, Deuteronomy and Joshua end with similar farewell speeches in which Jacob, Moses and Joshua on their death-beds lay out for their descendants the legacy which they leave (Gen 49; Deut 33; Josh 24). Other more contemporary parallels (Acts 20:17-35; Testaments of the Twelve Patriarchs) confirm that, although phrases and traits characteristic of the dying figure can be incorporated into these blessings and warnings, farewell discourses are not composed by the dying but by those left behind to honor their deceased parent or leader and to clarify matters of inheritance. In this Gospel the speech appears to be a cumulative voice of preachers, prophets and teachers who echo each others' words as they amplify Jesus' voice to reassure and instruct their community.[18] The statement, I am the way and the truth and the life, is probably spoken for Jesus by an inspired prophet or singer within the community, then adapted by a polemical contender in the sentence, No one comes to the Father expect through me, and finally set into dialogue and monologue by wisdom teachers who extend Jesus' response to Thomas with the confidence: If you knew me you would know my Father. And from now on you know him and have seen him (14:7).

In our contemporary debate over who spoke these words, the second round falls to the academy. It was not Jesus of Nazareth.

III. The Interpretive Context

But there remains a third round, due to a question that stands behind this question. Were the people who shaped this gospel deceived? And we can press this further to ask if we were being deceived when we were told Jesus said, "I am the way, the truth and the life." Did someone claim Jesus said these words and deceive others though he or she knew that Jesus did not in fact say them, thus making this guidepost to the way and the truth and the life into the wrong way and a lie, even into death?

To answer this requires us to determine how this claim and the other "I am" claims of this Gospel were understood in the community that shaped this tradition. We have seen above how the first person claims in this Gospel take forms found elsewhere at this time in inspired speech, whether in song or prophetic pronouncements. This suggests that the metaphoric "I am" invitations attributed to Jesus were generated within the worshiping community as a kind of continuing voice of Jesus, a voice not being handed down from the historical figure of Jesus of Nazareth but claiming Jesus' authority as his living

---

18 This phenomenon of one voice building on another has been recognized in recent research on the Fourth Gospel. But the scholars who are themselves writers tend to conceive this as relecture, a process of rewriting, rather than as re-speaking the tradition. Yet the right to keep building up the story must surely have developed in community life before writers could take it up. On the farewell discourse analyzed as relecture see Andreas Dettweiler's Die Gegenwart des Erhöhten. Eine exegetische Studie zu den johanneischen Abschiedsreden (Joh 13,31-16,33) under besonderer Berücksichtigung ihres Relecture Characters (Göttingen: Vandenhoeck & Ruprecht, 1995) andJean Zumstein's Kreative Erinnerung: Relecture und Auslegung im Johannesevangelium (2nd rev. ed., Zurich: Theologischer Verlag Zurich, 2004).

presence.[19] But if we look in this Gospel for a picture of the risen Jesus as a continuing and speaking presence, we do not find it. Jesus is understood to have returned to be with the Father and to be interceding with God for the community (16:23-28; 14:1-5, 11, 13, 20-24; 20:17).[20]

Yet there is an explanation within this farewell speech of how Jesus' voice speaks in the community. Jesus says he will ask the Father to send "another defender (helper, comforter, advocate)" to be with them forever, namely the Spirit of Truth who will stay with them and be in them, teaching them all things and reminding them of whatever he has told them (14:16-17, 25-26). This Spirit of Truth will on the one hand expose the world's sin, and on the other hand witness concerning Jesus and glorify Jesus, not speaking independently, but "that one will take what is mine and announce it to you" (15:26-27; 16:8-15). Jesus even says that it is better for them if he himself goes away so that he can send this Spirit. He explains, "I still have so much to say to you that you cannot bear now. But when the Spirit of Truth comes, that one will lead you into all truth" (16:7, 12-13).[21]

Yet this detailed explanation of how the Spirit will speak for Jesus what he couldn't say in his lifetime is itself part of the farewell speech, a speech composed in this community as they cultivate his legacy. How reliable is that? Jesus' assurance that his followers would receive God's Spirit is widely attested and may well be a tradition from Jesus of Nazareth (14:16, 26; 15:26; 2 Cor 3:17; Mk 1:8; 13:11; Mt 10:19-20; Lk 12:11-12; 24:49; Acts 1:4-5). But this community also attributes to Jesus the description above of their own particular experience of the Spirit's work. This means, on the one hand, that Jesus of Nazareth did not necessarily describe the Spirit in this way, nor can it be taken as a formula for the way God's Spirit will be present through Jesus in every place. But, on the other hand, it does demonstrate that those who were inspired to speak for Jesus in this community knew what they were doing, and that those who heard them were not deceived but understood that the Spirit was at work among them, simultaneously reminding them of what Jesus had said and leading them into truth that he could not have told them while he was with them.

To whom does this round fall? The witness of the Gospel is that by the work of the Spirit through a community of believers Jesus did say "I am the way, the truth and the life." Even the polemical twist on the invitation and promise in the words "No one comes to the Father except through me" is heard in their threatened setting as Jesus'

---

19 This is the proposal of Karlis Kundzin who identified the "I am" metaphors as words spoken by the resurrected Christ ("Zur Diskussion Über die Ego-Eimi-Sprüche des Johannesevangeliums," Charisteria Iohanni Kopp: Octogenario Oblata, Holmiae: Estonian Theological Society in Exile, 1954, 95-107). This thesis is argued in more detail in his less accessible Charakter und Ursprung der johanneischen Reden, Riva, Lativigas Universitate, 1939).

20 Matthew does understand Jesus to continue to be present wherever two or three gather, though apparently not to speak but to hear requests (1:23; 18:19-20; 28:20).

21 In key studies on the Spirit in this gospel Sigmund Mowinkel showed from a study of the few parallel texts the paraclete's judicial role as advocate or defense council who would vindicate those under attack ("Die Vorstellung des Spätjudentums vom heiligen Geist als Fürsprecher und der johanneischer Paraklet," ZNW [1933], 97-130). Ernst Käsemann argued that the Spirit in John's Gospel functions as the voice of Jesus, the Word that continues to speak to the disciples when he is no longer with them (The Testament of Jesus in John 17, Philadelphia: Fortress, 1966, 49, 84). Ulrich B. Müller recognized the Spirit as guarantor of continuity in Jn 13-14, but saw that only in the later development of Jn 15-17 did the Spirit function as judge of the world and giver of new revelation ("Die Paraklet im Johannesevangelium," ZThK [1974], 31-77).

reassurance of them. It appears that this round falls to the church. But it has taken the academy to ferret out how specific the Spirit's presence is in each place and how creative in each time.

We could call it a draw, or, better, a mutual teaching and learning moment on the field of religious contention today. But the possibility that a spark of life might catch on is, unfortunately, minimal. The challenge of the text is not just to understand who said what, but to hear the Spirit speak the continuing truth in another time and different place, and to point out the way here and now. The record indicates that neither the church nor the academy is prepared to do that.

Constructive Application

These articles reflect the location of their authors at the nexus of theology and politics, showing the implications and applications that the study of the Bible can have for the social-political realm

"Doers of the Word"
Public Theology as a Feminist Theology of Praxis: A South African Perspective

Denise M. Ackermann

This paper is an exercise in public theology as a feminist theology of praxis. Given the many faces of public theology, the South African context calls for a public theology that draws on the values of the reign of God as touchstone and articulates God's concern for those on the margins of society. Thus requires an explicit concern with the communicative impact of ethical practices, including those that come from "outside the camp". It also focuses on how gender roles are understood and lived out, by challenging the nature of transformative praxis in contextual situations. Thus public theology understood as a feminist theology of praxis pays particular attention to the need for a critical consciousness and social analysis, a concern with justice and imaginative praxis, and the ability to exercise restraint when necessary, but nonetheless to risk and to hope for a better world.

The Black Sash - an historical fragment[1]

One morning in May 1955 six women met in a home in the northern suburbs of Johannesburg, South Africa. All white and middle-class, they shared a common sense of frustration, outrage and the conviction that something had to be done to stop the Nationalist government of the day from removing the coloured people[2] from the common voters' role. The women viewed this strategy as a 'rape' of the Constitution and a blatant attempt on the part of the white minority government to ensure their re-election. Out of this meeting an organisation was born known as the Black Sash. Never large, it would for the next forty years work unremittingly for human rights in South Africa. By vigorously and publicly opposing the draconian apartheid laws, the Black Sash stood as a beacon of light through very oppressive times.

This organization was characterised by its imaginative practices, such as the public wearing of black sashes symbolising their mourning over the Constitution, and the organization's trademark from which its name is derived. In its early days, women of the Black Sash used to 'haunt' the public lives of prominent figures in the apartheid government. With members standing silently outside parliament, at airports, stations and public meeting places, with eyes downcast and black sashes across their chests, these early 'haunts' were acts of protest and conscientization that caught the imagination of the public. The press described with glee the ploys of cabinet ministers who tried to avoid this 'haunting'. "Ministers took to concealing their movements, ducking through side doors, arriving at parties or weddings without warning, buying theatre tickets under false names, asking meeting organizers not to announce scheduled speeches. Nothing helped. The women were always waiting" (*Time*, September 1955).

---

1 This paper picks up on certain themes raised in a former paper by me. See " 'The substance of things hope for': Women's imaginative praxis outside the church". *Emory International Law Review*, Vol. 14, 2000.

2 People of mixed racial origins were referred to as "coloureds". Today there is a movement among certain South Africans to reconstruct and reclaim the concept "coloured" with all its rich and varied cultural and linguistic backgrounds.

Holding 'stands' (as they were later known) became the organization's most characteristic form of public protest. The sight of white women standing with their sashes and holding spirited, often pungent placards, became a familiar one during the years of the struggle for democracy. Mary Burton, past president of the Black Sash tells of one of the more memorable taunts she was subjected to while 'standing': "...a man yelled as he drove past: 'Woman go home and cook!' " (*Fair Lady*, May 1986).

At the same time as they were 'standing', the women of the Black Sash were running advice offices, monitoring court proceedings, and actively putting their bodies on the line by being a visible presence in the townships during times of unrest, keeping vigils at trouble spots, being present when bulldozers demolished people's homes in order to forcibly remove them to newly designated areas, running workshops to train and inform people of their rights. They also met with opposition. Their offices were searched by security police and even bombed. Some were forced into exile; others were jailed, harassed and arrested. The image of 'nice' liberal ladies naively campaigning in defence of the constitution soon disappeared. The women of the Black Sash became seasoned campaigners for human rights. For their efforts they were nominated for many honours, including the Nobel Peace Prize in 1987. In 1994 the Danish Peace Foundation awarded its annual Peace Prize to the Black Sash. The highest accolade accorded them came from Nelson Mandela. On the historic day he was released from jail, he addressed a large and expectant crowd in Cape Town. In his speech he referred to the Black Sash (together with the National Union of South African Students) as "the conscience of white South Africans". The list of women, overwhelmingly black, who paid a high price for resistance to white racist policies is long and painful and one which is still be told in its fullness. The story of the Black Sash is but one small narrative which marks a turning point in the political awareness of certain white women.

In May 1995, one year after our first democratic election, the nature of the Black Sash changed. After much soul-searching by members as to its role in the new South Africa, a decision was taken at its annual conference to separate the advice offices from the membership organization known as the Black Sash. The latter as a predominantly voluntary white women's organization had served its role. From this decision a professional organization called The Black Sash Trust emerged. It continues to run the advice offices which cater to the needs of the poor and it continues to promote human rights and monitor their abuse.

Why the Black Sash?

Why this much abbreviated account of an avowedly secular organization like the Black Sash in a paper concerned with a particular approach to public theology? How can this historical fragment contribute to my contention that public theology, understood as *a feminist theology of praxis,* has a great deal to contribute to the cause of the reign of God on earth? What can it add to the challenge to believers to "be doers of the word" (Jm.1:22)? My attempt to answer these questions entails setting out my hermeneutical point of departure and what I understand by public theology, before discussing the limitations and the potential a feminist theology of praxis in the South African context.

The context out of which I write is one fraught with contradictions. South Africa is a new democratic nation. We have managed to move from an oppressive racist regime to a democratically elected government with little blood shed and with much hope. We are rated by the World Bank as economically sound. In these uncertain times, we are considered to be one of the world's safest tourist destinations. Yet, we have the second highest rate of HIV/AIDS infection in the world, unacceptable levels of unemployment, rampant poverty and, as a result, an increasing loss of hope among those who struggled for their freedom. Against this backdrop, a detour into the recent history of the Black Sash offers clues for transformative action that can contribute towards the shaping of a feminist theology of praxis in my context. This raises the further question: Why do I look to the story of the Black Sash rather than to the praxis in the Christian churches in the shaping of a such a theology? The answer is twofold.

First, the relationship of the churches to the social and political publics in South Africa has been and still is complex.[3] Apart from the overt justification of apartheid policies by the three white Afrikaans-speaking Reformed Churches, the role of the English-speaking mainline churches during those times was too often one of comfortable complicity.[4] Thus, the churches' relationship to apartheid was often disturbing, ranging from open support, evasion, lack of concern, to the courageous actions of a handful of individuals.[5] Today, the churches in South Africa are as divided as they were in apartheid times on issues of justice and social and transformative action. Take the case of HIV/AIDS. In the midst of a raging pandemic in which millions of people are infected and dying at the rate of 600 a day in my country, only one of the so-called mainline churches has publicly stood for treatment for pregnant mothers, newborn babies and adults and for the desperate need for an enlightened policy of prevention and care by the state in the face of the continuous denialist position taken by our state president and minister of health.[6] Others have remained silent, their leadership clearly concerned with not confronting the government, while their clergy bury members daily.

The second reason is the ever present spectre of gender discrimination within the church.[7] Women experience a huge gap in the church between its theory and its praxis. They are too often confronted with the paradox of a body which, on the one hand, affirms the humanity of all as made in the image of God, and on the other hand discriminates against women by denying them full participation in the church at every level. Yet, with equal facility, it proclaims the values of the reign of God as embodied in the person of Jesus but does not become involved in the visible praxis of these values. It is, therefore, not strange that given the ever present spectre of gender

---

3   See John W. de Gruchy, *The Church Struggle in South Africa* (Cape Town, David Philip, 1979), pp. 53-101.

4   See James R. Cochrane, *Servants of Power: The role of English-speaking Churches in South Africa:1903-193; Toward a Critical Theology via an Historical Analysis of the Anglican and Methodist Churches* (Johannesburg, Ravan Press, 1987) and Charles Villa-Vicencio, *rapped in Apartheid A Socio-Theological study of the English-speaking Churches* (Maryknoll, Orbis Books, 1988).

5   I acknowledge the prophetic impact of the Belhar Confession and the Kairos Document on church history in South Africa. However, both these documents were, in their social and ecclesial critique, blind to millennia of exclusion and discrimination suffered by women in the Christian churches.

6   The church in question is the Church of the Province of Southern Africa (Anglican).

7   From henceforth, "the church" refers to the church universal except where otherwise stated.

discrimination within the church, the women of the Black Sash, many of whose leaders were Christians, chose to work outside the framework of the church for the very values that the church should have been embracing.

Against this background, I found far more consonance between the Black Sash's theories on human dignity and justice and their single-minded application of a human rights praxis than I ever found in consolidated action in the Christian church. As such the Black Sash mirrored something of humankind's role in mending creation which the Christian community of faith would do well to emulate. With regard to the present crisis of HIV/AIDS there are, for instance, vibrant groups of women in the townships on the outskirts of South African cities tackling the need for care for the victims of HIV/AIDS with minimal resources.[8] More often than not these activities take place outside the formal structures of the church. Small groups of women come out bravely about their HIV positive status encouraging others to do so. Others run groups who feed, bath and care for the sick and dying. There are grandmothers living on meagre pensions taking care of children (recently I heard of one such grandmother who cared for 23 children at the age of 83 on a pension of just less than $50 a month). There are women who go to schools to talk to young people about their sexual practices in a context in which talk about human sexuality is taboo and others who counsel the fearful and the bereaved. These actions are often not initiated in the churches. They are conceived and driven mainly by women.

My contention is that such practices have a powerful communicative impact. Initiated and put into practice "outside the camp" (Heb. 13:13), the praxis of these diverse women has had a profound impact on the public sphere in which they function. Communicative praxis is a dialectical event. Christian actions are formed, informed, corrected and challenged by the actions of people "outside the camp" which are inherently compatible with the values of the reign of God. In view of this, what ought the church to hear from an organization like the Black Sash and from the groups of women combating HIV/AIDS in the townships of South Africa? Instead of church leaders telling, preaching, and teaching, they would do well to hear, absorb and understand these public acts for justice, love, care and healing and to be receptive to the critique that they offer and the hope that they bring. It is a salutary reminder that the prophets of Israel often listened to the people before they sought to bring wisdom and prophecy to contextual situations. The story of the Black Sash tells of a concrete struggle for justice carried out by a group of women with diverse religious convictions or with none at all. Their record is one which calls the church to account, even today. It is a record which communicates certain women's ability to act in the interests of others in the public arena reserved for men. So do the many small organizations which seek to combat HIV/AIDS. They challenge male-dominated hierarchies of the church to examine their own paucity of justice praxis. They hold out hope and encouragement for all who wrestle with what it means to become actively involved in the practice of one's faith. And, not least of all, they encourage us today to embrace activity over passivity, to take risks and to use our imaginations in the pursuit of a better world. It is

---

8   One such project is Hokisa, in Masiphumelele, Cape, a home that cares for children who are HIV positive. This project was conceived and implemented by a South African academic Karin Chubb and a German writer Lutz van Dijk, who raised the funds, had the buildings erected and who are at present training staff who will ultimately run the project themselves.

this kind of passionate engagement that has characterised the life and work of Herman Waetjen. His honest and unwavering wrestling with praxis for the reign of God, has encouraged many who, like me, have found his moral outrage against injustice an inspiration.

Reign of God

I have already alluded to the values of the reign of God in the above section. My hermeneutical point of departure is that all theology should be done in service of the fulfilment of God's reign on earth. The reign of God brings good news to people in terms of their life situations. It speaks of justice, love, peace and wholeness, of the flourishing of righteousness and *shalom*. The praxis of Jesus discloses the critical and transforming vision of what it would mean if the fullness of God's presence were to be known on earth. It call us, like Jesus, "to a radical activity of love, to a way of being in the world that deepens relation, embodies and extends community and passes on the gift of life."[9] This challenge to live by mutuality and reciprocity is never free from risk.

Theological reflection and theological praxis arise within the everyday messiness of Christian lives, because what we believe and how we act, embody our efforts to meet the problems that inevitably arise when we are challenged by the values of the reign of God in our particular contexts and time in history. Furthermore, those who profess the Christian faith are called to be God's agents for healing this world. This means that the reign of God, as embodied in the ministry of Jesus Christ, demands the *practical* realization of justice, love, freedom, peace and wholeness. As such it is a very public affair.

Public Theology

Public theology has many faces.[10] In order to clarify what I understand by public theology, allow me to say what it is not. First, public theology is not magisterial theological pronouncement from the church which claims to teach the public "out there" in an authoritative way. Public theology is not another grand endeavour which seeks to reclaim the polis for the church.[11] Second, public theology is not what Duncan Forrester calls "the in-house chatter or domestic housekeeping of a sect, concerned above all with its own inner life and with little interest in what goes on outside."[12] Third, public theology is not theological discourse that is obscure and inaccessible, technical and laden with academic jargon, with its own agenda understood only by specialists. Public theology is what it claims to be – theology which addresses the public and which must be accessible. Forrester goes on to describe public theology as "...confessional and evangelical. It has a gospel to share, good news to proclaim. Public theology attends to the bible and the tradition of faith at the same time as it

---

9   Beverly Harrison, *Making the Connections: Essay in Feminist Social Ethics* (Boston, Beacon Press, 1985, p. 18.

10 The notion of publics in theology was mooted by David Tracy, see his *The Analogical Imagination* (New York, Crossroad, 1981), chaps 2 and 3.

11 See Duncan B. Forrester, *Truthful Action: Explorations in Practical Theology* (Edinburgh, T & Clark, 2000), pp. 118-122 for a discussion on this issue.

12 *Ibid.,* p. 127.

attempts to discern the signs of the times and understand what is going on in the light of the gospel."[13]

Jürgen Moltmann also makes the link between public theology and the gospel through the metaphor of the reign of God. He says: "Theology for the sake of God is always kingdom-of-God theology. As kingdom of God theology, theology has to be public theology: the public, critical, and prophetic cry for God – the public, critical and prophetic hope for God. Its public character is constitutive for theology, for the sake of the kingdom of God".[14] Later Moltmann continues: "The theology of the kingdom of God is *theologia publica*, public recollection of God, grievance against God, and hope in God."[15]

Public theology is theology which talks about God in terms of God's own desires for the world in a manner that makes such truths accessible to all concerned with the pressing issues of the day. This does not mean that it simply takes over the agenda of the world. Although it takes the public sphere and what happens there very seriously, it seeks to articulate in the public sphere its own convictions about truth, goodness, freedom, justice, love and peace. Crucial themes in our common public discourse should reflect these values: the integrity and inviolable worth of every human being regardless of gender, race, class, ability, sexual orientation or whatever other categories tend to separate us; human rights in their widest possible application, including political, economic, and environmental rights; justice that is more than a call for equal treatment but which holds the common good and individual integrity as its goal; spaces where the voiceless can speak, in particular those who are marginalized because they have little means and diminished power; innovative and unending action for reconciliation and transformation, and solidarity which crosses denominational, ethnic, class and gender barriers.[16]

In the South African context the answer to the question as to which public sphere is addressed by public theology (as theology of the reign of God), is found in Christ's concern with those who are poor, sick and on the margins of society. Such a public theology seeks to bring to light the conditions and the hopes of those ignored by the powerful as well as to affirm redemptive hope. Because God is a God of life we are all supposed to live consistently with the values that our biblical traditions point to as pertaining to "the kingdom of God". Public theology is unqualifiedly engaged on behalf of life. It addresses all human beings concerning all spheres of life in the public space of civil society.

With the values of the reign of God as a touchstone, public theology can be evaluated in terms of how it is serving God's cause in the world. When, in apartheid South Africa, the church and the state had a cosy relationship, much public theology was present in political discourse. But it was a public theology which could not stand

---

13 *Ibid.* p. 128.
14 Jürgen Moltmann, Nicholas Wolterstorff and Ellen T. Charry, ed. By Miroslav Volf, *A Passion for God's Reign: Theology, Christian Learning, and the Christian Self* (Grand Rapids, Eerdmans, 1998), pp. 1-2.
15 *Ibid.,* p. 52.
16 See Helmut Peukert, "Enlightenment and theology as unfinished projects" in Don S. Browning and Francis Schüssler Fiorenza (eds.) *Habermas, Modernity, and Public Theology* (New York, Crossroad 1992), p. 62.

being measured against the values of God's reign. It stood for separating people on ground of race, for furthering the cause of one small section of South African society, denying justice and dignity to the majority of South Africans, and it certainly did not propagate justice, peace or love. Public theology, however, that seeks to engage on behalf of life, still fails to take sufficient cognisance of women's voices, women's experiences and women's contributions to the cause of justice, charity and hope. Once again the story of the Black Sash draws attention to women's accomplishments for such causes, albeit it outside the established churches. I see a nascent unintended feminist theology of praxis emerging from their history

A Feminist Theology of Praxis

The term "feminist theology" is contestable. There is no one feminist theology just as there is no one male theology.[17] Generally speaking, however, feminist theologies take a special interest in the lives of women, their stories, their hopes, their beliefs and their experiences of oppression and liberation. Christian feminist theologies want to bring women's lives into the "drama of the Christian message and explore how Christian faith grounds and shapes women's experiences of hope, justice, and grace as well as instigat[ing] and enforce[ing] women's experiences of oppression, sin, and evil".[18] Feminist theology in my context takes all women's experiences of oppression and discrimination very seriously, and it extends its concern to include all people who find themselves on the margins of our society and who know the violating effects of discrimination, either on grounds of gender, race, class, ability, sexual orientation or whatever, by remaining continually vigilant about the nature of the interlocking of systems of domination that contribute to such oppression.

A *feminist theology of praxis* requires further explanation. The term "praxis" points to intentional social activity. Rebecca Chopp describes praxis in Christian feminism as bringing together "a stress on the interconnectedness of historical existence and normative concerns of freedom on the one hand, and responsibility to change oppressive conditions into possibilities for human and planetary flourishing [on the other]...".[19] Feminist theology of praxis seeks not only to reflect on praxis but also seeks "actively to be a *form of praxis*: [my italics] to shape Christian activity around the norms and visions of emancipation and transformation".[20] It is always alert to the experience and place of women in its reflection. "Praxis as a starting point emphasizes the importance of everyday life and human bodiliness, as well as holistic anthropology, in order to overcome the dualisms private-public (individual-community), and body-soul (matter-spirit)".[21] Christian praxis is based on the willingness to be God's hands in the world, alleviating oppression and forming communities of endurance and hope and new understandings of what constitutes

17 The *Dictionary of Feminist Theologies* edited by Letty, M. Russell and J. Shannon Clarkson (Louisville: John Knox/Westminster Press, 1996) demonstrates this with its eight different entries for feminist theologies.
18 Serene Jones, *Feminist Theory and Christian Theology: Cartographies of Grace* (Minneapolis: Fortress Press, 2000), p. 14.
19 Rebecca Chopp, "Praxis" in Russell and Clarkson, *Dictionary*, p.221.
20 *Ibid.*, p. 222.
21 Elina Vuola, *Limits of Liberation: A Feminist Theology and the Ethics of Poverty and Reproduction* (London: Sheffield Academic Press, 2002), p. 98.

human flourishing. The vision of a world in which God is at home, in which love, justice, freedom, equality and peace thrive, needs more than the prayer "May your kingdom come". It requires the willingness of those who utters this prayer to translate it into deeds. Praxis is a central interpretative lens for my theology.

Feminist theologians have defined the conditions for their praxis. These conditions are first *accountability* which means that theologies of praxis are done in the interest of groups of people who experience oppression and discrimination. Second, praxis is conceived in *collaboration* with others. Third, all research, learning and teaching begins with our own *lives-in-relation*. We cannot do theology as isolated individuals but rather as members of particular communities. Knowledge is born in dialogue with others and is contingent upon the difference it makes to our lives and to others. Fourth, the *diversity of cultures* is a condition for feminist theological praxis. No theology can be applied universally – this women learnt when men's experience was given universal significance. The last condition is *shared commitment* because feminist theological praxis is strategic and action orientated.[22]

A feminist theology of praxis is explicitly concerned with the ethical, when issues such as sexuality and reproduction, violence against women and children, relationships between men and women, and relationships between human beings and nature are pursued. Theology that is explicitly ethical and contextual speaks from specific situations; names experiences; identifies suffering; and articulates possibilities of hope and transformation, testing them within a given moral and ethical framework. The relations between knowledge, power and interests is of ethical concern. This makes a feminist theology of praxis self-consciously contextual and historical and it knows that difference and particularity run throughout its deliberations.

In summary, a feminist theology of praxis starts with critical analysis of given contexts, with a particular focus on how gender roles are understood and lived out. It then seeks to engage contextual situations with liberating and transformative praxis in order to encourage human flourishing, undergirded by the belief that such theology is done in service of furthering God's reign on earth.

What might praxis for the reign of God in the public sphere look like? What should characterize it? Drawing on the example of the women of the Black Sash and holding myself accountable to those countless women who offer care to and solidarity with the suffering in often unrecognized and unheralded ways, I want to highlight several traits that typify praxis that witnesses to the reign of God in the public sphere.

Critical consciousness and social analysis

At a certain stage in South African history a handful of white women became conscious of the need to act in defence of what they perceived as justice and human rights. Today, other women who are actively involved in caring for HIV/AIDS sufferers, have decided to grasp the nettle and to forge ahead with care and education in the face of government intransigence. In both these cases critical consciousness is a response to a public need. Any change is precipitated by a process of discovery of either the self as suffering or oppressed, or of the necessity for solidarity with those

---

22 See Katie G. Cannon *et al*, The Mudflower Collective, *God's Fierce Whimsy Christian Feminism and Theological Education* (New York: Pilgrims Press, 1988), pp.23-27.

who are oppressed and suffering and the need to seek wholeness and affirmation. Critical consciousness dawns when social, political and economic contradictions are perceived and give rise to the desire to take action against oppressive elements of reality. This requires an awareness of who we are in the historical contexts in which we live. In this process, self-knowledge and social knowledge inform one another.

A critical consciousness that is socially informed requires ongoing social analysis rooted in particular contexts. As there is no such thing as "value neutrality" nor "pure disinterested knowledge" as such, a critical consciousness is forged in the rough and tumble of public debate and through knowledge that is acquired in conversation across ideological differences.

A feminist theology of praxis lives in an ongoing relationship with critical social, political and economic analysis, always open to revision and to renewal of our theological theories and tested continuously against the values of the reign of God. Justice, love, freedom, equality, wholeness and shalom provide the aim and the impetus for such praxis. The announcement that the "kingdom of God is at hand" pointed to something new and critical. Jesus' words and deeds embodied and clarified what it meant to live in the reign of God.

> He did not ask people to be "religious" in the well-recognized ways supported by the powerful religious leaders of his time. One way to characterize what he was doing is to say that he proposed a radical, alternative as understanding of what it meant to be "religious" or "spiritual", challenging many of the most influential and powerful conceptions of religiousness practiced in his culture....Living out this conception of "religion" brought Jesus into a great deal of conflict. It was obviously not in the interest of many people to encourage this sort of religion – an active, change-making praxis.[23]

Concerned with Justice

There is no single way of describing justice or one single theory of justice that satisfies everyone. From the perspective of a feminist theology of praxis the realities of injustice and the commitment to the common good lead to an understanding of scripture that holds that to know God is to do justice for our neighbour. The people of God must live under the stringent and unwavering expectation of communal right relationships. When these relationships are skewed through the abuse of civil, political, or economic rights, and suffering ensues, people should be roused to action. The sense that things are not right and that something must be done is common to both the women providing care in the townships and to those of the Black Sash. Neither groups are theorists about justice. But they know what Dorothee Sölle describes so well:

> Does the feeling of rage in the pit of your stomach have something to do with God? In every human being is a need for justice, a feeling about justice, and a knowledge of what is unjust and unacceptable. Without justice we wouldn't be able to live.[24]

---

23 Harrison, *Making the Connections*, pp. 217-218.
24 Dorothee Sölle & F. Steffensky, *Not just yes and amen: Christians with a cause* (Philadelphia, Fortress Press, 1983), p. 8.

The following elements are part of a Christian approach to justice: first, justice must be conceived of broadly as participating in the richness of the biblical tradition which regards justice as nothing less than 'right relationship' or righteousness; second, the righteous community – that is the one rightly related to God – is a community that is faithful to God through showing concern for the least privileged persons and groups; third, responsibilities are balanced with rights; fourth, the primary injustice is exploitation; fifth, since injustice is found in exploitation it must be corrected (primarily in rescue/resistance and in rebuke/reparations) and lastly, our concept of justice must be viewed as incomplete and partial.

Praxis for justice is seen as directed towards the creation of the common good, something that all who are oppressed and on the margins of society deserve. But the mere appeal to justice itself is not adequate. Justice as "communal right-relationship" becomes a basic theological hermeneutic for the proper understanding of spirituality.

Imaginative praxis

I am aware of the trend in post-modern times to predict the demise of imagination. At the outset let me concede that it is necessary to debunk the more naïve aspects of humanist imagination such as its belief in the inevitability of historical progress and some of its more messianic claims that emanated from the enlightenment.[25] The South African experience has, however, taught me that it is the courage of ordinary people (like the women of the Black Sash and those who tend to AIDS sufferers today) who dare to imagine what a better world would be like and who are prepared to back their hopes with creative actions, that shapes the course of history. People of faith can only echo Elaine Scarry who writes: "Belief is the act of imagining."[26] Belief in what?

At the heart of a feminist theology of praxis lies the belief in the role of human agency in the mending of God's creation. The hope for a redeemed creation runs through the Jewish and Christian scriptures; a hope for the feast which the "Lord of hosts will make for all people" (Is. 25:6), for the creation of new order in which "the wolf and the lamb shall feed together" (Is. 65:25). While we acknowledge that the whole of creation has been groaning in labour pains (Rom. 8:22), we are challenged by the announcement that "the Kingdom of God is at hand." Such is our utopianism – the belief that a better world is possible and that we are agents, rather like the hands of God in bringing it about. We are to be involved in change-making praxis. This requires Spirit-inspired imagination. The imagination is not a faculty which fabricates images of reality. It is a God-given power which forms images which surpass reality in order to change reality. The gift of imagination is the impelling energy in which the desire for a better world is born and nurtured. In imaginative praxis lies the birth of a restored world.

Imaginative praxis calls for the convergence of the poetic and the ethical. Through the years when we struggled in South Africa for liberation and justice, great emphasis was placed on the ethical. Yet, Christians express their faith through symbols, stories and metaphors, that is, through the poetic. The poetic does not exist in some abstract

---

25 In this regard see Richard Kearney, *The Wake of Imagination: Toward a Postmodern Culture* (Minneapolis, University of Minnesota Press, 1988), p. 360.

26 Elaine Scarry, *The Body in Pain: The making and Unmaking of the World* (New York, Oxford University Press, 1985), p. 205.

realm. The essence of what is perceived as real finds expression through poetic images because they are, in themselves, experiences of what is real. This is vividly expressed through the role of art and drama in situations of oppressions. Through creative imagination we express and enlarge our experience of reality. This is poetic creative activity. Now the women of the Black Sash are in essence driven by ethical considerations, but there were times when their resistance took on a poetic mantle as they found creative, refreshing and politically pungent ways of expressing their dissent.

It is also necessary to add that imaginative praxis is both an individual and a communal act. Conceived in the *geist* of the subject, once uttered, it takes on a collaborative mantle. From the sixties through the next three bad decades, a nucleus of no more than a few hundred women of the Black Sash kept the organization running. Their imaginative praxis was expressed in communal strategies for human rights. "Doing" the work of justice together, in unremitting resistance to apartheid, also forged robust bonds between these women which sustained them through difficult times. In the townships of South Africa today, groups of women are forging connections which offer support and collaboration in the fight against HIV/AIDS. Dorothy Qabashe who runs a programme of counselling and care for AIDS sufferers in Khayalitsha outside Cape Town finds that it is vital for her work to have links with a local feeding scheme which also disseminates nutritional advice to local people. Correct nutrition is but one of the strategies that are essential in the treatment of AIDS. Together the women who belong to both organizations are helping poor people to grow vegetables around their shacks which provide a much needed supplement to their daily diet and which can also provide them with an income.

The potential for the individual human subject creatively to imagine a better world is vital to our survival on this planet. Collectively, these acts of imagination inspire us to act in the interests of healing. Collaborative imaginative praxis is flexible and open, and at its best in small groups when not bogged down by bureaucratic rules or the power ploys of oppressive hierarchies.

Risk, restraint and hope

The processes I am describing require the willingness to take risks, to practice restraint and never to cease hoping. First risk. Imaginative praxis is often risky, even dangerous. Accompanying the spontaneity of imagination is its unpredictability. Unpredictability can degenerate into obsessive pathologies. It would have been hard to predict that in a world reeling from the horrors of Nazi racism, Afrikaner racism would invent its grand apartheid designs. In the face of these designs the Black Sash's praxis was a very modest but nonetheless effective strategy of resistance. But it was costly to some of the organization's members as attested to by the story I told at the beginning of this paper. Their praxis was clearly designed to be subversive. It was driven by a passion for the possible. Passion, like anger, kindles fire in the human spirit which makes people take risks. Imagination becomes a dangerous activity.

Second, restraint is required precisely because of the perilous nature of imaginative praxis. Passion and risk need to be contained by a self-reflective moderation which is willing to live within the limits of the possible. "Thembisa" who is HIV positive and is actively involved in the local branch of the Treatment Action Campaign,[27] has found that her passion for advocating state sponsored medication has involved her to such an extent that her fragile health has suffered. The women of the Black Sash knew the dangers of "burn-out". Small in number, they had to wrestle with boundaries between passionate commitment to the cause, and strategies which required them to harbour their energies.

The balance between commitment to a just cause and the acknowledging political and personal constraints is not easy.

Finally, a feminist theology of praxis is above all else hopeful. South African philosopher Johan Degenaar defines hope "in terms of creative expectation with regard to what is desired." The idea of expectation points to a future directness. It implies anticipation of what can happen which at the same times needs to be undergirded by the ability to wait patiently for hope to come about. The idea of "creatively" commits us to images that feed our hopes. Hope, unlike wishful thinking, is more directed and more realistic. Hope demands that we become creatively involved in making that which we hope for come about. It is also open to the unforeseen because we cannot predict the future with precision.

Erik Erikson argues that hope is often decisive in changing the world: Hope not only maintains itself in the face of changed facts – it proves itself able to change facts, even as faith is said to move mountains."[28] Such hope involves action, not stasis, passion not passivity. Once clear and concrete images of hope are formulated, and we are willing to work toward realizing these hopes, we risk disappointment, even despair. Our passion for the possible can sink into frustration, even hopelessness. Thus hope risks disappointment and is never without struggle. There is an even greater threat to hope: apathy. Apathy speaks of loss of all desire. During the bleak apartheid years, frustration, despair and even hopelessness were familiar emotions to those struggling to survive the onslaughts of racist rule. Today, I see signs of anger and of apathy as hope for a better life are frustrated and belayed. Years of being confronted with an intransigent minister of health on the issue of HIV/AIDS also causes despair, even apathy. But an apathetic citizenry will tolerate manoeuvres which can damage, and even ultimately destroy, the very democracy for which so many have paid a high price. Passion is the best antidote to apathy.

Feminist theologies of praxis in the community of faith, are vested in the human capacity to hope. The danger inherent in the notion of hope is that it can be embarked on too lightly. Cheap hope is nothing more than foolish optimism. Costly and risky hope faces despair, is unwaveringly realistic while it trusts in the One who promises us a healed creation.

Conclusion

In the letter attributed to James, the author cautions the faithful:

---

27 This organization is a vocal voice in civil society as it challenges the government to provide medication and care to AIDS sufferers, even to the extent of challenging the government in the Constitutional Court in 2002. This case was won by the TAC and the government was ordered to provide medication to pregnant women and newborn infants.

28 Erik H. Erikson, *Insight and Responsibility* (New York, W.W. Norton, 1964), p. 117.

> Be doers of the word, and not merely hearers who deceive themselves. For if any are hearers of the word and not doers, they are like those who look at themselves in a mirror; for they look at themselves and, on going away, immediately forget what they were like. But those who look into the perfect law, the law of liberty, and persevere, being not hearers who forget but doers who act – they will be blessed in their doing.[29]

A feminist theology of praxis takes the "doing of the word", as the measure by which its integrity and its authority will be judged in the public square. The witness of the church in the public sphere needs wise women (and men) whose actions are marked by stability, a concern for justice, courage to put their bodies on the line and fidelity to the teachings of the faith and the One who showed us the way. Then we shall be heard and respected.

---

29 James 1:22-25.

The Fragility of Truth

Tolerance, Discourse Ethics and the Formation of a Democratic Citizenry[1]

James R Cochrane

Toleration makes difference possible;
difference makes toleration necessary.
Michael Walzer[2]

A valued colleague at the University of Cape Town in the Department of Religious Studies recently welcomed European partners to a jointly organized conference on "diversity and ethos."

"Come to visit us, to see us, to understand us," he said in his opening address on *Embracing South Africa*.[3] But—as he poignantly concluded after probing the diversity of identities that makes up South Africa—by the mere act of saying the pronoun, "us," we have touched on the "discourses and forces, strategies and negotiations, by which the first-person plural is constructed." As he notes: This construction of the person as a plural reality presents "the most compelling challenges to theory and method" in the social sciences.[4]

Another way of putting it is this: If the social is also the political, then the political in our time is crucially about identity and difference.[5] It is the negotiation of identity and difference that shapes some of the most intractable conflicts of our time, almost irrespective of the particular economic conditions pertaining to a specific conflict. One need think only of the former Yugoslavia, of the complex set of conflicts which bedevil central Africa right now, of the Islamic Revolution, of the intractable battle between Israel and Palestine, of Northern Ireland—and many others!—to intuitively grasp the point.

1   This paper is made possible in part by grants from the National Research Foundation, South Africa, and the University of Cape Town's Research Committee, neither of whom are responsible for the views expressed here.
2   Michael Walzer, *On Toleration*, New Haven, Connecticut: Yale University Press, 1997, xii.
3   David Chidester, "Embracing South Africa, Internationalizing the Study of Religion," in David Chidester, Janet Stonier, & Judy Tobler (eds), *Diversity as Ethos*, Cape Town: Institute for Comparative Religion in Southern Africa, 1999, 23.
4   He said this of religious studies, but it would be equally applicable to social studies generally. The notion of a "plural reality" of the person is also given definition through the concept of hybridity, a term increasingly popular in the relevant literature on identity under "post-modern" conditions.
5   I adopt here a meaning of "the political" derived from Sheldon S. Wolin, "Fugitive Democracy," in *Democracy and Difference: Contesting the Boundaries of the Political*, Seyla Benhabib (ed.), Princeton, NJ: Princeton University Press, 1996, 31. Wolin distinguishes "politics" (legitimized, public contestation by organized social powers over access to resources—a continuous, ceaseless activity) from "the political" (an expression of the idea that a diverse society can, through public deliberation, promote or protect the well-being of the collectivity—a rare, episodic activity). In this view democracy is less a form of government (about "politics"), and more a project, a possibility, of ordinary citizens (about "the political").

The point has been more than intuitive in the case of South Africa. In what many now call our "negotiated revolution," we have had to concretize these issues in trying to build a new society. We had to do so initially under conditions which many others around the world also thought were, indeed, intractable—a bloodbath, after all, was the common prediction for our future as late as January 1989! By April 1994 the bloodbath was no longer expected, the sun had set on apartheid, and after a short night, the new dawn was present.

More importantly, in a country where difference and diversity had become *the* theory of politics under the apartheid regime; where identity had been inscribed in law as alienation from oneself and from the other; where otherness implied fear and hostility; and where tolerance was a swearword if it meant breaching or bridging our differences—in such a country we set out to reconstruct our differences and diversity again. We have done so with a new idea of tolerance, not a swearword this time but a word of hospitality and of generosity, of respect and of integrity. Reconstructed identities, redefined differences and a reconstitution of diversity mark the key tasks our society has undertaken in these years of transition from an oligarchic tyranny to a plural democracy.

I have repeatedly used the prefix "re" here. It bears one further comment. It is no surprise, if one thinks of the re-birth of Europe in the late medieval period, its celebration of new energies (its spirit, if you like) and its remarkable diversity, that our President Thabo Mbeki has used the term derived from that period in speaking of an African *Renaissance.*[6] It is a vague term, almost content-less in some respects. Yet it designates an intuitive conviction that Africa's material disasters, whatever their genesis, will only be turned around with a new will, a regenerated capacity to see new possibilities where old actualities have bred cynicism and despair. It requires a new spirit. In an odd way, it is a religious call, from a man not known for his religiosity. And yet it is right.

This is not to discount the material disasters which Africa suffers—from the rape by colonial powers to the subsequent mismanagement and corruption of new indigenous elites, from the desertification of huge tracts of lands to the pollution of waters so vital to life, from the degradation of over-used soils to the blasts of drought. They play no insignificant role in what is possible in Africa. They also impact upon conflicts which may be expressed through difference and identity. In short, competition for, and over, material resources is impossible to ignore. But to assume that material concerns are all that matter, or that non-material concerns such as one's identity and its difference from the identity of others are secondary, even superficial, is of a modernist mentality.

The flaw lies in some version or other of the assertion that history and human beings are essentially material—a view which shapes the left and the right of eighteenth and nineteenth century European theories of the political economy. Ironically, this view may even be said to lie behind those theories that have traditionally been named as idealist! The problems of this view lie both in an untenable

---

6   See, for example, Mbeki's "The African Renaissance Statement," 13 August 1998, at
     http://www.anc.org.za/ ancdocs/history/mbeki/1998/tm0813.htm.

essentialism—whether of history[7] or of the human being[8]—and in an equally untenable Nominalism.[9]

What I propose to do in this essay, in the light of these comments, is to develop the points made by looking at the question of tolerance in an emerging democracy, namely, ours. This I shall do, first, by commenting on the transition to democracy in South Africa, particularly in respect of the establishment and work of the Truth and Reconciliation Commission. Second, I shall unpack the discourse about nation-building which predominates since 1994. Third, a brief excursus on the question of religious diversity and political tolerance follows, in an attempt to show how the politics of identity and difference plays itself out in one, significant cultural form.

---

7   Historical sciences, including economics insofar as it is more than econometrics, are deeply interpretative forms of knowledge, yielding less laws (in the Newtonian sense of empirically verifiable rules) than perspectives (or, if laws, then of a kind more like Einstein's relativity theory and Heisenberg's uncertainty principle). The unpredictability of history is methodologically mirrored in this realization, as expressed in Thomas Kuhn's paradigm theory (*The Structure of Scientific Revolutions*, Chicago: University of Chicago Press, 1962). It prevents a retreat into the kind of historical science, positivist and certain of itself, that governed the major thinkers of the nineteenth century and earlier.

8   Michel Foucault's famous aphorism, that there is no longer any such thing as "man," only particular men (and women), expresses the anthropological basis of the critique of essentialism and a shift in philosophy.

9   I refer here to the critique of a colleague, Douglas McGaughey, in *Strangers and Pilgrims* (NY & Berlin: de Gruyter, 1997), who notes that the Nominalist movement, beginning with Occam, accepted that ideas are ectypal and not archetypal (25). The marriage in Copernican thought between Platonic physics (mathematical description) and Aristotelian metaphysics (the world of things as independent of our consciousness) further led to a grasp of physical phenomenon which became increasingly calculating, predictive, manipulative and controlling. The pragmatic results of this move are enormous, and persuade many to believe that "facts" are empirical and that truth has to do with the facts. The irony that mathematics, a non-sense faculty of the mind, is used to explain the sensual, is lost. The point returns with a vengeance in the more nuanced, magical (that is, framed by phantasms or mental fantasies which are then given mathematical form) world of contemporary cutting edge science, especially in particle physics and cosmology.

The transition from ideas as archetypal to ectypal, McGaughey suggests (29), can be traced in scholastic debates about the status of "universals." For the Nominalist, so-called "universals" are mere abstractions (names) for the real, which is the particular only, the material world. Appearances rather than substance, to use old terms, are taken to be the real—as good a description of the market driven consumer ideology as we might get. What we end up with in the "presumption of the mathematization of reality" (McGaughey, 447) is "that all experience can be explained on the basis of material reality and causal calculating rationality." We cannot go back behind the powerful gains made by the Nominalist view of the world and the materialist paradigm, of course (who wishes to give up cars, telephones, jets, computers, et cetera?). But the costs are high too, and the weaknesses of the paradigm are by now also apparent.

Besides actuality, to put it in a nutshell, human experience and understanding concerns possibility. A materialist paradigm deals well with actuality, but ignores the role of possibility, including the conditions of possibility which lie behind its own formulations. To grasp possibility requires more than *diairesis* or calculating rationality; it required *theoria* or contemplative reason; and it issues in "universals" (sameness, by which a recognition of identity is possible) which cannot be ignored any less than can particularities (difference). We are not bound to traditional orthodox views of universals here; we may take a defensible Platonic view on universals as tentative but enduring approximations of reality, lodged in memory, by which similarity within difference can be recognized and knowledge (of anything) constructed in the first place (McGaughey, 234). We only make sense of the flux of particulars by means of universals. Our reality is experienced or constructed in the way in which we combine the universal and the particular, ideas and materiality. In short, there is no direct access to the world through the senses, only mediated access through the filters of our imagination and reflection.

Finally, I shall turn to the theory of democracy, exploring the notion of tolerance in relation to identity and difference, and indicating my preference for a discourse ethics or deliberative theory of politics.

Memory, Amnesty and a Sunset Clause

I commented earlier that the sun had set on apartheid by 1994. This is not entirely accurate. Of course, the legacy of decades of harsh policies of separatism and the even longer history of entrenched racism were not wiped out by compromises and new constitutions.[10] We still struggle with this, and our struggle has to do with the question of tolerance, to which I will return. What I want to note rather, are two particular agreements that secured our "negotiated revolution."

The first was a proposal that broke the back of what looked to be a final and irresolvable impasse in the CODESA[11] meetings between the parties of the apartheid war. The impasse had to do with the patronage dished out by the apartheid regime to its supporters, in particular, the civil service. It was the civil service that had provided the National Party government with the capacity to offer employment to a legion of its supporters, beginning in 1948, something it had done with great consistency and efficiency. This was their political base and they were not prepared to do anything that would appear to betray it.

Ironically—because for many years he was publicly named by the apartheid regime as their "public enemy number one"—the leader of the South African Communist Party, Joe Slovo, was the one to make the proposal which dealt with the matter of the civil service, and which did the deal, so to speak. In essence, his proposal gave protection to the existing civil service, in the form of a guarantee of a further five years

---

Or in the terms of Kuhn, paradigms, not rules, are prior. This may be termed the *aporia* of knowing and unknowing (McGaughey, 240).

It parallels a second *aporia*, namely, that of the dialectical tension between logic and pragmatics in experience: on the basis of effects, we speculate about cause. In other words, causality—whether in nature or in history—is our paradigmatically shaped understanding determined by communal constructs about how reality functions. We do not perceive causes as such, except in the most trivial sense. At the same time, the effects of the physical world we perceive are real, and we would be in trouble if we ignored them.

A final *aporia* worth noting here, because it is pertinent to the general theme of this paper, is that which determines the resultant conception of truth. Truth is not a matter of correspondence (between matter and our ideas), and untruth simply a matter of the limits of our current capacity to explore correspondences. Truth, rather, always and everywhere, simultaneously reveals (the actual) as it conceals (the possible that has not been actualized) reality (McGaughey, 248ff.). It is more like disclosure (and closure) than it is like verifiable of falsifiable evidence. Truth in this sense is radically historical, though not simply material. History is about traces as much as it is about events.

10 Segregation policies were first formalized for the South African territory as a whole by the Sir Godfrey Lagden Commission of 1903-1905, under British authority. This included, among other things, the demarcation of "native reserves" (the basis of the later apartheid bantustans), the implementation of pass laws to control the movement of "natives," the establishment of "locations" for blacks in the urban areas (the basis for later townships like Soweto), and the restriction of women and children to the rural areas. Many of these policies were inspired by earlier nineteenth century experiments in control over indigenous people and land usage. All of this makes clear that economic interests were always part of the equation, though racism goes beyond the merely economic and racial oppression, like gender oppression, may in some respects be seen to be as fundamental.

11 Convention for a Democratic South Africa, the name of the negotiating forum that met for many months before 1994 to fashion a political resolution to the conflict.

employment (the period of the first post-apartheid government) for those who wished to stay, and of exceedingly generous retrenchment packages for those who wished to leave. The proposal was called by Slovo, and has been referred to since as, the "sunset clause."[12]

The second major element of the impasse had to do with the security forces, the other key base of the previous regime. All branches of the security forces—military, police, national intelligence and the State Security Council—had been deeply implicated in the atrocities of apartheid. On the one hand, they needed protection from prosecution. On the other hand, those who had suffered these atrocities were determined to root out the perpetrators, precisely to pursue their prosecution. The battle over this issue was protracted; overlaying it was the desire of the political leadership of the past to avoid responsibility for any deeds done which might be judged in court to be criminal.

Two things also constrained the leadership of the liberation movements in this context, the African National Congress in particular. Acute politicians among them knew well that the victory that had been won to date had not been secured on the battle-field itself. The liberation army forces never had any chance of overcoming the forces of the apartheid regime, even if a kind of stalemate had been reached in the violent daily experiences of what has been called "low intensity conflict."[13] A political solution was the only alternative to a protracted military struggle that neither side could win, and which would clearly damage the existing foundational structures of society to the point where little hope for a regenerated country would remain. That was the basic analysis.

But what precipitated things at the negotiations table was a report, commissioned by the African National Congress itself, on claims about atrocities committed in its own external camps in other countries at the time it was fighting the apartheid machinery. The Motsuenyane Commission Report duly arrived, and with it,

---

12 Slovo himself has since died of cancer while carrying out his duties as Minister of Housing in the new government.

13 The term comes from military theorists, including those of France, Britain and the USA, who had proposed "low intensity conflict" (LIC) as a way of dealing with insurgent, indigenous guerrilla forces where these could not finally be eliminated (see, for example, André Beaufre, *An Introduction to Strategy: With Particular Reference to Problems of Defence, Politics, Economics and Diplomacy in the Nuclear Age* (originally *Introduction À La Stratégie*), London : Faber & Faber, 1965; and *Strategy of Action*, London: Faber & Faber, 1967). The basic idea was to beef up security forces in all strategic areas, to give them control over the population through indirect and direct means, and to accept that a state of low intensity conflict would be a permanent feature of the society. The "stick" in this strategy was a co-ordinated structure of security forces at every level, capable of isolating resistance where necessary with whatever means were required (including disinformation, covert operations and assassinations). In South Africa the requisite structure was established through "Joint Management Centres" at local, district and regional levels, each incorporating police, military, intelligence operatives, local civic leaders (both white and black), key business people and even religious leaders. The "carrot" in this approach was offered in the form of personal rewards, preferential social development for co-operating sections of local communities, and political patronage. This latter aspect of the approach was often described in South Africa as the task of "winning the hearts and minds" of the people, particularly those upon whom the capacity and moral legitimacy of the liberation struggle depended. For an analysis of what was called the "total national strategy," the South African catch-phrase for the LIC model, see Gregory J.B. Mills, *South Africa: the Total National Strategy and Regional Policy During the Botha Years, 1978-1989*, Ph.D Thesis, University of Lancaster, 1990.

incontrovertible evidence of significant torture, even deaths, of ANC people suspected of being spies or informers, at the hands of ANC cadres. Debates within the ANC and without, led to a decision to set up the Truth and Reconciliation Commission, as an instrument of negotiation, to probe "gross human rights violations" on all sides of the conflict.

This was the opening which the apartheid regime needed. It offered a way of meeting the strong feelings among black South Africans about bringing perpetrators to book. But it restricted the process sufficiently that the perpetrators who would carry the guilt would be clearly identifiable front-line operatives. A limited form of amnesty would also be provided for, though no general amnesty. Senior leaders in both the political and military arms of the previous state were quite willing to sacrifice those lower down in return for the protection they now could expect to get.

As Dullah Omar, Minister of Justice in the first post-apartheid cabinet, tells the story, the discussions in the ANC about atrocities generally, produced the view that "what South Africa needs is a mechanism which would open up the truth for public scrutiny." It would be an attempt to establish moral responsibility at the same time as create a framework "to humanize our society."[14] For this reason, it was agreed that the proposed TRC would attempt something unusual: To hold hearings to establish accountability for gross human rights violations by allowing victims to speak; and at the same time, to provide for applications for amnesty from perpetrators under the Norgard principles.[15] The key shift, when compared to truth commissions elsewhere in the world, was captured in the term "reconciliation," to which I shall return.

Such was the stuff of compromise. Both the "Sunset Clause" and the TRC have been filled with ambiguities, and both remain the subject of heated debate. Both, however, signal a way of dealing with what appeared to be an intractable situation and a complete impasse. They may be regarded as expressions of the political practice of toleration, exercised in the desire to establish some foundation for a democratic state, in a bid to overcome war, fear, and the profound social damages which could otherwise be expected,[16] and which were likely to be irreversible.[17] Both compromise strategies have been messy processes, and they bring much into question, in practice and in theory. Not least, they raise questions about the meaning of truth, of democracy, of tolerance in a deeply divided society.

---

14 Reported in Antjie Krog, *Country of My Skull*, London: Jonathan Cape, 1999 (first published in South Africa in 1998 by Random House), 5.

15 In essence, these require that the amnesty applicant make full disclosure (which would have to be tested), and that a political motive for the deed be clearly established (which would require some evidence that a political party or body had directly or indirectly authorised the deed).

16 Of course, the social and economic damage done by apartheid and its precedents was already significant, and it continues to limit severely the policy options available to the present government.

17 Grounds for fearing an irreversible damage to the social fabric lay, indirectly, in a dramatic economic decline, increasingly expensive goods and outdated technologies in many areas as the sanctions campaign against South Africa deepened, internal conflict of a type that was making a wider range of local areas effectively ungovernable with no stable alternative in sight, and a depleting human resource base as those who could afford it left South Africa with their skills and those who could not battled with inferior education and a lack of skills. Growing damages to communal and family structures at one level because of apartheid policies and the costs of the apartheid struggle, and to the ecology of the country at another level—in both cases, with little hope of addressing these issues under the regime of the time—added to the pessimistic scenario which began to dominate analyses of this society.

Whose Truth, What Reconciliation?

Let me begin my further analysis by recounting a telling story. Some while ago I had the opportunity, together with the Anglican Archbishop of Cape Town, to spend an hour with our Minister of Finance, Trevor Manuel. In the course of our discussion, which was about South Africa's debt crisis, the conversation turned to the "Sunset Clause" invoked by Joe Slovo during the negotiations to end apartheid. It was now almost five years down the line. With exasperation, Manuel told us just what kind of sacrifice that had been, by citing an example in his own ministry in one of South Africa's provinces.

A senior Finance Ministry official had been found guilty of embezzling substantial sums of government money, and now sat in prison. But the agreement at CODESA meant that Manuel was obliged to continue paying his salary, even as a convicted thief. This money, and a great deal more like it, was of course vital to the capacity of the new government to deliver on its promises to build more houses, provide better education, supply adequate pension grants, construct roads, start irrigation schemes for poor areas, and so on. The compromises of the past had their costs in the present. And yet it could not have been otherwise.

In my view, this story expresses something of the depth of willingness among those who suffered under apartheid to give—to give a great deal!—for the sake of a hopeful and humane future. It has been, if you like, a massive exercise in toleration, if by that we mean generosity to the other. It is a spirit without which there would be no democratic South Africa.

With all its flaws and failings, this spirit remained at the core of the TRC process.[18] It was exemplified not least by its chairperson, Desmond Tutu.[19] What the TRC has allowed, in part at least, is for the voices of ordinary people, several thousands of them, to enter public discourse and shape our history. They are diverse voices, on both sides of the conflict. They are often searing in their pain. Surprisingly often, they speak of a readiness to enter into a rapprochement with those who caused that pain, for the sake of a joint future. Let me quote Cynthia Ngewo, mother of Christopher Piet, one of the "Guguletu Seven" who were, in the sanitized language of the security forces, "taken out" during the apartheid war. This is what she says: "This thing called reconciliation … if I am understanding it correctly .. if it means this perpetrator, this man who has killed Christopher Piet, if it means he becomes human again, this man, so that I, so that all of us, get our humanity back … then I agree, then I support it."[20]

---

18 The TRC itself was duly established as a Constitutional body. It consisted of three committees: the Human Rights Violations Committee which held public hearings around the country; the Amnesty Committee, made up of two Commissioners and three judges; and the Reparation and Rehabilitation Committee which had to formulate appropriate policies for government and parliament. The TRC also had a highly qualified Investigative Unit, and a Research Unit, the latter responsible also for the final TRC report. This report is now available as the *Report of the Truth and Reconciliation Commission, 5 vols*, Cape Town: Juta or London: MacMillan, 1999; an electronic version can be found at http://www.truth.org.za.

19 Desmond Tutu's own recounting of the process is contained in the just published *No Future Without Forgiveness*, London: Rider (Random House), 1999.

20 In Krog, *Country of My Skull*, op. cit., 109.

If, as Michael Walzer proposes, *tolerance* is an attitude or a virtue which is personal, and *toleration* a practice which requires political arrangements,[21] then we have in the voice of Cynthia Ngewo the attitude that makes possible the bridging of boundaries, the healing of enmities, and the stabilizing of a deeply divided society. Walzer identifies five basic possibilities which may be regarded as exhibiting the virtue of tolerance: a resigned acceptance of difference; a passive, benign indifference to difference; a principled recognition of the rights of others even if those others are unattractive; openness to others, even respect; and an enthusiastic endorsement of difference, either on aesthetic grounds or functional grounds. Cynthia Ngewo represents a form of the last possibility, believing as she does that human flourishing is the vital criteria of tolerance. In this regard, she gives voice to a deeply rooted African valuing of the human being in relation to other human beings, often called in South Africa the philosophy of *ubuntu*.[22]

What Cynthia Ngewo's voice does not represent, is a political arrangement, a successful *regime* of toleration. Walzer again: "… it is a feature of any successful regime of toleration that it does not depend on a particular form of this virtue [of tolerance]"; and further, "…political success doesn't depend on good personal relations" in any regime of toleration.[23] We are left with the political task of establishing a regime of toleration.[24] It may be, however, that people like Cynthia Ngewo contribute a great deal to the possibility of such a regime—at least under conditions where great divisions and enmities have been present and recent. In South Africa, post-apartheid, it has become common among government leaders, in political society generally, and in economic and civil society, to talk about the "moral fibre" of the nation.

Is a moral fibre necessary to building a nation, or is it secondary, superstructural, to use and old metaphor which no longer persuades? Thabo Mbeki, the economist, is one who believes it is necessary and in no way secondary. He calls on all sectors of society to "….join in the battle of ideas, or the debate, about the set of values needed to guide public policy if it is to be humane and just, honest and accountable."[25] These values are in some sense spiritual, a point Mbeki surprisingly makes in the presence of James Wolfenson, president of the World Bank, at a recent international conference on

---

21 Walzer, *On Toleration*, op. cit., xi.

22 *Ubuntu* can be translated in various ways, but its anthropological claim is best represented by the phrase, "we are human by virtue of other human beings." A philosophical exploration of this notion may be found in Augustine Shutte, *Philosophy for Africa*, Cape Town: University of Cape Town Press, 1993.

23 Walzer, *On Toleration*, op. cit., 12.

24 Of course, there are regimes on intolerance too, as many of us know well. Here difference is no longer prized in the "drive toward unity and singularity" (Walzer, *On Toleration*, op. cit., 83). We need to be clear here about what is meant here. Apartheid in South Africa, as the name suggests, was a system predicated upon difference—racial and ethnic difference. But its recognition of difference was based upon a unified, singular ideology into which all other differences were required to fit, or for whose purpose they were, indeed, constructed. It was not a matter of tolerance, but of segregation, or in crude terms, of divide and rule.

25 Thabo Mbeki, "Religion in Public Life: Engaging Power," in James R Cochrane (ed.), *Religion in Public Life: Multi-Event 1999 Conference Proceedings*, University of Cape Town, 1999, 50-52; also available at http://www.ricsa.org.za.

corruption held in Durban, South Africa.[26] This conviction is echoed in the United Nations Declaration on Tolerance which defines tolerance as "the virtue that makes peace possible, contributes to the replacement of the culture of war by a culture of peace."[27]

Even if we concede this point at some level, what kind of moral fibre is necessary to a regime of toleration, if any? The picture is not clear. Walzer, at least, believes that a regime of toleration may be stable even if no group likes any other group, as long as they are resigned to living with each other rather than fighting each other.[28] In the context of the many South African TRC debates, Rajeev Bhargava, from India, has suggested that the most one can hope for within the context of political transition is a "minimally decent society."[29] Does Cynthia Ngewo's kind of tolerance help then, does it contribute very much?

I don't think we can answer that question easily in the abstract. There are other testimonies that signal are far greater reluctance, even a repugnance, to forgive or accept in the way that Cynthia Ngewo has. Many even wonder whether the TRC, as such, has not been a colossal, expensive failure. We may put the question differently, therefore. Has the TRC helped us along the way of building a democratic regime of toleration? Has it added to the moral fibre necessary to build a nation that will work?

The legacy of the TRC cannot yet be judged with any great certainty. But some things have become clear. The process has been filled with contradictions, paradoxes and ambiguities. Many perpetrators have been named, some have already received amnesty,[30] many others have confessed. But virtually no-one in the higher reaches of government who planned and carried out apartheid policies, including the LIC programme, has been before the Commission or admitted to any direct responsibility. This has led many of their operatives who have appeared before the Commission to express a deep sense of betrayal. This in turn has meant that they have disclosed information which might otherwise not have come to light.

One of the major problems to arise with the TRC has been the question of the beneficiaries of apartheid, those who neither organized nor participated in its machinery, but who were happy to have it, both for their personal advantage and

---

26 His comments are: "In our own, national, case, we would make bold to say that a basic factor which informs corrupt practice is the disjuncture that has occurred between spiritual and material human needs. It seems clear that in that contest, the material has assumed precedence over the spiritual. In many instances, material values have gained their greater worth in the eyes of many people at the expense of spiritual values." Thabo Mbeki, "Address at the Opening of the 9th International Anti-Corruption Conference," Durban, October 10, 1999, at http://www.anc.org.za/ancdocs/history/mbeki/1999/tm1010.html.

27 Declaration of Principles on Tolerance, UNESCO, 16 November 1995, Article 1.1.

28 Although Walzer also notes that any regime of tolerance, even the most open one, carries with it the ongoing task of sustaining toleration: "toleration is always a precarious achievement," *On Toleration*, op. cit., 13.

29 Rajeev Bhargava, "Is the Idea of a Truth Commission Justified?," conference paper, International Seminar on Justice, Truth and Reconciliation in Transitional Societies, Geneva, December 1998.

30 The amnesty process still continues, though the TRC otherwise has shut down, simply because of thousand of applications for amnesty which must still be considered, each one requiring substantial time and resources to deal with adequately. This has in fact led one leading figure (Barney Pityana, Chair of the Human Rights Commission) to suggest that a general amnesty should now be applied, primarily to save finances which can be directed towards urgent, unfilled commitments to reconstruction.

because of their fear of black South Africans. They are people like myself, whites in the first instance, many "coloureds" and Indians too, a few blacks—people whose relative advantage now as a result of long-term acquisition of skills, resources and capital keeps the imbalance and inequality of our society in place.

Among those who have most strongly questioned the TRC on this point has been Mahmood Mamdani of Uganda, a leading African political scientist and until recently a colleague at the University of Cape Town. He wonders whether reconciliation, a defining term for the TRC, has turned into an embrace of evil. To be sure, many individual perpetrators have come forward, some of the revealing the real extent of the horror that characterized apartheid rule. But those who gained most from apartheid, yet who committed no individual crime, have virtually escaped censure, let alone taken responsibility for the past. These include not only the political leaders of the time, but all beneficiaries of apartheid—mostly, but not only, white South Africans. "What I still ask myself," says Mamdani, "is whether it is not easier to live with perpetrators than beneficiaries."[31]

Perhaps the most poignant reminder of the limits of the TRC came with the hearings at which ex-President F. W. de Klerk, a Nobel Peace Prize recipient along with Nelson Mandela, led the National Party delegation. Despite some relatively superficial words of apology for the past, the prevailing tone of their submission was one of avoidance of responsibility. As Antjie Krog describes the end of the hearing—when Chairperson Tutu's skin hung "dull and loose from his face," his shoulders "covered in defeat"—this was "The Day of the Undeniable Divide. One moment it was the closest, the next moment the farthest apart that people in this country have ever been."[32]

Perhaps we might filter differing views of our history, and hence of how our future should be organized, through the question of what constitutes a regime of truth? I do not propose an answer here, but I do want to put the question as starkly as possible, in the form of a brief anecdote from the TRC. The occasion was the amnesty hearing of a former apartheid torturer, Captain Jeffrey Benzien, about whom Ria Kotze, a psychologist who had been treating him for auditory hallucination, gave testimony. Throughout his lengthy recounting over several days of his deeds of torture (including a graphic demonstration of how he wet-bagged victims), Benzien experienced apparent memory losses regarding torture he had administered. Kotze was asked if she believed he was lying or telling the truth. Her disturbing comment was simple: "In my job there are, in a sense, no lies—all of it ties in, reacts to, plays upon the truth ...."[33] The undeniable divide in South Africa may be described as differing plays upon, or reactions to, the truth.

Building a Nation—Divided

This "Undeniable Divide," what is it then? If a regime of toleration is what South Africans have built for the moment at least, it is one which is not yet consummated. It might not be reflected in an attitude of tolerance at all, in fact.

31 Krog, *Country of My Skull*, op. cit., 112.
32 Ibid., 128.
33 Krog, *Country of My Skull*, op. cit., 78.

The TRC hearings and process offered us a double-vision of our society. On the one side, an astonishing array of ordinary people have had their voices placed into the public sphere in ways that penetrate the national consciousness, whatever one's reaction to what is revealed in the process. Their discourse has become indelibly part of the national discourse, in perpetuity. Whether "the truth" has emerged cannot be determined on the basis of facts in the first place, though those have played their role,[34] but only in terms of the validity of foundational, and perhaps founding, narratives.

The TRC, we might say, has contributed to the *reservoir* of memory upon which nationhood must be built, especially if that nationhood is to take into account the divided past in its present policies and programmes. It has also given South Africans a *repertoire* of stories, discourses, memorials, images and symbols by which we might measure ourselves as citizens and, in its recommendations, a *palette* of practical options by which we might engage in fashioning a new canvas of commonality in the face of a irreducible diversity. In short, the TRC in itself functions as a signifier of the task of expressing in political and social terms, the necessary link between the one and the many.

The other side of the double-vision we experience comes with the *aporia* between the one and the many, also captured by the TRC. There is some kind of resolution, and there is a painful realization on other levels that no resolution has been effected by the TRC. This is the "Undeniable Divide" I have mentioned. It is most powerfully articulated in narrative form by the rejection of any reconciliation with perpetrators on the part of victims of apartheid—and the TRC hearings had its fair share of such testimonies;[35] or by the kind of refusal of responsibility seen in the testimony by former President F. W. de Klerk and his party. The divide is most evident socially in the presence at hundreds of hearings of large numbers of black South Africans, and in the great majority of them, no white South Africans.[36]

The "undeniable divide" is best captured politically in a phrase often used by President Mbeki: he describes our South Africa as consisting in "two nations" and not one. To unpack this statement, let me turn to Mbeki's reply to the debate over his inaugural presidential address in Parliament earlier in 1999.[37] His analysis is predicated

---

34 Unsurprisingly, the "facts" are contested. A recent book which has received substantial coverage in the media, in part because its author has made great use of controversy and editorial letter pages to defend her position, is Anthea Jeffrey, *The Truth about the Truth Commission* (Johannesburg: South African Institute of RaceRelations, 1999); the book attempts to "expose" the weaknesses inherent in the TRC's investigations, criticises its standards of evidence, and documents "facts" which were not considered or could not be finally determined even though they are reported by the TRC. The critique has itself been widely criticized in turn.

35 Various reasons have been given for taking such a position, from a conviction that the truth has not been told and that the testimony of a perpetrator cannot therefore be trusted, to an inability not only to forget what was done but to forgive it (and no-one can judge this morally, as forgiveness is entirely in the hands of the one aggrieved), to a basic distrust of the TRC process because it was a political compromise of the negotiated settlement, to anger because the TRC process appears in some cases to undercut the possibility of bringing civil or criminal cases against perpetrators (an anger intensified by the lack of visible reparations to date, to those victims who have appeared before the TRC in trust that they will be given some form of reparation).

36 Even attempts by "anti-apartheid" Christian churches and ecumenical bodies to plead with white congregants to attend hearings for the sake of overcoming the visual evidence of the great racial divide produced very little fruit.

37 Thabo Mbeki, http://www.anc.org.za/ancdocs/history/mbeki/1999/tm0630.html. See also *New South*

less on racism—though he does not ignore the question—and more on differing visions or projects which drive national commitment. These are strongly ideological, and they have material grounds.

Briefly, Mbeki's speech embraces all opposition parties who take a consensus position on the task of national reconstruction,[38] and attacks the two parties he believes resist the consensus. One does so in the name of religion,[39] the other in the name of neo-classical market ideology.[40] That Mbeki tackles both these bodies, the one by venturing into theology (an unusual and risky move for Mbeki, of for any politician in an avowedly secular state), the other by recalling philosophical history, is interesting in itself for its dual emphasis. His attack on the African Christian Democratic Party (ACDP) touches deeply on the question of the *human values* he deems necessary to national reconstruction; and his attack on the Democratic Party similarly probes the economic vision by which *material goods* might be secured.

The ACDP he accuses of dealing in a theology of death rather than life, "a mean, angry, vengeful, soulless and retributive theology" at odds with the need to embrace diversity (including a publicly acknowledged plurality of religions) and build bridges across the hatred and distrust of the past. The exclusivist, absolutist claims the ACDP make undermine the national project at this level, for Mbeki. It should perhaps be noted at this point that Mbeki, though himself not religious, is not an enemy of religion, nor of Christianity in particular, though he has never been reserved in his criticisms of religion when it does not meet its own stated precepts in respect of human dignity and justice (precepts he derives in large measure from African humanism in conjunction with the humanists of the European Renaissance, and from Marx).

The DP he accuses of adopting wholesale the political theories—and accompanying material interests—of Jeremy Bentham in late 18th, early 19th century England. In particular, Mbeki singles out the linked claims that there is no such thing as society (only individuals), quoting Bentham: "the individual—the basic unit of the social sphere—is an atom and there is no self or individual greater than the human individual." In a state organized along such lines, Mbeki notes, it is inevitable that individual interests take precedence "over the interests of all other persons taken together." In this world-view is represented "the fundamental idea that everything must be left to the great leveller, the market, which is driven by the notion that 'self regarding interest is predominant over social interest'." This represents, Mbeki argues, a world-view incompatible with some of the key elements necessary for a common national project of reconstruction in the face of the heavy oppression of the past and the continuing, deep inequalities of the present.

The speech may, with justification, be seen as a clear statement of a conviction that South Africa still lives as "two nations"—one privileged and seeking to protect its

---

African Outlook, vol.1, no. 3, July 1999

38 In particular, the Pan Africanist Congress (PAC), the Inkatha Freedom Party (IFP), the Azanian People's Organization (AZAPO), the Freedom Front (the most conservative of the white Afrikaner parties in Parliament), and—of particular note—the National Party which drove apartheid in the past.

39 The African Christian Democratic Party, which considers the founding Constitution fatally flawed by its refusal to acknowledge the Christian God as supreme and which generally takes a position which might be described as anti-humanist on a wide range of policies.

40 The Democratic Party, whose approach to opposition politics and whose policies could be compared with Thatcher's Tories in England, and Reagan's Republicans in the USA.

privilege, the other seeking to build out of political freedom the foundations for broad-based economic and cultural freedom. It is the existence of these "two nations," in particular the overly powerful influence of the privileged one, that most bedevils the project of reconstruction and development and threatens the future of democracy.

If we then take the problem of nation-building to be that of the link between the one (nation) and the many (diverse particularities of its people), between sameness and difference, then the South African experience confirms at least six things.

First, the construction of a national identity, of a generalized sameness, is a task and not a final achievement.

Second, this task is not undermined by diversity and plurality, because both diversity and plurality can be politically institutionalized in ways which are productive and capable of producing a foundational consensus.[41]

Third, where the history of the nation is one of contestation and division, as is starkly the case in South Africa, a reservoir of memories able to integrate differing experiences of the past in ways which are constructive rather than destructive becomes particularly important; this requires a repertoire of discursive strategies and constructs by which the conflictual history of diverse groups may be brought into relation with each other short of ending relational possibilities—which would be to enter into violence.[42]

Fourth, any durable project of nation-building arising out of conflict and division depends upon some rapprochement between dominant groups and subjugated ones, in which the former are able to find guarantees for their survival even as the latter are able to find guarantees for their voice and presence to be honoured in word and deed (the alternative, again, is violence, and a chain of violence).[43]

Fifth, such guarantees cannot be made a priori; they are the stuff of negotiation (and breakdowns in negotiation), of meaningful sanctions to ensure the continuation of negotiations, and of compromises in all directions.

Sixth and finally, the task of nation-building requires that any enduring grounds for division be addressed, and be seen to be addressed; in the case of South Africa, this applies particularly to the two elements of our dominant political economy—"race" divisions, linked to class or economic divisions. Increasingly, we are seeing that gender divisions are equally significant, producing a range of political practices and acts which shape the public sphere in unprecedented ways.

To these six points, I would add one final comment concerning the project of building a nation. It is no longer self-evident that nationality, or oneness and sameness in this sense, is an adequate construct by which to understand contemporary politics

41 The South African Constitution is the first such instrument in our case, and it explicitly verbalizes the notion of national reconciliation in the light of a history of suffering and injustice as a founding principle in the preamble.

42 Of course, violence, if it is not gratuitous, aims at restoring the possibility of relationship in the face of a refusal of it from one side. It stops when that refusal turns to acceptance, though options to re-engage with violence might be held in the background until acceptance appears to be institutionally grounded and reasonably well-secured against further arbitrary refusals. The history of the period of negotiations in South Africa could readily be described as conforming to these axioms.

43 Of course, there will be no such process where the dominant group(s) feel secure in their domination and face no significant penalties for its continuance, as was the case with the apartheid regime until about the mid-nineteen eighties.

and hence the meaning of democracy.[44] Nation-states are products, practically and theoretically, of the modernist era. They continue to play a role—indeed, some would argue that they have a vital role in some configurations[45]—but they are also under attack or threatened by forces which pay no attention to national identities or boundaries, so called "globalization." We may like to think that these forces are new expressions of imperialism, no longer living on territorial conquest but rather on victory in cyberspace and virtual bodies (which is what I would call the modern market where it has to do with financial capital and speculative ventures), and to some extent there would be grounds for this.[46] But it certainly is nothing like any version of imperialism we know from the past in other respects, and many elements of globalization escape anyone's particular control.

On other grounds, both practical and ethical (with practical import), we may wonder about nation-states. In the case of South Africa, this concerns our relationship with neighbouring states, which under the apartheid regime and by virtue of South Africa's powerful relative economic presence, suffered in every respect the costs of the past. Do we now bring the shutters up or loosen borders to rectify this situation? Do we negotiate with richer parts of the world on our behalf alone, or on behalf of the Southern Africa Development Community (SADC)? Do we passively turn a blind eye

---

44 Samuel Huntington's famous thesis about "culture wars" as contained in his *The Clash of Civilizations and the Remaking of World Order*. New York: Simon and Schuster, 1996 is one example of an attempt to re-theorise international politics along different lines (civilizational identities rather than national identities). I would agree with David Skidmore ("Huntington's Clash Revisited," in *Journal of World-Systems Research*, Vol. 4, No. 2, Fall 1998, 181-188), however, that his case is suspect. Skidmore cites, among things, that Huntington fails to persuade both theoretically and empirically: he provides no adequate definition of what constitutes a civilization by which we might identify one and its difference to others; he offers a one-sided picture of underlying trends in the international system, including modernization, globalization and democratization; he claims a divergence among states without considering the evidence of widespread convergence in many respects; it is not clear, as he claims, that the West as a whole is in relative decline (especially after the recent "Asian crisis"!); and his argument does not cope well with a number of recent empirical cases (Bosnia, the Persian Gulf war, growing ties between China and the Middle East).

45 Political philosopher Jean Elshtain, in personal conversations, for example, has suggested that coalitions of nations, especially where they have some sort of regional integrity, may be important in resisting the centralizing controlling agencies of globalization. In this respect, it is interesting to note that the one example Michael Walzer denotes as a possible exception to the categories of regimes of toleration he enumerates may be the European community, which defies easy categorization or theorization; see Walzer, *On Toleration*, op. cit., 48ff.

46 There is little doubt, for example, that information technology and the communication systems will play a vital role in the economies of the next century. In both respects the USA is so far in the lead with its systems and resources that it is hard to imagine it not dominating much of what happens economically for some time to come, and thus politically too, of course. One example of the USA's centrality in what some call the "New Economy," is a recent mapping of the major internet backbones through which cyber transactions take place globally ("Spinal Tap," in *Intelligence*, vol. 5, no. 10, 1999, 13). It shows that the USA is the major hub for the rest of the world, and that virtually all traffic, no matter whence its origin, sweeps through the USA at some point. In short, US based e-commerce providers carriers and platform-providers are at the core of the "New Economy."

to xenophobia,[47] or do we actively structure our public institutions and political practices to counter-act it?

Here too comes a crucial test of what we mean by the one and the many, by identity and by difference, and hence, by toleration and by democracy. Whatever we now mean, it seems impossible to consider identity and difference without taking into account the radical plurality which impacts almost every society today, and hence, the complicated effects of experienced diversity. This is not new in some ways, as I might recall simply by noting my own South African origins, through four grandparents, to Scotland, Flemish territory, German aristocracy and Bengalese slaves, going back into the late 17th Century. But it is pervasive in ways that make for a qualitative difference. And that gives rise to our need to deconstruct the notion of the nation-state and national identity, though it is by no means clear what configurations of states and peoples will emerge out of that history. In this regard I do not share the high optimism of some post-Cold War theorists.[48]

Culture and Civilization through the Lens of Religion

Whether the divisions that characterize South Africa are racial, economic or gender-based, they are loaded with cultural weight. A large body of settlers or immigrants to the land have brought with them, beginning some 350 years ago, a diverse range of cultural fragments. The encounter with aboriginal peoples similarly meant another set of cultural fragments, almost as diverse in their own way.[49] Persistently, the cultural prism by which world-views are interpreted and communicated has been strongly religious, on all sides. While Islam arrived very early in the process, and Christianity from the outset, with African traditional religions long present, since then Jews, Hindus, Buddhists and Confucianists have also added significantly to the diverse character of the population. Christianity itself, by far the dominant religious tradition, has also become increasingly fragmented, and in many respects it can no longer be considered a single tradition.

Has religion contributed to tolerance, or has it engendered intolerance? The evidence is not strong on either side. A recent study on political intolerance and religion in South Africa shows the following.[50] First, it notes the existing literature on attitude surveys of political tolerance. This shows that South Africans exhibit a high degree of political intolerance, whose public face emerges in political and criminal violence, as well as in extraordinarily high levels of rape, child abuse, suicide and divorce. Second, using a large data set (3 031 respondents) based on interviews, the study shows that the relationship between political and religious (in)tolerance is minimal. Whether or not someone is religious, irrespective of what their particular

47 Xenophobia in South Africa is primarily directed against other Africans. A recent incident, for example, saw three African expatriates thrown to their death off a moving train, for no other reason than that their accents betrayed them, and with the argument that "these people are taking our jobs." The question of morality or spirituality intertwines once more with that of materiality.
48 Most notably Francis Fukuyama, *The End of History and the Last Man*. New York: Avon, 1992.
49 The major groups occupying South Africa in this period were Khoi, San, Nguni, Tswana, Pedi, and Venda, with some groups—the Nguni in particular—consisting in several major subdivisions (The Nguni, for example, include Zulu, Xhosa, Swazi, Ndebele, among others).
50 Amanda Gouws & Lourens M du Plessis, "Political Intolerance and Religion in South Africa," unpublished paper, 1999.

religion is, appears to have no direct bearing on their political attitudes. Equally, despite the fact that all the major religions include some value of respect or "love" for the other, the findings suggest that religion plays little role in engendering political tolerance.[51] In respect of religion, it must be noted that some level of religious tolerance, even under hegemonic Christian rule, has for long been the norm. Nevertheless, the study suggests, "the free exercise of religious rights could contribute to … 'reforming a free society' by working hard at 'reforming the individuals who make it up.' In this way religious tolerance can become the social laboratory for inculcating political tolerance too."[52] The study seems, therefore, to suggest that extending religious rights across society in the New South Africa has positive potential for building tolerance if, it also seems, faith communities focus on reforming their individual members by promoting respect for others outside of their communities. This is a very limited, rather individualistic view of the potential for tolerance among faith communities, analogous to the common religious idea that getting the person right gets the practice right. Still, it points perhaps to what others who speak of the moral fibre of a nation mean when they call for the building of virtuous character in citizens by religious communities.

With this thought, we are back to the issue of the moral fibre of the nation, and the view that a solid moral foundation is necessary to a healthy political society, and indeed, to a sustainable economy. The high levels of corruption in the South African state, its business community, and civil society generally, may be taken as an indicator of the pertinence of this view. It is not surprising, therefore, that the Mbeki administration has placed a premium on combating public sector corruption, and in calling on all other sectors of society to follow suit.[53]

At the same time, he and others have noted that the foundations for the kind of behaviour which would inculcate a different ethic in state bureaucracies, in business and elsewhere cannot be legislated or politically generated, though both legislation and political decisions and acts can encourage this. The foundations lie deeper, in the formation of the person. This, in turn, depends heavily upon relationships that are more immediate, in the first place (usually), the family.

Indeed, one of the significant contributory reasons for the high levels of crime, corruption and general moral malaise in South Africa probably lies in the destruction done to African families through the migratory labour system and the systematic undermining of family structures which accompanied this over almost the entire century. A personal sense of internal order and relational justice is difficult to establish under such conditions, especially in the face of very high and visible levels of

---

51 The single exception might be among the Jews, who evidence a relatively higher level of religious and political tolerance as a whole, perhaps, the report suggests, because "the persecuted have a better understanding of tolerance than those who do not have a history of persecution for religious beliefs do" (Gouws & du Plessis, op. cit.).

52 Ibid.

53 The details of the work that has been done, and some reflective essays, are captured in four volumes recently published by the Public Services Commission, namely, S Sangweni & D Balia (eds), *Fighting Corruption: Strategies for Prevention (vol.1)*; *Towards a National Integrity Strategy (vol. 2)*; *South African Perspectives (vol. 3)*; and V Mavuso & D Balia (eds), *Invitation to Ethics Management (vol. 4)*; all Pretoria: UNISA, 1999.

inequality in South African society.[54] This is complicated where the external trappings of justice appear as unjust, as was the case for black South Africans under apartheid, so that there is no experience of normative justice as a social pedagogy.

One significant location of a resistance to this kind of destructive patterning has been in the African initiated churches (AICs).[55] A good example is the Zion Christian Church (ZCC), inspired by the Pentecostalist movement of Zion City Church in Chicago earlier in the century. It claims some two million plus members. Its ethic is deeply rooted in its members, and includes strong sanctions against alcohol consumption and gratuitous sexual intercourse,[56] as well promoting a strong work ethic and honesty in dealings with others. All of this is bound up with what is emerging as a self-conscious claim to have harboured and treasured the best of African tradition, albeit transformed in its Christianized forms, precisely those values and virtues whose loss others now bemoan and for whose recovery they campaign.[57]

Focusing the lens of religion from one angle, then, it appears in the South African context at least, that religion and religious traditions offer resources for the shaping of the moral fibre necessary to sustain a regime of tolerance (or to push for it, if it is not yet in place) and build the capacity of persons to act as citizens in a larger unity than the one that defines them religiously or culturally. If I may rotate this lens a little, we may say that the human spirit grows in such places of particularity and identity, and that this growth of human spirit is consequential for a healthy society. This is true even if that same particularity and identity give rise in the accentuation of difference to intolerance at other levels.

As Gouws and du Plessis show in their study, it is not that religion correlates either way with political tolerance or intolerance, nor for that matter with the depth of democratic vision and practice which an open, plural society needs. Yet one may still claim with good grounds that religion (or cultural representations generally), once lodged in a context where a regime of tolerance has been established, offers important resources by which such a regime may be sustained.

Focusing the lens of religion from another angle, however, it must be said that the AICs which I have used as the case to establish the positive role of religion, appear in the analysis of Gouws and du Plessis as among those religious communities who exhibit the highest levels of political intolerance. Perhaps, the authors suggest, this is because they are inherently deeply conservative theologically and with respect to traditions. They are thus more inclined to suspect the outsider, the other—particularly any other whose world-view might threaten the tight orthodoxies or relatively rigid principles which lie behind their own success or viability. Religion, from this angle, is Janus-faced.

---

54 The Gini Coefficient for South Africa in most years is either the worst or the second worst among the sixty or so measurable countries, on a par with Brazil.
55 Also commonly called "African Independent Churches," or "African Indigenous Churches."
56 Which makes it a bulwark against the rampant HIV/AIDS epidemic.
57 This kind of claim is evident in the presentation to the TRC made by the ZCC in three days of hearing about the role of faith communities in apartheid. See James Cochrane, John de Gruchy & Steve Martin (eds), *Facing the Truth: South African Faith Communities and the Truth and Reconciliation Commission*, Athens, Ohio: Ohio University Press, 1999; in particular an essay by Robin Petersen, "The AICs and the TRC."

Moreover, religion, especially in as much as it is bound up with deep cultural traditions, is one face of what we might call the clash of civilizations in South Africa. The three hundred year history of Christian missions evidences this clash, as does the current recovery and public revival of African traditional religion in the face of the modernizing processes of globalization. But it would be an over-simplification to read into this merely a set of oppositions. It is not just identities predicated upon particular cultural and religious histories which are in conflict with one another, as between two prides of lions fighting over territorial boundaries. It is that no particular cultural or religious "civilization" is pure, without substantial and sometimes radically disparate internal tensions. No leading Africanist, to repeat something I said earlier, wishes to forego the benefits of modernity or of globalization—one merely needs to observe an African *sangoma* (traditional herbalist and healer) doing business with a cellphone to get the point!

In short, the articulation of religion and culture we see to be characteristic of our situation and time is one which is both internally and externally contested, fractured and diverse. Identity, even in the most rural and isolated areas of South Africa is seldom monomorphic. On the contrary, there is reason to accept that it is increasingly polymorphic, despite the wide variety of movements around the world which strive to reinvent and reimpose particular indentities.[58]

What then of Difference?

The set of explorations I have carried out by using the South African experiences of the TRC and discourse about nation-building, together with the excursus on religion and tolerance, leave me with one more move to make—a return to the theory of tolerance and democracy with which I began. The experience of the last few years convinces me, at least, that an enduring regime of tolerance under conditions where a deep historical scarring of the body politic exists, can only be built on the back of a commitment to deliberative politics in consensual mode. This is not the same as the characteristic Westminster mode in which it is assumed that opposition parties and groups in society have the primary role of being watchdogs over the ruling party, while seeking to maximize their opportunities to turn the scales (by any means, foul and fair, that will not tarnish them irrevocably). Nor, for that matter, can politics be as heavily delivered to the faceless bureaucrats of the civil service as is often the case in the Westminster mode.

In short, I find myself in sympathy (though not uncritically, for a variety of reasons) with the argument by Jürgen Habermas for a discourse ethics in political life. I am, however, less inclined than he is to aim for discourse practices which reduce the impact of traditions, or particularities, to giving good grounds for validity claims in open argument. The Enlightened intellectual, if you like, must not only make room for opinions on her terms, but also accept that other terms may have to be taken into

---

58 Indeed, these phenomena might well be seen as evidence for the rise of polymorphic identities, by virtue of the threats they pose to monomorphic identities and the resultant reactions. But more than than that, most programmes aimed at reclaiming particular identities (often of religious character) are themselves faced with having to suppress polymorphism internally, a contradiction that is often their undoing, or at least, which contains the seeds of the own destruction over the long run. The Taliban in Afghanistan offer a good example.

account—if for no other reason than that particularities, or group identities, however formed, have considerable capacity to allow for what I might call "backlash mobilization" against the Enlightened consensus.[59]

In a way this recapitulates what Walzer calls the twin modernist projects in relation to toleration and democracy. The first of these is democratic inclusiveness, which means that people, as citizens rather than as members of a particular group, enter the city as individuals. The second project, which deals with the inclination to separation as an alternative to entering the city, is "to provide the group as a whole with a voice, a place, and a politics of its own."[60]

But my argument goes with Walzer's one step further. It accepts, within the limits of Walzer's claim that various kinds of regimes of toleration work well even where the attitude of tolerance is not strong, the global situation as defined by the United Nations declaration on tolerance, that because of "the globalization of the economy and ... rapidly increasing mobility, communication, integration and interdependence, large-scale migrations and displacement of populations, urbanization and changing social patterns...escalating intolerance and strife potentially menaces every region. It is not confined to any country, but is a global threat."[61]

This is what we might call the condition of postmodernity. It produces a situation close to, but beyond Walzer's view on immigrant societies, or nation-states under immigration pressure. This is one where "people have begun to experience what we mighty think of as a life without clear boundaries and without secure or singular identities."[62] In a single family, ethnic, religious and cultural differences are part of the pattern. Hybrid, or "hyphenated" selves emerge, albeit predicated upon particular identities without which the hybrid itself would be unrecognizable.

This brings us back to where I began, with Chidester's welcome of visitors to South Africa. I remind you of his bold assertion that the use of the first-person plural—"us," "we"— touches on the "discourses and forces, strategies and negotiations, by which the first-person plural is constructed." Difference makes this statement necessary, because homogeneity, if it *has* been the nature of earlier societies in other times, is not characteristic of many sectors of many societies today, and increasingly almost everywhere. Difference is also no longer simply between "them" and "us." It is increasingly internal to us. Fundamentalism, Walzer suggests, is basically a response to this situation—the ideological form of a longing for "more coherent communities and a more unified consciousness" in the face of perceived secular confusion and anarchy.[63] Intolerance may then become an attack on the present order for the sake of a putatively redeemed one. At least this would be the desire which fuels attitudes, and in many cases, action.

Yet the postmodern, if that is what it is, is not a putative stage in a progressive development of history, but an alternative in the midst of the modern. In Walzer's view, this means that any new understanding of tolerance, for now at least, must

---

59 There are more positive reasons for accepting this, among them a valuing of the other and a respect for their dignity *as defined by them.*
60 Walzer, *On Toleration*, op. cit., 85.
61 Declaration of Principles on Tolerance, UNESCO, 16 November 1995, Article 3.1.
62 Walzer, *On Toleration*, op. cit., 87.
63 Ibid., 88.

tolerate difference twice—"on a personal as well as a political level."[64] The mix of a unified national project such as the one South Africa has now embarked upon, and the public recognition of diversity in the population of the nation, is a necessary programme of building a larger "us" without sacrificing the smaller foundations of "us-ness," to coin a word, and the concomitant acknowledgement and hospitality to those who we designate "them" amongst us.

If we return to the example of the Truth and Reconciliation Commission, we might recall the words of a psychiatrist who was involved in dealing with many of those who testified of the horrors to which they had been subjected, or of which they had in fact been the agents. Dr Sean Kaliski: "But there will be no grand release—every individual will have to devise his or her own personal method of coming to terms with what happened."[65]

Here there is an understanding of the memories of the past, of the task of the present, and of the ambiguity of the future which gives us no easy answers, but sets us out on a project without end. A regime of toleration is necessary which will allow this to happen, and Walzer is right—it does not matter at this stage whether an attitude of tolerance derives from resignation at the one extreme, or enthusiastic embrace at the other, so long as toleration is a political arrangement with requisite measures in force to establish and sustain it.

Yet, and yet, it does matter that a Cynthia Ngewo speaks of humanity and seeks to embody it. It does matter that regimes of toleration encourage this kind of attitude or mind set. It does matter that differences are accorded some measure of respect. It matters not because this is the only way to stabilize a political order—for it clearly is not the only way—but because human being and human becoming lives off possibility, even it is has to live in actuality. And possibility transcends, and keeps transcending actuality. It is a human characteristic that one gives oneself to this whenever one can— even in abject poverty, even in solitary confinement, even under torture, even on death row.

If you like, politics has to do with the material ordering of relations in a society. But, as many societies know to their cost, if that is all politics is without remainder, the possibility of something else will rear its head, and the human spirit—the spirit of new possibility—will break forth. That is a political fact, as much as it is an anthropological one.[66] In all the stories of the TRC, there are what Krog calls "under-stories," matrices which determine what is left out, what is used, how it is used, in a narrative—and an invisible audience for whom one constructs one's story: family, colleagues, new rulers, and so on.[67]

Every listener decodes and encodes the story again, in order to construct a truth. That is the fragility of our being. This does not mean a lack of commitment to a particular social vision, a particular justice order, a particular regime of toleration. It

---

64 Ibid., 91.

65 Krog, *Country of My Skull*, op. cit., 129.

66 That it is an anthropological fact is not merely a theological claim, though it certainly is that as well for most religions. It is also supported by a wide range of human scientific studies, both in positive claims and by virtue of those negative counter-experiences which we call "pathologies" or "anomie" or "clinical depression," and the like.

67 Krog, *Country of My Skull*, op. cit., 85.

means that toleration is the sine qua non of political life in our time—and violence its end. That is why we live with the fragility of truth, and die by the hand of those who seek to possess it as their own.

The Radical Jesus
You Cannot Serve God and Mammon[1]

Douglas E. Oakman

Based on philological considerations and contextualization of the very earliest Jesus traditions, especially Luke 16:13, this article argues that at the core of the concern of Jesus of Nazareth was a critique of Mammon, carried on under the proclamation of God's ruling power, that may still today leave Christians in an Age of Mammon with an uneasy conscience.

Introduction

A very common interest among U.S. Christians today, especially in the multitudinous "Bible churches," is the guidance offered by Scripture and in particular the biblical example of Jesus Christ. Indeed, the Bible might seem more important in American culture today than the Constitution of the United States. Under such impulses a few years ago, people began wearing bracelets inscribed with the acronym "WWJD," standing as most readers probably know for "What Would Jesus Do?"

A number of presuppositions are wrapped up with any answers to such a question – for instance without in any sense attempting to be comprehensive, the presuppositions that the gospel material recounting Jesus' example or words stems by and large from Jesus himself, or that Jesus' example or words should somehow be directly relevant to our situation without further investigation, or that nothing between Jesus and us has shaped Christian sensibilities and ethics.

All of these deserve more thorough exploration than can be given here. Suffice it for now to say that even scholars have versions (perhaps more sophisticated) of this interest and these presuppositions. I need only cite three instances: In 1953, Ernst Käsemann launched the Second Scholarly Quest of the Historical Jesus with his well-stated repudiation of teacher Rudolf Bultmann's position that Jesus was simply the presupposition of Second Testament Theology. Käsemann argued that Christianity would be reduced merely to an ideology if there were no critical principle of its meaning in Jesus; conversely, the Second Quest attempted to show the points of continuity especially between Jesus' proclamation and the *Kerygma* or proclamation of the early Christian movement. More recently in 1972, John Howard Yoder's fine study *The Politics of Jesus* assumed that Jesus had a politics and that it is important for Christian reflection on political life. Yoder's treatment, however, lacked refinements of scholarly study of the gospels so that his Jesus turned out essentially to be that of the Gospel of Luke. Finally, the strenuous efforts of the Third Quest for the Historical Jesus, on-going since 1980 and caught between the horns of the dilemma of a socially irrelevant apocalyptic or cynic Jesus and a socially relevant politically-engaged figure, shows the persistence of concern with the Man at the Root of the Christian Tradition, the Radical Jesus (Herzog 23-33).

---

1   This essay was published previously in *Biblical Theology Bulletin* 23 (2004): 122-29 and is used by permission of the Editor.

The portrait of a socially irrelevant Jesus is to some extent the editorial product, based in scriptural and theological interpretation, of the scribes of the first-century Jesus traditions. Critical sifting of the earliest traditions, closer to the Galilean soil, shows that at the core of the concern of Jesus of Nazareth was a politically charged critique of Mammon, carried on under the proclamation of God's ruling power. Let us proceed, then, by way of a careful investigation of the Jesus-saying preserved in the Q tradition, "You cannot serve God and Mammon" (Q/Luke 16:13). Q refers to the collection of Jesus' words in the Sayings Gospel, the earliest material about Jesus that we possess (around 50 CE). Q passages are cited today by their location in Luke, and that convention will be followed in this discussion (Robinson, Hoffmann, Kloppenborg 9).

Luke's Moralistic Treatment of the Saying

Some years ago, I wrote an essay attempting to "locate" the ideology of Luke, the writer of the Third Gospel of the Second Testament, and concluding that he had transformed the social register of Jesus' original message:

> What was originally a radical social critique by Jesus and his followers of the violent and oppressive political-economic order in the countryside under the early empire becomes in Luke's conception a rather innocuous sharing-ethic ambiguous in its import for rural dwellers. ... For Jesus, the kingdom of God was world reconstruction, especially beneficial for a rural populace oppressed by debt and without secure subsistence. For Luke, political expediency demands that the world restructuring be limited to alleviating the harshest aspects of political economy within the local Christian community by benefaction and generalized reciprocity. (Oakman 1991: 177)

This assessment involves the judgment that Luke's gospel represented an "elite-directed moralism." It is likely that Luke-Acts is one of the first in a line of apologetic works for the early Christian movement. Luke dedicates his two volumes to Theophilus, perhaps an elite city councillor somewhere in the late first- or early second-century Roman Empire. Luke-Acts has the general theme that the Jesus movement represents no threat to the Roman order. Luke's propaganda can be styled "moralistic" because Luke glosses over the harsher aspects of Roman relations and expresses a message of heart-felt concern for the poor which at bottom is an appeal to *noblesse oblige*.

Luke presents several sayings of Jesus about Mammon in chapter 16, immediately following the Parable of the Unjust Steward. The context has long been seen to be an artificial literary construction, since the Unjust Steward parable, which appears only in Luke, is followed by a series of appended applications that do not belong to the parable proper (Jeremias 46-7). Included here is the statement of Jesus to "make friends by means of the Mammon of Injustice." These application statements in turn are followed by the sayings about faithful stewardship and the impossibility of serving two masters or God and Mammon. The sayings about two masters and Mammon are found in identical order in Q (as can be seen from Matthew 6:24). From the Gospel of Thomas 47, however, the saying about two masters had another trajectory in the tradition where it was paired differently with sayings about the impossibility of riding two horses or stretching two bows.

The Meaning of Mammon

Appreciation of Luke's moralistic applications and this brief tradition analysis give us license to inquire as to the meaning of these statements for Jesus himself, especially the Q word "You cannot serve God and Mammon."

The term Mammon offers a fascinating word study, of which we can only give the outlines here. The word appears four times in the New Testament, and only in connection with sayings of Jesus: Luke 16:9, Luke 16:11, and of course Q/Luke 16:13/Matt 6:24. Though the earliest collection of Jesus' sayings we can reach historically – the Q sayings – are already in Greek, Jesus' mother-tongue was Aramaic, the language of the first-century Palestinian village. This shows in numerous places in the early Jesus traditions, for instance, in the Aramaic address of God as *Abba* ("Father"; Mark 14:36; Rom 8:15; Gal 4:6; Aramaic probably stands behind the Greek of Q/Luke 11:2), or nicknames like Cephas (the "Rock," as Jesus called Simon), or idioms like "son of man," or phrases like *talitha koum* (in Greek transliteration, "little girl, arise," Mark 5:41; see Brown 203-73).

The word Mammon likewise is Semitic. Though the noun *MMÔN* does not appear in the Hebrew Bible, it emerges in later Hebrew and Aramaic. "Mammon of Injustice" – translated "Mammon of Unrighteousness" in the Authorized and American Standard Versions, "unrighteous Mammon" in the Revised Standard Version, and "dishonest wealth" in the New Revised Standard Version – becomes a stock expression *MMÔN DŠQR* in the targumic and rabbinic traditions after 70 CE, where Mammon has the standard meaning of wealth, money, or property (BGAD 614; Black 139). However, the simplex reference to Mammon in Q/Luke 16:13 is probably closer to the authentic speech of Jesus in the 20s CE. Mammon is set in stark contrast to "God," without the suggestion at all that there could be a "Mammon of Justice," an acceptable and legitimate Mammon or *MMÔN ŠL 'MTH*, as allowed in later targumic and rabbinic traditions (Hauck 389).

Without more detailed first-century evidence, etymological considerations are indispensable for apprehending Jesus' meaning. Old Latin translations of the gospels confused etymological discussion by doubling the middle 'm'; this spelling carried over into late Greek manuscripts, early Protestant translations of the Bible, and modern English. However, the best Greek manuscripts have a single 'm', with the accent on the last syllable of the word. This suggests that the Greek transliterates the Aramaic word *MMÔN'* in the emphatic state, that is, *The* Mammon (Hauck 388; Nestle 2913). Four roots come into discussion: 1) *MNH* or *MÔN* to count or apportion, 2) *HMH* to roar, hence in noun form, to represent a crowd or metaphorically abundance, 3) *MN* to conceal, lay up, and 4) *'MN* to confirm, support, or trust. The play on words in Luke 16:11 (faithless with unrighteous mammon, entrusted with righteous mammon) gives a very powerful indication that Jesus' intention and meaning was closest to root 4 – *'MN*, to trust (Nestle 2914). From *'MN*, we get the familiar English transliteration Amen, truly. What is trustworthy is true; what is untrustworthy is false. This attitude comes from an ancient culture where epistemology is rooted in social relations and strong-group perceptions (Malina 58-79). The meaning of Mammon is bound up with trust and true and false social perceptions of reality.

But what is it that is falsely trusted in the usage of Jesus? The linguistic evidence points to Mammon as signifying wealth collected in the bank, or the storehouse, or the treasury, wealth which then becomes the object of trust for the powerful-wealthy to the exclusion of God and neighbor. More importantly, Mammon is based in a system that exploits the many for the benefit of the few. To serve Mammon is to be alone in one's self-sufficiency; to serve God is to have concern for others and to practice reciprocity. To trace the further meaning of Jesus' critique of Mammon, we need to investigate and see more clearly his central interests in context.

Jesus' Critique of Mammon

At the time of Jesus' historical activity (late 20s CE), Galilee had stood under Roman provincial arrangements for nearly a century (Pompey 63 BCE). Herod the Great wrested the area from bandits and Hasmoneans, and managed to have the Roman Senate declare him King of the Judeans (37-4 BCE); at his death, when Jesus was a small child in Nazareth, a Galilean insurrection resulted in the intervention of the Syrian Legate Varus and the destruction of Sepphoris just down the road from Nazareth. Herod Antipas, the son of Herod the Great, subsequently rebuilt Sepphoris, making it according to Josephus into the "ornament of all Galilee" (Josephus *Antiquities* 18.27). Builder-families such as those of Joseph and Jesus perhaps even participated in this work. Around 20 CE, Herod Antipas began construction of his other major Galilean city, Tiberias by the Galilean Lake. He did this, I believe, to secure greater control over the tax revenues from fishing. Perhaps Jesus participated in this building work as well; but not long thereafter, Jesus appeared at Capernaum on the north end of the Lake delivering his message about the Kingdom of God.

It is increasingly persuasive, based on historical evidence and comparative social science, that Jesus' message held social significance. Exorbitant taxation and debt seems to have been a central concern, as is often the case among peasants. Agrarian tax systems, which have no formal checks and balances to protect the village cultivator, are typically oppressive. Early Roman imperial taxes were fixed and levied in imperial silver. These were exacted from an agricultural base, hence had to be "converted" from agricultural produce into money. Fixed or invariable taxes showed no respect for natural variance in product. When villagers were unable to pay, tax debts were tabulated in written records kept in royal and imperial archives. James C. Scott's comparative political studies of peasantry offer us helpful perspectives on the general issue. For instance, Scott writes in his book *Domination and the Arts of Resistance*:

> ... in the region in which I have conducted fieldwork [farmers] have resented paying the official Islamic tithe. It is collected inequitably and corruptly, the proceeds are sent to the provincial capital, and not a single poor person in the village has even received any charity back from the religious authorities. Quietly and massively, the Malay peasantry has managed to nearly dismantle the tithe system so that only 15 percent of what is formally due is actually paid. There have been no tithe riots, demonstrations, protests, only a patient and effective nibbling in a multitude of ways: fraudulent declarations of the amount of land farmed, simple failures to declare land, underpayment, and delivery of paddy spoiled by moisture or contaminated with rocks and mud to increase its weight. (89)

Scott's category of "everyday peasant resistance" is helpful for contextualizing Jesus' activity. Traditional peasantries have employed a number of means of day-to-day resistance (Scott's "fraudulent declarations of the amount of land farmed, simple failures to declare land, underpayment, and delivery of paddy spoiled by moisture or contaminated with rocks and mud to increase its weight"), though none of these ever does away with the systemic problem.

Ancient peasant revolts were infrequent because of the perennial localism of peasants and the highly organized means of violence in the hands of elite groups. Not surprisingly, the great Judean Revolt of 66-70 CE was accompanied by tax remedies. The Jerusalem debt archives were burned during the initial phases (Josephus *war* 2.427), and Simon bar Giora later announced the release of prisoners and the liberation of slaves (Josephus *war* 4.508). When recounting the burning of the Jerusalem archives, Josephus refers to them as the "sinews of the city." He might have said empire as well.

According to Josephus also, the Roman tax arrangements implemented when Judea became an imperial province in 6 CE were met with stiff resistance. Judas of Gamala (in Gaulanitis, the present-day Golan Heights to the east of the Galilean lake) and a certain Zaddok the Pharisee, insisting that there is no God but God and that paying taxes to Rome is a sign of servitude, advocated armed resistance. I quote briefly two passages from Josephus:

> But a certain Judas, a Gaulanite from a city named Gamala, who had enlisted the aid of Saddok, a Pharisee, threw himself into the cause of rebellion. They said that the [tax] assessment carried with it a status amounting to downright slavery, no less, and appealed to the nation to make a bid for independence. (Josephus *Antiquities* 18.4, LCL)

> As for the fourth of the philosophies, Judas the Galilean set himself up as leader of it. This school agrees in all other respects with the opinions of the Pharisees, except that they have a passion for liberty that is almost unconquerable, since they are convinced that God alone is their leader and master. (Josephus *Antiquities* 18.23, LCL)

One cannot but be struck by the proximity of Judas and Jesus, and the similarity of their messages. At the time of the census, Jesus would have been about ten years old and living only thirty miles from Gamala. Moreover during the time of his own historical activity, Jesus spent most of his time in the environs of the Galilean lake. Capernaum is within eyesight of Gamala, and vice versa.

Another significant datum about Jesus of Nazareth is his association with "tax collectors and sinners" (attested in Q and in Mark). "Why does he eat with tax collectors and sinners?" (Mark 2:16) Why indeed? John Kloppenborg, one of the preeminent American scholars studying Q, offers a clue in terms of that document's origins:

> If one asks, who would be in a position to frame the Sayings Gospel as it has been framed, the answer would appear to be village and town notaries and scribes. .../ There is ample evidence from Egypt to indicate the presence of a variety of scribes, of varying educational levels, in towns and villages, some serving in the apparatus of the provincial administration and others functioning as freelance professionals. The [village scribe] was concerned with tax and census matters. (200-201)

Jesus's associated with "tax collectors and sinners" around the table, hence had to do with the sharing of real goods and perhaps the mitigation or even elimination of burdensome debts and taxes. The tax collectors possessed the social technology – writing – by which debt and tax collection was enforced. Ironically, the same technology enabled Jesus' oral Aramaic words eventually to be recorded for posterity. Jesus' message held special resonance with the fishingfolk, and Jesus' closest followers were fishermen like Simon and Andrew (sons of John), and James and John (sons of Zebedee). So a tax collector Levi, son of Alphaeus, turns up among Jesus' retinue. Interestingly, a fourth-century inscription found during the archaeological excavations at Capernaum reads: "alfu, the son of Zebidah, the son of Yoanan, made this column. May he be blessed" (Tzaferis 294). It would seem from this inscription that the association of the Alphaeus, Zebedee, and John families persisted for many centuries. If so, then the tax collectors were the fishers' relatives, and Jesus' meal program gathered together to some extent both the indebted and their creditors. There was mutual benefit.

The Radical Jesus

At the root of Christian origins, then, there stands a disaffected group and a social concern. Jesus proclaimed a socially transformative power, "the Kingdom of God," which appealed to the indebted and the outcast. Lake-fishers were in debt to the tax-farmers; prostitutes were in debt to their pimps, who undoubtedly paid a regular tax; and village-farmers were obligated to the large estate holder. Rents and taxes meant debt and arrears, for sooner or later (and usually sooner) people fell behind on their payments and were permanently put on record. The Romans encouraged this situation by infusing coined money into provincial agrarian economies, which in turn led to money loans and further debt. The provincial banks, which in Greek are called "tables" (*trapezai*), were held by powerful-wealthy interests. These tables represented exploitation, while the table of Jesus promoted reconciliation and reciprocity.

Jesus was attempting to mitigate the situation of the indebted, and perhaps went even so far as to promote peasant resistance in the form of subversion of the imperial tax system in Galilee. This subversion would have operated both in terms of tax evasion and distortion of the tax records. Jesus also focused on debt-forgiveness in the name of God's ruling power in order to mitigate the situation of the indebted.

Additional corroborations for these assertions are found in a variety of excellent Jesus material. The remission of enormous tax debt in Matt 18:27 (special Matthew) is noteworthy, and the slaves are expected to follow suit. In a very different light, the political significance of Luke 16:1-7 lies open for scrutiny. A royal steward manipulates tax records in his own interests and against those of the *kyrios*, the master. These manipulations are viewed positively (in v. 8), and the steward anticipates "being welcomed into (villagers') houses." More subtly, Mark 4:3-8 (The Sower) and Gospel of Thomas 97 (The Empty Jar) intimate possible evasion tactics—when seed sown on impossible ground or lost meal becomes available for tax-free gleaning. The tax question is addressed ambiguously at Mark 12:17 and Matt 17:26 (special Matthew). Even at the redactional level of the evangelists, good evidence of such resistance might still be preserved, for instance in Luke's Zacchaeus (19:1-10) or in Luke 23:2 (both special Luke) when Jesus is accused before Pilate of advocating tax evasion.

The evidence of the very earliest Q material, stemming as we have indicated from Tiberian scribes in the administration of Herod Antipas, is particularly important (see further Oakman 1999: 140, 147). Early Q reflects on the ethos and largesse of God's alternate kingdom. With roots in Passover meditation (as I see the Q beatitudes) and perhaps the example of Moses (who violently resisted Egyptian corveé, Exod 2:11-12), early Q has in view a liberation praxis (Robinson 1995: 259-74).

Indeed, early Q takes on a fascinating light when read against the concerns of "tax-collectors and debtors." "Love for enemies" (Q/Luke 6:27) and "Golden Rule" (Q/Luke 6:31) are not meant then as generalized ethical norms, but as supports for reversing the normal dynamics of imperial taxation. This value is stated positively in Luke 16:9, "Make friends with unjust Mammon." Behind both Q/Luke 6:32 and Q/Luke 11:4, Jesus' oral-Aramaic speech patterns are in view. As Matthew Black and others have noted, the Greek reflects the ambiguity of the Aramaic *OV'* (Black 140). While the related Greek word *hamartôlos* could be understood within a Judean theological frame to refer to the morally disreputable, i.e. "sinners," *OVYN* could equally denote those in indebted circumstances. With this translation adjustment in view, the saying contrasts balanced reciprocity and the general reciprocity ethic of debt- and tax-forgiveness commensurate with God's ruling power. Jesus' prayer concretely brings into focus his praxis, especially through the petition, "Release us (that is, tax-collectors) from debt, as we release those in debt to us (that is, those who owe taxes)" (Q/Luke 11:4).

Rostovtzeff, the great ancient historian, remarks on the frequency during the Hellenistic period of those who turned in royal opponents (including tax-evaders): "[In Ecclesiastes, under Ptolemy II] The spies of Ptolemy, who are so ubiquitous that 'a bird of the air shall carry the voice' of him who cursed the king in secret, were presumably both fiscal and political *mênytai* (Greek, 'informers')" (Rostovtzeff 350). The same pattern continues into the Roman period. The Q-words of Luke 12:2-3 have in mind such damaging revelations of secrets, so the connection to bodily danger in 12:4 is not accidental. This consideration throws a striking light onto Judas Iscariot, the Betrayer of Jesus.

Hatred of family members (understood ironically in Q/Luke 14:26) implies that one's actions for the sake of God's rule put family members at grave risk. Gospel of Thomas 55 and 100-101 juxtapose hatred of family with either the tax question or the cross. Besides Matt 18:25, there is the interesting story told by Philo about the actions of an Egyptian tax-collector:

> Recently a man was appointed tax collector among us. When some of those who were supposed to owe taxes fled because of poverty and in fear of unbearable punishment, he carried off by force their wives, their children, the parents, and the rest of their families, striking them, and insulting them, and visiting all manner of outrages upon them in an effort to force them either to inform against the fugitive or else to make payment in his stead. (*Special Laws* 2.19.92-94, qtd. in Lewis & Reinhold 400)

Thus, Q/Luke 14:27 and Gospel of Thomas 55 provide an important crux for this line of argument. For these sayings indicate very clearly Jesus' consciousness of the political consequences deriving from his praxis. The Q writers and Thomas hardly say a word otherwise about Jesus' death. If the cross saying is hyperbole, as some scholars think, why would it be associated with family and bodily danger? The saying's literal meaning must then be taken seriously. As the Roman jurist Paulus wrote in the early second century CE, "People who plot sedition and riot or who stir up the masses are, according to the nature of their social rank, either crucified, or thrown to wild animals, or exiled to an island" (*Opinions* 5.22.1, qtd. in Shelton 13).

Jesus' criticism of Mammon – the money and wealth stored at the bankers' tables or in creditors' storehouses or in the imperial treasury – resonated with the concerns of other contemporary Palestinian documents focused especially upon the elites of Judea. The Damascus Document from the Dead Sea Scrolls records:

> Unless [the priests] are careful to act in accordance with the exact interpretation of the law for the age of wickedness: to separate themselves from the sons of the pit; to abstain from wicked wealth which defiles, either by promise or by vow, and from the wealth of the temple and from stealing from the poor of the people, from making their widows their spoils and from murdering orphans ... (CD 6.14-17, Martínez 37)

Testament of Moses 7:3-8 likewise indicates a general feeling about Herodian Judea:

> Then will rule destructive and godless men, who represent themselves as being righteous, but who will (in fact) arouse their inner wrath, for they will be deceitful men, pleasing only themselves, false in every way imaginable, (such as) loving feasts at any hour of the day–devouring, gluttonous.

> ... But really they consume the goods of the (poor), saying their acts are according to justice, (while in fact they are simply) exterminators, deceitfully seeking to conceal themselves so that they will not be known as completely godless because of their criminal deeds (committed) all the day long, saying, "We shall have feasts, even luxurious winings and dinings. Indeed, we shall behave ourselves as princes." They, with hand and mind, will touch impure things, yet their mouths will speak enormous things, and they will even say, "Do not touch me, lest you pollute me in the position I occupy ..." (Priest 930)

Whether fictional or historical, the recollection in the gospels that Jesus attacked the tables in the temple points to an incompatibility of social perspective and interest. Forty years ago, Eppstein supposed on the basis of Mishnah Shekelim that Jesus would not have taken offense at money-changers because he "understood their necessity both in the provinces and, assuming that he had previously kept the Passover, in the Temple" (Eppstein 45-46). It is likely, on the contrary, that Jesus understand all too well the nefarious political consequences for provincials of the tables, money-changing, and debt. His attack enacts the basic idea of the Q saying, "You cannot serve God and Mammon" (Q/Luke 16:13). The tables represented deposits of money in trust, bank-deposits that could then be loaned out, *mamônas*, and correspondingly something trusted to the detriment of other human concerns and values, such as familial sharing, which the Jesus movement championed. Moreover, the tables represented tax-collection points and perpetual debt and arrears. Jesus' table, by contrast – consonant with his central concern of debt-forgiveness – was the gracious Passover table, the feast of the gracious and compassionate God of Israel to which all the hungry and indebted were invited.

Jesus' historical activity, in this reading, was centrally about provincial politics, the social realities of Mammon or the wealth-concentrate in the hands of the powerful, and not centrally about theological debates. The activity of historical Jesus signified debt-release and possibly tax evasion in the name of God's ruling power. While Jesus' historical resistance to imperial realities left its traces in early traditions, it is also true that later scribes shifted from Jesus' focus on political relations to theology. By Luke's day, Jesus could be seen as innocent of any Roman charges. In this sense, the Second Testament made an early contribution to obscuring the meaning of Jesus' peasant resistance.

WWWD–What Would We Do?

How does this meet with our situation today? Certainly there are analogies. However, I do not think we can simply leap from the first- directly into the twenty-first century without further considerations. So much has happened since then. Karl Polanyi gave important indications in his book *The Great Transformation*; Ernst Troeltsch traced other lines in his monumental *The Social Teaching of the Christian Churches*; H. Richard Niebuhr demonstrated complex historic possibilities in the relationship between *Christ and Culture*. But Robert Wuthnow's recent study *God and Mammon in America* indicates the on-going resonance of these themes. Perhaps, therefore, the real question is not so much What Would Jesus Do, but What Would We Do now?

This kind of historical investigation places certain developments in the Christian tradition in a significant light. It suggests that we look for places in the Christian tradition that are socially and culturally resonant with Jesus' critique of Mammon. To name two examples ready to hand, Francis of Assisi and Luther come to mind. The wealthy Francis gave away his substance to stand in solidarity with the poor and all creation (Tawney 23; Troeltsch 355). Luther too came to a moment of theological clarity through the radical grace of God, and restated Jesus' radical aims thus (in the words of Luther's *Large Catechism*):

> ... the trust and faith of the heart alone make both God and an idol. If your faith and trust are right, then your God is the true God. On the other hand, if your trust is false and wrong, then you have not the true God. For these two belong together, faith and God. That to which your heart clings and entrusts itself is, I say, really your God. (Tappert 365)

Luther further had none-too-kind things to say about money loans and usury, and he called bankers of his day "extortioners" (Tawney 74). Arguably, the Lutheran Reformation itself had as a central concern the clarification of basic human values that had been obscured by narrow economic interests. Exemplary figures in the Christian tradition, then, provide signs of the on-going power and influence of Jesus' vision and commitment.

Relative to our time, Jesus' critique of Mammon suggests that a capitalism without equity and distributive justice has not measured up to his radical vision of human fulfillment. And his critique is not just for the Christians. The engines of industrial and technological capitalism have produced the greatest boon in history, so as to provide the resources to address poverty and hunger on a global scale. But enormous imbalances in control and distribution of this cornucopia leave most on the planet in a state of abject poverty. Moreover, the great wealth of capitalism, in the name of security, is increasingly diverted into expensive weaponry, defensive social structures, and wars that perpetuate fear and misunderstanding. Necessary investments in the right kind of education – one that would promote genuine understanding and that perfect love which might finally cast out fear (1 John 4:18) – fall far behind. Meanwhile, the gross injustices of global capitalism and corresponding cultural dislocations give ready excuse for violent terrorism.

In this respect, the searching critique of individualism by Robert N. Bellah and his colleagues points to the tyranny of the isolated self that can only be the cultural consequence of capitalistic Mammon. Critique of the social and environmental insustainability of an economics promising endless growth in a world of limits has been powerfully advanced by Herman Daly and John Cobb in their book *For the Common Good*. They urge a thorough reconsideration of arrangements that place wealth into a few hands, where the many hold tokens while the real dividends are paid only to the few.

Indeed, there is need to rethink in broadly-representative democratic assemblies arrangements of capital, trade, and taxation, and to pursue policies that promote a more just and humane social order. There is need for a new kind of leadership to move the debate in legislatures and congresses beyond draconian budget cuts and tax relief for the wealthy. And there is need to see fiduciary and trust arrangements not as mere opportunities for personal gain, or the stock market as a rich man's lotto, but to see wealth as a community-trust to benefit all.

Finally, in an age of increasing fear and insecurity, Jesus' critique of Mammon compels thought about how we might see, how we might live, and how things might *be* if the ultimate heart of the universe is loving mercy and grace. It was Jesus, after all, who was remembered as having said:

> If you love those who love you, what credit is that to you? For even debtors love those who love them. And if you do good to those who do good to you, what credit is that to you? For even debtors do the same. And if you lend to those from whom you hope to receive, what credit is that to you? Even debtors lend to debtors, to receive as much again. But love your enemies, and do good, and lend, expecting nothing in return; and your reward will be great, and you will be [children] of the Most High; for God is kind to the ungrateful and the selfish. (Q/Luke 6:32-35)

Hardly the sentiments of an Enron executive or a Pentagon general, but words that might still be taken seriously by Christians, or a "Christian nation," or even a global civilization. Indeed, these are sentiments that do not sit comfortably at all in an age of corporate exploitation and the global politics of terror, but might provide a radically different basis for rapprochement between very different cultures and peoples. If everything *has* been given in radical grace, what then will we do now?

Works Cited

BGAD = Bauer, Walter, and Frederick W. Danker. 2000. *A Greek-English Lexicon of the New Testament and Other Early Christian Literature*. Third edition. Chicago and London: University of Chicago Press.

Bellah, Robert N., Richard Madsen, William M. Sullivan, Ann Swidler, and Steven M.

Tipton. 1996. *Habits of the Heart: Individualism and Commitment in American Life.* Updated edition. Berkeley: University of California Press.

Black, Matthew. 1998. *An Aramaic Approach to the Gospels and Acts,* with an introduction by Craig A. Evans and an appendix by Geza Vermes. Third edition. Peabody, MA: Hendrickson Publishers.

Brown, John Pairman. 2001. "The Foreign Vocabulary of Jesus' Aramaic." Pp. 203-73 in *Israel and Hellas, Volume 3. The Legacy of Iranian Imperialism and the Individual.* Beihefte zur Zeitschrift für die Alttestamentliche Wissenschaft, 2999. Berlin and New York: Walter de Gruyter.

Crossan, John Dominic. 1991. *The Historical Jesus: The Life of a Mediterranean Jewish Peasant.* San Francisco: HarperSanFrancisco. 1998. *The Birth of Christianity: Discovering What Happened in the Years Immediately After the Execution of Jesus.* San Francisco: HarperSanFrancisco.

Daly, Herman, and John B. Cobb, Jr. 1994. *For the Common Good: Redirecting the Economy Toward Community, The Environment, and a Sustainable Future.* Second edition. Boston, MA: Beacon Press.

Eppstein, Victor. 1964. "The Historicity of the Gospel Account of the Cleansing of the Temple." *Zeitschrift für Die Neutestamentliche Wissenschaft* 55: 42-58.

Hauck, Friedrich. 1967. "Mamônas." Pp. 388-90 in *Theological Dictionary of the New Testament, Volume 4,* edited by Gerhard Kittel and translated by G. W. Bromiley. Grand Rapids, MI: Eerdmans.

Herzog II, William R. 2000. *Jesus, Justice, and the Reign of God a Ministry of Liberation.* Louisville, KY: Westminster John Knox Press.

Jeremias, Joachim. 1972. *The Parables of Jesus,* translated by S. H. Hooke. Second edition. New York: Charles Scribner's Sons.

Josephus, Flavius. 1926-81. *Josephus,* translated by St. J. Thackeray, Ralph Marcus, Allen Wikgren, and Louis H. Feldman. 9 volumes. LCL = Loeb Classical Library. Cambridge, MA: Harvard University Press.

Käsemann, Ernst. 1964. "The Problem of the Historical Jesus." Pp. 15-42 in *Essays on New Testament Themes,* translated by W. J. Montague. Philadelphia: Fortress Press.

Kloppenborg Verbin, John S. 2000. *Excavating Q: The History and Setting of the Sayings Gospel.* Minneapolis: Fortress Press.

Lewis, Naphtali, and Meyer Reinhold. 1955. *Roman Civilization, Volume 2. The Empire.* New York: Columbia University.

Malina, Bruce J. 2001. *The New Testament World: Insights from Cultural Anthropology.* Third edition, revised and expanded. Louisville, KY: Westminster John Knox Press.

Martínez, Florentino García. 1996. *The Dead Sea Scrolls Translated: The Qumran*

Texts in English, translated by Wilfred G. E. Watson. Second edition. Leiden: E. J. Brill.

Nestle, Eberhard. 1913. "Mammon." Pp. 2912-15 in *Encyclopaedia Biblica, Volume 3*, edited by T. K. Cheyne and J. Sutherland Black. New York: Macmillan.

Niebuhr, H. Richard. 2001. *Christ and Culture*. San Francisco: HarperSanFrancisco.

Oakman, Douglas E. 1991. "The Countryside in Luke-Acts." Pp. 151-79 in *The Social World of Luke-Acts: Models for Interpretation*, edited by Jerome H. Neyrey. Peabody, MA: Hendrickson.

———. 1999. "The Lord's Prayer in Social Perspective." Pp. 137-86 in *Authenticating the Words of Jesus*, edited by Bruce Chilton and Craig A. Evans. Leiden: E. J. Brill.

Polanyi, Karl. 2001. *The Great Transformation: The Political and Economic Origins of Our Time*. Second edition. Boston, MA: Beacon Press.

Priest, John. 1983. "The Testament of Moses." Pp. 919-34 in *The Old Testament Pseudepigrapha. Volume 1. Apocalyptic Literature and Testaments*, edited by James H. Charlesworth. Garden City, NY: Doubleday.

Robinson, James A., editor. 1990. *The Nag Hammadi Library in English*. San Francisco: HarperSanFrancisco.

———. 1995. "The Jesus of Q as Liberation Theologian." Pp. 259-74 in *The Gospel Behind the Gospels: Current Studies on Q*, edited by Ronald A. Piper. Supplements to Novum Testamentum, 75. Leiden: E. J. Brill.

Robinson, James A., Paul Hoffmann, and John S. Kloppenborg, editors. 2002. *The Sayings Gospel Q in Greek and English, with Parallels from the Gospels of Mark and Thomas*. Minneapolis: Fortress Press.

Rostovtzeff, Michael. 1941. *Social and Economic History of the Hellenistic World*. 3 volumes. Oxford: Clarendon Press.

Scott, James C. 1990. *Domination and the Arts of Resistance: Hidden Transcripts*. New Haven and London: Yale University Press.

Shelton, Jo-Ann. 1988. *As the Romans Did: A Source Book in Roman Social History*. New York and Oxford: Oxford University Press.

Tappert, Theodore G., translator and editor. 1959. *The Book of Concord: The Confessions of the Evangelical Lutheran Church*. Philadelphia: Fortress Press.

Tawney, R. H. 1954. *Religion and the Rise of Capitalism: A Historical Study*. Holland Memorial Lectures 1922. New York: Mentor Books.

Troeltsch, Ernst. 1931. *The Social Teaching of the Christian Churches*, translated by Olive Wyon. 2 volumes. New York: The Macmillan Company.

Tzaferis, Vassilios. 1993. "Capernaum." Pp. 291-6 in *The New Encyclopedia of Archaeological Excavations in the Holy Land, Volume 1*, edited by Ephraim Stern. New York: Simon & Schuster.

Wuthnow, Robert. 1998. *God and Mammon in America*. New York: The Free Press.

Yoder, John Howard. 1972. *The Politics of Jesus: Vicit Agnus Noster*. Grand Rapids, MI: Eerdmans.

The Historicity of Myth and the Myth of Historicity

Locating the Ordinary African 'reader' of the Bible in the Debate

Gerald West

Introduction

There is, I have discovered, an important place for socio-historical resources in the interpretative interface between socially engaged biblical scholars and ordinary 'readers' of the Bible. Somewhat ironically, I have found myself making this point quite frequently of late (West, 2002d, West, 2002b, West, 2000).[1] I say ironically, because much of my early work has been in debate with those who sought to privilege socio-historical modes of biblical interpretation (within biblical studies in general and liberation hermeneutics in particular). While I appreciated the contributions of Norman Gottwald, Elisabeth Schüssler Fiorenza and Itumeleng Mosala, I was unpersuaded by their insistence that their socio-historical modes of reading were more appropriate to liberation hermeneutics than, for example, the allegedly 'neo-orthodox' literary modes of reading favoured by Phyllis Trible, Allan Boesak and Desmond Tutu. I argued vigorously that literary modes of reading were as coherent and theoretically well_grounded for the purposes of a biblical hermeneutics of liberation as their socio-historical cousins. Furthermore, I also argued that literary modes of biblical interpretation were more egalitarian and empowering than socio-historical approaches when it came to reading the Bible 'with' ordinary 'readers' of the Bible (West, 1995).

While the lines between literary and socio-historical modes of interpretation are not as starkly drawn as they used to be, it is not this relaxation of the boundaries between them that has precipitated my move. It has been my work with ordinary African 'readers' of the Bible. In my ongoing work with ordinary African 'readers' of the Bible I have come to realise the significant role our scholarly biblical resources play when socially engaged biblical scholars and ordinary non-scholarly 'readers' interpret the Bible together. In brief, I believe that our interpretative resources supplement and complement the resources they already have and so enable them to more readily find resonances between their 'working' theologies and the biblical tradition in which they stand and with which they are sustained (West, 1999).

I have also come to recognise (and here I am summarising the argument I have put forward in the essays cited above) that while many of their connections are with the biblical *text*, they also long to find lines of connection between their realities and the *historical* realities which lie behind the biblical text. Like Gottwald, Schüssler Fiorenza, and Mosala they want to know that their lived realities are connected with the lived realities of those who have gone before them in the faith; and in both instances these lived realities have clear historical dimensions. It matters to black

---

1 Another version of his essay is to be published in the journal *Neotestamentica*.

unemployed youth whether early 'Israel' emerged from among the marginalised classes of Palestine (Gottwald, 1979); it matters to African women whether women in early 'Israel' were part of a nonhierarchical society (Meyers, 1988); it matters to African university students whether Jesus was an organic intellectual working among the poor and marginalised (Horsley, 1994); it matters to African women who feel called to leadership in the church whether women were an integral part of early Christianity (Fiorenza, 1983). For the dispossessed it matters whether those like them had a place in the formation of a tradition that is meaningful, powerful, and true for them,[2] but who do not find themselves represented in its dominant discourse. Rosemary Radford Ruether says it well when she argues that to express contemporary experience in a cultural and historical vacuum is both "self_deluding and unsatisfying."

> It is self_deluding because to communicate at all to oneself and others, one makes use of patterns of thought, however transformed by new experience, that have a history. It is unsatisfactory because, however much one discards large historical periods of dominant traditions, one still seeks to encompass this 'fallen history' within a larger context of authentic and truthful life. To look back to some original base of meaning and truth before corruption is to know that truth is more basic than falsehood and hence able, ultimately, to root out falsehood in a new future that is dawning in contemporary experience. To find glimmers of this truth in submerged and alternative traditions through history is to assure oneself that one is not mad or duped. Only by finding an alternative historical community and tradition more deeply rooted than those that have become corrupted can one feel sure that in criticizing the dominant tradition one is not just subjectively criticizing the dominant tradition but is, rather, touching a deeper bedrock of authentic Being upon which to ground the self. One cannot wield the lever of criticism without a place to stand (Ruether, 1983:18).

No wonder ordinary 'readers' of the Bible have an interest in history. No wonder too that socially engaged biblical scholars like Gottwald, Schüssler Fiorenza, and Mosala have expended so much energy and expertise in attempting to track the traces of marginalised sectors in biblical history. Being in collaboration with the struggles of the socially and politically dispossessed, they have struggled to return to them a place in the biblical tradition; a place often denied to them by the dominant trajectories they encounter in their churches.

I still want to maintain, however, that the way into this history must remain via the text. To circumvent the text disempowers ordinary 'readers' of the Bible and they are forced to become dependent on the scholar. Besides, it is only by engaging with the text that ordinary 'readers' are able to pose *their* socio-historical questions. Socio-historical research is not an exact science and is driven as much by the interests and ideologies of the researcher as by the data available. So it is important that the poor, the working class, and the marginalised be allowed to pose their questions to the world behind the text.

In our fifteen years of work in the Institute for the Study of the Bible & Worker Ministry Project (ISB&WM) it has become apparent that those with whom we work do want to know about the socio-historical realities behind the biblical text. In fact, as I

---

2   I use this phrase "meaningful, powerful, and true" in the sense that it is used by Linell Cady (Cady, 1986, see also West, 1995:chapter 5).

have said, it is this that has persuaded me to reflect more substantially on the importance of this mode of reading. Daniel Patte misunderstands the import of my attempts at clarifying the needs of ordinary 'readers' in this regard. I am not claiming that "Experts are necessary to refine the poorly or wrongly formulated interpretations by ordinary readers," placing the latter, therefore, "in a subaltern position" (Patte, 2002:379). He correctly discerns my concern when he goes on to say that I pay "particular attention to the importance for believers that they have a sense of continuity between the scriptural text and themselves" (Patte, 2002:379). However, when he goes on to suggest that historians as experts "are required to establish this sense of continuity" he again misses my emphasis. Like him I want to assert that his students and the ordinary 'readers' with whom I work are able to establish their own forms of continuity with the Bible. Like him I have insisted that there definitely is more than one way of conceiving of this continuity. And like him I would not want to conceive of this historical continuity in an exclusively Western conceptualization of history (Patte, 2002:379).

I do envisage a more active role for the biblical scholar than Patte does in the encounter between scholar and non-scholar. But this is only because our work in the ISB&WM has indicated that the particular resources biblical scholars commonly employ as part of their trade provide *additional useful* resources for ordinary 'readers' in their attempts to articulate, to own, and to bring into the public realm their inchoate and incipient working theologies (West, 1999). And while my early work has emphasised the contribution of literary modes of reading, I have been forced by our reading practice to recognise a contribution from socio-historical modes of reading.

I really liked Patte's example of Lewis Baldwin's exposition of the deep sense of continuity between the experience of African-American slaves and Jesus. It is an excellent example of the profound resources ordinary 'readers' have forged in their determination to find lines of continuity between their lived reality and the biblical witness. Patte is right in two respects:

> First, the slaves perceived continuity between themselves and Jesus is not something they needed to be taught; it is found in their existing interpretations. Second, in this case, this sense of continuity involves a typological view of history (according to which "there is no before and after in Torah," as the rabbis said), which is commonly found in the Bible itself (see, for instance, the interpretations of the law and prophets in Matthew and Paul) but also in many non-Western cultures today – including, for instance the Zulu culture, according to which the ancestors remain present with the living (Patte, 2002:379-380).

I have no argument with this whatsoever and I applaud Patte for his recognition and celebration of the reading resources of ordinary 'readers'. What I do want to reflect on more fully in this paper is the contribution of *Western-style historical studies*. Having opened the door to them, I now have to walk through and examine their contribution more carefully.

Before I begin, however, let me reiterate what I have said. I do not want to grant any privilege to historical modes of reading the Bible. With Patte I would insist that

> historical interpretations (for which what is significant is *behind the text* as "window" upon some historical entities) are on the same plane as, for instance, narrative , literary,

and structural interpretations (for which what is significant is *in the text*) and rhetorical, political, feminist interpretations (for which what is significant is *in front of the text*). An interpretation is as meaningful and as legitimate whether it chooses to ground itself "behind," or "in," or again "in front" of the text (Patte, 2002:379).

In fact, as I have also said, I would want to privilege literary modes of reading as the entry point for collaborative reading acts between socially engaged biblical scholars and ordinary African 'readers' of the Bible. But I have been led by these selfsame ordinary 'readers' to recognise and to respond to *their requests* for historical information (and, hopefully, historical continuity), requests that have come from their engagement with the biblical text. So not only do I not want to privilege historical modes of reading, I also do not want to privilege *the ('assured') results* of the historical work of biblical scholars, because the questions that drive their quests for historical information are derived largely from their middle-class and mainly white male realities and ideologies. Socially engaged socio-historical biblical scholarship must place itself in the service of the questions of the poor, the working-class, and the marginalised (West, 2002d, West, 2002b, West, 2000).

The Myth of Historicity

All of this does bring me to an analysis of how we might go about appropriating socio-historical modes of reading in our work with ordinary 'readers' of the Bible. The first remark I want to make has to do with the danger such modes present to the collaborative reading process. Socio-historical modes of reading tend to retain an aura of objectivity that is missing with literary modes. Ordinary 'readers' quickly realise that they can contest the interpretation of text, particularly when they are working with Bible translations in their own vernaculars. However, even well organised and articulate ordinary 'readers' tend to defer to the socio-historical expert in their midst. It is not easy, for example, to contest a particular historical reconstruction of the Pharisees' role in the Jerusalem temple. The myth that there is a realm of "what really happened" behind the text is an enduring one. Of course, historiography has come a long way since L. von Ranke's "wie es eigentlich gewesen" [what actually happened], but we have yet to fully shake off what John Huizinga so long ago referred to as "the naive historical realism which represents the initial attitude of educated men [sic] in general and no less of a great many historians" (Huizenga, 1936:5). This naive historical realism supposes "that history strives to relate *the* story of *the* past" (Huizenga, 1936:5). This "common sense" view of history, as another early philosopher of history, Louis Mink, informs us, presupposes "that historical actuality itself has narrative form, which the historian does not invent but discovers, or attempts to discover. History-as-it-was-lived, that is, is an untold story. The historian's job is to discover that untold story, or part of it, and to retell it even though in abridged or edited form" (Mink, 1978).

Alluring as this common sense view of history is, particularly for biblical scholarship, built as it is on a historical-critical legacy, even we must move on. Much has happened in historiography and biblical studies must shake itself from its slumber (Whitelam, 1986). Traditional narrative historiography, the most common form of biblical history, has long been questioned by other forms of historiography, most notably by three major strands within historiography: the social-science orientated French *Annales* school (of scholars like Fernand Braudel, Francois Furet, Jacques Le Goff, Emmanuel Le Roy Ladurie) who regard "narrative historiography as a non-scientific, even *ideological representational strategy*, the extirpation of which was necessary for the transformation of historical studies into a genuine science"; semiotically orientated literary theorists and philosophers (like Roland Barthes, Michel Foucault, Jacques Derrida, T. Todorov, Julia Kristeva, Umberto Eco) "who have studied narrative in all of its manifestations and viewed it as simply one discursive 'code' among others, which might or might not be appropriate for the representation of 'reality,' depending only on the *pragmatic* aim in view of the speaker of the discourse"; and the hermeneutically orientated philosophers like Hans-Georg Gadamer and Paul Ricoeur "who have viewed narrative as the manifestation in discourse of a specific kind of time-consciousness or structure of time" (White, 1984:7-8).[3] Even the champions of narrative historiography, the Anglo-American analytical philosophers (like W.H. Walsh, Patrick Gardiner, William Dray, Authur Danto, Louis Mink) "who have sought to establish the epistemic status of narrative, considered as a *kind of explanation* especially appropriate to the explanation of historical, against natural, events and processes" (White, 1984:7) have acknowledged the constructed nature of narrative.

Arthur Danto reminds us that "any narrative [including historical narrative] is a structure imposed upon events, grouping some of them together with others, and ruling some out as lacking *relevance*" (Danto, 1968). Louis Mink makes a similar point when he says that narratives, including historical narratives, contain "indefinitely many ordering relations, and indefinitely many ways of combining these relations". It should be clear, continues Mink, "that a historical narrative claims truth not merely for each of its individual statements taken distributively, but for the complex form of the narrative itself". "The cognitive function of narrative form, then," concludes Mink, "is not just to relate a succession of events but to body forth an ensemble of interrelationships of many different kinds as a single whole" (Mink, 1978, see also Mink, 1966:181). Even more significantly, Mink indicates the direction in which we need to look for an analysis of these ordering relations. In an earlier article Mink had suggested that "history is akin to poetry" in that its significant conclusions "are represented by the narrative order itself" (Mink, 1966:181). Which is precisely where Hayden White makes his contribution. History, like poetry, writes White, is also a form of literary patterning, "only here the patterning in question is not that of sound and meter so much as that of the rhythms and repetitions of motific structures which aggregate into themes, and of themes which aggregate into plot-structures" (White, 1984:20, see also White, 1973).

To put it succinctly, but accurately, history is *constructed* rather than found (White, 1984:2). We do not *find* the historical story in the 'factual' primary source data that historians collect, we *fashion* it (White, 1975:59). And even the *Annales*-type social-scientific historiography which has something of a following in biblical studies (Whitelam, 1986), though hardly a sustained one, is not exempt from this fashioning,

---

3   The scholars mentioned here and below are all discussed by White in the article cited.

even if they eschew narrative sources and narrative representations. For as White so aptly puts it:

> The point is this: even in the simplest prose discourse, and even in one in which the object of representation is intended to be nothing but fact, the use of language itself projects a level of secondary meaning below or behind the phenomena being 'described'. This secondary meaning exists quite apart from both the 'facts' themselves and any explicit argument that might be offered in the extradescriptive, more purely analytical or interpretative, level of the text. This figurative level is produced by a constructive process, poetic in nature, which prepares the reader of the text more or less subconsciously to receive *both* the description of the facts and their explanation as plausible, on the one side, and as adequate to one another, on the other (White, 1978).

The persistence of a naive historical realism is not found in these quarters but among "certain historians who can be said to belong to no particular philosophical or methodological persuasion, but speak rather from the standpoint of the *doxa* of the profession, as defenders of a *craft* notion of historical studies, and who view narrative as a respectable way of 'doing' history (as J.H. Hexter puts it) or 'practicing' it (as Geoffrey Elton would have it). But, as White, goes on to argue, "this group does not so much represent a theoretical position as incarnate a traditional attitude of eclecticism in historical studies – an eclecticism which is a manifestation of a certain suspicion of theory itself as an impediment to the proper practice of history enquiry, conceived as *empirical* inquiry" (White, 1984:8). These are the "educated men" Huizinga warned us about so long ago.

The point of this brief resume is to remind the historically interested socially engaged scholar who works with ordinary 'readers' of the Bible of the myth of historicity. We must embody a more nuanced view of history in the very act of imparting historical information in our collaborative work with non-scholars. The illusion that we know "what really happened" must be shattered, and we must find ways of *showing* this when sharing historical knowledge, particularly when we are providing (requested) information concerning those especially significant *founding* moments of our faith.

I add this final clause because, as Keith Whitelam reminds us, the (re)construction of the past "is a struggle over the definition of historical and social identity", particularly when we are dealing with originary events, what V. Dharwadker refers to as those "first moment[s] of true civilization", moments which are especially significant in the history of any people (cited in Whitelam, 1996:234). Mainstream biblical scholarship has tended to monopolize the originary moments of early Israel for its own purposes, as Whitelam's book *The Invention of Ancient Israel* amply articulates. Whitelam makes a persuasive case for an intricate and intimate link between biblical criticism and the cultural and political agendas of contemporary developed states such as Western Europe, Israel, and North America. By claiming the right to represent the origins of 'ancient Israel' mainstream biblical studies has, according to Whitelam, "collaborated in an act of dispossession, or at the very least, to use Said's phrase, 'passive collaboration' in that act of dispossession". The construction of ancient Israel (retrospectively) in the images and likenesses of

European visions of itself "has silenced the history of the indigenous peoples of Palestine in the early Iron Age" (Whitelam 1996:222), and has contributed to the marginalization of the Palestinian people in Israel today (Whitelam 1996:225-227).

This is not all; more can be laid at the door of the dominant socio-historical discourse in biblical studies. Not only have Palestinians been dispossessed; others too have been dispossessed. By controlling the originary moments of early Israel (and early Christianity) through their representations, the dominant sectors of biblical scholarship have participated in dispossessing others of their place in these defining moments. Representing the past is a social and political act that has important ramifications for the present "because personal or social identity is either confirmed by or denied by these representations" (Whitelam, 1996:12, see also Tonkin, 1992:6).

In this section I have made two related arguments. First, I have argued that history is fashioned and not found and that socially engaged biblical scholars who work with ordinary 'readers' of the Bible ought to be honest about their lack of direct access to "what really happened". Second, I have briefly reiterated my argument elaborated more extensively in essays already cited that the formative moments in a tradition are especially susceptible to the agendas of the dominant discourses in biblical scholarship and so socio-historically orientated socially engaged scholars should tread warily when they take up these socio-historical resources. We need to realise that we are contending with powerful 'myths', which may or may not have historical validity. What further complicates our task is that these scholarly myths are not the only ones we have to contend with; the church too generates and perpetuates a range of powerful myths which can all too easily take on historical proportions. Myths of an ethnic and/or geographical 'Israel', myths of God ordained conquest, myths of empty promised lands either to occupy or to return to, myths of an anti-Jewish Jesus, myths of an anti-Palestinian Jesus, myths of an androcentric early Christianity, myths of a God who punishes the people of God with a deadly Human Immunodeficiency virus, and many other myths.

One of the profound contributions of Western (Enlightenment) historical-style reading resources is, as Robert Carrol reminds us, that they are able to probe the historicity of these myths (Carroll, 2000). This is the enduring legacy of the historical-critical approach and its more recent (Lategan, 1984) socio-historical manifestations.

The Historicity of Myth

These concluding comments lead nicely into the second section of my essay. I begin again with the naive historical realism of "educated men", for it seems they have a point. Having argued persuasively how difficult it is to distinguish between history and fiction, maintaining as he does that the difference between history and fiction is not a cognitive one (see also Bann, 1981:367-368), Mink goes on to insist that "our understanding of fiction needs the contrast with history as our understanding of history needs the contrast with fiction. The quality of our responses to imaginative fiction and its uses in our lives require the willing suspension of disbelief; but we could not learn how and when to suspend disbelief except by learning how to distinguish between fiction and history as making different truth-claims for their individual descriptions" (Mink, 1978). "If the distinction were to disappear", Mink goes on to explain, "fiction and history would both collapse back into myth and be indistinguishable from it as from each other". He then, quite remarkably, adds, "And though myth serves as both fiction and history for those who have not learned to discriminate, we cannot forget what we have learned" (Mink, 1978).

While I will not attempt a thorough exegesis of Mink's remarks, one way of reading this final sentence is to maintain that there are those who do not discriminate between history and fiction, for whom all narrative is myth, but that there are also those who have been educated by the Enlightenment's historical legacy to (try to) make and maintain a distinction between historical narrative and fictional narrative. Whether I have properly understood Mink or not, what I have gleaned here is enough for my purposes in this second section of my paper, providing me as he does with a useful (albeit minimalist) notion of 'myth'.

I think Mink is right (and if I have misunderstood Mink then I take full credit for the insight), some people do not distinguish between historical and fictional narrative; for them the narratives in their tradition which are meaningful, powerful, and true (ie. mythic), are meaningful, powerful, and true for reasons other than their historical truth claims. Patte's example mentioned earlier of the "typological view of history" of African slaves in America might then be a good case of a mythic understanding of narrative. Whether these narratives are fiction or history, in the Western-historical sense, does not matter. The biblical narratives are meaningful, powerful and true mythically. Others of us, however, are bewitched by the Western sense of history and so constantly try to differentiate between historical and fictional biblical narrative, basing our estimate of how they are meaningful, powerful, and true for us differently, depending on whether we adduce them to be (primarily) historical or fictional. For biblical scholars like Gottwald, Meyers, Mosala, Schüssler Fiorenza, and Whitelam the difference does matter, and so they attempt to reconstruct another historical narrative of "what really happened", though none of them would do this naively. As I have said, for them part of the reason for this imperative to reconstruct another (more historical) narrative is because of their commitments to present sites of struggle in which Bible readers (whether literate or not) yearn for a *historical* connection between their *historical* realities and *historical* realities in and behind the biblical text. "There is the graduate student in a seminar on *Tribes*", writes Norman Gottwald, "who wrote me a thank-you note that said, 'It was satisfying to have a historical reconstruction well explained that I actually desire to have existed: an "elsewhere" that I like!'" (Gottwald, 2002:181).

It would, of course, be crass to too quickly conclude from my discussion that this graduate student represents the product of an Enlightenment education and so has learned the distinction between fiction and history and that the African slaves in America represent those "who have not learned to discriminate" between fiction and history and for whom all significant narratives are mythic. While there may be communities that fit neatly into this divide, my experience suggests otherwise.

At this point I want to nuance the distinction between narratives as mythic on the one hand, and narratives as either history or fiction on the other. In our work with ordinary 'readers' of the Bible in South Africa, it is with considerable ease that participants find and forge lines of connection between their lived realities and biblical narratives. But, as I have already said, these same participants will also ask historical-type questions, questions that probe the received narrative either for further historical information or an anticipated (or hoped for) reconstructed historical narrative. In other words, at times participants seem content to engage with biblical narratives as narratives that are meaningful, powerful, and true for them with no (overt) consideration of whether they are historical or fictional; at other times, participants continue to probe the narrative for its historical truth claims – they want to know the historicity of this myth.

Given the ambiguous history of the Bible in South Africa, most generations of South African Bible 'readers' come to the biblical text with both a hermeneutic of suspicion and a hermeneutic of trust. The Bible is both a problem and a solution (Mofokeng, 1988). Perhaps, again given our history, the hermeneutic of suspicion always has a historical sensibility. Most black South Africans – the ordinary 'reader' I refer to – have learned, to use Mink's loaded verb, the distinction between history and fiction, so while they have the cultural and hermeneutic capacity and propensity[4] to engage with biblical narratives mythically, they also have moments of caution in which they want to ask historical questions. And given the pervasiveness of the powerful church-based myths mentioned in the earlier section and the popular forms of scholarly myths that find their way into the public realm, the wariness of ordinary African 'readers' is not misplaced. Whether it be the myth that Israel has some special place in God's plan or the latest myth of the Jesus Seminar to make the cover of *Time* magazine, the historical dimensions of the hermeneutic of suspicion of ordinary African 'readers' is to taken seriously by the socially engaged biblical scholar and an appropriate historical response formulated.

In summary, I have argued in this section of my paper that while biblical narratives may function mythically for many Bible 'readers', we must not make too much of Mink's distinction. Even when biblical narratives are granted mythic significance – that is, they are signified as meaning, powerful and true irrespective of their historical claims – historical questions may not be far away.[5] And when they do surface, the task of the socially engaged biblical scholar is to respond with critical responsibility to the academy and with social accountability to our context.

The Shape of our Historical Task

For those of us socially engaged biblical scholars who work collaboratively with ordinary poor, working class and marginalised South African 'readers' of the Bible and who have been called upon from time to time to provide historical information the task is not straightforward. Socio-historical biblical scholarship is not uncontested! We must, therefore, give some thought to what historically we provide when invited to do so.

Motivated as we are, as socially engaged biblical scholars, by our declared ideological commitments, our choices are not innocent and we should not pretend they are. Our resources are as plotted (to use White's image) as the next biblical historian's.

---

4   This phrase deserves a fuller analysis than I can provide here (but see as a start West, 2002a).

5   Here too there is much that requires further reflection; for example, do most ordinary 'readers' of the Bible operate less with a mythic understanding of biblical narrative and more with a naive historical realism? Can any of us really escape modernity's insistence on truth as historical?

If, however, we have allowed our scholarship to be partially constituted by experiences and questions of those non-scholars we read 'with',[6] then we must grant an epistemological privilege (Frostin, 1985, Frostin, 1988:3-4) to what their experiences and questions delve from the historical record. To be sure, we must with Huizinga, Danto, Mink and White refuse to succumb to an irresponsible historical scepticism. While historians clearly fashion their scholarly constructs, this "fashioning process need not – be it stressed – entail violations of the so-called 'rules of evidence' or the criteria of 'factual accuracy' resulting from simple ignorance of the record or the misinformation that might be contained in it" (White, 1975:60).

Doing primary historical research or reading secondary historical works guided by the experiences of those we read 'with' will shape both what we *find* and what we *fashion*. For example, being partially constituted by the realities of my reading partners guides me to prefer Richard Horsley's Jesus ((Horsley, 1994) to Gerd Theissen's Jesus (Theissen, 1978) because Horsley's Jesus speaks more directly to these realities. While I am aware of the dangers involved in making (and owning up to) such a choice, this is what socially engaged biblical scholars do when they read with ordinary 'readers' of the Bible and are asked to share socio-historical information. They make responsibly critical yet ideology influenced choices. Just as the primary scholarship of Theissen and Horsley are shaped by a whole range of (often undeclared) social and ideological forces and factors, so to is the scholarship of those who use (or do not use) their work in their collaborative reading 'with' ordinary African 'readers' of the Bible. I use the word scholarship in the sentence above quite deliberately. What Theissen and Horsley do, while having different outcomes, is biblical scholarship. They employ the training and tools of and are responsible to their scholarly communities in the doing of their work. Similarly, those of us who engage with their primary scholarship are also accountable to our discipline (West, 1999:118-120). If we take our responsibility as biblical scholars seriously, and I do, then when we choose to use Horsley rather than Theissen we do so not only for ideological reasons but also for scholarly reasons. As Hayden White insists, there is no excuse for sloppy scholarship.

However, while some scholars are paralysed by the plurality of biblical scholarship or by the lack of prospects of a convincing consensus in biblical scholarship (Watson, 1994:58), those of us who work with ordinary African Christians must choose. As I have said before (West, 1999:119-120), I must choose, both in what I find in the Bible and biblical scholarship and what I fashion from this because I am also accountable to those ordinary African 'readers' who have called me to read the Bible 'with' them. When I do choose among the primary and secondary resources available, my choices are shaped both by my scholarship and by my social location among ordinary African 'readers' of the Bible.

Given my commitment to begin with the Bible in a form that is most accessible to those ordinary 'readers' with whom I work, I am particularly excited when I come across biblical resources that show a profound appreciation of both the Bible as text and the Bible as reconstructed socio-historical context. So I am particularly impressed,

---

6 I have argued that this is a characteristic of African biblical scholarship in general (perhaps because African biblical scholars find it harder than their Western compatriots to sequester themselves in the corridors of the academy) (West, 2002c).

— (2002) Response to contributors, in *Tracking The tribes of Yahweh: on the trail of a classic* (Ed, Boer, R.) Sheffield Academic Press, Sheffield, pp. 172-185.

Horsley, Richard A. (1994) *Sociology and the Jesus movement,* Continuum, New York.

Huizenga, Johan (1936) A definition of the concept of history, in *Philosophy and history* (Eds, Klibansky, R. and Paton, H. J.) Claredon Press, pp. 1-10.

Lategan, Bernard C. (1984) Current issues in the hermeneutic debate. *Neotestamentica,* 18, 1-17.

Meyers, Carol (1988) *Discovering Eve: ancient Israelite women in context,* Oxford University Press, Oxford.

Mink, L.O. (1978) Narrative form as a cognitive instrument, in *Literary form and historical understanding* (Eds, Canary, R. H. and Kozicki, H.) University of Wisconsin, Wisconsin, pp. 129-149.

Mink, Louis O. (1966) The autonomy of historical understanding, in *Philosophical analysis and history* (Ed, Dray, W. H.) Harper and Row, New York, pp. 160-192.

Mofokeng, T. (1988) Black Christians, the Bible and liberation. *Journal of Black Theology,* 2, 34-42.

Patte, Daniel (2002) Reading with gratitude: the mysteries of "Reading communities reading Scripture", in *Reading communities reading Scripture: essays in honor of Daniel Patte* (Eds, Phillips, G. A. and Duran, N. W.) Trinity International Press, Harrisburg, pp. 361-382.

Ruether, Rosemary Radford (1983) *Sexism and God-talk: towards a feminist theology,* SCM, London.

Theissen, Gerd (1978) *Sociology of early Palestinian Christianity,* Fortress, Philadelphia.

Tonkin, E. (1992) *Narrating our past: the social construction of oral history,* Cambridge University Press, Cambridge.

Waetjen, Herman C. (1989) *A reordering of power: a socio-political reading of Mark's gospel,* Fortress, Minneapolis.

Watson, Francis (1994) *Text, church and world: biblical interpretation in theological perspective,* Eerdmans, Grand Rapids.

West, Gerald O. (1995) *Biblical hermeneutics of liberation: modes of reading the Bible in the South African context,* Orbis Books and Cluster Publications, Maryknoll, NY and Pietermaritzburg.

--- (1999) *The academy of the poor: towards a dialogical reading of the Bible,* Sheffield Academic Press, Sheffield.

--- (2000) Gauging the grain in a more nuanced and literary manner: a cautionary tale concerning the contribution of the social sciences to biblical interpretation, in *Rethinking context, rereading texts: contributions from the social sciences to*

for example, by Herman Waetjen's Jesus (Waetjen, 1989), a Jesus who inⁱ
contours of both the text and his socio-historical context. A feel for bᵉ
dimensions of the Bible is, unfortunately, quite rare. But it must be cultivatᵉ
by biblical scholarship generally, then certainly by the socially engaged biblicaⁱ
who works with the Bible among the poor, the working class and the marginaliˢ

If our God is indeed a God who observes the plight of the poor and oppressᵉ
hears their cries, and who knows their suffering (Exodus 3:7) then we may be
respond to the socio-historical questions put to us with socio-historical reconstrᵘ
that are both satisfying and that we desire to have existed. But if we are true
(Western) historical craft then we may at times also have to admit, as Nᵒ
Gottwald did when asked what he thought about life in early Israel: "'I would not
wanted to live there!'" (Gottwald, 2002:183). In elaborating on this instinctive ᵣ
Gottwald aptly describes the shape of the task before us as we strive to be accounⁱ
both to our scholarly communities and to communities of the poor, working class,
marginalised who have called us to read the Bible 'with' them:

> My reply was shorthand for the impossibility of resuscitating early Israel, or any otheⁱ
> past elsewhere for that matter, not only because it would be naive but because it would
> be undesirable. Recognizing past "elsewheres" and "days of justice" does not mean
> canonizing them but drawing on them as a resource for asking and answering what
> peace and justice require of us in a situation of technological and social complexity
> with outmoded political organization overrun by the juggernaut of economic
> globalization. Because elsewheres and days of justice have existed in our past, they are
> not idle dreams but open-ended historical possibilities (Gottwald, 2002:183).

Bibliography

Bann, Stephen (1981) Towards a critical historiography: recent work in philosophy of
history. *Philosophy,* 56, 365-385.

Cady, L. E. (1986) Hermeneutics and tradition: the role of the past in jurisprudence
and theology. *Harvard Theological Journal,* 79, 439-463.

Carroll, Robert P. (2000) (South) Africa, Bible, criticism: rhetorics of a visit, in *The
Bible in Africa: transactions, trajectories and trends* (Eds, West, G. O. and Dube,
M.) E.J. Brill, Leiden, pp. 184-202.

Danto, Arthur C. (1968) *Analytical philosophy of history,* Cambridge University Press,
Cambridge.

Fiorenza, Elizabeth Schussler (1983) *In memory of her: a feminist theological
reconstruction of Christian origins,* SCM, London.

Frostin, Per (1985) The hermeneutics of the poor: the epistemological 'break' in Third
World theologies. *Studia Theologica,* 39, 127-150.

--- (1988) *Liberation theology in Tanzania and South Africa: a First World
interpretation,* Lund University Press, Lund.

Gottwald, Norman K. (1979) *The tribes of Yahweh: a sociology of the religion of
liberated Israel, 1250-1050 B.C.,* Orbis, Maryknoll, New York.

biblical interpretation (Ed, M. Carroll R., D.) Sheffield Academic Press, Sheffield, pp. 75-105.

--- (2002a) The Bible as *bola*: among the foundations of African biblical apprehensions. *Journal of Theology for Southern Africa,* 112, 23-37.

--- (2002b) Disguising defiance in ritualisms of subordination: literary and community-based resources for recovering resistance discourse within the dominant discourses of the Bible, in *Reading communities reading Scripture* (Eds, Phillips, G. A. and Duran, N. W.) Trinity Press International, Lewisburg, PA, pp. 194-217.

--- (2002c) Indigenous exegesis: exploring the interface between missionary methods and the rhetorical rhythms of Africa; locating local reading resources in the academy. *Neotestamentica,* 36, 147-162.

--- (2002d) Reading abused female bodies in the Bible: interpretative strategies for recognising and recovering the stories of women inscribed by violence but circumscribed by patriarchal text (2 Kings 5). *Old Testament Essays,* 15, 240-258.

White, Hayden (1973) *Metahistory: the historical imagination in nineteenth-century Europe,* Hopkins University Press, Baltimore.

--- (1975) Historicism, history, and the figurative imagination. *History and theory,* 14, 48-67.

--- (1978) *The tropics of discourse: essays in cultural criticism,* Johns Hopkins University Press, Baltimore.

--- (1984) The question of narrative in contemporary historical theory. *History and theory,* 23, 1-33.

Whitelam, Keith, W. (1986) Recreating the history of Israel. *Journal for the study of the Old Testament,* 35, 45-70.

Whitelam, Keith W. (1996) *The invention of ancient Israel: the silencing of Palestinian history,* Routledge, London and New York.